The
Morning
After

The Morning After

AMERICAN SUCCESSES AND EXCESSES 1981–1986

George F. Will

COLLIER BOOKS
MACMILLAN PUDLISIIING COMPANY
NEW YORK

Collier Macmillan Publishers
London

Macmillan Publishing Company
866 Third Avenue, New York, N.Y. 10022
Collier Macmillan Canada, Inc.

Library of Congress Cataloging-in-Publication Data
Will, George F.
  The morning after.
  Includes index.
  1. United States—Politics and government—1981–
2. Conservatism—United States.   I. Title.
E876.W55   1986b   973.927   87-14589
ISBN 0-02-055450-8 (pbk.)

Macmillan books are available at special discounts for bulk purchases for sales promotions, premiums, fund-raising, or educational use. For details, contact:

Special Sales Director
Macmillan Publishing Company
866 Third Avenue
New York, N.Y. 10022

First Collier Edition

10 9 8 7 6 5 4 3 2 1

Printed in the United States of America

To Jonathan Frederick Will

Contents

II. SKIRMISHES ON THE HOME FRONT

Introduction

Happiness is not always all it is cracked up to be. That is particularly so in politics, where the pursuit of happiness involves the pursuit of power. Attainment of power begets responsibility, and a run-in with reality. That takes a terrible toll on ideology, and on the sense of purity and virtue that is compensation for the frustrations of being out of office.

For American conservatives, and not only for them, the realization that happiness is rarely unalloyed has given a bittersweet tinge to the experience of the 1980s. In 1981 the conservatives' hour came 'round at last. They elected a President who was not only conservative, he was Mr. Conservative. But beginning in 1981 many Americans—a not-at-all-silent majority—had their bluff called. They had grown comfortable with the rhetoric of complaint about "big government." What Reagan gave the country in the first half of the 1980s was a rolling referendum on domestic spending. The country took a crash course in the federal budget and found that conservatism could be uncomfortable.

Conservatism quickly became the belief that it is time to cut thy neighbor's subsidy. However, in this middle class country the budget is primarily a menu of benefits for . . . the middle class. After a cold shower of facts the country was wiser. But it also was sadder, because it had to forgo the fun of feeling virtuous merely by striking the pose of forthright opposition to the indefensible. It turns out that almost anything the government does has defenders.

Many conservatives have discovered, to their dismay, that the American people are conservative. That is, the voters who enabled Reagan to carry 93 states in 48 months did not ratify a revolution against the post-New Deal role of the Federal government. Indeed, some conservatives—those whose stock-in-trade is antigovernment thunder—may come to rue the day that Reagan came to Washington. While giving America government with a grin, he has rehabilitated government's good name. He ran against government for years and years, and then capped his career by making Americans comfortable once again with the dominating and tone-setting institution of government, the Presidency.

In the process, Reagan killed a cottage industry of intellectuals. In the late 1970s there was a spate of books and articles suggesting that the country is "ungovernable" and that the Presidency is too demanding for one person. Reagan's predecessor, who often was up late and waist deep in details, emphasized the burdensomeness of it all. Reagan chose to communicate a different message: "This is a piece of cake. Now, it's 3 p.m., so let's go riding." The fact that he was having so much fun should have been an early and alarming clue to conservatives who expected a "Reagan Revolution." Revolutionaries frown on fun. They are people with pursed lips and furrowed brows. And Reagan? He is a Reaganite.

During the 1930s and 1940s the U.S. Communist Party specialized in fierce and expressibly foolish factional fights. One such concerned the alleged deviationism of a factional leader, Jay Lovestone. This fight contributed to the comic lore of our politics a slogan hotly used by his enemies: "Lovestone is a Lovestoneite!" They had him there.

A partial summation of the Reagan years is: "Mr. Conservative is a conservative." That explains his reluctance even to try to kick over the traces of the welfare state. This has displeased some conservatives, and perhaps some liberals who hoped for more turmoil than the placid President has occasioned. But revolutions require steam and during Reagan's tenure—perhaps at the hour of its beginning, as the hostages left Iran—America went off the boil.

Regarding foreign affairs, some Americans hoped and others expected that the year 1981 would someday be etched as sharply in American history as 1958—the year de Gaulle launched the Fifth Republic—is in French history, marking an abrupt rupture with the past. In foreign policy, where the stakes are especially high, a sharp departure from the policies of the recent past was most needed. It is regarding this foreign policy that a feeling of disappointment is, I think, most justified.

However, there is a seamlessness in politics. In 1981 the nation was ready for what Reagan was temperamentally suited to supply—a period of cheerfulness. Cheerfulness tends to color a country's view of the external world, and makes a country complacent. That is a dangerous flaw in democracies. They find it difficult to be content with their domestic situations yet vigilant about the unchanging challenge of the totalitarians.

The 1980s have been years of mixed emotions, of happiness alloyed with anxiety, of celebration tinged with a nagging sense of the vast inertia in the life of a great nation. Hence *The Morning After*. Events have given a theme to, and hence have suggested a title for, this collection. In politics, but not only in politics, the 1980s have been years in which Americans have had the sharp sensations of morning—freshness and sobriety and a second chance.

Americans are fortunate in many things, not the least being the fact that they live in a country in which politics does not loom over life. Many of these essays concern matters that are "off the news." These are not merely matters that appear "below the fold" of the front page of a newspaper. Rather, they are things that do not normally count as news, things like children and other amusements.

People, a metaphysician once said, have more fun than anyone. Certainly, we who are privileged to comment regularly on the antic parade of American life have no excuse for not having fun. Midway through the 1980s it is midday in America and, as always, it is a splendid place to be.

PART 1

Broadening Incidents

"The Last Virgin in America"

This broadening incident from an all-too-broadening life occurred, as most of life seems to, in a station wagon. On a typical Saturday in autumn or spring, the highways in suburban Maryland are congested with station wagons—Democrats in Volvos, Republicans in Pontiacs—carting young players, male and female, to and from soccer games.

A parent tough enough to keep his or her ears open gets a shattering sense of the mind and vocabulary of the nation's nine-year-olds. It confirms the proposition that Mowgli, the boy raised by wolves in Kipling's *Jungle Book*, is not really unlike children raised by normal parents, who are members of a different species.

Recently, the Will wagon, brimful of the anarchy that nine-year-olds secrete, was inching through coagulated traffic opposite a shopping center where a movie marquee announced: "The Last Virgin in America (R)." Now, it is a well-documented fact that the average child who is blind as a brussels sprout when looking for the sneaker he left in the middle of the living room can read a movie marquee that is still over the horizon, especially if the movie being advertised has received the tantalizing accolade of an "R" rating.

On this occasion, the nine-year-old culture critics said: "*The Last Virgin in America*—Ohoooooooo." And the driver thought: Arrrrggghhhhh—what is the decorous thing to say when one of the creatures asks what a virgin is and why America is down to its last one?

The *Shorter Oxford English Dictionary* (no station wagon should be without one) offers a useful salad of definitions that could have been given to the soccer players. One definition is: "A female insect producing fertile eggs by parthenogenesis." The soccer players would not have been satisfied with that.

Another definition is "Of a fortress city, etc., that has never been taken or subdued." The *OED* gives this example: "In Africa, the highest mountain is still a virgin." That is, surely, a retrograde use of the word, because it suggests that sex is a conquest, a form of aggression. Nine-year-olds of my acquaintance, of both genders, should not be told that there are unexplored fields for their overflowing aggressions.

The first *OED* definition is charged with theology: "An unmarried or chaste maiden or woman, distinguished for piety or

3

steadfastness in religion." The second definition is similar, but the third is: "A young woman or maiden of an age and character affording presumption of chastity." That raises more problems than it solves, because the average driver of a station wagon boiling with nine-year-olds does not want to conduct a conversation on the admittedly fascinating question of at what age, in 1983, the presumption referred to evaporates.

I have asked other parents what they would have said about what a virgin is. One father suggests: "Tell them a virgin is a girl without a boyfriend." But that definition postulates a correlation that is dubious—and defeatist. Anyway, the *OED* is not so sexist as to say a virgin must be female. Its fifth definition is: "A youth or a man who has remained in a state of chastity."

Perhaps as the traffic crept along I should have fallen back on the last resort, the truth. Perhaps I should have said the idea of virginity has to do with sexual intercourse. But a station wagon is no place for a sex-education seminar.

Some occasions call for all that the brain can manage in the way of circumlocutions. I have always admired the character who mastered the use of the triple negative, as in the phrase "not unmeaningless." Slip that labyrinth of a phrase into a conversation and it will swallow up the conversation, setting you free from tiresome talk. But circumlocutions and ruses were not so necessary back when movie marquees caught children's attention with titles like *Commanche Comeuppance.*

Nothing is more striking to this parent than how early and strongly children feel the pull of popular culture. Today the social atmosphere is heavily dosed with invitations to think about what are loosely called adult topics. But, fortunately, the average nine-year-old cannot think about anything for very long.

So when one of them said, "What's a virgin?" I answered by shouting, "Chuck E. Cheese's [a pizza emporium and games arcade] coming up on the right!" The answer was, I know, a bit oblique, and perhaps a dereliction of duty. But some of life's duties should be left for those occasional intervals when one is not in a station wagon.

June 9, 1983

Autopsy on the Sixties

Forty-Seventh Street partakes fully of the Times Square ambiance—traffic congealed into puddings of irritability, food aromas that alone can elevate your cholesterol level, street people with complexions that resemble blue cheese. In this tangy precinct of the theater district there is a cultural event indicative of the changed political climate. Conservatism is no longer "Off Broadway," metaphorically or literally.

Michael Frayn's play *Benefactors* is an autopsy on a particular social sensibility. The title is sardonic; would-be helpers often are not. Although set in London, the theme is transatlantic, and timeless. It begins, in flashbacks, in 1968, the emblematic year of recent radicalism. It ends about a dozen years later, with this message: "It was people. That's what wrecks all our plans—people."

David, an architect, has plans to develop public housing in a run-down neighborhood. The people he would benefit? "They're going to get their houses pulled down whether they like it or not. And we don't need to ask them what they want instead because we know." And: "I'm not going to build towers. No one wants to live in a tower."

But what begins as an idealistic venture in "building the new world" becomes, in maddeningly minute steps, the torture of a thousand cuts. Politics and bureaucracy and economics and society—in a word, reality—compel compromises that drive David toward building high-rise towers. His cynical neighbor warns of "progressive collapse," a technical term for a form of disaster in tall buildings. In Frayn's hands the term has another meaning.

Frayn has not written anything so tiresome as a play "about"—heaven forfend—public housing. And it is not *Waiting for Righty*, a Thatcher-era emulation of Clifford Odets's *Waiting for Lefty*, the archetype of a play as a political cartoon featuring cardboard heroes and villains. Many political plays, like many political persons, are barren of ambiguity. Frayn's play is about ambiguity, about how personal relations and social actions have, in the end, unanticipated consequences, and how they have, at the beginning, unacknowledged motives.

Frayn has mastered the delicate art of making a point without preaching. *Benefactors* is primarily about the troubled marriages of two couples who become ruinously entangled as they try to "help" each other. However, the private and public situations become mutually reinforcing metaphors. Marriages are, Frayn says, like public works of architecture, plagued by unexpected complexities, changing conditions, defective materials.

Architecture has frequently been invested with political hopes, especially by behavioralists who believe that social nurturing can overcome human nature. They say: Reform the social environment and you will reform man. Urban renewal can evict the old Adam. In the 1930s, a bright light of the literary left, W. H. Auden, wrote in a poem about "new styles of architecture, a change of heart." That thought now looks like a quaint stick of period furniture from a mentality that has all but vanished. (There actually are photographs of the collapse of liberalism—the 1972 dynamiting of St. Louis's huge Pruitt-Igoe public-housing project. It had become unlivable, a paradigm of giantism and overreaching by liberal social engineering.)

In *Benefactors* the reality principle is incarnate in David's wife Jane, played with icy force by Glenn Close. Jane is an anthropologist, a student rather than a savior of people: "Look, I'm not trying to help anyone. . . . I'm just trying to count them." For David, the retreat from "building high" is, in several senses, a matter of coming down to earth. When his neighbor says of architecture, "It must be wonderful to change things," he replies: "No, it's not, Sheila. It's heartbreaking. It's always just warped windows and condensation problems. It was going to be so new and amazing, and it never is, it's always just like everything else."

The area he was supposed to benefit is called a "twilight area"—not a slum, "a bit gray and exhausted, that's all." And so, in the end, it remains, and David, the would-be benefactor, resembles it.

Frayn's conservatism is not Reaganite conservatism with a smiling face, conservatism singularly lacking in a tragic sense of life, gloomy only about government and cheerfully convinced that everywhere else—a.k.a., the "private sector"—is a realm of harmony and limitlessness. Political stances often are products more of sensibilities than philosophies, and Frayn's sensibility is of chastened hopefulness. It is sensibility congenial to an older conservatism.

In the 1960s Frayn was a wonderfully unenthralled columnist in "swinging London" amidst the postimperial giddiness of Carnaby Street and pop music. Today *Benefactors* is playing next door to *Oh! Calcutta!*, a soiled remnant of the 1960s, years when people were told to solve the problems of living by "getting in touch with their feelings." *Benefactors* performs conservatism's thankless task, saying: It's more complicated than that.

February 6, 1986

The Democracy of Angling

NEWPORT BEACH, CALIF.—It is 4:15 A.M. and down in the galley of the good boat *Freelance* money is changing hands. In the predawn darkness the barracuda and bass off the coast are sleeping the untroubled sleep of the just. But trouble is heading their way in the form of sport fishermen, some of whom—regulars on the *Freelance*—are playing poker for nickels as the crew readies to shove off for a day of strenuous fun.

A Will boy, 11, who was up at 3 A.M. fine-tuning his tackle, is bright-eyed and eager to buy his breakfast: a microwaved burrito and a 3 Musketeers candy bar. The boy's cousin, 15, a grizzled old boy of the sea, is delivering, for the edification of his tenderfoot uncle from the East, a nonstop and terrifyingly erudite disquisition on offshore fishing. The uncle—your correspondent—is barely conscious but is conscious enough to be wondering why, in his hobby of dreaming up oxymora ("married bachelor," "Lebanese government") he had not thought of "family vacation." We are given children to test us and make us more spiritual. Fishing with energetic boys actually is good for a father's soul, and for the boys' souls, too—assuming, on the basis of ambiguous evidence, that boys have souls.

The *Freelance* chugs out of the channel into the ocean before the sun is up and before the barracuda have had their shredded wheat. It arrives at a fishing ground when the gray rolling sea is still a seamless universe undifferentiated from the gray horizon. Soon a fierce-looking deckhand, who could be a reject from a pirate ship but who is the soul of helpfulness, will stand up on the bait tank and toss scoops of live anchovies over the side to attract fish. Well, most of the anchovies will go over the side. Bits will land in our hair. Such fishing is not for the fastidious. Anyway, better to have anchovies in one's hair than on one's pizza.

Just as there are food fascists who would outlaw french fries and force everyone to breakfast on bran muffins, there are fishing fascists who despise the use of live bait. But such dogmatism is out of place in the democracy of angling. Fishing, properly approached, is like the political philosophy of a civilized society: It is less a creed than a climate of opinion. Fishing is a way of life resembling what the incomparable Aristotle considered the best regime. That is, it combines democratic and aristocratic elements.

It is democratic in that it is open to all. Adequate equipment is not expensive. And fish are broad-minded. They are uninterested in the social class of the hand that holds the rod that casts the line. Fishing is aristocratic in that there is a hierarchy of skill and achievement. Excellence is respected by other fishermen and rewarded by the fish, whose broad-mindedness does not make them indifferent to skill. It is aristocratic in that it encourages development of the nobler virtues, including both tenacity and resignation, when each is appropriate. Good fishermen are aristocratic in their possession of elegantly understated manners. These involve adherence to a code of honorable behavior that would have earned nods of approval in a medieval tournament. There are distinctions between sporting and unsporting methods, and respect for the social space of others, who are pursuing what should be, as much as possible, an almost solitary sport. This last is especially important for children because a child's life nowadays tends to be too organized, programmed, collectivized.

Sensible adults use artifices, such as fishing, to recapture, fleetingly, the harmony of sense and spirit that seems spontaneous in healthy children. Fishing gives an adult's mind the satisfaction of focusing on a manageable task. Einstein said he liked chopping wood because it was the only thing he did that produced immediate results. Fishing is like that, even when the fish are obdurate. In fact, their obduracy is itself a satisfying challenge.

Fishing leaves formative lines on the soft wax of a child's temperament. A boy who is painfully shy when required to say even a simple "hello" to an adult in a social setting can suddenly become bold about calling out to adults in other boats or on opposite riverbanks to find out what lure they used to hook that pike. It is stirring to see one's son engaged in earnest conversation, on a basis of perfect equality, with a stranger five times his age, concerning the relative merits of squid slices and casting jigs as bass bait.

Children need some field of knowledge in which they can savor the pleasure of deeply understanding something. For some, the activity involves collecting things—stamps, beer cans, whatever. (If you think there is not a lot to know about beer cans, you have not read the literature produced for the intelligentsia among can collectors.) For other children, knowledge of baseball—Andy Pafko's batting average, how to calculate slugging percentage, when to hit behind the runner—gives the first sense of mastery. Baseball long ago gave some of us our last sense of mastery, but better one than none. Certainly a young person in the grip of a passion for fishing is awakening to the joys of proficiency.

John Buchan was a passionate fisherman and an unsurpassed memoirist. His autobiography, *Pilgrim's Way*, published in 1940, was John Kennedy's favorite book. Buchan wrote that fishing satisfies a boy's desire for tangible results and his innocent passion for loot. Buchan's description of the rewards of a classical education, of the close study of masters such as Plato and Thucydides, also describes the rewards of fishing. Fishing, like the classics, teaches patience, humility and the joy of life. The classics extinguished in Buchan any inclination toward being a rebel, because they made him "profoundly conscious of the dominion of unalterable law." A wholesome lesson, that, and one a child learns when matching his talents against the wiles of a mature trout. A fisherman soon comes to terms with the fact that there are many forces and mysteries beyond his ken or control.

Fishing, like more formal education, teaches the talent of living worthily, but it is not, as healthy children try to argue, a wholly satisfactory substitute for the lamp of learning that is relit indoors every September. However, in August school is a dark cloud on the horizon no larger than a man's hand, a cloud smaller than the bass that every boy knows his next cast will catch.

August 19, 1985

Bruuuuuce

What I did on my summer vacation:
My friend Bruce Springsteen . . .
Okay, he's only my acquaintance, but my children now think I am a serious person. I met him because his colleague Max Weinberg and Max's wife, Rebecca, invited me to enjoy Max's work,

which I did. He plays drums for Springsteen, who plays rock and roll for purists, of whom there are lots. For ten shows in New Jersey, he recently sold 16,000 $16 tickets in the first hour, all 202,000 in a day. His albums can sell one million copies on the first day of release.

There is not a smidgen of androgyny in Springsteen who, rocketing around the stage in a T-shirt and headband, resembles Robert DeNiro in the combat scenes of *The Deerhunter*. This is rock for the United Steelworkers, accompanied by the opening barrage of the battle of the Somme. The saintly Rebecca met me with a small pouch of cotton—for my ears, she explained. She thinks I am a poor specimen, I thought. I made it three beats into the first number before packing my ears.

I may be the only 43-year-old American so out of the swim that I do not even know what marijuana smoke smells like. Perhaps at the concert I was surrounded by controlled substances. Certainly I was surrounded by orderly young adults earnestly—and correctly—insisting that Springsteen is a wholesome cultural portent.

For the uninitiated, the sensory blitzkrieg of a Springsteen concert is stunning. For the initiated, which included most of the 20,000 the night I experienced him, the lyrics, believe it or not, are most important. Today, "values" are all the rage, with political candidates claiming to have backpacks stuffed full of them. Springsteen's fans say his message affirms the right values. Certainly his manner does.

Many of his fans regarded me as exotic fauna at the concert (a bow tie and double-breasted blazer is not the dress code) and undertook to instruct me. A typical tutorial went like this:

Me: "What do you like about him?"

Male fan: "He sings about faith and traditional values."

Male fan's female friend, dryly: "And cars and girls."

Male fan: "No, no, it's about community and roots and perseverance and family."

She: "And cars and girls."

Let's not quibble. Cars and girls are American values, and this lyric surely expresses some elemental American sentiment: "Now mister the day my number comes in/ I ain't never gonna ride/ in no used car again."

Springsteen, a product of industrial New Jersey, is called the "blue-collar troubadour." But if this is the class struggle, its anthem—its "Internationale"—is the song that provides the title for his 18-month, worldwide tour: "Born in the U.S.A."

I have not got a clue about Springsteen's politics, if any, but flags get waved at his concerts while he sings songs about hard times. He is no whiner, and the recitation of closed factories and other problems always seems punctuated by a grand, cheerful affirmation: "Born in the U.S.A.!"

His songs, and the engaging homilies with which he introduces them, tell listeners to "downsize" their expectations—his phrase, borrowed from the auto industry, naturally. It is music for saying good-bye to Peter Pan: Life is real, life is earnest, life is a lot of work, but . . .

"Friday night's pay night, guys fresh out of work/ Talking about the weekend, scrubbing off the dirt . . . / In my head I keep a picture of a pretty little miss/ Someday mister I'm gonna lead a better life than this."

An evening with Springsteen—an evening tends to wash over into the A.M., the concerts' lasting four hours—is vivid proof that the work ethic is alive and well. Backstage there hovers the odor of Ben-Gay: Springsteen is an athlete draining himself for every audience.

But, then, consider Max Weinberg's bandaged fingers. The rigors of drumming have led to five tendonitis operations. He soaks his hands in hot water before a concert, in ice afterward, and sleeps with tight gloves on. Yes, of course, the whole E Street Band is making enough money to ease the pain. But they are not charging as much as they could, and the customers are happy. How many American businesses can say that?

If all Americans—in labor and management, who make steel or cars or shoes or textiles—made their products with as much energy and confidence as Springsteen and his merry band make music, there would be no need for Congress to be thinking about protectionism. No "domestic content" legislation is needed in the music industry. The British and other invasions have been met and matched.

In an age of lackadaisical effort and slipshod products, anyone who does anything—anything legal—conspicuously well and with zest is a national asset. Springsteen's tour is hard, honest work and evidence of the astonishing vitality of America's regions and generations. They produce distinctive tones of voice that other regions and generations embrace. There still is nothing quite like being born in the U.S.A.

September 13, 1984

Realism Creeps into Academia

Realism may be coming on little cat feet into places from which it recently was expelled—universities, and discussions of what universities are for. This bit of realistic graffiti has been seen at a university: "The meek shall inherit the Earth—but the strong shall retain the mineral rights." And the *New York Review of Books,* which was once full of tolerance for the follies of the young, recently published some constructive crankiness from two men of many years and much understanding.

It seems like only yesterday that the *NYRB* printed on its cover a diagram of a Molotov cocktail. That was in 1967, when the *NYRB* was, to say no more, tolerant about the ferment on campuses. Today the *NYRB* is less titillatingly but more genuinely provocative when it publishes sensible things, such as Jacques Barzun's essay about "the wasteland of American education."

Barzun is an emeritus professor at Columbia University, and his essay is an introduction to a reissue of his 1945 book, *Teacher in America.* His theme is that secondary schools have abandoned "the old plan and purpose of teaching the young what they truly need to know," and the idea of a university as a seat of learning has been lost. The implication of his argument is, I think, that the condition of American education poses a danger of social disintegration vaster and more lasting than anything Molotov cocktails can produce.

Barzun speaks unsparingly about the deceits by which secondary schools disguise the fact that they are disgorging millions of functional illiterates. The deceits include academic credits for almost anything (the "photography is as good as physics" doctrine), "social promotion" (which includes "high school" graduates with eighth-grade reading abilities), and a multitude of derelictions of duty encompassed by "bilingual education."

The hottest domestic issue of the 1980s may be, and probably should be, the collapse of a kind of confidence that once was a defining characteristic of America—confidence in public secondary education. And the condition of universities may justify equal alarm.

Enticed by government largess, universities in the postwar period embraced the ideal of "relevance," understood as "meeting social needs." There was a hot auction for scholars who could attract to universities the grants offered by government. High salaries were important, but so were promises that the scholars would be virtually exempt from teaching.

Barzun much too charitably attributes the campus disorders of the 1960s to the students' sense that "teaching was regarded as a disagreeable task, and students as obstacles to serious work, meaning research." I spent all of the Sixties on campuses, as a student or professor, in three countries, and I am convinced that radical students and their faculty applauders had two unattractive reasons for desiring the academic degradation that Barzun detests.

Many students were on campus only because they were carried there by the preposterous notion that every high school graduate is suited to college education. Many faculty members were on campus because the education boom made the academic job market undemanding. Thus, many students and teachers were bored by scholarship, and their self-esteem and comfort were threatened by traditional academic standards. So they had powerful incentives to demote those standards and elevate vague and shifting standards of social utility ("relevance") in the hierarchy of academic values.

Furthermore, student and faculty "reformers" rejected the idea of a core curriculum of necessary knowledge because they embraced an idea that severs moral philosophy from reason. In an essay in the same issue of the *NYRB*, J. M. Cameron, emeritus professor at the University of Toronto, argues that the disarray of college curricula reflects a mistaken doctrine of modern philosophy. It is the doctrine that all values are equally arbitrary, so the "selection" of values, like the selection of items in a cafeteria, is purely a matter of "taste."

"Such thoughts," writes Cameron, "may have odd consequences for the curriculum. Boys and girls who couldn't write on a sheet of paper, or put into speech, even the rudest outline of what Christians or Jews believe and who couldn't recount accurately a single story from the Old or New Testament, may be given instruction in Hindu and Buddhist metaphysics; this, lest the teachers commit the offense of proselytizing on behalf of the traditional European culture."

The collapse of the idea of a core curriculum for society is, ultimately, a political event. It has been well argued that Homer was a founder of the Greek people because he gave them what made them distinctive—a particular moral understanding, potently expressed in poetry rich in embodiments of virtues and vices. A corpus of great books—the Bible, Shakespeare, and others—once was regarded as suited to serve a similar unifying and civilizing function.

The abandonment of this corpus, and this function, is a political problem, because citizenship is a shared and nurtured state of mind.

October 29, 1981

Ah, Idealism

Ah, spring. The sap is rising and so is what passes for idealism on campuses where love of justice is expressed by shouting down conservative speakers. Mobs at Berkeley and Minnesota have disrupted speeches by Ambassador Jeane Kirkpatrick, and Jill Conway, president of Smith College, has, in effect, disinvited Kirkpatrick, who had been invited to deliver the commencement address this spring. Conway said Smith could not guarantee order. Rubbish. To guarantee order Conway had only to say that disruptive students would not graduate, disruptive faculty would be fired and police would attend to outsiders.

Conway probably (and Berkeley certainly) would have used napalm to prevent conservatives from silencing a liberal speaker. Conway did not act strongly because she did not feel strongly about keeping order for Kirkpatrick. Conway's assertion that Smith could not do what it certainly could do is an example of exertion apportioned according to political persuasions. It is a timely example. It comes as many academic administrators are saying that it would be unbearably burdensome (and contrary to their exacting principles) to help enforce the law linking student aid with compliance with draft registration.

Last year Congress voted to deny education aid to men who do not comply with the law requiring them to register. To register, a man merely fills out a short form at any post office. Conscientious objectors do not compromise their case because registration is not held to be a declaration of willingness to serve. About 96 percent of all men required to do so have complied. Most of the 500,000 who have not probably just do not understand the requirements. However, a judge can almost always be found to block a government action that is not congruent with the liberal agenda. A judge has held that the law linking aid and registration probably is unconstitutional.

He says it may be a bill of attainder, imposing punishment by legislation, rather than judicial process. But is it "punishment" to restrict access to a federal benefit to persons in compliance with the law? And what, then, of the routine practice of making federal aid or tax-exempt status for institutions conditional on compliance with civil-rights laws? The judge also thinks the law may violate the Fifth Amendment guarantee that no person "shall be compelled . . . to be a witness against himself." But where is the compulsion? No one is compelled to break the law or apply for aid.

Critics of the law say that persons who are "unable to prove their innocence are automatically found guilty." But no one is unable to prove innocence in this matter. Some persons are unwilling to be innocent. Besides, the law does not assign guilt. It just adds one more eligibility requirement that students must meet.

Critics say the law violates the "equal protection" clause because it "discriminates" on the basis of wealth (it does not affect the very rich) and has a "disparate impact" on blacks and other minority students because a high proportion of them receive aid. But federal aid for students is principally a subsidy for the middle and upper-middle classes. A student from a family with an income of more than $60,000 can be eligible. And if we are supposed to purge American law of all provisions that have a "disparate impact" on the poor and minorities, we can begin with the deductibility of mortgage-interest payments and charitable contributions, sales taxes and the new gasoline-tax increase. Social security, too, is flawed because lower-income people start working younger and die younger than others, so they work longer and receive benefits for a shorter period.

Such "disparate" impacts are an inescapable facet of life in a complex society. Persons who want to worry about fairness might try worrying about why a 19-year-old construction worker who complies with the draft-registration law should see his taxes subsidize college education for a privileged few who will not comply.

Some academicians have suddenly developed a new scruple: Educational institutions should not be involved in enforcement of social policies. But their scrupulosity is selective: They do not object to being enforcement agents for "affirmative action" requirements. Federal regulations applicable to postsecondary schools fill 635 pages of small print—272 pages about how colleges must comply with federal-aid measures, 86 pages concerning compliance with antidiscrimination laws. But now some academicians say: The burden of verifying draft registration—the burden of asking an applicant for the letter he receives from the Selective Service System—is intolerable.

What is going on? What went on at Smith, in this sense: Colleges have no enthusiasm for doing something that is unpopular with an aggressive and trendy minority, so the colleges are saying they cannot do it.

One of the nation's principal problems is the cost of entitlement programs. But a bigger problem is the "I'm entitled" mood, the mood of those who say that simply because they are alive they are entitled to all society's privileges and it would be repressive to connect a privilege with a responsibility. That means there are no privileges, properly speaking; there are only unconditioned rights. Where do people get such ideas? Perhaps in school.

Yale's president, A. Bartlett Giamatti, is praised as "outspoken." In 1981 he spoke out to warn Yale's entering freshmen. Young persons about to spend four years at Yale need to be warned about many things. Giamatti chose to warn them about the menace of . . . Jerry Falwell. Such outspokenness is not brave. In January, in an action now emulated elsewhere, Yale announced that it would subsidize defiance of the law by arranging grants or loans for students whose tender consciences will not permit them to register. It is not brave for Yale to teach, as its policy does, that a person's enjoyment of society's generosity does not even entail an obligation to obey the law.

Teaching that to America's most privileged young men is a betrayal of the university's civilizing mission. Remember this axiom: You can argue about exactly what hospitals should do, but surely they should not spread disease.

March 28, 1983

AIDS and The Community

SAN FRANCISCO—Well, says Mervyn Silverman, suppose someone opened a Russian-roulette parlor, where adults so inclined could go risk their lives. Could the city be indifferent? Silverman recently resigned as director of health in this city, where there is currently a death a day due to AIDS (acquired immune deficiency syndrome). Two new cases are reported each day, which means that a year from now there will be two deaths a day.

This city is—depending on your idea of civic virtue—famous or notorious for its tolerant attitude toward homosexuality. Ten to 15 percent of the population (75,000–100,000) are male homosexuals. Among many such men, unlike among lesbians, there is a pattern of promiscuity.

Bathhouses, featuring private rooms and saunas or whirlpools, are relics of a generation ago. Before homosexuals felt able to "come out of the closet," such establishments were used for assignations by people who felt they had nowhere else to do what they were determined to do. Today, Silverman says, bathhouses are less used for that, although they still are used by, for example, bisexual married men or others who desire secrecy. But bathhouses are symbols of "homosexual rights," so there was protest last April when Silverman promulgated regulations to prohibit "unsafe sex" in bathhouses.

San Francisco's yeasty political process stopped the regulations, so Silverman ordered the bathhouses closed. The owners "won" in court, but the court, in allowing them to remain open, essentially imposed Silverman's "unsafe sex" regulations, requiring monitoring of activity, forbidding private rooms and requiring lights to remain on. Silverman argues that because of AIDS (and some less harmful diseases) bathhouse sex is inherently unsafe. Bathhouses are frequently used for forms of group promiscuity that should not be described in a newspaper.

To persons who say that the regulations will merely change the venue, not the quantity or nature, of homosexual activity, Silverman says: If couples meet in separate locations, the quantity of especially dangerous contacts will decline because group sex will decline. He says this is already happening under the tutelage of death: Watching a friend die is educational. When we see a wreck along a highway, Silverman says, we drive more slowly for the next few miles, then soon speed up. But AIDS has a more lasting deterrent effect.

San Francisco spends several million dollars a year on education and counseling about sexually transmitted diseases. Information is, Silverman thinks, the primary reason for the changed behavior that has resulted in a 75 percent reduction in cases of rectal gonorrhea. Sexually transmitted diseases are paradigms of many of today's principal public health problems, such as traffic accidents, cancer from smoking, alcoholism. They are "optional" diseases in the sense that they can be radically reduced by the dissemination of information that modifies freely chosen behavior.

Silverman is opposed by libertarians who say the regulations violate "civil rights." They say that publicity about AIDS has been so effective that almost everyone is informed, and that sexual activity in private between informed and consenting adults, even when dangerous, threatens only the consenters and thus is no business of government.

Silverman argues that even if the facts about AIDS have passed the threshold of public understanding that can be called "common knowledge," there are still victims who have never given "informed consent" to the risk of infection. Victims include women who have sexual relations with bisexual men, drug addicts who use tainted needles and recipients of tainted blood.

But the argument for Silverman's policy is most interesting when it moves beyond nuances about informed consent, and beyond the sort of argument used to justify laws requiring seatbelt use, or requiring motorcyclists to wear helmets. (If a cyclist scrambles his brains and becomes an invalid, his act is not just, as philosophers say, a "self-regarding" act. Rather, it is "other-regarding" because, thanks to the insurance industry and extensive government involvement in the provision of medical resources, we have socialized the burdens that result from individual irrationality, however consensual.)

The form of ethical argument natural to Americans and favored by libertarians favors libertarianism. It turns on strict individualism—the individual's information, the individual's consent and the individual's rights, including his right to have government share the burdens he incurs. Such an argument skews policy debates because it excludes communitarian concerns, especially concerns for community values.

The soul of Silverman's argument is that the city is not interfering with anyone's right to commit any sexual act, but only with the bathhouse owner's right to facilitate dangerous sexual activity. He says the reason the city is right to interfere is the same reason that a civilized city would close a Russian roulette parlor: Life is good, and the law, a powerful teacher for good or ill, should affirm the preciousness of life by discouraging behavior that cheapens it.

Is this an argument for "legislating morality"? Yes.

Sex as Tabasco Sauce

By the time peace spread her gentle wings over the Minneapolis city council it had, by a 7 to 6 vote, done something innovative. In doing so it showed how awkward are attempts to act wisely on unwise premises.

The council came out for censorship, declaring pornography to be a form of illegal sex discrimination. Had the mayor not vetoed the measure, even the panorama of skin that assaults the senses of anyone approaching a normal newsstand would have violated the civil rights of all Minneapolis women, regardless of whether they are exposed to or affronted by it.

The amendment to the city's civil-rights law would have defined pornography as the practice of "exploitation and subordination based on sex which differentially harms women." That is part of a remarkable statement of "findings":

"The bigotry and contempt (pornography) promotes, with the acts of aggression it fosters, harm women's opportunities for equality of rights in employment, education, property rights, public accommodations and public services; create public harassment and private denigration; promote injury and degradation such as rape, battery and prostitution and inhibit just enforcement of laws against these acts; contribute significantly to restricting women from full exercise of citizenship and participation in public life, including in neighborhoods; damage relations between the sexes; and undermine women's equal exercise of rights to speech and action. . . . "

Although most of those assertions may be true, or true enough, it is hard to say how they constitute "findings." The assertions (here is another: "pornography is central in creating and maintaining the civil inequality of the sexes") are overreaching, a tactic of desperation. Why is such extravagance necessary? Because the logic of today's jurisprudence requires such unreasonableness before reasonable action can be taken.

It should not be necessary, before using law to sustain minimal decencies, to pretend that one can demonstrate that the polluting touch of pornography produces this or that particular behavior. But the Minneapolis law bristles with such assertions because today's judicial fashion holds that (in Felix Frankfurter's words) "law is concerned with external behavior and not the inner life of man."

It would be more sensible to say, as proper conservatives do:

Behavior is a consequence of the inner life. Besides, the soul of the citizenry reveals the success of the country. We judge a nation by the character of its citizens, and common sense unassisted by sociological "findings" tells us that pornography is coarsening, and hence injurious to the community, and especially to women. Even more destructive than pornography are libertarian laws that express the doctrine that law should be indifferent to the evolution of the nation's character—to the inner life. So censorship of the most execrable material is wise.

Alas, the First Amendment as currently construed proscribes common sense. The freedom of speech clause looks as though it has been trampled by a naked dancer, which in a sense it has. Various courts have decided that the clause was designed to protect not just speech—a capacity connected with reasoning and ideas, and hence self-government—but "expression," including that of naked dancers.

The mayor of Minneapolis said the measure went beyond the regulation of conduct to the impermissible regulation of "the transmission of ideas which may or may not have a causal relationship with illegal conduct." It is odd to speak of "ideas" being transmitted in pornographic movies, but that is not the only example here of the brittleness of the inapposite language of liberalism.

Proponents of the amendment, including some famous liberal feminists, obviously, and sensibly, considered it a measure to protect the moral tone of the community. Yet, they rattle on and on about individual rights and equality. Contemporary liberalism is a doctrine of such severe individualism that liberals, including the amendment's authors, cannot use the vocabulary of collective concerns. They cannot speak about the needs and rights of communities combating a $7 billion industry in pornography.

A wise woman once wrote that sex is the Tabasco sauce that a nation with an adolescent palate sprinkles on every course in the menu. But the Supreme Court has left local authorities with some power over the crudest uses of the sauce. Local standards can be consulted when regulating material that appeals to prurient interests and is without literary, artistic, political or scientific value. If women can find more convincing language to use when pressing the point they made in Minneapolis, and I wish them well, they will alter community standards and thereby perhaps expand the power of local authorities to regulate pornography.

January 8, 1984

Herpes and Full Disclosure

America the prolific may be about to invent yet another right. It is the right to be told in a timely manner if one's sexual partner of an idle hour has herpes.

Susan Liptrot is suing the man with whom she says she slept once, after a brief acquaintance. She says she noticed (sorry: This is a family newspaper but these are not family times) sores on his genitals. But, she says, "he said he didn't know what it was. I didn't think anything about it." After moral reflection, she thinks the law should compel him to give her more than $100,000. "Hey, you know, why should this person not have any responsibility for what his actions were?" Hey, why do so many people develop such convenient theories of jurisprudence? She "didn't think anything about it," but now is out to develop a new law of sexual responsibility.

The law has recently, through "palimony," sanctioned the idea that persons who reject the legal responsibilities of marriage can nonetheless use the law to impose responsibilities on others when that becomes convenient. One does wish that today's free spirits, who are too emancipated to conform to the law's codification of social values regarding marriage, would at least have the consistency not to come running to court seeking the help of a society whose codified values they reject.

When Liptrot called to tell her partner he had infected her, he said: "Oh, I'm sorry." You thought love meant never having to say that? But who said anything about love? Well, actually the *Washington Post* did. Its headlines spoke of a "lover's right to be told of herpes." Its story spoke of putting "before a court a question facing a large number of unmarried Americans: whether and when to tell potential lovers about herpes."

Hold it. We are supposed to be unflinchingly candid about sex, and Liptrot's suit is about making candor compulsory, so let's not use language that can fog judges' minds. If courts are going to start refereeing such grievances as will arise between persons who choose to be governed by their glands, judges should at least understand that they often will be dealing with persons who are not "lovers" as any sensible person understands that term.

Liptrot, who became litigious when the man asked her not to tell his girlfriend, says, "It's just like if a guy got a woman pregnant and just walked out." But, for the record, women can give herpes to men. And herpes is a well-publicized epidemic. Persons who get it should spare us the argument that they have a right to claim the cherished status of victim. Victim of what? Presumably of society's failure to make life, however foolishly lived, risk-free.

Emancipated persons say that sex is a private matter—none of the law's business. They say that freedom is the absence of restraint—"the silence of the law." But in the cultural climate that comes with such thinking, millions of persons are passing around an infectious and, at this point, incurable disease.

Law and life would be well served by allowing the sanctions inherent in the situation to function: People are free to disdain society's old morality, but society should not foot the bill for arbitrating disputes arising from the epidemic associated with the new morality. Unfortunately, free spirits, male and female, are going to come to court, talking about (other persons') "responsibilities" and wanting to apply the law as a poultice to the hurts that life attaches to the way they choose to live.

Liberalism teaches that society is an abstraction, that the law should take cognizance only of individuals' desires. Liberal jurisprudence teaches that law has no business attempting to shape society's moral climate, least of all concerning a private matter like sex. But in the resulting dissolution of social mores and other restraints, liberal jurisprudence attempts to translate every unhappiness into a justiciable conflict of individual rights. So some judge is apt to pioneer a law concerning herpes.

Let's see: Are there privacy rights of the infectious to be weighed against the information rights of the infected? And distinctions must be drawn: The rights of short-term partners may differ from those of a married person whose spouse contracts herpes in an extramarital affair. (Three wives have sued their husbands.)

Where will it end? It won't. The lesson, constantly taught and never learned, is that society gets a drizzle of dumb, little laws when it abandons the wise, big laws of life.

February 24, 1983

Norman Mailer, Economist

Rejoice! Economic recovery is at hand: Norman Mailer and Sophia Loren have put their pretty heads together in Paris at a conference of intellectuals—broadly defined, obviously.

The conference was paid for by François Mitterrand's socialist government. It thinks writers and movie stars should help solve the world economic crisis. "Just as war is too important to be left to the generals, so is an economic crisis too important to be left to the economists or the 'practical men',," said John Kenneth Galbraith, who is not guilty of belonging to either group.

Kate ("Sexual Politics") Millett did her number, complaining about the "severe lack of representation of women." She is a writer who is not picky about the meaning of words: Her complaint was, presumably, about insufficient representation, not "lack of representation." Melina Mercouri was there. (She is minister of culture for the Greek socialist government.) Sophia was there. And so, of course, was Susan Sontag, whose economic theories have, in the past, been, well, vigorous: "America is a cancerous society with a runaway rate of productivity which inundates the country with increasingly unnecessary commodities."

The Sontagian definition of "necessary" is obscure. But Sontag's books are, presumably, necessary commodities, as is her theory connecting commodities and conduct: "To us, it is self-evident that the *Reader's Digest* and Lawrence Welk and Hilton Hotels are organically connected with the Special Forces napalming villages in Guatemala."

Her theory resembles Mailer's justly famous White Bread Theory of History. White bread, he said, is the "embodiment" of, among other things, "corporation land which took the taste and crust out of bread and wrapped the remains in wax paper and was, at the far extension of this same process, the same mentality which was out in Asia escalating, defoliating. . . . The white bread was also television. . . . "

It probably was this ability to see the big picture that caused Mitterrand to seek Mailer's counsel. That, and the fact that Mailer shares Mitterrand's enthusiasm for things Third World. In the history of literature, there is no love as affecting as that which Mailer felt for Castro 20 years ago. "It was," Mailer once wrote of Castro, "as if the ghost of Cortez had appeared in our century riding Zapata's white horse."

Peter Ustinov enjoyed the conference: "Governments of the left are always much better at this sort of thing because they give the appearance at least of wanting to learn, while governments of the right want only to teach." Actually, governments of the left are careful to seem to want people like Ustinov to teach. One thing that made Sontag limp with admiration for Castro's police state was the fact that "intellectuals in a revolutionary society must have a pedagogical function." Yes, "must" is the right word. Intellectuals who do not accept their function go to jail. The likes of Sontag go back to Manhattan, content to praise totalitarian pedagogy from a safe distance.

The conference was organized by France's anti-American minister of culture, Jack Lang. Sontag is sad that the United States does not have a minister of culture—except that if we did, she says, the minister might be Clint Eastwood. In that case, Americans would never be raised to the Cuban level of joy. "The Cubans know a lot," she once wrote, "about spontaneity, gaiety, sensuality, and freaking-out. They are not linear, desiccated creatures of print-culture." There is nothing like a steady diet of communist print, edited by a minister of culture, to cure linear tendencies.

News reports were disappointingly silent about Sophia Loren's thoughts on our economic difficulties, but reports agreed that discussions tended to be a bit "vague." And what good came of it at last? "Well," said Galbraith (perhaps seriously, perhaps not; I do not know how to tell when Galbraith and Mailer are being serious), "I found Norman Mailer's proposal for a tax on plastics very interesting." Besides, Galbraith said, "Only a journalist would ask if this was actually useful."

Utility is a concept important to economists, but it would be tacky to allow utilitarian considerations to spoil the fun of living well on other people's money. French taxpayers paid the bill the government incurred renting these intellectuals.

Mitterrand's policies are failing, so he wants to change the subject. Cultural posturing suits the timeless French vanity and today's French austerity. Even after a decade of inflation, intellectuals come cheap. For all their bold talk about an adversary stance toward power, they are quick to play the game of a leftist government that provides plane tickets and hotel rooms.

February 17, 1983

This Crime Wave Wants You!

Today I urge American travelers to join me in a crime wave. Let's start stealing hangers—or, to be precise, parts of them—from hotel closets.

I see you nodding vigorously; you know exactly what I mean. I mean the hangers designed for times when the hotel is renting rooms to John Dillinger or Karl Marx or someone else who lacks respect for private property. The part of the hanger that holds the garment detaches from the part that is fixed to the closet rod.

Shrewd thinking, hotel owners: Were it not for your precautions, none of us would buy Christmas presents. Why, even when it came time for the traveler to remember his wedding anniversary he would steal a matched set of your hangers for his helpmeet.

These theft-proof hangers, expressing the hotel's estimate of the guest's character, are moral insults added to the aesthetic and sometimes physical injuries that often are visited upon guests. Here you are, weary traveler, entering your room, for which you are paying perhaps $125 per night. The walls are made of tissue paper that has been pounded like veal scallopini to make it thinner, the better to enable you to hear the interesting things said and done by your neighbors. (It is said that Americans have lost all sense of community. Hotel guests often have an acute, not to say oppressive, sense of togetherness.) The wonder is that on walls so thin the management can hang those fluorescent prints of wide-eyed Mexican waifs.

But your innkeeper is nothing if not eager to please, so in the bathroom you will find a cornucopia, a little plastic basket brimming over with gifts: shampoos that are semi edible (they contain eggs or beer or coconut), a shoehorn, a shoeshine cloth, a shower cap, a needle and thread, a tiny bottle of mouthwash, bubble bath crystals, and other elixirs and ointments.

But these delights are not sufficient compensation for the instrument that involves the guest in the dangerous game of shower roulette. I refer to the high-tech shower faucet. You cannot manipulate it unless you have done doctorate-level work at MIT and have the dexterity of a brain surgeon, or André Watts.

Remember in the dark ages, when showers had two faucets? One regulated the hot water, the other the cold. You fiddled with them until the water was an agreeable temperature. Alas, the human race has grown up and gone to town. Now there is a single shower faucet which when pulled (wrenched, really) forward starts the water flowing and begins the roulette. The faucet (or one or more levers on it) is turned to regulate the temperature. The faucet may have a dial containing lots of numbers, and several lines of different colors, and maybe a button or two. But the line that matters is the thickness of a hair and is unmarked. It divides freezing from scalding.

I will herewith suspend my Dante-esque tour of the hotel room and return to the closet where lurk the offending hangers. Some ethicists with whom I have conferred say that the proper retaliation for the clear insult conferred by the hangers is for the insulted—all of us—to steal something of real utility—say, the bath mat. The ethicists' spirit is commendably aggressive, but their theory is faulty. It is that if hotels are going to assume we are all crooks, they deserve to have their assumption be self-fulfilling.

That tactic is the wrong response to injured honor. What is called for is a grand gesture, one than metes out condign punishment but expresses austere, aristocratic disdain for benefit. Therefore, the sound response is to steal the removable part of the hanger, which is useless, so the act is purely punitive, with no taint of utility.

It has been said that such is human vanity, we often are offended by praise because it seems to assign a limit to our merits. But it is right to resent hangers that do not even pay us the tribute of suspecting us of an interesting vice.

The world's random suspicions are with us always. In the drug store we are watched in round, overhead mirrors; in department stores by television cameras. We are electronically frisked in airports. But we should draw the line at the closet door.

June 7, 1984

" . . . and the home of the brave play ball."

The Bible, which devout baseball fans consider the *Sporting News* of religion, counsels patience. But what did Job and other supposed sufferers know of the interminable cultural drought of the baseball off-season? My patience is exhausted—with the deficit, the Mondale administration (no point waiting on that one) and all sports that are not baseball.

Jefferson's tombstone lists three achievements: author of the Declaration of Independence and of Virginia's statute for religious freedom, and father of the University of Virginia. Not bad, but not a patch on what my tombstone will announce: Here lies the holder of the Major League record for distance sprinted to a league championship series game—Paris to Chicago in October, 1983, for a game that started at 2:20 A.M. Paris time.

I planned to use the winter to hone a new argument against the American League's designated-hitter rule. The argument was to be that the rule is a middle-class entitlement program (it entitles some men to play extra years) and hence is partly to blame for the federal deficit. But Baltimore's dh, Ken Singleton, is one of nature's gentlemen, and helps the Orioles win, so a theory I favor must yield to a fact I love. I support the dh until Singleton retires. That is creative principledness: I learned it in Washington.

Since winter began—since the last out of the World Series, in a Sunday dusk in Philadelphia—there has been nothing to do except pout about the rottenness of a universe in which the regular season is just 162 games long. Pout, and study useful facts, such as:

There is no non-pitcher in the Hall of Fame named "Bob." To "dial 8" means to hit a home run. (On hotel telephones you dial 8 to get long distance.) Only one player's last name is also the name of the capital of a Mediterranean island republic (Steve Nicosia). Aurelio Lopez is the only pitcher in history whose first name contains all five vowels. Ed Figueroa is the only pitcher in history whose last name. . . .

Never mind. The last days of deprivation, before the great getting-up morning of April 2, have been softened by the arrival of Robert Creamer's biography *Stengel: His Life and Times.* The story is a reminder of how young America is. Casey Stengel, who died in 1975 at age 85, was a 20-year-old ballplayer when his fellow Missourian, Mark Twain, died. Twain could have written this exchange:

Stengel: "I won't trade my left fielder."

Sportswriter: "Who's your left fielder?"

Stengel: "I don't know, but if it isn't him, I'll keep him anyway."

If you disregard the (I guess) sexism, you can not deny the beauty of this utterance: "What about the shortstop Rizzuto who got nothing but daughters but throws out the lefthanded hitters in the double play?"

After managing the mighty Yankees, Stengel became the first

manager of the Mets, who in their first season (1962) lost 120 games. The first player the Mets picked in the expansion draft was a relentlessly undistinguished catcher, Hobie Landrith. Stengel explained: "You have to have a catcher or you'll have a lot of passed balls."

Creamer says the Mets were early counterculture, a harbinger of the long hair, short skirts and loud music of the Sixties. The Mets certainly were ghastly and that did, come to think about it, make them emblematic of the Sixties. Stengel ("Canzoneri is the only defensive catcher who can't catch") was just the fellow to lead them beneath his banner: "They say you can't do it, but sometimes that isn't always true." Once when a Met batter was going to the plate, Stengel pointed to the foul lines and said: "Do you know what them lines are for? They are there to hit the ball on, and those other ballplayers are all out there in the middle." That is explaining a subtle sport with middle-Western concision.

Baseball, like Stengel's long life of peaks and valleys, is like spring itself. It illustrates regeneration, resurrection and life's second chances. Forty years ago, when all able-bodied young men were fighting to make the world safe for baseball, the St. Louis Browns, for the first and last time (you can look it up), won the American League pennant. The Browns had been, and soon were again, a byword for futility and, in 1954, in the most blessed journey since the Israelites left Egypt for the Promised Land, the Browns moved to Baltimore, land of crabs and coleslaw, which beats milk and honey.

There, Studebaker became General Motors: The Browns became the Orioles and became a dynasty. They have baseball's best won–lost record over the last 28 seasons. And there, on Monday, after the World Championship flag is raised, winter will end with the last eight words of the National Anthem, which are, as every real American knows, " . . . and the home of the brave play ball."

March 29, 1984

Let Us Now Praise Anger

If New Yorkers do as they are bidden by their moral tutors, they will quit taking pleasure from the action of the subway "vigilante." I hope they tell their tutors to buzz off.

The man shot and seriously wounded four young men who accosted him. In the argument about this episode a word is getting mangled and two topics are getting tangled. The word is "vigilante," which usually has meant a member of a group organized for the suppression of crime. From what is known as this is written, what the man did in the subway may have been self-defense. If he was at all like a vigilante it was because he was armed, and perhaps angry. Also, although he may not have been looking for trouble, he does not seem to have been trying to stay out of its way.

One of the tangled topics is the moral status of what the man did. The other is how to characterize the city's rejoicing. Let us get the easy part over by saying, straightaway, that it is wrong "to take the law into your own hands," and the state should have a monopoly on the use of violence. But such moral near-absolutes wobble when the law seems increasingly unable to cope with crude violence or the community comes to feel that the state chooses not to act vigorously against such violence as the 12,000 felonies reported in New York's subways in the first 10 months of this year. When citizens believe that their city, or a sector of it, is a Hobbesian state of nature (a New York subway ride can be nasty, brutish and long), resort to violent self-help becomes predictable and less obviously reprehensible.

Social theories and their consequences—government policies—have been teaching irresponsibility: The poor are not at all responsible for their condition, men are not responsible for the children they father, women are not responsible for becoming pregnant, criminals are not responsible for their actions. Vigilantism is an individual saying: "I've got to be responsible for my own safety." Vigilantism is private enterprise in the justice business. It is apt to occur when public-sector institutions of justice fail on a wide scale. Public officials are right to insist that what the man did to the youths—at least three had criminal records—cannot be condoned. But officials should be shaken by the vehemence of the public's reproach, expressed in visceral approval of the man's deed. New York City is a welfare state. Its comprehensive solicitousness is expressed in hundreds of ways, from rent control through subsidized arts. But it has failed to provide an essential prerequisite of civilization— safety in public places.

The army of psychiatrists and psychologists who, not surprisingly, find business brisk in New York are busy pontificating about the man's inner life and the public's sickness, and a city columnist, the invaluable Jimmy Breslin (he unfailingly indicates where wisdom lies by taking positions diametrically opposed to it), says the public's cheering should stop because one of the four men is now paralyzed and if he lives to 80 the public cost may exceed $2 million. Not even Breslin can think that is the important point. (It costs New York City $40,000 a year to incarcerate a criminal, more than the annual expense Breslin imagines for the paralyzed person. Is punishment itself too costly for Breslin?) A cost-benefit analysis of this episode should acknowledge the social benefit of episodes that exercise people's capacities for healthy anger.

Many New Yorkers are angry because they believe justice is a rare accident. They believe that few violent criminals are caught, that many fewer are convicted, that most of those convicted plea-bargain their way to leniency. That is true. In 1983 in the city there were 84,043 reported robberies. There were just 7,351 convictions, all but 663 by plea-bargaining. There were 26,808 reported felonious assaults, just 727 convictions, all but 61 by plea-bargaining. Persons dependent on the subway—a nightmare of spray-painted graffiti that underscores the menacing environment of lawlessness—can become desperate.

Let us now praise anger, and especially anger in the form of a desire for justifiable vengeance. Ours is an age that overvalues the "well-adjusted" person without inquiring as to the nature of the circumstances to which we are supposed to adjust ourselves. (A well-adjusted subway rider would worry me.) We have been plied and belabored with the notion that anger is invariably a dysfunction, a "failure to cope" with our "environment." Great literature from Homer on (Nicholas Nickleby was splendidly angry) teaches otherwise; it teaches that anger can be necessary for coping. We are told that a desire for vengeance is primitive and shameful. But Hamlet's desire was noble.

When a society becomes, like ours, uneasy about calling prisons penitentiaries or penal institutions, and instead calls them "correctional institutions," the society has lost its bearings. If prisoners are "corrected," that is nice but it is an ancillary outcome. The point of imprisonment is punishment. The idea of punishment is unintelligible if severed from the idea of retribution, which is inseparable from the concept of vengeance, which is an expression of anger. No anger, no justice. A society incapable of sustained, focused anger in the form of controlled vengeance is decadent. What the man did in the subway pleased the community because it satisfied a desire for vengeance against the enemies of serenity. The community's pleasure, although not thought through (and perhaps only because it is not thought through) is wholesome.

If we lived in a world in which vengeance really was "senseless," so would life be. Life would be, as Macbeth said, "a tale told by an idiot." But *Macbeth* is about justified anger producing virtuous vengeance. If you will not take Shakespeare's word for it, take Clint Eastwood's—or else. Because of the "Dirty Harry" movies, Eastwood is a megastar. Harry is a cop who is, shall we say, pre-Miranda in his methods. The movies express an idea that is debatable (that liberal court rulings have unjustly helped criminals). But the movies satisfy a longing we should want to keep strong—a longing for justice. It is healthy anger that causes New Yorkers to take pleasure from what the man did in the subway and it is not obvious that what he did was unhealthy.

January 7, 1985

Washington's Little Miracles

In Washington's shopping and dining district, on a small triangular island where Connecticut Avenue and 18th and M streets cross, a statue of Longfellow sits, brooding: "Life is real! Life is earnest!" Every evening, when (as he was wont to say) darkness falls from the wings of night, he sees that life is indeed like that. A ramshackle truck—in its youth it was a Good Humor truck—parks beneath his pedestal. From the shadows, and silent as shadows, comes a trickle of street people, many of them homeless, to receive soup, sandwiches and coffee.

Upward of a hundred come, eat ravenously and silently steal away, back into the crevices of the metropolis. One reason drifters drift into this opulent area of the city is that bins behind fine restaurants are full of discarded food. Ah, the balance of nature: Expense accounts encourage diners to order to excess; vanity—fear of fat—causes them to leave much uneaten; desperation brings other diners to the remains.

The truck, like another operating in rougher neighborhoods, comes from Martha's Table,* a kindly place on a mean street. Veronica Maz, the head of the Table, and her volunteers operate behind three storefronts at the corner of 14th and W streets, across from what once were stables for the White House. Many windows on the street have been boarded up since the rioting after the assassination of Martin Luther King. Today the block is infested by drug dealers. The sea of social distress surrounding Martha's Table drives normal souls to despair. But if Longfellow had ever met Maz, he never would have wasted ink on that comparatively spiritless youth who bore 'mid snow and ice a banner with the strange device, "Excelsior!" Maz—short, compact: a hyperkinetic fireplug— is always up and doing with a heart for any fate.

In an unheated room (utility bills are recurring crises), bundled in a cardigan, Maz radiates serenity. She is a sociologist who 12 years ago ran smack into society and experienced an epiphany. She came to Washington to teach about poverty and took students to see some. On a wintry evening on North Capitol Street she saw men clustered around a fire in a metal barrel, cooking soup from chicken claws. Suddenly she knew her vocation. She opened a soup kitchen and began scrounging (her word for what she does).

Maz asked a North Capitol Street resident to contribute a spoon and to get a neighbor to contribute one. Shortly, the resident showed up with 80 spoons. Maz believes there is enough of everything out there, but that the distribution needs attending to. Maz goes from churches to school cafeterias and elsewhere seeking gifts of food and money. From a nonprofit "food bank" she buys supplies—principally bread—for 1,200 sandwiches a day.

Her sandwich factory also functions as a daytime shelter for children. It is not unusual for her to arrive at 7:30 A.M. and find a semidressed four-year-old ("You know how children dress themselves") who has been up since 4 A.M., or has not been to bed and whose parent, or guardian, is out—just "out." At Martha's Table, Maz says, a child finds something it may not have elsewhere, "its own little corner." The small children are looked after by 14-year-

*At 2124 14th Street NW, Washington, D.C. 20009, for those who would like to help.

old girls who have the grown-up steadiness, at once wonderful and sad, of children who have passed too fast through childhood.

Longfellow warned that into each life some rain must fall, some days must be dark and dreary. The people who sup at Maz's mobile tables, or collect clothes from her storeroom, could teach the poet a thing or two about life's deluges. They are not in poverty; poverty suggests an inadequate income. They have sunk through poverty, into another dimension of precariousness.

Many have been poor for a long time and have given up. Others come to the truck first in a clean white shirt; within days they are too dirty to seek work. Many have downward-pulling problems, such as alcoholism or mental illness. Social events, like a recession, and social policies, like the careless deinstitutionalization of the mentally ill, swell the ranks of the street people. So do changes in social values: The increasing numbers of young homeless persons reflects an increasing readiness of parents to discard troublesome children. But Maz also believes that the problems she struggles with have almost nothing to do with what Washington worries about: national policies and changes of administration.

The food truck moves from Connecticut Avenue to Lafayette Park, across from the White House, not as a political gesture but for a practical purpose: When some bewildered persons arrive in the city, they seem drawn, like iron filings by a magnet, to the one place they know of.

No social safety net, however tight its mesh, could prevent many such persons from falling through. The fortunate ones fall into the care of little miracles like Martha's Table. By "miracles" I mean only that such organizations are gloriously inexplicable. Many thinkers are ready, at the drop of a sociology textbook or a government-grant application form, to explain badness. The explanations are always in terms of this or that correctable flaw in the social environment. Washington has a growth industry devoted to such explanations. There is less interest in goodness, perhaps because it is not a "problem" and hence is boring to the professional classes that consider themselves society's problem solvers.

But how do you explain—really explain—Maz, or her volunteers, most of whom are poor enough to have enough problems of their own? Longfellow said that everyone is either an anvil or a hammer. If anvils are people who are pounded upon by life, the street people are anvils. However, Maz and others like her are hardly hammers, out to pound the world into shapes they prefer. There are plenty of hammers in Washington, thank you. But Maz, who is white, and her helpers, most of whom are black, are . . . well, just say they are good, and be done with it. Whatever invisible hand winds their inner springs had better keep doing so. When winter winds curl around Washington's monuments they carry a chilling damp, a reminder that there are rivers nearby and a swamp not far in the city's past.

December 5, 1983

Well, *I* Don't Love You, E.T.

The hot breath of summer is on America, but few children feel it. They are indoors, in the dark, watching the movie *E.T.* and being basted with three subversive ideas:
Children are people.
Adults are not.
Science is sinister.
The first idea amounts to counting chickens before they are hatched. The second is an exaggeration. The third subverts what the movie purports to encourage: a healthy capacity for astonishment.
The yuckiness of adults is an axiom of children's cinema. And truth be told, adults are, more often than not, yucky. That is because they are human, a defect they share with their pint-size detractors. (A wit once said that children are natural mimics who act like their parents in spite of all efforts to teach them good manners.) Surely children are unmanageable enough without gratuitously inoculating them with anti-adultism. Steven Spielberg, the perpetrator of *E.T.*, should be reminded of the charge that got Socrates condemned to drink hemlock: corrupting the youth of Athens.
It is not easy to corrupt American youth additionally. Geoffrey Will, 8, like all younger brothers in the theater, swooned with pleasure while sitting next to his censorious father watching the little boy in *E.T.* shout across the dinner table at the big brother; "Shut up, penis breath!" *E.T.* has perfect pitch for child talk at its gamiest. Convincing depictions of a child's-eye view of the world are rare. George Eliot's "The Mill on the Floss" and Henry James's

"What Maisie Knew" are two. But those delicate sensibilities could not have captured the scatological sounds of young American male siblings discussing their differences.

I feel about children expressing themselves the way Wellington felt about soldiers. He even disapproved of soldiers cheering, because cheering is too nearly an expression of opinion. The little boy in *E.T.* did say something neat: "How do you explain school to a higher intelligence?" The children who popped through C. S. Lewis's wardrobe into Narnia never said anything that penetrating. Still, the proper way to converse with a young person is:

Young person: What's that bird?

Older person: It's a guillemot.

Young person: That's not my idea of a guillemot.

Older person: It's God's idea of a guillemot.

I assume every American has spent the last month either in line to see, or seeing, *E.T.* In the first month it earned $100 million—$17.5 million during the Fourth of July weekend. But in case you have been spelunking beneath Kentucky since May, *E.T.* is about an extraterrestrial creature left behind in a California suburb when his buddies blast off for home. He is befriended by a boy in the American manner: The boy tosses a ball to E.T. and E.T. chucks it back.

It is, I suppose, illiberal and—even more unforgivable—ethnocentric (or, in this case, speciescentric) to note that E.T. is not just another pretty face. E.T. looks like a stump with a secret sorrow. (Except to another E.T. As Voltaire said, to a toad, beauty is popeyes, a yellow belly and spotted back.) E.T. is a brilliant, doe-eyed, soulful space elf who waddles into the hearts of the boy, his big brother and little sister. But a wasting illness brings E.T. to death's door just as a horde of scary scientists crashes through the door of the boy's house.

Throughout the movie they have been hunting the little critter, electronically eavesdropping on the house and generally acting like Watergate understudies. They pounce upon E.T. with all the whirring, pulsing, blinking paraphernalia of modern medicine. He dies anyway, then is inexplicably resurrected. He is rescued from the fell clutches of the scientists by a posse of kid bicyclists and boards a spaceship for home. This variant of the boy-sundered-from-dog theme leaves few eyes dry. But what is bothersome is the animus against science, which is seen as a morbid calling for callous vivisectionists and other unfeeling technocrats.

A childish (and Rousseau-ist) view of children as noble savages often is part of a belief that nature is a sweet garden and science and technology are spoilsome intrusions. But nature is, among other things, plagues and pestilences, cholera and locusts, floods and droughts. Earlier ages thought of nature in terms of such afflictions. As Robert Nisbet says, this age can take a sentimental view of nature because science has done so much to ameliorate it.

Disdain for science usually ends when the disdainer gets a toothache, or his child needs an operation. But hostility to science is the anti-intellectualism of the semi-intellectual. That is in part because science undercuts intellectual vanity: Measured against what is unknown, the difference between what the most and least learned persons know is trivial. *E. T.* is, ostensibly, an invitation to feel what we too rarely feel: wonder. One reason we rarely feel wonder is that science has made many things routine that once were exciting, even terrifying (travel, surgery). But science does more than its despisers do to nurture the wonderful human capacity for wonder.

U.S. missions have revealed that Saturn has braided rings and a ring composed of giant snowballs. The space program is the greatest conceivable adventure; yet the government scants it and Philistine utilitarians justify it because it has yielded such marvels as nonstick frying pans. We live in (let us say the worst) an age of journalism: an age of skimmed surfaces, of facile confidence that reality is whatever can be seen and taped and reported. But modern science teaches that things are not what they seem: Matter is energy; light is subject to gravity; the evidence of gravity waves suggests that gravitic energy is a form of radiation; to increase the speed of an object is to decrease the passage of its time. This is science; compared with it, space elves are dull as ditchwater.

The epigram that credulity is an adult's weakness but a child's strength is true. Victoria Will (21 months) croons ecstatically at the sight of a squirrel; she sees, without thinking about it, that a squirrel is a marvelous piece of work—which, come to think about it, it is. For big people, science teaches the truth that a scientist put this way: The universe is not only queerer than we suppose, it is queerer than we can suppose.

July 19, 1982

Technology That Cares

From windows facing west you see the spires of Michigan Avenue's "Magnificent Mile," a milieu for those who are nimble on the ladder of life. Facing east you see traffic streaming lickety-split along Lake Shore Drive. Chicago, Chicago: The city sings with energy. But behind the windows of the Rehabilitation Institute of Chicago are many persons for whom nimbleness is at most a memory, and the smallest motions require draining exertions, physical and emotional. Here an increasingly important kind of medicine is taught, practiced and enlarged.

The director is Henry Betts, 52, chairman of Northwestern University's Department of Rehabilitation Medicine. Tall and slender, he looks as delicate as porcelain, but his work demands a spirit as strong as bridle leather. His hair is the color of pewter, his manner is laconic, his wit is arid. His vocation is vital to more than just the 35 million Americans who are to some degree disabled. "Disabled" is a label that designates the most inclusive minority. Most Americans will at some point be in it. America is a land of speed and industrialism. But rehabilitative medicine serves persons chronically ill as well as persons disabled by injury. Hence it will be increasingly central to the health system as life expectancy increases and so does the incidence of such disabling afflictions as stroke and arthritis.

In other times and places, the infirm elderly and other disabled persons were put on ice floes, fed to dogs or thrown off mountains. Our society has been more, but not sufficiently, tender. It has often offered only cold custodial care, warehousing broken bodies and disregarding bruised but lively spirits. Until the middle of this century, treatment of the disabled was largely a system of rejection. This was partly a failure of moral imagination—out of sight, out of the range of empathy—but it also reflected the felt impotence of the medical profession. Today, treatment of the disabled reflects two related advances, medical and moral, as society expands its technical capacities and its desire to make American life more inclusive.

Technology is providing marvelous devices to make the most of the few muscles that function for the severely disabled. Machines to control a home environment (lights, appliances) cost less than attendant care. The device that enables a quadriplegic woman to be a telephone operator at the institute, handling calls through a computer she operates by sucking and blowing through a small tube, has made an invalid into a happy taxpayer.

Were America to curtail handguns and limit drunken driving substantially, the burden on rehabilitation resources would be vastly reduced. At a European conference on rehabilitation, Betts asked why a chart listing the principal causes of disability did not even mention gunshots. The response to his question was incredulity. A walk through the institute's physical-therapy rooms is an antidote to sterile libertarian arguments against passive restraints in automobiles (airbags, for example) or laws requiring use of seat belts. Such laws, common in Europe, would, Betts believes, contribute more than any other single measure to reducing the soaring expenditure on rehabilitative medicine.

In the children's ward one day recently, there were eight patients with spinal-cord injuries. Four were victims of youth-gang violence—shootings and stabbings. A tiny black infant with a serious congenital disability was in the institute for, among other things, simple nourishment. Another black baby (a boy with a rare syndrome that includes elongated and contorted fingers and toes) was being cared for while social workers tried to find a mother for him. Children at the institute are disproportionately black. Being conceived in the ghetto is hazardous to your health. Unhealthy factors can include your mother's diet, your pre- and postnatal care, the lead content in your home's interior paint and the ambience of the street and other places of play. In allocating risks, life is severly regressive.

A severely handicapped person must strive for serenity with minimal help from circumstances. But circumstances can be medicinal. Talking to a few new employees at the institute—a security guard, a billing clerk, an outpatient nurse—Betts emphasizes that a recently disabled person is sensitive to every nuance. He is apt to be depressed, filled with dread about the future, afraid he will never love or be loved again, and nagged by feelings of guilt. So, Betts says, everyone from the doctors to the billing staff who comes into contact with patients and their families must understand the complexity of the traumas and dilemmas.

Medicine is both a limited science and a subtle art. Most medicine, but especially rehabilitative medicine, depends on patients who abstract the best of themselves. When a rehabilitation hospital is run right, it gives patients the first experience in their lives in which they are surrounded by people who are entirely supportive.

Betts believes that rehabilitative medicine has much to teach the entire medical profession about the limits of "solo doctoring." Rehabilitative medicine is a paradigm of what most medicine should become. It is collaborative work—something few doctors have much experience with—and it often depends on collaboration with families and the community. Being a doctor, Betts says, is not a matter of 30 dramas a day. Surgeons may be the fighter pilots of medicine, but surgery is not the norm. Much—perhaps most—illness involves an emotional dimension, and treating it requires treating the person as a person. That requires medicine that is more than technological virtuosity.

Most of our lives are as soft as soufflés. It is hard for the hale to realize that even the strongest body is a twig easily broken by the sharp edges of life. Charles Dickens, who had the painful gift of empathy and a genius for awakening empathy in others, wrote: "There are many lives of much pain, hardship, and suffering, which, having no stirring interest for any except those who lead them, are disregarded by persons who do not want thought or feeling, but who pamper their compassion and need high stimulants to rouse it." The Institute's work, like Dickens's fiction, is such a stimulant.

November 8, 1982

Government as Black Hole

The government may have to force the Universe to file an environmental-impact statement. Evidence suggests that you should put your patio furniture in the garage, lest it get demolished, as the dinosaurs did, by a meteorite. There is a hypothesis that with monotonous regularity—every 26 million years—a star that orbits in tandem with our sun pelts Earth with a shower of meteorites. And it seems likely that 65 million years ago—the day before yesterday on the Universe's calendar—something plowed into Earth and stirred up so much debris that sunlight was radically filtered, temperatures dropped, lots of vegetation died, and soon the dinosaurs did, too. Welcome to the thrill-a-minute world of "catastrophism," the theory that the physical history of this planet has been emphatically affected by periodic natural cataclysms.

Other planets have undergone radical changes relatively quickly. Data from Viking probes launched nearly a decade ago indicate that Mars, unlike Arizona, has an abundance of water. It is frozen or in deep underground pools. But just a few billion years ago Mars was hot and humid, sort of like Florida without people. Mars seems to have changed by a domestic dynamic rather than an interstellar event of the sort that did in the dinosaurs. That one is the subject of a *Science* magazine report by three University of Chicago scientists who found something they were not looking for in clay in Denmark, Spain and New Zealand.

They found 10,000 times more carbon than normal in the geologic time zone of 65 million years ago. It is a worldwide layer of soot that may have fallen after gigantic wildfires were ignited by a meteorite six miles wide. Such a fast-moving fragment of space stuff would make a crater 85 miles wide and 20 miles deep. Because there is no such crater, the meteorite probably hit water, perhaps the Bering Sea, generating a cloud of steam and scattering white-hot rocks over 1,000 miles. The amount of soot suggests that much of the Earth's vegetation burned, and perhaps fossil fuels did, too.

However, some of the fun of science comes from the fact that people are forever popping up to say, "On the other hand. . . ." Scientists from Berkeley have found a bed of dinosaur bones north of the Arctic Circle in Alaska—appropriately, west of the town of Deadhorse. The remains of the duckbilled brutes that stood 15 feet tall prove that some dinosaurs could live in cold and in months-long nights. Arctic life may have slowed the creatures' metabolic rates, making them peckish and less affected than others by the reduction of flora and fauna farther south. This does not refute, but interestingly complicates, the "bombardment" theory about mass extinction in the Big Chill.

The fact that big things occasionally bang into Earth is not surprising, considering how much matter (and antimatter, more about which anon) has been whizzing around since the Big Bang. If you hold a penny at arm's length, you block from your field of vision a thousand galaxies 350 million miles away, which is just next door in our little backwater of the Universe. But although there is a lot of stuff, there is a lot more space. If there were only three bees in all of Europe, the air of Europe would be more crowded with bees than space is with stars. But that does not mean the patio furniture is safe from collisions. On June 30, 1908, nine years too soon, the Universe evidently landed a stiff jab on what is now the Soviet Union. Many eyewitnesses saw a flaming something plummet earthward, flattening and scorching a vast expanse of Siberian forest. The flash was seen 400 miles away; the crash was heard even farther, and seismographs on the other side of the globe sat up and took notice. Strangely, there is no crater.

David Quammen, summarizing hypotheses in *Outside* magazine, suggests that a comet, which is a loose aggregation of matter and ice and gas, burned up explosively as it roared into Earth's atmosphere. A couple of American physicists say the devastation might have been caused by a black hole. A black hole is the result of a star's gravitational collapse, in which gravity becomes so powerful that even light is pulled back into it. A black hole the size of an atom could generate a devastating shock wave from its gravitational force because it would have the compressed mass of a large asteroid. On the other hand, perhaps the forest was felled by antimatter. That stuff (antistuff?) includes positrons. A physicist says, not very helpfully, that we can think of a positron as "an electron moving backwards in time." Anyway, perhaps the reason there is no hole in the Siberian ground is that what hit Siberia was a hole. Got it?

Any bit of new knowledge about anything is of literally immeasurable value because you cannot predict its fecundity. My idea of Heaven is endless knowing. But last week we learned that we shall defer, yet again, knowing more about the heavens. NASA announced that because of budget constraints it is scrapping plans to launch an unmanned spacecraft that would have intercepted and traveled with a comet for 850 days.

Comets are especially rich sources of intimations about the origins of our solar system. The comet in question, which has the wonderful name Wild 2, was not discovered until 1978 and is the biggest and brightest of the comets that regularly sidle past Earth. An intercept may someday be scheduled, but for now it is prevented by the piddling price of $400 million over six years. That is $66 million a year. Federal farm subsidies devour that sum every 46 hours.

As one grows older and sees more of this world, one's sensibilities become, mercifully, numb. Most of the folly and philistinism fails to shock. But unless your capacity for indignation has entirely atrophied, this cancellation, forced on NASA by deficits produced by political choices, should disgust you. It is, strictly speaking, antihuman: It devalues the distinctively human capacity for curiosity and frustrates the noble urge to assuage it. What is at stake is exploration of the 99.9 (and a trillion trillion more 9s) percent of the Universe beyond Earth's atmosphere. Our government will not pay the price of 46 hours of farm subsidies to increase knowledge of the Universe and man's place in it. Such a government is itself a black hole, swallowing light.

October 28, 1985

The Genius of Winchester, Kansas

Bill James lives as a solitary genius in Winchester, Kansas. Well, not quite solitary. He has, he says, a wife to neglect. Does she, too, like baseball? "She does now," he says tersely. All James does—I'm not criticizing, he does enough—is compile, each year, *The Bill James Baseball Abstract*, the most important scientific treatise since Newton's *Principia*.

More than anyone since Pythagoras (who thought that the essence of everything could be expressed arithmetically), James believes in numbers. He also believes in looking at evidence.

For example, in 1981 careless persons said the Yankees had an "incredible" won–lost record, 51–3, in games in which they led going into the eighth inning. But James found that the average record for American League teams leading after seven innings was 49–5. The Cleveland Indians, part of baseball's Third World, were 42–3. And James found that the Yankees' remarkable won–lost record was 0–41 when they were behind after seven.

Round the clock and through the calendar, James sees things no one else sees, and disproves things that "everyone" knows are true. Next time conversation flags at a cocktail party, say: "In 1982, the Indians made 61 fewer double plays than their opponents, and no other team in the league had a differential of more than 31. The Twins were the only team that had a losing record even in games when they scored a run in the eighth inning." If people do not burst into applause, you are at the wrong cocktail party.

Two moral imperatives are: Be as intelligent as you can be at whatever you are doing, and savor the sweetness of life. James does so by marinating himself in the mathematics of baseball. Baseball statistics gave many of us our first sense of mastery, our first (and for some of us our last) sense of what it feels like to really understand something, and to know more about something than our parents do.

Baseball people are Pythagoreans, but there are limits in life to what can be quantified. I knew I was in the wrong profession when, as a graduate student in political science at Princeton, I opened a scholarly article on "The Judicial Philosophy of Justice Robert Jackson" and found a mass of equations and graphs. Part of baseball's charm is the illusion it offers that life can be completely reduced to numbers. But how would you like it, reader, if everyday from coast to coast newspapers printed a box score of your accomplishments and errors at work the previous day?

Mathematics now has proved what clear-thinking moralists always hoped would be true: The American League's designated hitter rule, America's worst mistake since electing President Buchanan, is a deserved affliction to its perpetrators. *Sports Illustrated's* Jim Kaplan, a prophet who will not be without honor in his country while I draw breath, notes that for the first time the National League has won four consecutive World Series with four different teams. Also, the National League has won 19 of the last 20 All-Star games. Some MIT mathematicians told Kaplan that the odds against such a result between equals is 23,800 to one, so Kaplan concludes the leagues are not equals.

Writing with a judgmental tone not heard since the Old Testament prophets were cataloging the shortcomings of the Israelites, Kaplan says to the American League: Your failures are the wages of sin, and the dh is sin. True, Kaplan cites other factors, such as better farm systems, and fewer small parks that encourage mindless, swing for the fences baseball. But the dh also has made managers dumber: "Because pitchers don't bat in the American League, managers have tended to leave them in the games when they are losing. As a result, there has been less thinking, less strategy, less managing." With the dh, teams lust incontinently for a big inning, so there is less aggressive scrambling for runs. Sloth. Sin.

I have warned Ronald Reagan: He will be judged by whether he rids the nation of the dh. He has not lifted a finger, preferring to squander his time on lesser matters, like arms control. I am remaining uncommitted for 1984 until I hear where Alan Cranston stands on the dh.

However, God gave us baseball so that we should not have to think about missiles or the money supply all the time. An old man once said that if he could get through March, he usually found he lived till the end of the year. Old man, wherever you are: We made it.

April 7, 1983

Looters in a Queue

Britain may soon learn what America learned: Worse than the physical damage done by rioters is the moral damage done "explaining" them.

Britain has unemployment, racial tensions and riots. But Zurich's rioters complain about the boringness of prosperity. In Amsterdam the rioting is supposedly about housing; in West Berlin, about something else.

Some British disturbances have been racial. But some mobs have been integrated. Unemployment? Many rioters are too young to be rioting for anything but the fun of it, something they may have learned from Britain's soccer fans or youth gangs. (People who think the British are uniformly placid know Britain only from Trollope.) Riots that began spontaneously became organized, with cars stolen to carry away the loot.

Before the smoke clears from any rioting, advanced thinkers are explaining that the rioting was a "cry for help" from people oppressed by some social inadequacy. But then come photographs (as from Britain) of people excitedly looting appliance stores. From Watts to Detroit to Liverpool the "cry for help" seems to be a cry for a free color TV.

Newsweek reports from Liverpool: "As the officers fell back, looters followed, including local women with shopping bags and children as young as eight. Some stood calmly in line waiting for their turn to steal food, television sets, suits and dresses. Housewives hurried away with baby carriages piled with loot." Only British looters would queue up. But the basic story is familiar.

During the New York riots of 1977, a woman looter wandered

through the second floor of a furniture store looking for end tables and complaining to other looters, "I just can't use a thing up here."

During the 1960s many Europeans blamed America's disorders on "the streak of violence" in American life (the frontier, John Dillinger, John Wayne, etc., etc.), and America's "racist society," and, of course, "alienation." Recently, Europeans have been a bit too busy to condescend to Americans—too busy failing to deal with their comparatively trivial ethnic problems. But if the British would like to benefit from our experience, they should read Midge Decter's "Looting and Liberal Racism," published in *Commentary* magazine after the rioting that followed the New York power failure of July 13, 1977.

The 1965 power failure had occasioned no rioting. What had changed by 1977? The moral climate, says Decter.

In the intervening 12 years the flow of government money to the urban poor had become a flood. The urban poor had become the focus of a social work industry with a professional stake in convincing its clients that they were not just disadvantaged, they were "victims."

The looters of 1977 "had been given permission" to riot, Decter said, by attitudes and policies "proclaiming that race and poverty were sufficient excuses for lawlessness." Permission had been given by politicians who clearly believed that appropriations were the correct response when minority "leaders" (you remember—Huey Newton, H. Rap Brown, Stokely Carmichael) threatened "long, hot summers."

Decter wrote: "Young blacks are getting the message from the liberal culture, more subtly but just as surely as from any old-time Southern sheriff, that they are, inherently and by virtue of their race, inferior. There are virtually no crimes they can commit that someone with great influence does not rush in to excuse on the grounds that we had no right to expect anything else. . . . They must not be judged by the standards that apply to everyone else in schools or in applying for or performing a job." The "very liberal and very racist idea" was "that being black is a condition for special moral allowance."

But throughout American cities in the 1960s, as in New York in 1977, the vast majority of blacks did not riot. And they must have wondered why not, by the time white liberal "explainers" were finished.

It is dismaying to note that British officials are reading the

Kerner Commission report which fatuously blamed America's riots on "white racism." A danger Britain faces is the emergence of an official "explanation" that will demoralize the vast majority of un-employed whites and immigrants who are not lawless.

British officials would do better to read Decter, who reports that after the 1977 riots, two young black boys were asked why they had not participated in the looting that had swirled around them. One said: "I was scared of the cops." The other said: "Because my mamma would have killed me." There is more to be learned from those two boys than from a thousand volumes from the liberal "explanation industry."

July 16, 1981

The Indignation Industry

Richard Lamm's thick shock of hair was gray long before he said that dreadful thing, but the reaction to what he said was enough to bleach white anyone's hair. And the reaction illustrated a recurring, growing and dismal aspect of public discourse. The phenomenon is indignation exhibitionism.

America spends a large and growing portion of its wealth on medical care, much of it in the final months of patients' lives. So last year Lamm, Colorado's governor, then 48, meeting with some health lawyers, said society has ethical questions to answer about prolonging life. It should not automatically allocate scarce re-sources and technological miracles to produce short extensions of life for persons who are terminally ill. He said we all have "a duty to die and get out of the way with all of our machines and artificial hearts and everything else." He could have given this issue a wide berth. Or he could have touched it with soft, round-edged language that would have caused neither contention nor, of course, reflec-tion. Instead, refusing to prettify things, he used the stern word "duty." What he produced was a Krakatoa of indignation.

Part, but only part, of the problem was that he was misquoted as saying the terminally ill and elderly should get out of the way. (One headline was: LAMM TO ELDERLY: DROP DEAD.) The misquo-tation was quickly corrected and the correction was quickly for-gotten, lest it spoil the fun of the folks who were reeling about and acting scandalized. By raising a difficult problem Lamm was exercising leadership. He was rewarded with the stigma of "insensitivity."

Washington is home for many advocacy groups and has an unreasonably high ratio of television cameras to human beings. In Washington when an official says something that might ignite some advocates (for the poor, the teachers, the trout and trees . . .) the camera crews fan out, knocking on doors, collecting statements of outrage. The statements come not from the unorganized masses. (Lamm's mail indicated that most elderly Americans think he spoke common sense.) Rather, the really blistering stuff comes from people who specialize in strong feelings, persons whose job is to advocate. No advocate, nervously looking around him, can dare to seem less indignant than the other advocates, lest he seem insufficiently sensitive.

Do you remember when Ed Meese said there is no hunger in America? No, you do not because he did not say that. He said some people go to soup kitchens because they prefer not to pay for food, and he said he had not seen "any authoritative figures" establishing that there are hungry children. Now, he could have raised the issue he wanted to raise—that there is more passion than precision in arguments about poverty; that compassion can stand to be leavened with information—more delicately. But we were off and running in the sensitivity sweepstakes. Many Americans earn their living by striking moral poses. They are participants in an unending moral Olympics, a competition in spiritual preening—the more-sensitive-than-thou event. For a week or so Meese's words were a public-works project, providing work for the indignation industry.

This advisory panel, said Jim Watt jokingly, has "a black, a woman, two Jews and a cripple. And we have talent." One reason for the firestorm that followed was that Watt was being playful with a piety—with the ethnic and sexual spoils system that has grown behind the euphemism "affirmative action." But his cardinal sin was the word "cripple." Handicapped people understandably do not like that word. But in this case there was not even an opening phase when people pretended that the issue was substantive. It was sensitivity, all the way, which brings us all the way to Bitburg . . .

Whoa! Do not throw this magazine across the room. I raise the wrung-out subject of Bitburg to put that controversy into a pattern. The two low points were when the president suggested we should somehow put the Holocaust behind us and when he seemed to say that many German soldiers were not just victims but as much victims of Nazism as Jews were. His problem was not mere insensitivity, it was stark intellectual chaos. But by the time he got to Bitburg he and his writers had put down on paper, as precisely as the language makes possible, the truth: We should work at remembering the ghastly consequences of Nazism, including the fact that for thousands of young Germans Nazism meant only "a brutal end to a short life."

However, an hour later a leader of the American Jewish Committee was on network television declaring that Reagan "seems again to be equating the nature of the deaths and the nature of the killings between those who died fighting for Hitler and those who were the victims of Hitler." That was simply and flagrantly false: Reagan had done no such thing. Perhaps by then nothing he could have said—he could have spoken as eloquently as Pericles; he could have read a Pizza Hut menu—would have prevented some persons, impelled by the momentum of indignation, from insisting that he had repeated his blunder. It was almost as though Reagan had done something unfair by correcting himself. He had no *right* to recover.

Our addiction to indignation is going to compound the problems of governance. Already we have institutional gridlock; soon we may have intellectual paralysis. As the inability to write a budget demonstrates, the government is bound down by thousands of thin but cumulatively immobilizing threads. The government among the client groups is like Gulliver among the Lilliputians. If the trafficking in indignation continues, public discourse is going to become more and more bland and homogenized. Everyone in public life may eventually practice too much self-censorship, lest any thought give some hair-trigger group a pretext for the fun of waxing outraged. The result will be timid, frozen, boring thought.

On an old radio program a character used to say, "If it makes you happy to be unhappy, then be unhappy." That character was admirably broad-minded, but it is not easy to be so placid about people who, luxuriating in indignation, are infecting public life with a moralism that is shrill, sterile, perfunctory and unconvincing.

May 27, 1985

Teenagers and Birth Control

Victoria Will is two years old and perfect. That is, she is perfectly like a two-year-old, which means she has the executive disposition of Lady Macbeth:

Me: "What is your name?"

She: "No!"

That word will stand her in good stead in about 15 years. Until then I live in blissful ignorance of the special tribulations of a parent of an adolescent daughter. But as a citizen as well as a father, I favor the Department of Health and Human Services' rule requiring federally funded birth-control clinics to notify parents whose daughters 17 or under are receiving prescription contraceptive drugs or devices.

Opponents call this the "squeal rule," implying that it is dishonorable for the government to codify the fact that parents have an interest in knowing of a minor daughter's receipt of prescription materials related to sexual activity. Notice, the rule does not require parental permission. A child may need parental consent even to take a school trip to the zoo, but the HHS rule requires only parental notification, and only after prescriptions have been filled.

A civil liberty, correctly understood, is a liberty central to the functioning of democracy. The American Civil Liberties Union evidently thinks it is a civil liberty for children to be given federally subsidized contraceptive measures and counsel, in secret. In response to an ACLU suit, a judge has blocked implementation of the rule, arguing that it would lead to an increase in teenage pregnancy and thus constitute "blatant disregard" for Congress's intent in supporting family-planning clinics. Arguing against the rule in another court, a lawyer said it would cause 33,000 such pregnancies annually. Amazing, how folks can know these things.

It is devilishly difficult to prove cause-and-effect relationships between social policies and social changes. But this is clear: The problem of teenage pregnancy has grown as contraceptives and sex education have become increasingly available. I am not saying the availability caused the growth. But it would be rash to say the availability is irrelevant. And many of those who today are predicting with such certitude awful results from the HHS rule predicted that teenage pregnancies would decline as contraception and sex education became more available.

Supporters of the rule note that prescription birth-control measures can have serious side effects. Opponents reply that pregnancy is more dangerous than contraception, especially to adolescents. That is true, but hardly an answer to this argument: In a society where most schools will not give a child an aspirin without parental consent, parents have the minimal right to be notified after a minor daughter has received a drug related to sexual activity. Besides, adolescents have a third choice between contraception and pregnancy. It is continence.

Opponents of the rule say it constitutes governmental intrusion into family relationships. But surely the government subverts family relationships when it subsidizes 5,000 clinics that purvey to children medical treatment and counsel on morally important matters, and do so without informing those who have legal, financial and moral responsibility for children—parents.

Opponents say that if parents are told that their minor daughters are on the Pill, some daughters will be deterred from seeking contraceptives, but will be no less sexually active. This is true. But the law that the HHS rule implements does not say that all values shall be sacrificed to the single aim of reducing pregnancy. Indeed, the law stipulates that subsidized clinics must "encourage," to the extent practical, "family participation." Again, the HHS rule does not require parental participation. It does not, for example, require that parents accompany the child to the clinic. It does not even require that contraceptive drugs or devices be withheld until parents are notified. It requires only that parents receive after-the-fact information that parents can act on as they please. It is hard to imagine a more minimal compliance with Congress's mandate to "encourage" parental participation. The rule is just an executive-branch attempt to balance the various values Congress affirmed.

It has provoked a disproportionate response. The New York Times has editorialized against the rule at least six times, denouncing it as "cruel." The Times says the rule would increase bureaucracy, which in this case the Times is against. The Times says the rule is an example of intrusive government, which in this case the Times is against. (Force busing? Fine. Parental notification of drugs prescribed for unemancipated minors? Too intrusive.) Why such uproar over a halfhearted rule that barely constitutes compliance with Congress's unexceptionable affirmation of parental involvement? Perhaps the decay of liberalism into a doctrine of "liberation" has led to this idea: Even children must be "liberated," even from parental knowledge of even their sexual activities. Perhaps the extreme individualism of today's liberalism finds "repressive" even restraints associated with a collectivity as basic as the family.

Many opponents of the rule seem to think that realism consists of accepting as irreversible the recent increase in teenage promiscuity. (Be honest, readers: how many of you think the value-laden word "promiscuous" is illiberal?) Granted, governments can do nothing to make teenagers less sexually ardent. And when traditional mores are dissolving as fast as ours are, trying to arrest the dissolution with a law is like trying to lasso a locomotive with a thread. However, policy need not passively reflect and accommodate itself to every change, however destructive. It need not regard social change as a process that is or ought to be entirely autonomous, utterly immune to the influence of judicious interventions. The HHS rule is such an intervention.

Law should express society's core values, such as parental responsibility. If HHS's mild rule is declared incompatible with public policy, what, for goodness's sake, is that policy? What values does it affirm, or subvert by neglect? HHS's rule at least does not express complacent acceptance of the inevitability of today's rate of teenage sexual activity. Obviously the trend is against sexual restraint. But as has been said, a trend is not a destiny.

February 28, 1983

At First Blush

Here is a question that might cause you to blush: What causes you to blush?

When considering the campaign against "porn rock"—vulgar and obscene lyrics in rock music—consider that question, and this one: Would you want to live in a world in which no one, not even the young, blushed?

Various parents' groups are putting wholesome pressure on recording companies, radio stations and the makers of rock videos to exercise discretion and self-restraint. Approximately one-third of the nation's radio stations have rock formats, and many are behaving responsibly. But the sort of people who profit from aggressively marketing porn rock have the morals of the marketplace, and the marketplace is the place to get their attention. In addition, putting labels on records with vulgar lyrics is going to help parents exercise supervision.

Rock music has become a plague of messages about sexual promiscuity, bisexuality, incest, sado-masochism, satanism, drug use, alcohol abuse and, constantly, misogyny. The lyrics regarding these things are celebratory, encouraging or at least desensitizing. By making these subjects the common currency of popular entertainment, the lyrics drain the subjects of their power to shock— their power to make people blush. The concern is less that children will emulate the frenzied behavior described in porn rock than that they will succumb to the lassitude of the de-moralized.

As people become older they become less given to blushing. This is, in part, because they lose that sweet softness of youthful character that is called innocence and makes one's sensibilities subject to shock. People blush for various reasons. Sometimes it is because we suddenly have embarrassing attention called to ourselves. Sometimes we blush when utterly alone, when we think of something about ourselves that is shaming—such as the fact that almost nothing causes us to blush.

Often people blush because they are exposed to something that should be private or is shameful. This may be an endangered species of blushing, thanks to omnipresent vulgarities like porn rock making even the vilest things somehow banal.

Walter Berns, the political philosopher, asks: What if, contrary to Freud and much conventional wisdom, shame is natural to man and shamelessness is acquired? If so, the acquisition of shamelessness through the shedding of "hang-ups" is an important political event. There is a connection between self-restraint and shame. An individual incapable of shame and embarrassment is probably incapable of the governance of the self. A public incapable of shame and embarrassment about public vulgarity is unsuited to self-government.

There is an upward ratchet effect in the coarsening of populations. Today's 12-year-olds cannot enjoy—can hardly sit still for— the kind of 1950s Westerns that enthralled their fathers. Today's 12-year-olds are so addicted (that is not too strong a word) to the slam-bang nonstop roar of Steven Spielberg movies, their attention is not held by, say, John Wayne in *She Wore a Yellow Ribbon*.

The social atmosphere is heavily dosed with sexuality, from the selling of blue jeans to the entertaining of prime-time television audiences. Thus it is perhaps reasonable to have feelings of fatalism. Perhaps societies, like rivers, run naturally downhill. Perhaps the coarsening of a public is irreversible, especially when the coarsening concerns a powerful and pleasurable appetite such as sex. But it is demonstrably not true that societies cannot move away from coarseness toward delicacy of feeling.

In the first half of the 18th century, the dawn of the Age of Reason, a form of English merriment on Guy Fawkes nights was to burn an effigy of the Pope. The belly of the effigy was filled with cats whose howls of agony in the flames were supposed to represent the voice of the devil emanating from the Catholic Church. That kind of cruelty to animals is, by today's standards, obscene. Sensibilities can change for the better. So fatalism is wrong and the porn rock fight is worth fighting.

Mass culture, and especially music, matters. Nothing is more striking to a young parent than the pull of popular culture on even three- and four-year-olds. And perhaps good music can make good values more adhesive to children.

People can reasonably argue about what is the second finest work of music—a Mozart concerto, a Beethoven symphony, this or that Bach tune. But everyone knows that the acme of the art of music is the currently popular song that says, "Put me in, coach, I'm ready to play. . . . Look at me, I can be centerfield." The Republic has a fighting chance as long as the popularity of porn rock can be rivaled by the popularity of its moral opposite, baseball rock.

September 15, 1985

The Shocking Bourgeoisie

The rising sun spreads a rug of light through St. Louis's Gateway Arch and across a less loved artifact 11 blocks away. That object is a "sculpture" called *Twain*, named after a Missouri boy who became a master of realism. It covers most of a block and consists of eight panels of rusting steel placed in a formation that resembles a triangle drawn by a quavering hand. *Twain* was perpetrated by Richard Serra, a "postminimalist" entrepreneur who once exhibited, as art, a 97-pound pig in a cage. His arrogance is almost a work of art. He says: "I don't think it is the function of art to be pleasing." He thinks it is the function of the public to give people like him money and space and limitless license. In fine, the public is to pay up and shut up. *Twain* is, in part, your tax dollars at work. The federal government chipped in.

Today there is rising over St. Louis a dark cloud of insurrection, a cloud as impressive as the one that rose over Toledo (Spain, not Ohio) and stirred El Greco, an artist who did not work in rusty metal. Some St. Louisans have seen *Twain* steadily and seen it whole and have seen enough of it. Not since opposition to the Dred Scott decision—Scott's case was tried in a nearby courthouse—has there been such an admirable opposition movement. St. Louisans are hospitable, ready to scale the skies and pluck out stars and strew them at your feet. But when provoked they are as turbulent as the tornadoes that frequent the region. Serra also is finding New Yorkers tiresome. In Manhattan there is a move afoot to junk Serra's *Tilted Arc*, 73 tons of rusty steel 12 feet high and stretching 120 feet across the plaza of a federal building. (Yes, more tax dollars.) It is not just an eyesore, it is a nuisance, impeding pedestrians.

The natives are restless elsewhere, too. Chicagoans have never been considered among Nature's hamsters—tame—and some of them are up in arms about what they consider graffiti applied to the walls of a library and called a "fresco." In a world gone wonky, nowhere is safe. In Paris, the artist Christo is preparing to wrap the most beautiful Seine bridge, the 16th-century Pont Neuf, in shiny beige nylon, as a "sculpture." This treatment of the bridge is like the treatment of Michelangelo's *Pietà* at the 1964 World's Fair, where it was illuminated with flickering blue light, presumably to improve it.

Time was when artists wanted to shock the bourgeoisie. Today the bourgeoisie is running around with open wallets, trying to call forth art with cash. But art is not a commodity like pretzels. Strong monetary demand for pretzels increases the supply of pretzel makers. Their products are recognizably pretzels, and the best pretzel makers prosper. The market for art is different because the supply of good art is not similarly elastic. Unless, of course, you suspend all standards. There will be an abundance of fine art if you declare that fine art is anything that anyone calling himself an artist calls fine art. One way to expand the supply of anything is to define it so permissively that limiting standards evaporate and almost anything can be included. But as a 19th-century politician from across the Mississippi River, up in Sangamon County, Ill., once said: If I

call a tail a leg, how many legs has a dog got? Five? No, because
calling a tail a leg doesn't make it a leg.

Such is the docility and gullibility of many city governments
and corporations, it is almost dismaying when they decide to commission works of art. Of course, the disproportion between the large
demand for art and the small supply of serious artists is not an argument against patronage. Pope Julius II did posterity a favor with
his "jobs for the boys" program for artists. His boys included Michelangelo and Raphael. Today, patrons must have considerable
prudence and self-confidence when the ratio of charlatans to serious
artists is as high as it is.

Some Serra defenders say his First Amendment rights are being
trampled. But the issue is not a person's right to "express" his whims
in rusty steel. The issue is the public's right not to be saddled with
the results forever. Even if the public's hostility were just a whim,
so what? Artists who peddle their whims as art, counting on an
absence of critical standards, cannot suddenly claim to have standards superior to the public's and incomprehensible to the public.
And they cannot hide behind this crashing non sequitur: Great in-
novations in art often have met hostility, therefore whatever pro-
vokes hostility must be a great innovation. Joan Mondale says the
public should give *Tilted Arc* time to prove its "eternity." Sounds
like a long wait.

Today Philistines often march under the banner of anti-Phil-
istinism. Serra's defenders stigmatize his detractors as a backward
mob slow to recognize genius. This is deliciously ironic, considering
that abstract art once was defended as "democratic." It was supposed to be art purged of "academicism," art immediately and
equally "accessible" to everyone, art "understood" by even the un-
tutored eye. Actually, it is anti-intellectual "art" enveloped by ludicrous intellectualizing.

For example, this is how one critic "understands" Jackson Pollock's canvases covered with drips: "Pollock's strength lies in the
emphatic surfaces of his pictures, which it is his concern to maintain and intensify in all that thick, fuliginous flatness. . . ." One
wishes that critic had reviewed Serra's movie that featured nothing
but a hand holding a wad of cloth at arm's length until the arm
was exhausted and the cloth dropped. One Serra fan brings his art-
Babel to a rolling boil to praise the "savage elegance" of Serra's
"resilient" and "insistent" stuff.

The emptiness of postminimalist and other fads of nonrepre-

sentational art has elicited floods of theorizing from a clerisy of critics. They have acquired importance as the assigners of importance
to substanceless "art." Theirs is not tiring work. The assigning can
be capricious because the critics are not inhibited by the presence
of any content in the art they construe. The exegesis of effortless
art is effortless. If human beings were dominoes, such critics and
the artists they inflate would be double blanks. In their formative
years they must have been spanked with rolled-up learned journals
of fine arts. How else explain their contempt for mind, and their
seeming attempt to give art a bad name?

September 16, 1985

Art and the Conscientious Janitor

Art lovers are heartened by New York's decision not to prosecute the fellow who put what the police called a bomb atop the
Brooklyn Bridge. The fellow, who calls himself an "environmental
artist," says the bucket full of fireworks was "kinetic sculpture."
Well, it would have been if the "sculpture" had not had a defective
fuse.

A British gallery has a new work, *Room Temperature*, featuring two dead flies and a bucket of water, in which float four apples
and six uninflated balloons. A gallery official says the work left him
"amazed by its completeness, its oneness, its apparent obviousness.
Yet it had the ability to tease, to make me wonder, and question,
to lead me in other directions. Why? This is air and this is water.
Have you looked at them, have you actually seen these elements
before? Here they are."

Matisse said he hoped his art would have the pleasing effect
of an armchair on a tired businessman. Matisse, alas, is not around
to meet the artist who fired a revolver at an airplane taking off from
Los Angeles, and called his act a work of art. In 1929 Walter
Lippmann said art had "ceased not only to depict any theory of
destiny but has ceased to express any important human mood in the
presence of destiny." But pistol-packing "artists" express a mood:
Anything goes.

In 1977, one of Joseph Beuys's masterpieces—a child's bathtub
flecked with sticking plaster—was mistakenly used to cool beer dur-

ing a party at the museum that owns it. But, then, a conscientious janitor would have cleared away the pile of bricks that was a display at London's Tate Gallery. The bourgeoisie of Hartford, Connecticut, questions the wisdom of spending $87,000 for 36 boulders which an artist-entrepreneur placed in some green space and called "stone field sculpture."

But an American foundation paid $300,000 to finance *Vertical Kilometer*, a brass rod one kilometer long, buried in a hole one kilometer deep. The same artist also perpetrated *Lightning Field*, a patch of New Mexico made into a pin cushion by metal rods. Ah, wilderness: Consider *Spiral Jetty*, a curling path of rocks bulldozed into Utah's Great Salt Lake.

Claes Oldenburg, who makes large toothbrushes and other banalities (Philadelphia has a giant clothespin) once said: "I am for an art that is political-erotical-mystical, that does something other than sit on its ass in a museum." His masterpiece, *Two Cheeseburgers with Everything* (a burlap-and-plaster model of just what the title says), sits in the possession of New York's Museum of Modern Art.

Roy Lichtenstein (he paints large snippets from comic books) once said his aim was to paint a picture so ugly nobody would buy it. The harder he tried, the hotter became his sales. The avant-garde was a 19th-century idea of revolutionary daring in the face of stultifying elite standards of acceptable taste. Pity the poor artist today: Where there are no standards, there can be no avant-garde.

Robert Hughes, *Time* magazine's art critic and author of *The Shock of the New*, says that every five years America's art schools graduate more people than lived in Florence in the last quarter of the 15th century, and that there probably are more galleries than bakeries in New York. But college credit in "art" has been given for photographing 650 San Diego garages, and for spending a week in a gym locker (a work—or act—of art called "a duration-confinement body-piece").

The broadened definition of art to include doing anything, as well as making anything, is a triumph of democracy: Everyone can be—indeed, cannot help but be—an artist. Hughes notes that Richard Tuttle "was chosen to represent America at the 1976 Venice Biennale with a stick rather longer than a pencil and three-quarters of an inch thick, cut from a length of standard 1-inch lumber, unpainted, and placed in solitary magnificence on the wall of the U.S. Pavilion." Your tax dollars were at work in that display of purely democratic art: Having no content, Tuttle's "art" was immune to the charge of "elitism."

New York City, which evidently has cash to spare, is considering requiring that works of art be purchased for all new or renovated municipal buildings. In an age when sticks count as art, the supply of art is sure to expand to satisfy the economic demand.

In 1915, Paul Klee said: "The more fearful the world becomes, the more art becomes abstract." What can be inferred about the world when art becomes absurd?

August 2, 1981

Miami Wild

MIAMI—"Look," says the mayor, turning at the lunch table and gesturing toward the window and beyond at this city's erupting skyline. "If it's so bad, how come the big players in real estate are here?" And he rattles off a list of those players.

Well, maybe some of the real estate boom derives from the fact that there is a lot of bad money looking for things to buy. And one reason many banks and corporations have offices here is the same reason a few things are bad here: Latin America is just over the horizon. So are the drug traffickers.

"Look," says Mayor Maurice Ferre, 49, using a knife to draw a line on the tablecloth. "Draw a line due south to the South Pole. Every major airport in South America is to the east of Miami. If you want to fly from Lima to Los Angeles, the quickest way is through Miami." And among the things coming through Miami is a flood of "controlled substances," which barely are. Controlled, that is. The drug traffic continues in spite of Crockett and Tubbs, the characters—and how!—on the television show *Miami Vice*.

Viewing that program is like being locked inside a rock video with two boys who, having overdosed on chocolate donuts, are hyperactive and should be sent to their rooms. Crockett and Tubbs are police officers. Sure they are. When not roaring around in a speedboat, they are roaring around in a Ferrari, and in $500 Italian linen jackets and sleeveless, peach-colored T-shirts.

Does this shoot-'em-up portraying Miami as crime-ridden bother the mayor? No, Ferre says equably, people are trying to explain Miami's vitality in terms of the wrong chemicals. It started with Dow, not drugs.

About 15 years ago, he says, Dow Chemical Co. decided it could not efficiently run its Latin American operations out of Michigan and did an elaborate study which highlighted Miami's advantages. That study circulated widely, and soon the city's commercial base achieved a critical mass, with European and American banks and corporations creating "symbiotic energy." The mayor is in his sixth two-year term and, like the city, is revved up.

Energy, symbiotic or other, Miami has, some people think, in excess. It had ample energy even before Castro flooded it in 1979 with refugees lacking proper character references. But the mayor insists that Miami is a Latin American city only the way Boston is Irish or Milwaukee is Polish and German.

Miami has been called "the Hong Kong of Latin America," but the mayor prefers to compare it to Beirut—before the civil war, he hastens to add. He says Miami is to Latin America what Beirut was to the Arab World: a center for commerce, pleasure and cosmopolitanism. The big difference, the mayor says, is "the American flag"—the FBI, the Constitution, the law. But some Miamians think the difference is not as big as it should be.

Of the drug money sloshing around Miami, the mayor says: "Is it a great part of Miami? Of course." Look, he says, Miami is the cocaine capital of the world only because the United States is the main cocaine market.

If all international cocaine merchants formed a single American company, that company would rank with the Ford Motor Company near the top of *Fortune* magazine's list of largest corporations. It would be three times larger than the movie and recording industries—combined. Recently some cocaine was found here in the cargo on a Colombian 747 airliner. The street value of the cocaine was $800 million—five times the value of the 747.

Drug runners have the best boats, planes and electronic equipment. Miami, says the mayor, can not help but be awash with drug money. Dealers can load the cash into jets and deliver it to numbered accounts in Bahamian or other "offshore" banks and then have it transferred, electronically, back to Miami. And such laundering is not always necessary. If someone comes into a showroom offering $60,000 cash for an automobile, not many salespersons are going to call the police.

Look, the mayor says cheerfully, geography is destiny and

Florida always has attracted adventurous spirits because it is "the end of the line." So it is, and so it has been home for aviation pioneers, land speculators and other high-spirited folks including, it is safe to say, America's only mayor who compares his city to Beirut—before the roof fell in, of course. The end of the line: That was the Wild West when it was a frontier. Miami is a sort of frontier. It is the Wild South, and the sheriff wears a sleeveless, peach-colored T-shirt.

April 18, 1985

"Ex-cel-lent!"

I well remember my first adventure with Indy. Indiana Jones, that is. I am, I feel, on a first-name basis with him, we have been through so much together.

Our first adventure was three summers ago, and I had a seven-year-old on my lap. I was ready to steady and comfort him during the assault of what I had been warned were jolting scenes in *Raiders of the Lost Ark*, such as the early scene where gobs of tarantulas fall on Indy's back. That scene, even though anticipated, was a turn-the-bones-to-jelly shocker, for father. The seven-year-old sighed contentedly and said in the measured cadence of that season's sophistication: "Ex-cel-lent!"

Parents are pleased to believe, against all evidence, that their children's souls are sensitive flowers—orchids, not marigolds—and that, therefore, care must be taken lest the little creatures be traumatized by exposure to this or that cultural excess. Actually, they are more durable—perhaps "impervious" is a better word—than we think. But there are limits to what they should experience, and *Indiana Jones and the Temple of Doom* oversteps those limits.

I have now had my second adventure with Indy, the archaeologist with the bullwhip and the thirst for excitement. *Raiders* are stimulating enough, thank you, with pits of vipers, villains diced by airplane propellers, faces melting and corpses perforated by arrows, like San Sabastian. But *The Temple of Doom* sets a standard for violent action at which subsequent movies will shoot, in vain, I hope.

A football game is approximately nine minutes of action and

a couple of hours of standing around and sorting things out. This movie is about nine minutes of relative calm, and 109 minutes of violent action punctuated by intervals of mere repulsiveness.

I saw it with an exacting critic, a 12-year-old who was impatient for the snakes to slither on stage, the snake motif being strong in this genre. He was soon satisfied, because the eating of live little snakes is part of a meal that includes beetles, eyeball soup and chilled monkey's brains served from staring skulls. That meal was comic relief from giant roaches and other creepy crawly things, and from children flogging sadists who are led by a live wire who with his bare hands plucks the hearts from the chests of victims.

The frolicsome movie proceeds without undue expenditure of nuance, which is fine, but suddenly it becomes ugly. There is salacious cruelty in the torture scene where a fellow is roasted alive. But then, that is sort of the way it is apt to be with your basic torture scene.

The flogging, roasting, and heart-plucking are not suitable for children. The movie concedes as much by warning that some scenes may be too "intense" for young children. The adjective "intense" is the sort of mushy word that committees settle on when they are groping for a way to circle the truth without barging into it.

The truth is that this movie, as fare for children, is unsuitable and, as a cultural symptom, is depressing. It is not just another example of the inexorable tendency toward excess, like halftime shows at Super Bowls. It is an example of the upward ratchet effect of shocking extremism in popular entertainment. This march toward the shocking is producing a generation that would yawn through the parting of the Red Sea. We who, when children, considered Hopalong Cassidy and Randolph Scott the last words in excitement now know better, but we doubt that our children are more fortunate.

The two persons responsible for *Temple of Doom*, Steven Spielberg and George Lucas, are commercial geniuses. The noun is right but it is severely limited and devalued by the adjective, which also is right. Their obsession with juvenile obsessions (repulsive creatures and foods) may be evidence of their arrested development, which is their problem. But the sensory blitzkrieg they have produced to coin money is apt to stunt the imaginations of children, and that is our problem. This movie is perfectly made for perfectly passive children—for children raised on electronic images rather than on reading, which requires imaginative involvement.

Movies can engage the imagination but doing so requires art. And whatever else art involves, it involves proportionality and subtlety—the ability to approach the edge of excess without falling in. This movie leaps in exuberantly, and that is why there may not be a third Indy epic. What is left to happen to him? If the future takes such revenge for today's excess, well, ex-cel-lent.

May 31, 1984

Miss Manners's Ignoble Savages

The three children under my jurisdiction are in for it now. Mrs. Will and I imprudently produced them before Judith Martin produced her new book, but now we are going to buckle down to bringing them up by the book. Ms. Martin, hitherto the author of *Miss Manners' Guide to Excruciatingly Correct Behavior*, has just published *Miss Manners' Guide to Rearing Perfect Children*. The oldest Will child is 12 and the youngest is about to wage her fourth birthday party (more about which anon), so we have our work cut out for us. But Miss Manners says a parent's duty to persevere is absolute. Miss Manners is a Miss after my heart because she deals exclusively in categorical imperatives. She has not got the word that the theory of relativity not only revolutionized physics but supposedly knocked morals (of which manners are a dimension) into a cocked hat.

Like Plato, and unlike the political candidates crashing around in the underbrush, Miss Manners knows there is one subject of ultimate social significance. It is—no, silly, not arms control or even the new federalism—childrearing. If parents did it right—which includes preparing the children to rear children—in one generation the world would be civilized, forever. Not since Edmund Burke's *Reflections on the Revolution in France* has there been a counterrevolutionary trumpet call as ringing as Miss Manners's. Her aim is restoration of the *ancien régime*, the belief that children actually need rearing and lots of it.

In the 1960s the theory was that a serious childrearing interferes with the free flowering of the child as a creative individual. In the 1970s (when some of the products of the 1960s were becoming parents) the theory was that the work—and it is that—of childrearing interferes with the free flowering of the parent as a creative individual. Those theories produced children who were "free, creative and honest"—which is to say, unmannerly, ignorant and rude. Miss Manners is magnificently impatient with the idea that children are noble savages. The savagery she concedes; the nobility she thinks is missing and needs inculcating.

Hence she says that being taught to share toys "goes directly against human nature and is therefore an important step in the opposite direction, toward civilization." As she says, every child is born ignorant and oafish and is civilized by two things, example and nagging. "It takes 18 years of constant work to get one into presentable enough shape so that a college will take him or her off your hands for the winter season, and it can easily take another 10 years of coaching and reviewing before someone will consent to take the child on permanently." For the transmission of civilization, Miss Manners preaches three virtues: intolerance, inflexibility, insincerity.

Inflexibility? Children, given their druthers, are rigid traditionalists. "The devotion to ritual exhibited by the average toddler in regard to his bedtime routine would make a 19th-century English butler look like a free spirit." Children want to know where they stand, what the rules are. They are programmed by nature to ask "Why?" and the full text of the correct response to "Why?" is "Because."

Intolerance? Only of bad form. Miss Manners is like Lincoln, who warned against seeking a middle ground between right and wrong. He was talking about slavery and she is talking about the evil of putting the milk carton on the breakfast table, but the principle is pretty much the same. She contends—only a braver man that I who would gainsay her—that people who are latitudinarian about milk cartons on breakfast tables will be wishy-washy on big questions, such as slavery or the correct placement of teaspoons. (Miss Manners knows it is easier to be a friend of a political or sexual scoundrel than of someone who scoops up gravy with his knife.

Insincerity? Sincerity has its charms—there is a time and place for everything—but carried too far it causes civil war. People who praise candor should be reminded that if everyone went around saying and acting exactly as they think and feel, society would disintegrate. Against the vice of immoderate honesty Miss Manners urges the virtue of hypocrisy. That is why childrearing involves giving children acting lessons, as in "act like a lady" or, more often, "act like a human being—please."

Sometimes a child needs acting lessons to express the feelings he really has. A parent who asks a child, "Would you like to pig out on pizza?" is apt to get this response: "Uh huh." The child does not know how to act—how to say, "Thank you, I'd love to!" More often children need lessons in how to act in ways highly unnatural to them—how to act fascinated by what Aunt Min is saying about her petunias or interested in what a sibling is saying at the dinner table or appreciative of a birthday present the child already has two of. Which brings me to the grim subject of birthday parties.

Miss Manners wonders why children, who do not drink, flirt or converse, wish to give parties. Well, why did the Vikings pillage? For booty, which is also the point of birthday parties. There are few spectacles as soul-searing as that of a birthday child jerking a present from the hands of a guest (children have an infinite capacity for regarding largess as no more than their due), ripping off the wrapping and delivering a sincere, honest, candid opinion of it. The guest then curls at the edges like scorched paper. But if social acting is taught, even birthdays can be bearable, and parents can concentrate on planning for the day when eroticism dawns in their darlings.

Miss Manners urges parents to practice saying, with just the right inflection, "Well, Dear, we're sure he must have qualities we can't see." And I have put a paper clip on the page where Miss Manners deals like Metternich with the diplomacy required of parents when a child invites home from college a roommate the parents mistakenly assumed was of more or less the same gender as their child. Miss Manners has much to say about sex, but *Newsweek* readers, being perfect products of fastidious parents, blush easily. So suffice it to say that, regarding sexual instruction, Miss Manners recommends describing the basic physical practice to children when they are still at the age when children listen to the description and then ask, "Why would anyone want to do *that?*"

October 8, 1984

Light at the End of the Day

Americans consume 20 tons of aspirin a day, so they need pleasure at the end of the day, and many are getting it from reading their children *A Light in the Attic*, poems by Shel Silverstein. Amazingly, this volume concerns neither sexual gymnastics nor a sauerkraut-and-fudge diet, but nevertheless is near the top of the best-seller list. So a lot of moppets are being read Silverstein's "Prayer of the Selfish Child":

> Now I lay me down to sleep,
> I pray the Lord my soul to keep,
> And if I die before I wake,
> I pray the Lord my toys to break.
> So none of the other kids can use 'em. . . .
> Amen.

A generation reared on such searing knowledge of the human heart may turn out a bit grim, or may become the Emerging Republican Majority. But it will be better for having known "The Little Boy and the Old Man":

> Said the little boy, "Sometimes I drop my spoon."
> Said the little old man, "I do that too."
> The little boy whispered, "I wet my pants."
> "I do that too," laughed the little old man.
> Said the little boy, "I often cry."
> The old man nodded, "So do I."
> "But worst of all," said the boy, "It seems
> Grown-ups don't pay attention to me."
> And he felt the warmth of a wrinkled old hand.
> "I know what you mean," said the little old man.

Silverstein's sales and, even more, the sales of C. S. Lewis's "Narnia" series suggest that many parents are giving their children the two essential things: thought and time. It helps if children have two caring parents, but in the 1970s births to unwed women increased 50 percent and now amount to one in six births. This scandal is a calamity because the more we learn about children, the more certain we are that many things (emotional stability and social competence, to name two) depend on attentive, skillful parents.

It is often difficult to be such a parent at the end of the day. But it is principally by the quality of their attentiveness that parents help children achieve the serenity and self-esteem that can enable children to be masters of their destinies.

All of us, big and small, are, to an annoying extent, influenced by our physical natures—by our chemical and electrical mechanisms. Studies now link minor nutritional problems in infancy and in pregnant women with emotional instabilities when children reach school age. The emotions of adults, too, can be determined physical phenomena. Hot, dry winds like the sharav in Israel and the Santa Ana in Southern California alter the ion concentrations in the atmosphere of a region, producing increased tensions, irritability and slower reactions. High levels of positive ions raise, and high levels of negative ions lower, the blood levels of a hormone important to behavior. Concentrations of both types of ion seem to reduce brain levels of the hormone, and reduced levels of the hormone have been found in the brain tissue of suicides.

You may resent evidence that suggests we are, to some extent, marionettes dangling at the ends of long strings that run back deep into nature. But high-quality parental attention can be scissors that snip some of those strings. It enhances a child's self-esteem, and hence self-control, and thus expands the range of real autonomy, at the expense of physical determinants.

All children have a sweet tooth for praise, and there is no praise as sweet as being taken seriously, for example by a parent who reads to you. But most of all, children like the sense that their parents are realists and truth-tellers. How else can children value their parents' praise? So it is good for their souls to hear a parent read Silverstein's poem "God's Wheel," in which a child is speaking:

> God says to me with kind of a smile,
> "Hey, how would you like to be God awhile
> And steer the world?"
> "Okay," says I, "I'll give it a try.
> Where do I set?
> How much do I get?
> What time is lunch?
> When can I quit?"
> "Gimme back that wheel," says God,
> "I don't think you're quite ready yet."

The smile, part shy and part sly, that flickers across the face of a listening child—a smile of rueful recognition—is, for an adult, more therapeutic than aspirin ever can be.

November 12, 1981

Baltimore Sunrise

You know the feeling you get watching the steamier Greek tragedies, when dynasties are falling and sons are marrying their mothers and everyone is behaving badly and you are thinking: Really, things can not go on like this. That is how March makes proper Americans feel. Life is vain, the world is a moral void, the universe is an empty shell. Then proper Americans look toward April, the horizon where the sun will rise. The sun is baseball.

Baltimore is the best place to watch the sunrise. I will explain why, after dealing with this disagreeable business: Peter Ueberroth must go. His reign as baseball commissioner is already six months old and the wicked Designated Hitter rule has not been repealed. Worse—infinitely so—he is talking about taking an opinion poll on the subject. The mind reels. The thought occurs: Death, where is thy sting?

Who needs polls to discover if Michelangelo is superior to Andy Warhol? Some judgments should be beyond the reach of majorities. Democracy has, I suppose, its place, but in baseball? Perhaps public opinion must influence government, but baseball should not be a plaything of that turbulent, hydra-headed monster: the mob. Do we submit theories of astrophysics to referenda? Surely even in an open society there are closed questions, and this is one: Should baseball be desecrated by the dh rule, which allows degenerate, footballesque specialization?

If Ueberroth's baseball bolshevism is the bad news, the good news is that our can-do country has gone and done it. It has produced a baseball book that almost contains all the information citizens ought to be required to master before being allowed to vote. The book is *The 1985 Elias Baseball Analyst.*

Do you have a Gibbonesque fascination with declines and falls? The book reveals that the 1984 White Sox were only the eighth team in 50 years to suffer a decline of 150 percentage points in their won–lost record compared with the immediate preceding season. In 1984 Cleveland extended to 24 its record for the most consecutive seasons (excluding the 1981 strike season) finishing more than 14 games behind the league or division leader. Before the 1984 Milwaukee Brewers did it, the last team to go in just two years from the best record in the league to the worst was during the Johnson administration. The time before that, Woodrow Wilson was in his first term.

AccDecSyn (Accelerated Decline Syndrome) exists when three criteria are satisfied: A team wins 10 fewer games in season X than in season X minus 1; it had a losing record in X minus 1; it had a winning record in X minus 2. The 1984 Giants suffered AccDecSyn.

But enough about incompetence. Let's go to Baltimore, where last Monday the Orioles, who will beat the Cubs in a six-game World Series, began what will be their 18th consecutive season over the .500 mark. Only the 1926–64 Yankees have done better, and no team has a better winning percentage (.565) over the last 29 seasons. Why are they so good? Hey, as Ring Lardner, born 100 years ago this spring, used to say, you could look it up.

The Elias book says Cal Ripken, the O's shortstop, has baseball's best on-base average (.452) when leading off an inning. With the opening game tied in the eighth inning on Monday, Ripken led off and got on base. Next came Eddie Murray. The book says that last year he batted .459, with a .838 slugging average, in late-inning pressure situations with runners on base. On Monday he drove in Ripken with a home run.

As Murray began his regal, relaxed lope around the bases (Prince Charles could take lessons from Murray about the business of kingly bearing), baseball's magical mix of science and serendipity was on display.

A 162-game season is, like life, a study in cumulation. Things tend to even out, and talent tells. Ripken and Murray are gods, but there are lots of lesser but useful talents, and in a town like Baltimore, where they make good steel and sausage and baseball, they know how to make use of scraps. Who led the American League last year in the percentage of runners driven in from third with fewer than two outs? Elias knows: Jim Dwyer, Baltimore.

Past performances give rise to averages, on which managers calculate probabilities about future performance. The more you study, the less surprised you are. But no matter how hard you study, you still are surprised agreeably often, and the surprises that come to the studious are especially delicious. This is true in baseball and in the lesser stuff that is the rest of life.

April 11, 1985

Don't Beep in My Outfield

It has been said that baseball is to the United States what revolutions are to Latin America, a safety valve for letting off steam. I think baseball is more serious than any Latin American revolution. But, then, I am a serious fan.

How serious? I like *Sports Illustrated*'s baseball issue even more than its swimming-suit issue. I would sell my soul for the thrill of hearing a manager say of me what Joe DiMaggio's manager said when asked if DiMaggio could bunt. The manager said he didn't know and "I'll never find out, either." The last words my four-year-old daughter hears at night are " . . . at the old ball game." (On the "as the twig is bent" principle, my parenting involves the use of "take me out to the ball game" as a lullaby.) I have one son who even knows the names of first-base coaches. That is like knowing the name of the secretary of commerce. I have told my other son that if he can hit a slider when he is 16 he can quit school. I believe in incentives, and Rogers Hornsby, who said: "Don't read, it'll hurt your eyes." So much for my credentials, OK? Now, listen up. The Japanese have gone too far.

I am not talking, as everyone else is, about how crummy the Japanese are being about American exports. I am talking about a Japanese export, another electronic gadget. It is a sonar system that beeps to warn an outfielder chasing a fly ball that he is approaching the fence. My objection is not that the technology is Japanese. My nationalism stops short of that of the Cub pitcher who, when asked if he threw spitballs or otherwise violated the rule against doctoring the ball with foreign substances, replied: "I don't put any foreign substance on the baseball. Everything I use on it is from the good ole U.S.A." My objection to talking fences is not patriotic but esthetic.

The thought of beeping fences intrudes jarringly on April, a month of buds and box scores. The philosopher in us is consoled by the thought that, although ours is an age of dizzying flux, baseball retains a healthy Luddite hostility to modernity. But already some degenerate teams are using infernal machines, rather than honest manual labor with a fungo bat, to propel balls for fielding practice. And now beeping fences? If this insensate lust for high-tech baseball does not abate, baseball will become as bad as—this is harsh, but it must be said—football.

The fact that football fans have coarse characters and frayed moral fibers cannot be a matter of mere chance. The explanation has something to do with a fact noted here before: Football combines two grim features of American life, violence and committee meetings (huddles). It also has something to do with football's lunatic fascination with technology. The coaches stalk the sidelines wired up like astronauts so they can talk to the assistant coaches with whom they have spent the previous six days doing computer analysis of game films. The NFL is even considering "helmet radios" so that quarterbacks calling plays at the line of scrimmage can be heard clearly by receivers.

Baseball's emphasis is not on machinery, it is on mind, although some players modestly deny this. Bill Lee, Red Sox pitcher, said: "When cerebral processes enter into sports, you start screwing up. It's like the Constitution, which says separate church and state. You have to separate mind and body." Rot. Baseball's emphasis on mind accounts for its fine sense of moral nuance, as in the batter who, after being brushed back by a pitch, said: "They shouldn't throw at me. I'm the father of five or six kids." Mind, in the form of mastery of facts, is also required of baseball fans.

Martin Nolan, who edits the editorial page of *The Boston Globe* but is not otherwise dangerous, is a typical fan. The highlight of his life was when he walked into a saloon and answered that day's question: Name the only player active when Ruth hit his last home run and Aaron hit his first (Phil Cavaretta). Heinie Groh boasted that he held the record among non-Yankee, non-switchhitting third basemen for playing in the most World Series with the largest number of different teams. Ah, but somewhere out in this broad land there is a young, right-handed, non-switch-hitting third baseman with visions of the glory that will be his when he breaks Groh's record. As baseball folks say (stop me if you've heard this), records are made to be broken. Or, as Yogi Berra wired Johnny Bench when Bench broke Yogi's career record for home runs by a catcher. "I always thought the record would stand until it was broken."

One baseball scholar whose mind may have snapped assures me that Harry Chiti, who was a catcher, sort of, holds this record: He is the only player ever traded for himself. Detroit traded him to the Mets for cash and a player to be named later. The Mets looked him over and designated him the player to be named later. Chiti was, of course, an ex-Cub. Before the Cubs attained their current grandeur, Cubness was the subject of a quiz compiled by a sadist and sent to masochists like me: 1. What Cub slugger dislocated his shoulder carrying his suitcase down to the hotel lobby? 2. Why was it bad that Cub pitcher Bill Hands recorded 14 straight strikeouts? 3. What Cub batter holds the major league record for leaving the most runners stranded on base in a nine-inning game? 4. What Cub right fielder, trying to throw a runner out at the plate, beaned the bat boy? 5. Cub catcher Cuno Barragon hit a homer in his first major-league at bat. How many did he hit in his career? 6. The Cubs once set a major league record by scoring five times in the bottom of the 11th inning. Who won? 7. The Cubs once blew a 13–2 lead and lost on a home run. Who hit it? 8. The Cubs scored 22 runs and lost on a home run. Who hit it? You could look it up. But you only need to look below.

Last week baseball posed, for this fan and other Tories, a metaphysical puzzle. It expanded the league championship series from best-of-five to best-of-seven games. This puts in conflict two principles that are moral absolutes. One is: The more baseball the better. The other is: Everywhere, but especially in baseball, change is deplorable. Well, some absolutes are more absolute than others, and the former principle is absoluter.

April 15, 1985

Answers: 1. Dave Kingman. 2. He did it as a batter. 3. Glen Beckert, 12. 4. Mike Vail. 5. One. 6. The Mets, who scored six in the top of the inning. 7. and 8. Mike Schmidt.

Academic Thought Police

Charley McCaffrey, a cop in the ranks of the thought police, saw his duty and did not flinch. McCaffrey, president of California's University of the Pacific, saw what William Bennett said and withdrew an invitation for Bennett to receive an honorary degree. "We simply cannot honor a person holding these views."

I know little about the University of the Pacific, but I will wager that it resembles most universities and therefore is broad-minded about the expression, and even the teaching, of the view that America is racist, sexist, imperialist, militarist, etc. So what did Bennett, the new secretary of education, say that caused McCaffrey, he of tender sensibilities, to recoil and become the toast of the faculty club?

Among other things, Bennett said that for budgetary reasons subsidies to middle-class students should be cut. Specifically, families with incomes above $32,500 should not be eligible for federally guaranteed loans (that would mean they would have to pay perhaps 12 rather than 8 percent interest).

There are many Americans—including, I suspect, Mc-Caffrey—in whom the flame of thought flickers so weakly that they only feel vital and engaged with history when they are indignant. America's indignation industry makes neither shoes nor butter nor poetry. Rather, it makes mandatory blandness by practicing moral intimidation. Its intimidation works on people who can be intimidated by the denial of the honor, such as it is, of a degree from the hands of the likes of McCaffrey.

Blandness in public utterance is encouraged by television journalism, which, because of the tyranny of the clock, specializes in what are known, in televisionspeak, as "sound bites." It defines, and distorts, individuals with brief, telegenic "bites." A nation that knew nothing of secretary Bennett got its first glimpse of him in a "sound bite." He was saying that for some students the cut in subsidies might mean having to forgo a stereo or car or spring vacation at the beach.

A typical viewer probably got this glimpse on television at dinner time. The baby was crying and so was the Cuisinart, the phone was ringing and so was the viewer's head because Billy, 14, and his cassette player blasting out Madonna's "Like a Virgin." It was all background music for the 15-second sound bite that introduced Bennett to the nation.

Sound bites are more than adequate to present all the thoughts of some people. But Bennett is not one of them. He is the only member of the president's Cabinet who has spent his life taking serious ideas seriously. That is what makes him dangerous to the academic division of the indignation industry.

Bennett says that there can be no "right" for every student to attend the university of his or her choice. Anyone who disagrees with that has a peculiar understanding of the allocation of public

goods, especially goods such as university admissions that are valued in part because of the various forms of status they can confer.

Bennett says (well, he said it once, he probably will not say it
again because departures from blandness cause too much turmoil)
this: He can imagine not being dismayed if his son someday wants
the money saved for university tuition to be used instead to start a
business.

Bennett is not expressing a philistine preference for money over
mind, he is expressing dismay that so many universities serve the
mind poorly. This point, which he has been making forcefully for
three years as head of the National Endowment for the Humanities,
has been missed by persons eager to strike a pose of indignation.
Which brings us back to McCaffrey, who has disinvited Bennett.
Why? "Because I find your views to be directly contrary to those
held by me and our University of the Pacific. . . . "

The aid plan Bennett defends will preserve all aid for the least
affluent students who, without aid, could not go to any college. It
would make less expensive public institutions better able to compete
with private institutions, such as the Univeristy of the Pacific, for
middle-class students. The aid plan is debatable. But dishonorable?

The hysterical condemnation of Bennett illustrates the moral
exhibitionism of people like McCaffrey. It also reveals that the academic lobby—like, say, the tobacco lobby, but with more moral
pretenses—has become an organized appetite. Bennett has interrupted its concentration on the social pork barrel by raising disturbing questions about academic purposes and competence.

McCaffrey's approach to controversy is not new. "Why should
we bother to reply to Kautsky?" Lenin asked. "He would reply to
us, and we would have to reply to his reply. There's no end to that.
It will be quite enough for us to announce that Kautsky is a traitor
to the working class, and everyone will understand everything."
McCaffrey should know that everyone understands him.

February 21, 1985

Chicago's Favorite Sons

Real men don't eat quiche? Real Chicagoans won't even eat veal. Red meat rare, please. Big-shouldered, wheat-stacking Chicago fancies itself hairy-chested. But it has a baseball team, named for baby bears, that has been a byword for wimpishness. However, the Cubs now are, to coin a phrase, back and standing tall. Their fans—gosh, how many there suddenly are—are sitting atop the world on a pink cloud with rainbows draped over their shoulders. The rest of you had better brace yourselves for a spate of sociology. To understand the peculiar fervor of Cubs fans you must understand Chicago's temperament.

Chicago accommodates high culture (perhaps America's finest university, finest symphony, finest novelist and, for its size, finest art museum) but does not wallow in it. One Cubs broadcaster once said on the air to another, "I picked up the *Sun-Times* this morning and saw Sparky Anderson's [then manager of the Cincinnati Reds] picture on the front page. I wondered, what's Sparky done to get his picture on the front page? It turns out it wasn't Sparky at all. It was a writer named Saul Bellow who won the Nobel Prize."

Bellow, the novelist, is one of my pinups (my only pinup who cannot hit behind the runner). He moved back to Chicago from New York, in part because of Chicago's healthily relaxed attitude about the literati. Chicago writers are not expected to declaim about everything under the sun. Joseph Epstein, a man of letters living in the Chicago area, notes that when Susan Sontag gave a speech in New York announcing her recent discovery that communism is a bad thing, she caused a stir. It is inconceivable that Bellow would utter such a banality, or that anyone in Chicago would notice if he did.

Augie March, one of Bellow's characters, says with nice concision that Chicago is "not mitigated." Chicago takes life neat: no ice, no water. One mayor told his machine, truthfully, "I'll do any damned thing you boys want me to do"—a thought often thought but ne'er so well expressed. When someone asked a judge to require Sally Rand to wear something beneath her two ostrich-feather fans she (a mediocre dancer but a great entrepreneur) had bought on credit, the judge snorted, "Some people would like to put pants on horses." That was an opaque but very Chicago-like contribution to jurisprudence, which in Chicago has some built-in elastic. Chicagoans used to carry $10 bills folded with their driver's licenses to settle matters when they were stopped for speeding. That is why Mort Sahl called the Outer Drive "the last outpost of collective bargaining."

Chicago, wrote Nelson Algren, "has grown great on bone-deep grudges." The deepest are against New York, and not just because of decaying New York's insufferable snootiness about thriving Chicago. There also is the atrocity of Sept. 8, 1969, the low point of a low decade. I don't want to beat a dead horse to death but Tommie Agee was out at the plate that night.

The Cubs were in New York playing the Mets, a parvenu outfit that did not exist until 1962, when it lost a record 120 games. What was the first team to finish below the Mets? The 1966 Cubs. The Cubs still have not won a pennant since 1945, when all but the lame were fighting the Axis. But in 1969 the Cubs led the pack until a September swoon, the crucial moment of which was the first game of the two-game series the Mets swept. The Mets won it 3–2 when Agee scored from second on a single by a dinky .218 hitter. At least the umpire said he scored. I say the umpire's scandalous decision was the beginning of Watergate. The image of Agee scoring—a summation of all the insults visited on Chicago by New York—is burned on every Cubs fan's mental retina. The wound will not heal until there is mighty vengeance from the Midwest, perhaps this year.

Baseball is heaven's gift to struggling mortals, but has meant more thorns than roses for Chicago. The other team, the White Sox, has won only four pennants in 83 seasons. The 1919 "Black Sox" took a dive in the World Series. The 1906 "hitless wonders" had an anemic batting average of .228 but still managed to win the series, beating—who else?—the Cubs. It has been said that the test of a vocation is love of the drudgery it involves. Being a Cubs fan is a vocation because the memory of man runneth not to a time when rooting for the Cubs was not mostly drudgery.

Today's Cubs are a tribute not to husbandry but to entrepreneurship. Few players were grown down on the Cubs' farm teams. Most were traded for by Dallas Green, an executive with the breezy eloquence of the Wife of Bath and the administrative flair of Lady Macbeth. Such wheeling and dealing strikes some purists as the summit of crassness, but this is a Republican era, so sharp practices are without moral taint.

A theory, contentedly expounded by the comfortable, is that

suffering makes us spiritual. (John Wesley wrote to his sister Patty: "I believe the death of your children is a great instance of the goodness of God toward you. You have often mentioned to me how much of your time they took up! Now that time is restored to you . . . you have nothing to do but serve our Lord.") To those who say that passing through a fiery furnace is good for one's soul—that we learn in suffering what we teach in song—I say: One can have too much soul.

Real Cubs fans are 99.44 percent scar tissue. A fast start by the Cubs causes them no palpitations. Such feints are traditionally followed by faints. But now it is August and, wonder of wonders, the team is still in the thick of things. Dull despair has yielded to flaming hope, which is building like steam in a pressure cooker. Also, true Cubs fans are as mean as most winners unaccustomed to winning and are busy repelling late-boarders from their gravy train.

Remember, this year baseball is politics carried on by other means. And in America, politics is most bitter when what is at issue is status. The Cubs are William Jennings Bryan, a prairie uprising against highfalutin Eastern plutocrats wearing spats, the Mets and Phillies. "Arise ye prisoners of starvation!"—that is the Cubs' anthem.

Chicago, wrote Algren, is "an October sort of city even in spring." The numbed nerves of Cubs fans are sensing the possibility that this year it could be spring—resurrection, regeneration—in October.

August 13, 1984

Baseball: "We Do This Every Day."

Where is Trotsky, now that we really need him?

I have been done hideous injury by a malefactor of great wealth, a capitalist pest called CC Assets Distribution Corp. That is the clanking, officious name for what until recently was called, melodically, the Chicago National League Ball Club.

The Cubs, who have notoriously few atheletic assets, invented trickledown baseball. They acquire aging players (Dizzy Dean, Ralph Kiner) as their careers trickled down to a level suitable for the Cubs, a team forever trickling down in the standings. And now the Cubs' pestilential new management has engaged in a rapacious business pratice that makes me think the Russian Revolution treated capitalists about right.

The brutes at the CC Assets Distribution Corp. inform me that they are exercising their right—a *right*, mind you: Is this America or Poland?—to buy back my one share of Cub stock. Because these robber barons are conscienceless, and because the law is deaf to the voice of justice, I am no longer a baseball owner.

If this is the capitalist system Ronald Reagan wants to save, I say bring on Walter Mondale to destroy it, root and branch. Peremptory letters from faceless financiers; mere money given in exchange for a piece of my soul—Hell must be very like this.

But on a spring day, when all of Nature seems to shout, "Play ball!" even Cub fans can enjoy one exquisite baseball pleasure. They can read Thomas Boswell's nifty new book, *How Life Imitates the World Series*.

Sports serve society by providing vivid examples of excellence. So do sports pages when graced by Boswell's by-line. He is the thinking person's writer about the thinking person's sport. Like baseball itself, he is graceful, subtle, elegant, inexhaustibly interesting, and fun.

Baseball is for all of us who feel as Pete Rose does: "I was raised, but I never did grow up." Boswell is for all who like fine writing. Baseball, like Pericles' Athens (or any other good society), is simultaneously democratic and aristocratic: Anyone can enjoy it, but the more you apply yourself, the more you enjoy it.

Boswell has applied himself. His father works at the Library of Congress and one day smuggled his son into the closed stacks, to the sacred precincts of deck 29, and said: "Okay. Here is every book on baseball ever written. Don't go blind." Heaven must be very like that.

Bill Veeck, who, like me, is a former baseball owner, thinks it is to baseball's credit that when the times were out of joint, baseball was out of step: "The Sixties was a time for grunts or screams. . . . The sports that fitted the times were football, hockey and mugging." One of Boswell's (and my) pin-ups, Earl Weaver, the philosopher-king who manages the Baltimore Orioles, says: "This ain't a football game. We do this every day." An Orioles coach says: "In this game it's never going to be third-down-and-one. You don't hit off tackle in baseball, and you can't play the game with your teeth gritted. Muscles are fine. But this is a game of relaxation, conditioned reflex, and mental alertness."

That is why Boswell says a good team depends on "the ability to achieve a blend of intensity and underlying serenity which, in daily life, we might call mental health. . . . Baseball is to our everyday experience what poetry often is to common speech—a slightly elevated and concentrated form." Boswell, an English major from Amherst, says, "Each team's season is like a traditional nineteenth century novel, a heaping up of detail and incident about one large family."

Yes, but some teams' seasons call to mind Dickens's *Great Expectations*, an eventful progress toward a happy ending. The Cubs' seasons are Dostoyevskian—*Crime and Punishment* and *The House of the Dead*—full of angst and gnashing teeth. It is the Karamazov family at play.

But the CC Assets Distribution Corp. is about to erupt from the dugout for another crack at life without a safety net. Recently (since the days when fans drove to the park in Hudsons and Packards—since 1946) the Cubs have had two problems: They put too few runs on the scoreboard and the other guys put too many. So what is the new management improving? The scoreboard.

Management recently chastised the players: "The Cubs have gained the reputation of being somewhat laissez-faire in their approach to work." At Wrigley Field, they handle words the way they handle ground balls.

March 28, 1982

Detroit's Craftsman

Thirteen months ago I bought my first Elmore Leonard novel, in Cleveland, his kind of place. Since then I have read 10 others. Recently, a newspaper story announced his new novel, *Glitz*. I put down my sandwich and drove to a bookstore. It was a peanut butter and pickle sandwich, so you know Leonard is good.

Today he is taking lunch in style, at the Manhattan Ocean Club. You say good news never gets into newspapers? Read on. Last week, after publishing 23 novels in 32 years, he finally made the *New York Times* best-seller list, just barely, in 15th place. This week he is seventh. His good luck is good news because luck had nothing to do with it. Craftsmanship has been rewarded.

Leonard lives in Birmingham, Michigan, a suburb of Detroit, the city where some of his stories are set. The description of Detroit as "Cleveland without the glitter" could come from his novels. Detroit is not Bloomsbury, but Leonard, 59, with a gray beard and a wardrobe consisting mainly of a tweed jacket, says he is not an artist, just an entertainer.

His books are not exactly crime novels, although crimes occur and guns go off. The novels are about marginal people, small people incompetent at petty crime, or quiet professionals who, like Leonard, are underestimated for a long time. There are no verbal flourishes, no arresting descriptions, but his style is as strong and personal as Van Gogh's brush strokes. He has perfect pitch for the street talk you might hear from armed robbers who are not very good at armed robbery.

Assistant professors being what they are, there are turgid essays thick with coagulated paragraphs about such novels as sublimations of the class struggle. I recently read (well, started to) an essay that says detective stories are popular because secret crime and subsequent discovery are associated in the reader's subconsciousness with (I am not making this up; I could not) the "primal scene," a psychoanalytic term referring to a child's imagining of sexual intercourse between his parents.

Leonard, too, has suffered overinterpretation. A reviewer once said of him: "The aesthetic sub text of his work is the systematic exposure of aesthetic pretension." Leonard retaliated. In his novel *LaBrava*, the protagonist, a photographer, refers to an exhibition of his pictures: "The review in the paper said, 'The aesthetic subtext of his work is the systematic exposure of aesthetic pretension.' I thought I was just taking pictures."

Leonard's insistence that he is just a storyteller expresses pride, not humility. He has a craftsman's pride that being a fine craftsman is good enough, thank you. He sold his first fiction in 1951, to *Argosy* magazine, and his first novel, a Western, in 1953. His mother wishes he were still writing Westerns, because the language would be less gamy. Until he sold his novel *Hombre* (voted one of the 25 best Westerns of all time by the Western Writers of America) to

Hollywood, he had to work full time writing advertising copy. Well, Wallace Stevens worked in an insurance office, T. S. Eliot at a bank, Anthony Trollope at the post office.

After *Hombre*, Leonard stopped writing Westerns and started making books the way a custom cobbler makes shoes: steadily, with no wasted motion. He writes from 9:30 A.M. to 6 P.M.

He has been called the Dickens of Detroit because of the colorful characters he creates from the seamier side of life. But he reminds me of Trollope. This is not, Lord knows, because of his subjects—there are no Pallisers in his pages—but because of his approach to his craft.

Trollope kept a meticulous diary of the pages he wrote. He noted that such discipline is considered beneath a man of genius. But, he said cheerfully, not being a genius, he had to be disciplined. You say that anyone who works with his imagination should wait for inspiration? Trollope said it would be just as absurd to say that a shoemaker should wait for inspiration. Writers, he said, should sit themselves at their desks as though they were clerks, and should sit until their daily writing quota is filled. If they adopt his quota, they will produce a book in four months.

Elmore Leonard's "sudden" success—he is an "overnight sensation" after 32 years of hard plugging—is a tribute to America, where people are not homogenized, and cream rises. If you want a sip of the cream, start with his novel *Swag* and then read *Stick*. Then, if you are not hooked, go watch television. It will serve you right.

February 17, 1985

The Rain Forest in the Lobby

CHICAGO—Here, at last, I have hit upon a moral reflection commanding universal assent: Hotel lobbies should not be hostile environments. This, surely, is a golden precept of civilization: A lobby should not resemble the flight deck of an aircraft carrier during the battle of Midway, or a rain forest, or one of those mazes scientists design to test the average rat's breaking point.

Indications of decadence are rife, but nowhere more so than

in modern hotel lobbies. In such lobbies it is possible to suffer vertigo as a result of the architecture and decor, and it is well-nigh impossible to find a quiet place to sit while waiting for the vertigo to pass.

Atlanta's Peach Tree Plaza has a lobby that Lewis and Clark could not have found their way across. Actually, the concept "across" hardly applies. It is a trackless waste in the fourth dimension. Pity the poor traveler who has screwed his courage to the sticking point just to get through Atlanta's new airport, which is about the size of Vermont. Then he is decanted from a cab into the inferno of escalators, elevators, coffee shops, gifte shoppes and counters that is the Peach Tree Plaza's cruel caricature of a lobby. There is, of course, a pondlike body of water—Walden in everything but charm—in which you can drown yourself, which you might wish to do.

In Detroit, there are, I'll wager, delegates—shells of their former selves—left over from the 1980 Republican Convention, wandering with blank stares and broken spirits along the endless concrete ramps and corridors that fill the cavernous space that should be the lobby of the Renaissance Plaza. The man nominated in Detroit should base the MX missile in that "lobby." The Russians will never find it.

It is prodigiously sly of hotels to design themselves so that the weary traveler can only sit in a place where money is spent. One such place is a sunken saloon smack in the middle of the "lobby," where drinks are served at 10 A.M. by young ladies dressed not at all the way their mothers recommended that they dress at 10 A.M. Many Hyatt hotels have capacious lobbies, but they are surrounded by tiers of rooms rising 20 or more stories. Being in such a lobby is like being at the bottom of a well, which is agreeable if you are a newt, but not if you're not.

The lobby of the Bonaventure in Los Angeles is like . . . well, suppose the Santa Monica and San Diego freeways intersected near the headwaters of the Amazon River. It is concrete, with green growing things and a monsoon.

I have been brooding about the Lobby Question for many seasons, but a visit to Chicago has moved me to take up my pen in praise of the few remaining proper lobbies. They are scattered like rubies across the Republic—the Hotel Utah in Salt Lake City comes to mind—but Chicago has three. The Drake is venerable. The Park Hyatt is distressingly new and shiny, but the lobby has a harpsichord, so all is forgiven. But the essence of lobbiness is in the Loop, in the old Palmer House.

It has large stately potted plants. No nonsense here about foliage suspended from wires, making the place look like an explosion in a florist's shop. The lobby is surrounded by balconies and ornamented by high brass light stands and, of course, a legible clock with Roman numerals. There are chairs and couches so deep that you seem to settle for several minutes before coming to rest.

High above, the ceiling is a wonderful protest of romance against the everydayness of life. There are paintings of ladies of almost Rubenesque dimensions. (They reflect the taste of a bygone era, before Richard Simmons and best-sellers titled *Thin Thighs in Thirty Days*.) The ladies are disporting themselves with gentlemen of vaguely Athenian aspect. All in all, the Palmer House lobby is like the Sistine Chapel without the chapel's infernal roar of tourists' cameras clicking.

I know that the Lobby Crisis is nothing compared to the wrestling match between Paul Volcker and M-1. I know we are not put on earth for pleasure alone, and that we are naught but bubbles on the surface of Eternity. But the modern hotel lobby, with its insensate pursuit of perfect discomfort, is intolerable.

For years Detroit made cars that looked like sharks or spaceships—anything but cars. And the cars did everything well—inspired, entertained, expressed their owners' primal urges—everything, that is, except get people to and fro with minimal expense and risk. Detroit has recently, and in the nick of time, remembered: As clipper ships showed, what is functional can be beautiful. Let the designers of hotel lobbies remember that, or be sentenced to live in what they design.

November 28, 1982

Neurobiology and Us

It was a headline that arrested the eye:
Einstein's
Brain Was
Different
Not news, you say? Wrong. The news from neurobiology is large enough to subvert our sense of ourselves.

Having obtained bits of Einstein's brain from the pathologist who conducted the autopsy in 1956, a scientist at Berkeley has discovered that Einstein's brain had 73 percent more "support cells" for every neuron than are found in average brains. The Einstein samples reportedly came from the part of the brain responsible for "the deepest thinking"—presumably the part we use to ponder the infield fly rule.

We are learning a lot—perhaps an alarming lot—about what we are. Increased knowledge of the brain already has brought a reduction of misery through pharmacological treatments of such diseases as depression and schizophrenia. But that knowledge seems to threaten us—that inner something that makes us individuals. It seems to portray us as merely physical, as more comprehensible and quantifiable than we want to be.

It was bad enough when Copernicus evicted us from where we think we belong: the center of the cosmos. Since then, many systems of thought have seemed to imbed us stickily in the world in ways that compromise our sense of autonomy.

Darwin embedded mankind in the mud of the planet that Copernicus had made peripheral. Darwin asserted a continuum between mankind and lesser (are we sure?) matter. The historicisms of Marx and others asserted that political and social change are governed by iron laws of social evolution, not the choices of autonomous human beings. Freud said there are within us uncharted depths with their own turbulences.

Now comes neurobiology, suggesting . . . what? It really does not suggest that anyone with 73 percent more support cells per neuron than average could have said, as Einstein did, "Hey: Increase the speed of an object and you contract the passage of its time." (Einstein was always saying things like that, and may even have understood the infield fly rule.) Neurosciences do not make such extravagant claims.

In the current issue of the *New York Review of Books*, Israel Rosenfield of the City University of New York offers a balanced assessment. Suppose particular mental events—feelings, emotions—can be associated with particular chemical events. That does not mean that, say, the feeling of love or patriotism or whatever can be expressed as a chemical formula. Neither does it mean that when you read *Hamlet* you should say, "Ah, yes. This is the product of beautiful brain chemistry."

What has been learned about brain functioning has advanced therapy more than it has understanding. We can improve the functioning of the brain without really knowing how to explain what is being done, aside from the correction of a chemical imbalance. As Rosenfield writes, "Just as we cannot know the role an actor is playing by studying the basic electrical patterns in his brain, no analysis of the circuits of a computer can tell us whether the computer is playing chess or predicting the weather." While it is better to treat certain mental illnesses by administering drugs rather than confining the patient to an immobilizing chair, "we should have no illusions that we really know what we are doing when we use many of the therapies administered today."

The chemistry of memory, the chemistry of sorrow. . . . We would feel diminished in dignity by such ways of speaking. But certain foods contain amino acids which pass into the blood and alter moods. Indeed, simply seeing food evidently can trigger physiological mechanisms that produce weight increase. Gracious.

Human beings became comfortable with the thought of themselves as creatures composed of flesh and blood and also something grander. Now neurobiology makes problematic the idea that we are both bodies and quite distinct minds or spirits. The idea of "the ghost in the machine" may be yielding to the idea that we are machines. Are we just the sum of the chemical reactions bubbling within us?

Happily, the more we know, the less we know. The more we know about the brain, the more we are awed by how much there is to know, not only about the brain but about the totality of creation that has culminated (we are the culmination . . . aren't we?) in a gadget as intricate as man. The neuroscience behind the news that "Einstein's Brain Was Different" calls to mind a recent *Chicago Tribune* headline. It was a story about the aftermath of the Israeli airlift out of Ethiopia: "20th Century Stuns Ethiopian Jews." I know just how they feel.

February 28, 1985

When Homicide Is Noble

It is said that hard cases make bad law. But bad law can be made by pretending that hard cases are not cases.

Consider the case of Hans Florian, who on March 18 shot to death the woman to whom he had been married for 33 years. His act was loving, brave, even noble. Nevertheless, it was not an act about which society should be indifferent or permissive, or about which the law should be agnostic. Yet a Florida grand jury refused to indict him.

Alzheimer's disease began destroying his wife's mind in the late 1970s. There is no known cause or cure for the disease. It causes the brain to shrivel and fill with bubbles and granules. Soon his wife could not drive or write, and would panic when he stepped away from her. He and his son by an earlier marriage cared for her, forcing her mouth open for food, and bathing her and changing her clothes five or six times a day as she soiled them.

For most of the past two years, whenever she was not heavily drugged she howled constantly, and screamed two words, "fire" and "pain," in her native German. Finally, she had to be put in a nursing home for her own safety. Hans Florian is 17 years older than she was and he did not want to die leaving her alone.

This case did not involve any of the multiplying dilemmas occasioned by the sophistication of modern medicine, the mechanical and pharmacological technologies that can prolong a painful process of dying, without altering the prognosis. This was not the sort of case for which hospice care is most suited. Such care is designed for the predictable final period of a terminal disease, during which the patient can lead a tolerable life enhanced by pain management. Alzheimer's disease can run on and on.

This was not a case where a person had sunk into a condition where, by some arguable definition, death could be said to have occurred. Mrs. Florian's mind was destoryed, but brain death had not happened. Because Alzheimer's disease is terrifying, irreversible and protracted, Florian's case underscores this fact: There is no way entirely to exclude "quality of life" considerations from all controversies in biomedical ethics.

Many persons feel proper anxiety about casual, incoherent injections of "meaningful life" rhetoric in the 1973 Supreme Court abortion ruling, and in rationalizations for infanticide even against newborns with easily remediable physical defects. Therefore, many persons have tried to assert "sanctity of life" criteria that would enable all decision-making to proceed without consideration of the quality of life a subject can lead.

Quality of life assessments are fraught with difficulties and dangers. Current practices offer abundant examples of mistakes and abuses. However, when "heroic" medical measures are employed, or when there is a decision to intervene in a person's life to alter the course nature would take in "taking its course," this is true: You cannot judge the morality of what is done without reference to the quality of life that has been extended by heroic medicine or ended by extreme action.

However, the law cannot quite countenance such extreme measures as Florian's, even when, as in this case, the situation is extreme. Obviously Florian was in an unsettled frame of mind when carrying out his considered decision to shoot the woman he loved. But he did not try to diminish his responsibility for his action. And there was no ambiguity concerning competent consent: Florian obviously substituted his judgment for that of a person incapable of choosing.

It is, therefore, hard to see how the grand jury can have properly refused to indict. Surely there was probable cause for finding that a crime—homicide—had been committed. Grand juries require less to indict (a finding of probable cause to believe that a crime has been committed) than a trial jury requires to convict (proof of guilt beyond reasonable doubt).

The proper place for society to express compassionate understanding in cases such as Florian's is at the sentencing stage. There should be ample discretion at that stage to enable society to avoid the practice of not indicting when a homicide undoubtedly has occurred. Such a practice would express the dangerous doctrine that certain homicides are matters of indifference to society.

Some cases are hard because this is true: A homicide can be noble without properly being, in the eyes of the law, permissible.

April 14, 1983

The "Twinkie Defense"

In the increasingly peculiar annals of American law, Dan White is less notable for his lurid offense than his imaginative defense, the "Twinkie defense." This San Francisco case and another in Detroit demonstrate a growing disgrace: sentences as shocking as the crimes for which they are imposed.

Just five years ago—November 27, 1978—White entered San Francisco's city hall, killed the mayor, George Moscone, and supervisor Harvey Milk, a homosexual activist. White had impulsively resigned his elected office as supervisor, and Moscone, backed by Milk, had refused to reappoint him.

White was given the maximum sentence under a minimal charge: voluntary manslaughter. His sentence was seven years, eight months—minus time in jail before trial, with one-third off for good behavior. Why a sentence so light that his parole date is less than a month away (January 6)? Because the jury bought his argument of diminished mental capacity. He was, he said, depressed by financial pressures and political setbacks; and the chemical effects of junk food—Twinkies and stuff like that—subverted his self-control.

The sentence sparked a six-hour riot. Today, as White's parole approaches, tensions are rising in San Francisco, where the desire for proportionate punishment—for civilized vengeance—was frustrated by a court that compounded White's crime. He destroyed two persons. It destroyed him by treating him as just a tossed salad of impulses, without the human dignity that punishment presupposes.

It is tempting to say that San Francisco has earned such trouble. It is vain about its tolerance, and it is too hospitable to the idea that anything goes because whatever is going on is to be explained, not judged, and explained by quarter-baked nostrums, such as that Twinkies diminish moral accountability. But what did Detroit do to deserve the Chin case?

On June 19, 1982, Vincent Chin, 27, a Chinese-American, was being given a bachelor party at a Detroit tavern. Ronald Ebens, an unemployed autoworker, and his stepson, Michael Nitz, became unpleasant ("It's because of you we're [many Americans] out of work") and were asked to leave. Later, armed with a baseball bat, they fell upon Chin and while one held him down, the other beat him. He died four days later.

They were first charged with second-degree murder, for which the maximum penalty is life in prison. They plea-bargained to manslaughter, for which the maximum sentence is 15 years. But the judge sentenced each to three years' probation and a $3,780 fine. The judge said they were "not the kind of people you send to prison." Could have fooled me.

The judge found it an extenuating fact that both killers were employed. He pronounced himself certain that they will not harm anyone else—got it out of their system, don't you know—and, besides, prison would not do any good "for them or for society."

The Detroit and San Francisco judgments demonstrate the arrogance of "progressive" law. The Detroit judge believed the law should be an arena for his improvisations, where he makes utilitarian calculations about what is suitable for individuals and society. In San Francisco, the law was made into a handmaiden of passing theories that locate in chemistry or society primary responsibility for an individual's behavior.

In California, paroles have become a political issue, a court having held that "awareness of public hostility" can be a reason for denying parole. That is a perverse way for the legal system to accommodate the public's desire for proportionate punishment. Many California leaders urged the Justice Department to stretch a federal statute and try White for violating Moscone's and Milk's civil rights. The statute properly applies only where persons are killed because they are campaigning for office. However, under another federal civil rights section, Chin's killers have been indicted for violating his rights because of his race.

The element of retribution—vengeance—does not make punishment cruel; it makes punishment intelligible, distinguishing it from therapy. But a "progressive" aspiration has been to make people feel guilty about certain sentiments, such as (concerning crime) outrage and desire for vengeance, that are essential for social decency.

Persons who share that aspiration should note arrival of Clint Eastwood's *Sudden Impact*, the fourth film about Dirty Harry, a cop—in San Francisco—who does not follow the Warren Court in his approach to due process. That is at least the seventh film (*Death Wish, Star Chamber*, etc.) about vengeance as a private enterprise. When courts frustrate the desire for moral symmetry between crime and punishment, vengeance becomes the business of vigilantes.

December 11, 1983

Metaphysics in Pittsburgh

On the morning of what was to be a momentous day, I decided to dip a toe into the rushing stream of the modern world by seeing the movie *Flashdance*. Little did I then suspect that this movie, about which the intelligentsia has been quite rude, actually unlocks the mystery of the human race's place in the cosmos.

It is about a young lady welder (no kidding) in Pittsburgh who in the evenings performs in a blue-collar bar where she dances like a dervish and twists her comely self as though she is auditioning for the role of a soft pretzel.

Like *Breaking Away*, which was set in Bloomington, Indiana, and *Personals*, which was set in Minneapolis–St. Paul, and *Diner*, which was set in Baltimore, *Flashdance* is almost lyrical about a place that does not often evoke lyricism. ("O Pittsburgh"? "Let us now praise Bloomington"?)

Our lady welder is to her gender, and her end of Pennsylvania, what *Rocky* was to Philadelphia. She is a monument to upward mobility through sweat. By grit and pluck (and pumping iron) she dances her way into, yes, of course, our hearts, but also into ballet school. In the last scene she is in the arms of her lover, another upwardly mobile type who has risen from a rough nieghborhood to a Porsche, and owns the dark, satanic mill where our lady welds.

Her language is, I gather, a badge of emancipation these days. That is, it would cause blushes beneath deck in a troop ship. But her clothes have become a commercial force. In the Juniors department at Woodward & Lothrop in Chevy Chase, Maryland, and across this broad land, you can buy the *Flashdance* look.

When our heroine wends her weary way home after a hard day over the acetylene torch, she slips into something . . . well, "comfortable" hardly does justice to it. It is so loose she almost slips right out again. The Flashdance look is a ragged sweatshirt hanging off one fetching shoulder and barely hanging on the other. A tear or two is required, and at stores that know their stuff you can now buy pretorn and elegantly unfinished garments. For half-hearted flashdancers, some garments come equipped with snaps that can snap up the torn look and make the thing whole for, I guess, formal occasions.

What is the world coming to? To a place it has been before. In his new book, *Lost in the Cosmos: The Last Self-Help Book*, Walker Percy recalls that when Wallis Warfield Simpson appeared at Ascot with the second button of her blouse inadvertently unbuttoned, lots of women began leaving their second buttons unbuttoned. And when John Wayne was filming *Red River*, and his belt buckle slipped to one side, lots of men slipped their buckles sideward.

What is going on in such cases? The pursuit of happiness, of course. But why, Percy wonders, does such behavior produce happiness?

Cosmos? I thought we were in places like Pittsburgh. Percy says: Pittsburgh, cosmos, what's the difference? The fading of religious explanations of mankind's place in the cosmos has left the self dislocated and without identity. So people put on new identities—Mrs. Simpson's, or John Wayne's, or our lady welder's.

Liberated by skepticism from the restraints of religion, by democracy from social oppression, by technology from drudgery, the modern individual is free to do as he or she pleases. And what does it please him or her to do? Unbutton the second button, slip the belt sideward, don a pretorn jersey.

This is not to say that modern life is problem-free. Percy cites this letter to Dear Abby: "I am a 23-year-old liberated woman who has been on The Pill for two years. It's getting pretty expensive and I think my boyfriend should share half the cost, but I don't know him well enough to discuss money with him." That lady may be lost in the cosmos, and so may we all be, whether we know it or not. But the lady welder, unlike those derivative selves who want to dress like her, is comfortable in the cosmos, and not just because her clothes are so comfortable.

She is like two persons Percy mentions—Franz Schubert, who sat in beer halls writing lieder on the tablecloths, and Pablo Picasso, who sat in restaurants molding animals out of bread. She is so totally absorbed in a vocation—both a gift and a mastering passion—that she has no time to be absorbed with the self's worries about itself. And that is the moral of the story: You can pursue happiness by wearing a torn jersey. You can catch it by being good at something you love.

You thought *Flashdance* was just music? It is metaphysics, of which they have some in Pittsburgh.

August 14, 1983

Einstein Revealed as Brilliant Youth

Damn.

The rotten news for parents was put succinctly in a *New York Times* headline: "Einstein Revealed as Brilliant in Youth." That may not strike you as any sort of news, but it is, and it blasts a hope that has sustained some of us.

It has long been said that Einstein was a slow starter. The legend, to which many parents have clung for comfort, was that Einstein was dim in primary and secondary school and even failed his college entrance examinations. He did fail those examinations, but primarily because he had trouble learning French, which trouble I consider a sign of superior spirit.

The rest of the legend turns out to derive from a misreading of the grading system at his Swiss school. It now has been learned, as a result of the preparation of his papers for publication, that the kid was something of a prodigy. He excelled at college physics before he was 11, was gifted at Latin and Greek, and was a "brilliant" violinist.

The science (or so we are invited to regard it) of "parenting" incites the hope that we can learn practical lessons from conspicuous successes. So I have been looking into the rearing of little Al Einstein. My findings are not entirely encouraging.

At age five he was tutored at home, but only briefly—until he had a tantrum and threw a chair at the unfortunate woman doing the tutoring. So far, so good: The Will children certainly have had that Einsteinian phase.

Now for the bad news.

It is said that when at age four or five he received a compass from his father, he trembled and became cold from the thrill of thinking: Because the needle always points in the same direction, something unseen in space must be compelling it; therefore space is not empty.

He was stirred to the depths of his soul (it had more depth than I usually see in children's souls) by a book of Euclidean geometry which, he thought, gave him a glimpse of perfection. Now, admit it: If you gave your child a book of geometry, he or she would not take his or her nose out of the Michael Jackson biography he or she is reading. If you give him or her a compass at 9 A.M., and it has not been lost by 10 A.M., by 11 A.M. it will have been traded for a Moosehead beer can.

Little Einstein was perhaps slow to speak, but once he got the hang of it he said attention-getting things. As the Will children fill the dinner hour with ad hominem remarks about one another, spiced with digressions concerning the enveloping subject of Michael Jackson, my mind turns to this fact: Young Einstein was given to wondering aloud, "What would the world look like if I were riding on a beam of light?"

(Don't say: "Blurry." Einstein was being serious, and the correct answer is: "Frozen." Jacob Bronowksi explains it: Suppose you are riding away from a clock tower on the beam of light with which you were seeing that the clock reads "noon." You will travel 186,000 miles away from the clock in a second. But the clock, as you will see it over your shoulder, will not change at all, not even a second. Why not? By keeping up with the beam of light, you have escaped from the passage of time.)

When asked on his 74th birthday whether the compass and the geometry book really influenced his growth, Einstein said he thought so: "But a man has little insight into what goes on within him. When a young puppy sees a compass for the first time, it may have no similar influence, nor on many a child." I love the equation of puppies and children. And I wonder: What about the second time the puppy sees the compass?

You can, Einstein said, postulate theories, but you will never find the answer to the riddle of what determines the reactions of individuals to particular influences. Therefore, parents, the science of parenting is, it seems, severely circumscribed.

Thank God. How intolerable would be the burden of responsibility, and how sad would be the death of mystery, were we able to control the maturation of creatures we let loose on the world. So it is cheerfully that I, with a flourish that puts me on a par with Einstein at, oh, age four, offer this sunburst: Parenting is a science of single instances.

June 10, 1984

"Chicago Ain't Ready for Reform"

I spent my childhood in Champaign, Illinois, pondering two slogans of the divine Steak 'n' Shake restaurants: "It's a meal" and "In sight it must be right." Now I think I understand. The former is rhetorical minimalism: Could you claim less for food than that it is a meal? The second slogan means: Shucks, food is just food, so what more need be said for a restaurant than that it is here, now. Today, Chicago's mayoral contest involves Steak 'n' Shake politics.

Congressman Harold Washington believes in "it's a meal" minimalism. A TV commercial closes with: "Washington: the Democrat." You can hardly say less for him, but in Chicago, where most voters have Democratic chromosomes, that should suffice. His Republican opponent's slogan is: Vote for Bernard Epton "before it's too late." Or: shucks, he is not Harold Washington, so what more need be said, other than that he is here, now.

Welcome to Chicago, where even the feast of Saint Valentine is associated with bloodshed. Chicago politics, like Chicago baseball, is not for the squeamish.

Epton, 61, is an extremely liberal Republican, which is like being a High-Church Unitarian: It is possible, but why bother? He is wealthy, Jewish, a state legislator and too fond of wisecracks. In a recent "debate," during which the candidates audited each other's tax returns, Epton said: "*George* Washington you're not." Washington said he had already confessed that.

Washington also confessed to "negligence." He was jailed for not filing tax returns for four years. The prosecutors claimed he did not file for 19 years. He was suspended from practicing law for taking fees for legal work he did not do. Epton claims Washington's wages have been garnished for nonpayment of bills. On Palm Sunday, with a penitent Walter Mondale in tow (Mondale endorsed someone else in the primary), Washington went stumping at a mass in a church in a white neighborhood. The vulgarity of the visit was exceeded by the nastiness of the mob that protested. Mondale, without a shred of evidence but pronouncing himself an "expert on demonstrations," declared Epton responsible for the mob. Washington, an ingenious ethicist, said Epton was responsible "no matter who inspired it." After mature reflection, Washington said everything was being orchestrated by Reagan, of course. Of Epton he says: "In his cooler moments he is a rational man," a transparent reference to Epton's having had psychiatric tests. (Before ulcers were discovered, Epton thought his stomach pains might be psychosomatic.)

It has been said that the succession of heavyweight champions was a rough measure of black emancipation. Joe Louis established the right of a black to be quiet and talented. Sonny Liston, a convict, established the right to be mean and talented. Muhammad Ali established the right to be obnoxious and talented. Harold Washington gives blacks access to a feeling other ethnic groups have often experienced because of their candidates: embarrassment.

Although Chicago's lakefront skyline is unsurpassed, Chicago is as horizontal as the prairie. It is a city of small houses, representing the owners' achievements and aspirations. Politics can be driven by anxiety about property values. Two-thirds of Chicago's neighborhoods are 95 percent white or 95 percent black, which means that there is a bit, but only a bit, more racial isolation than in many other cities.

It is being said that such is the bitterness of this campaign that Chicago will be ungovernable no matter who wins. But Chicago has lived a long time with ethnic tensions. The first serious fiction I remember reading was the Studs Lonigan trilogy by James T. Farrell, a Chicagoan who had a sure sense of the city's unmelted and unreconciled ethnic blocs 50 years ago. It remains an illuminating primer on the strong sense of territoriality, and the border skirmishes, that are facets of life in this unhomogenized city. But of all Chicago's blocs, none can match the black population, which is larger than that of all but two black African cities.

Chicago was built by railroads. Before Chicago gave the world *Playboy* and the Big Mac, back when Messrs. Sears and Roebuck met there, and Montgomery Ward opened his first store there, and Messrs. Swift and Armour began butchering hogs there, Chicago radiated rails. I grew up watching the Illinois Central's streamliners, the Panama Limited and the City of New Orleans, streak toward Chicago. The IC also carried a lot of Southern rural blacks with one-way tickets and dreams of better days as urban Northerners. Long ago the City of New Orleans got, as the song says, the disappearing railroad blues. And a lot of dreams faced a cold dawn in Chicago, south of the IC's 12th Street Station, which also has gone. Harold Washington is an unworthy vessel for those dreams. But whether he wins or loses, Chicago will remain the great laboratory of our democracy.

This city of the plains is the great American city. It is a bit like Florence when the Guelphs and Ghibellines were at each other's throats. The unsavory political life is no measure of the city's creativity, commercial and cultural.

In 1893, when Henry Adams visited the Columbian Exposition, Chicago was a city of 1 million. It had had 300 residents just 60 years earlier, when incorporated. Adams wrote: "Chicago asked in 1893 for the first time the question whether the American people knew where they were driving . . . Chicago was the first expression of American thought as a unity." Ninety years later, in its sesquicentennial year, Chicago still exemplifies the essence of American history, and American yearning. America's story is about the tension between the celebration of energy, expressed in restless individualism, and the desire for community, which must be inclusive and exclusive.

Chicago is energy incarnate, and a mosaic of fiercely self-conscious communities. In 1956, when Richard Daley beat a "reform" Democrat in the mayoral primary, Paddy Bauler, a saloon-keeper-alderman, announced: "Chicago ain't ready for reform yet." Is it ready for the role history has assigned it, the role of reconciling dynamism and communitarian values? Ready or not, here it is, and I say: In sight it must be right.

April 11, 1983

Eeeek! Heterosexism!

In London's borough of Brent, a move is afoot to eliminate "heterosexism." This new front in the battle for social perfection was opened in response to a poster for an afternoon tea dance. The offending poster showed men and women dancing together. Well!

Some local improvers said there was no reason why posters should not show men dancing with men and women with women. Guidelines for elimination of "heterosexism in publicity" have been submitted.

The Greater London Council has focused its moral microscope on another social defect. Blue plaques are placed as historical markers on London homes where famous people have lived. The Council thinks the plaques are inadequate. They tell who lived there, and the nature of his or her claim to fame, but do not announce the person's sexual "preference." The proposal is to right this wrong by having certain plaques proclaim that certain persons—say, John Maynard Keynes or Oscar Wilde—were homosexuals. Plaques will remain reticent about heterosexuality.

Oh yeah, the Council also has decided to offer children free membership in the new center it funds for lesbians and homosexual men.

Many Americans, too, believe that thoroughness in the pursuit of equal treatment of everything is no vice. However, in Syracuse, some Episcopalians have been roiled because one of their churches is allowing its facilities to be used by a church that performs homosexual "marriages."

In San Francisco, a man whose male lover committed suicide took some time off work. The company says it extends bereavement leave in cases of the deaths of spouses but not lovers. A court test may decide whether the lover counted as a "spouse."

Controversies like the one in San Francisco are the predictable next step in the accelerating campaign to establish in law and social mores the doctrine that sexual "preference" is as much a matter of moral indifference as a preference for oysters rather than clams.

Many employers thought ending discrimination against homosexuals in hiring would be the end of the controversy. But the modern corporation, like the modern state, offers many entitlements to employees and their "spouses" and "families." Those categories are targeted for radical redefinition by some "homosexual rights" groups. They say nondiscrimination requires elimination of "heterosexism" in the definition of "family" and "spouse."

The Supreme Court's recent brush with the subject of homosexuality must be understood in the light of such indiscriminate assaults on discrimination. The Court voted against reviewing an appeals court decision concerning a bisexual woman who lost her job as a guidance counselor in an Ohio high school. A jury had ruled against the school district, holding that she had suffered impermissible injury. But the appeals court overruled the jury, holding that no constitutional principle prohibits the school district from making her sexuality a ground for dismissal.

Now, the question is not whether the school district acted wisely or justly. The question is whether the Constitution, which guarantees neither perfect wisdom nor perfect justice, protects the woman's right to hold her job, or whether the community has a right to act as it did in expression of its convictions.

In a steaming dissent, the Court's two liberals, Justices Brennan and Marshall, say the court should have taken the case. Clearly they think the woman's First Amendment rights of free "expression" and a free-floating "privacy" right were violated, as well as her Fourteenth Amendment right to "equal protection."

Her sexuality became known through her casual remarks. The two dissenters call them "nondisruptive" remarks, although it is unclear how they know the effect of the remarks on the community. Anyway, because her remarks revealed her sexual "preference," the dissenters present this as primarily a "free speech" case.

Furthermore, the dissenters, although emphasizing that the remarks were private and casual, insist that the remarks "necessarily and ineluctably involved her" in a "public debate" about an "explosive issue." Therefore, they seem to think, her remarks were especially deserving of protection as political speech.

This argument is absurd because it is absurd to say that the issue was her words describing her sexual behavior. The issue was her behavior, which the community considers deeply offensive and potentially harmful to others. Brennan and Marshall dismiss the community's values as "prejudices."

Brennan and Marshall must think that any moral and psychological disruption of the community by the "nondisruptive" words does not count. Their position is not "neutrality" regarding homosexual behavior. Their evident aim is to force communities to adopt policies that express the notion that homosexuality is a matter of indifference. In the name of free expression, Brennan and Marshall would stigmatize as immoral the community's expression of its values.

March 3, 1985

Baseball Is a Worrying Thing

Drenched in Florida sunshine, the spring training game was under way and everyone was as bubbly as ginger ale. Everyone, that is, except the Baltimore Orioles' batboy, who had a large lump in his cheek: his first chaw of tobacco. In the fourth inning he turned as green as grass and departed. Spring is a season for manly rites of passage, and in spring, especially, a lad's reach should exceed his grasp.

The next day the batboy was back, and so was the lump. And among the spectators, the columnist with his eight-year-old recalled Rolfe Humphries's poem, "Polo Grounds":

> Time is of the essence. The crowd and players
> Are the same age always, but the man in the crowd
> Is older every season. Come on, play ball!

Baseball's soothing continuities were exemplified that day by the gentleman seated nearby. Jack Dunn works for today's Orioles. His grandfather owned the minor league Orioles and signed a kid off Baltimore's sandlots, a kid named Ruth.

Today baseball reflects the Stockmanization of life: too much talk about money. David Stockman is duty-bound to talk about it incessantly, but it is tiresome when sports pages read like releases from the Office of Management and Budget. The Yankees' Dave Winfield hits about .280 and earns a salary the size of the Kemp–Roth tax cut. In 1929, Lefty O'Doul hit .398 with 254 hits— a National League record never surpassed. It earned him a $500 raise. In 1932 he hit "only" .368 and his salary was cut $1,000.

With terrible swiftness players become men in the crowd, older every season, so they should read this 1914 editorial in Baseball magazine:

"It is, as a rule, a man's own business how he spends his money. But nevertheless we wish to call attention to the fact that many men do so in a very unwise manner. A very glaring instance of this among baseball players is the recent evil tendency to purchase and maintain automobiles. Put the money away, boys, where it will be safe. You don't need these automobiles. That money will look mighty good later on in life. Think it over, boys."

Baseball recently provided some timely food for thought: a reminder that in spite of the risks, it is still nice to be President, in part because just about anyone you invite will come to lunch. Three days before he was shot, Ronald Reagan lunched with Sandy Koufax, Ernie Banks and some other boys of other summers: baseball immortals. The two most testing jobs in America are President and radio broadcaster for the Chicago Cubs. Reagan has now held both, and kind of combined them at that lunch.

One table was adorned by a broken-down Yale first baseman (George Bush), a Cardinal first baseman (Stan Musial), a Cub second baseman (Billy Herman) and a Pirate outfielder (Ralph Kiner, who spent, as many now do, some of his declining seasons with the Cubs). In addition, some relatively new Washington hands got into a genteel rhubarb with an old Washington hand.

Joe Cronin was player-manager of the last Washington Senators team to win a pennant (1933). He is a defender of the American League's sinister Bolshevism that already has inflicted the "designated hitter" on baseball and may, unless checked, produce even worse desecrations.

Paul Volcker, a rangy righthander from the Federal Reserve Board, told Cronin that the American League's incontinent social experimentation, its restless lust for novelty, is the cause of inflation. Jim Baker, the crafty portsider who is White House chief of staff, is a man of soft but wounding words, and he compared the American League's tinkering with baseball to the Anglican communion's tinkering with the Book of Common Prayer. Bush maintained a discreet silence. He may want to run for President some day. And supporters of the designated hitter rule are, alas, allowed to vote.

Baseball resembles politics. Consider the analysis by Stanley Coveleski, a Cleveland Indians' pitcher and metaphysician: "The pressure never lets up. Doesn't matter what you did yesterday. That's history. It's tomorrow that counts. So you worry all the time. It never ends. Lord, baseball is a worrying thing."

It isn't for Jonathan Will who, noting his father's blighted life, has become an Orioles fan. Over the last 22 seasons they have won more games than any other team. For this father, a Cubs fan, the worry is:

As the Cubs enter the 36th year of their rebuilding effort, there is the possibility of a player strike. If the Cubs' players withhold their labor, will we be able to tell the difference?

April 12, 1981

Movies as Child Abuse

Whoever authored the prayer "God protect us from fire, steel and contemporary literature" should have expanded the list of menaces to include movies like *Scarface*. Consider the dismemberment, by chain saw, of one drug dealer by another.

When the ratings board gave *Scarface* an X because of violence and vile language, the movie was jeopardized because many theaters will not show X-rated material. So changes were made. Now viewers do not see the chainsaw make contact with flesh; they must be content with splattering blood. Even after such tinkering, the board sensibly favored an X-rating but was overruled.

The board was created 15 years ago by the studios and theater owners to forestall local censorship ordinances. Its seven members are all parents whose job is to make empirical, not moral, judgments. It is a majoritarian institution, making educated guesses about community standards—about what entertainment most parents consider proper for children.

The appeals board, composed of movie industry people, has often overruled the ratings board at the ratings board's request. The automatic-language rule requires an R when there are harsh sexually derived words. So the ratings board gave perfunctory R-ratings to *The Right Stuff* and *Terms of Endearment*, and then asked to be overruled, and was.

In the last 10 years the ratings board has classified 3,500 films. Aside from pro forma language rule appeals, the ratings board has been overruled just 12 times. Each time the rating was lowered. Nine times the issue was violence, three times sex. An X means children under 17 (18 in a few places) cannot be admitted; an R means they must be accompanied by a parent or guardian.

In classifying *Scarface* X, the ratings board unquestionably made a correct assessment of how most parents would judge the movie. Floating face-down, drowned in a bath of blood, is the corpse of what could have been a valuable movie about what drug money is doing to south Florida. To say that the movie is morally constructive because it shows the squalor of drug addiction, and because the bad guys get massacred, misses a large point, which is: Realism is no all-purpose defense in art.

Yes, even the chainsaw scene is not without basis in fact: The brutality in the drug trade is hair-curling. But it is unnecessary, and artistically lazy, to achieve impact by relentlessly dwelling on shocking things. What can be true of sex can be true of violence, too. Intimation can be more powerful than indiscriminate, pitiless detail. Within the restraints of 19th-century literature, *Madame Bovary* managed to have a moment as erotic in its way as episodes in today's explicit novels. Violence hinted at, but left at least somewhat to the viewers' imagining, should suffice.

Pamela Hansford Johnson has written: "Only a minority of people act out what they have seen (or read). But I believe a great number become desensitized by being exposed to scenes of, or ideas of, violence. I have seen the young become increasingly unshockable by the screened or staged display of cruelty. What would it be like if they met with the real thing? Such as Hitler's public humiliation of the Jews? Crowds excitedly gathered round old Jewish victims in Vienna. They were laughing. Are we preparing ourselves for a good laugh?"

About the young I, too, can attest. I remember *Marathon Man*, a serious movie but one involving torture with a dental drill. The most alarming thing was that my reaction (I nearly ran from the theater) was eccentric. The rest of the audience—like most movie audiences, mostly young—was unfazed.

The principal worry is not that repeated exposure to depictions of cruelty will make persons act cruelly. Rather, it is that it will produce persons who can respond only to depictions of excess. A generation raised on what are known as "slash films" (*Prom Night, Halloween, Friday the Thirteenth,* etc.) may become unable to enjoy subtlety, nuance or delicacy. That is, they may be rendered immune to art.

The ratings board deserves praise for taking gratuitous violence as seriously as degrading sex. But how will it rate things when the "slash film" generation becomes parents? While the ratings board tries to conform to community standards, the movies are driving those standards steadily down.

The night I saw *Scarface,* a couple brought their daughter, who was not yet 15. She must have found interesting the 175 uses (the official count, I am told) of what the Will boys decorously call "the f word." The ticket-taker, appalled by the movie, anguished about whether to warn the parents, and did not. Exposing a child to 170 minutes of torture, gore and obscenity is child abuse as serious as an act of physical violence.

December 15, 1983

The Noblest Use of Cinema

There has never been anything like it, or its subject, so there is something flat about saying that *Shoah* is the finest film ever. So say this: It is the noblest use to which cinema—the technology, the techniques—has been put, ever.

Claude Lanzmann's nine-and-a-half hour masterpiece *Shoah* (the Hebrew word for annihilation) contains not a frame from the 1940s. It is an elicitation of memories of the Holocaust and it proves that the unspeakable is not inexpressible.

No subject is too large or lurid to be encompassed by words well chosen. And when words are joined with pictures that do not subordinate the words to visual values, even plain words are set like diamonds in platinum.

Cinema rarely rises from a craft to an art. Usually it just manufactures sensory blizzards for persons too passive to manage the active engagement of mind that even light reading requires. Cinema, with its enervating bath of sights and sounds, usually is a medium for modest attention spans. But, paradoxically, *Shoah*, a near-perfection of cinematic art, is brilliant because it is an act of cinematic modesty. It uses pictures—usually of people plainly framed or landscapes slowly panned—as a sort of silent music behind the words.

Rhetorical flourishes are few and far between. (A death camp survivor says: "If you could lick my heart, it would poison you.") There are some moments of savage illumination, as when an SS veteran replies to a question about how many were killed at a particular place: "Four something—four hundred thousand or forty thousand." As eloquent as even the most eloquent words are the silences, the pauses, the flickering expressions as facial muscles register the struggle for composure.

The most stunning episode in this shattering film lasts about five minutes and involves "only" the talk of a barber now in Israel. While he clips the hair of a customer he talks, never needing to raise his voice to be heard over the small sounds of a familiar ambience. He describes his duties in Treblinka, cutting hair from naked women on the threshold of the gas chamber, and the day a fellow barber saw his wife and sister enter the room.

The film's recurring image is of trains rolling across Poland's flat terrain. There is a sinisterness, a menace in the mere clackety-clack of wheels rolling down a single track between lovely pines toward a shimmering clearing, a camp. A locomotive engineer, old now, his face the texture of elm bark, tells how he was plied with vodka to enable him to push to unloading platforms the freight cars packed with Jews dying of thirst.

One reviewer got it exactly right when he described Lanzmann as a "cinematic pointillist." He works in minutiae which, cumulatively, become portentous. He asks a question such as, "Was this road asphalted then?" and the person questioned begins to talk and a narrative builds, detail piled upon detail, until you have hell in a monotone, and it is the more hellish for its matter-of-factness.

One person, after seeing *Shoah*, wrote to Lanzmann that it was the first time he had heard the cry of an infant in the gas chamber. He had not, of course. What he had heard was the quiet description by an Auschwitz survivor of the way bodies were jumbled when the gas chamber doors opened, and what that jumble of flesh and blood and vomit and excrement told about the final minutes in the dark when fathers lost their grips on their sons and the strong climbed over the weak as the gas fumes rose.

Here is a task—a duty—for Jewish and other organizations: Subsidize the sale of cassettes of this film. No church or school should be without it. Lanzmann's little questions ("What color was the truck?") wind up answering one big question: What was it like? The answer to that contains the answer to another big question, the question that is the title of the only other film Lanzmann has made: "Why Israel?"

The Nazi project was to erase European Jewry—not just kill but erase traces. So the Nazis ground to dust the bones that would not burn and threw the dust in rivers and lakes. *Shoah*, like Solzhenitsyn's *Gulag*, is an act of continuing resistance to a continuing atrocity.

Continuing? Yes, it is an assertion of memory against a program of erasure, a program that will not be fulfilled until memory fades and indifference reigns. Lanzmann cites a philosopher's statement that Europe's massacred Jews "are not just of the past, they are the presence of an absence." Wherever *Shoah* is seen, and for as long as it lasts, they are present.

November 14, 1985

Literary Voyeurism

Sooner or later, a ready pen and a blank piece of paper awakens the fiend that sleeps in most of us, and we write intemperate letters. The cause is usually personal pique rather than public-spiritedness. (As has been said, it is a pity that people resent insults more than fallacies.)

If you are wise, you enjoy the catharsis of writing such a letter but won't mail it. If you mail it and are fortunate, the recipient will not wait until you die and then publish it, injuring your reputation and perhaps causing pain to others.

Ernest Hemingway was not fortunate. So if you have a thick wallet and thick forearms, you can pick up *Ernest Hemingway: Selected Letters, 1917–1961* (921 pages, $27.50). In it you will find various letters containing injunctions such as "Never mention any of this to anyone. . . . Bury all this," and "This is only for your information."

There is a childishly vituperative letter to Cardinal Spellman. A biographer of Hemingway, A. E. Hotchner, who has reviewed this volume of letters for *New York* magazine, was with Hemingway in Cuba when Hemingway "stormed into his study and rattled off this 'letter,' which he presented to me to read. 'It's not for sending,' he said. 'It's for the letting-off-steam file.'" Although never mailed, it has now been published.

To an editor at his publisher, Scribner's, Hemingway wrote: "I think you or the family should take great care that nobody gets hold of [my letters]. The personal letters are often libelous, always indiscreet, often obscene and many of them could make great trouble." And great pain.

Hemingway never met the late James Jones, author of *From Here to Eternity*, but Hemingway wrote to Charles Scribner about Jones: "I hope he kills himself as soon as it does not damage his or your sales. . . . He has the psycho's urge to kill himself and he will do it." In another letter Hemingway calls Jones a "whimpering neurotic" and "a coward. . . . I wish him no luck at all and I hope he goes out and hangs himself as soon as possible."

Hotchner wonders how Jones's widow and children will feel about such letters. I wonder what interest is served by publishing them—what interest sufficient to justify the costs involved in disregarding the desires of the dead and lacerating the feelings of the living. What interest beyond "the public's right to know"—a right frequently invoked but rarely defined by those (publishers and journalists) whose commercial and professional interests are served by invoking it.

Publication of these letters was authorized by Hemingway's widow, Mary, who, Hotchner suggests, might rethink the matter of discretion in publishing if Hotchner published some of Hemingway's letters to him which refer to Mary. ("In lots of ways she reminds me of Leo Durocher. . . . I have never seen her be kind except to servants.") As Hemingway said, "In a letter there is not the time you need to be just."

Hemingway is but the most recent victim of an emphatic, almost aggressive, disregard for discretion. In his last will, Somerset Maugham, who had good reasons, expressed the wish that there be no biography of him, and asked that his letters be destroyed. Obviously no one can legislate from the grave against the writing of biography, and he who wants private correspondence to remain private should see to the destruction of it before he dies. But it was crummy of Maugham's literary agent to disregard Maugham's wishes and help bring into being a 711-page biography. Another "friend" gave the biographer 600 letters.

In a prefatory note, Maugham's agent wrote that "many people may think I acted wrongly," but he rationalizes what he did on the ground that the biographer did not "pass any moral judgment" on anybody. Even were that true, which it is not, it would be beside the point. It may be that Maugham had the sort of "friends" he deserved, but that, too, is beside the point. The point is that it is not nice to cause unnecessary pain, or to violate the wishes of the dead, just to satisfy the curiosity of the reading public.

When Henry Stimson was secretary of state (1929–33), he said of attempts to crack other nations' diplomatic codes: "Gentlemen do not read each other's mail." That standard must be bent for reasons of state. But not for reasons of commerce, or literary voyeurism.

April 19, 1981

Summa Contra Super Bowl

When Saturday night at length with slow retreating steps departs, dawn will break like thunder on Super Sunday and on the sterile violence of indoor football in air conditioning on plastic grass on the banks of the Father of Waters. Turn up your rhetorical rheostats, America, it's gonna be a Stroh's Light Night.

But first, at 3 P.M. EST, the sauna of spectacle will get steaming with a two-hour pregame show during which commentators will plumb the shallows of the subject, explaining that on any given day any team can beat any other team because all the players have come to play and they all put their pants on one leg at a time although Willie Gault's speedy legs, well, when he's dashing down the field he and his quarterback are in different zip codes and both quarterbacks are gamers and role models and everyone will be giving 150 percent like Sweetness who goes for the gold when he gets near the goal line like all the money players who know that intensity is the name of the game when there is no tomorrow, especially with the 12th man in the game, those great fans from the two great cities who have enjoyed themselves so good like haven't we all in this great city of New Orleans where this great game in spite of all the glamour will be decided in the trenches where the blue-collar boys of the offensive line will establish the running game so they can establish the passing game because defense is the name of the game because good defense beats good offense and vice versa so special teams are the most important ingredient as is the kicking game and the offense because the other guys can't score when you've got the ball, so key on the seam-splitting nose guards who are flooding zones with stunting nickel defenses to see who can be most opportunistic about turnovers with both quarterbacks audibilizing over the roar of this crowd that knows, oh sure, there is money at stake but by golly there is a lot of little boys in the big men who play hurt not for money but for a little thing called pride, which is why there is such a lot of America in this great game of football.

Now this: tastesgreatlessfillingflamebroiled. Now back to . . .

It must have been someone who saw a Super Bowl telecast who said he preferred rogues to fools because rogues sometimes take a rest. Having had the brass to begin, the wonder is that the broadcasters ever stop. They won't, until they have stomped the last vestige of shape from the mother tongue.

Charles Krauthammer has well described the "absurd Augustan ritual" of the Super Bowls: flags the size of Rhode Island or the Dallas–Fort Worth Airport or the West Bank (whichever is biggest), military honor guards, presidential coin tosses, platoons of vestal virgins (well, vestals, anyway). The Super Bowl is a movable feast unanchored to anything except the core principle of commerce: The highest bidder (among cities) gets it. As Krauthammer says, "It would be played in Krakow, if the Krakow Bowl had enough skyboxes."

Bits of football will be slipped between "officials' times outs" and "two-minute warnings" and other excuses for commercials. Then come the male bonding scenes—the towel-snapping thrill of victory in the winner's locker room and the bluff, hearty, bravely borne agony of defeat in the other. The game itself will be interlarded with 25 minutes of commercials, fifty 30-second spots sold for $550,000 apiece. It was born in the U.S.A.—the $1.1-million minute.

The best minute will be NBC's 60-second "intermission." It will by 60 seconds of blessed nothingness. It is supposed to help make the other 25 minutes worth what advertisers are spending.

In the otherwise silent watches of the night, advertisers sit bolt upright in bed and scream in terror: Suppose when their beer commercial comes on, 50 million fans (about half the viewers) head for the kitchen or the bathroom? This does happen during what broadcasters call "a break in the action"—as though football is not mostly such breaks: six seconds of grunting followed by committee meetings called huddles.

During NBC's blank minute there will be nothing on the screen, in the hope that viewers will make themselves comfortable before the serious stuff (no, silly goose, not football—commercials) begins. This will take a great weight off advertisers' minds that are buckling beneath the burden of getting their message noticed in the cacophony.

For this Sunday, Timex spent $1 million just to produce a commercial for a $34.95 watch. The commercial features a 60-foot watch 50 feet beneath the surface of the Red Sea. The commercial has the delicacy and nuance suited to this Sunday.

January 26, 1986

Sport and Civility

In March—basketball tournament time—this middle-aged man from the Middle West relives in memory the athletic glory of his youth.

Well, not exactly glory. As an athlete I subscribed to the maxim that anything worth doing is worth doing badly. That is, anything worth doing is worth trying, even if you make a hash of it. I played on a high school team that fitted a coach's famous description of his team: "We're short but we're slow." I was a "scrappy playmaker" (that means: no finesse, no shot) for the University of Illinois High School.

Known as "Puny Uni," the school had too many faculty brats who spent too much time reading books and too little time practicing the old give-and-go. (I was a faculty brat, but read nothing except *The Sporting News*.) I hung up my black hightop sneakers before Uni got the national attention it deserved for losing 96 games in a row. But in my senior year we rolled to a 2–16 record, twice beating a small rural school which, perhaps spurred by shame, soon consolidated with another school. Uni's 1958 yearbook snickered that things got so bad that the coach, in an act of existential despair, even allowed Will to start a few games.

God in His infinite mercy gave us basketball so that we would have something besides supply-side economics to talk about between the end of the World Series and the beginning of spring training. Basketball isn't baseball but, hey, Cézanne wasn't Rembrandt. There are games of sporadic action (baseball, football) and games of flow, like basketball, a marvelous mixture of concentration and instinct. Sport is one of America's remaining meritocracies, a realm where quality rises and excellence wins. If America produced good products (or economists) as prolifically as it produces basketball talent, it could work miracles—maybe even balance the budget.

There is a sad side to this profusion of talented players. Most of the best are black, and many are motivated by a chimera, the lure of astronomical professional contracts. Of the thousands of collegians playing big-time basketball this year, perhaps 100 will have serious pro careers. It is a sad commentary on the experience of many black fathers that so many sons invest so much concentration in honing talents for careers that are open to so few. Too many young black players generate huge sums for universities and networks, only to be used up and discarded, barely educated but schooled in cynicism by sleazy recruiting and other practices. (During Watergate a wiseacre said that when we got to the bottom of the scandal we would find a basketball coach.)

Frederick C. Klein of the *Wall Street Journal* thinks college basketball is confirming a law of sports decline: "The more prosperous a sport becomes, the more likely it is to destroy the reasons for its prosperity." The primary reason for college basketball's prosperity is exuberant play. But increasingly that is being suffocated by stalling tactics. Today there are large arenas to fill and large television contracts ($70,000 per appearance) at stake. Coaches get their teams on television by winning, appease alumni by winning, attract recruits—the key to winning—by winning.

The NCAA Tournament has been expanded to 48 teams, each of which will get a minimum of about $121,000. So some coaches will play any way—including not really playing in long stretches of the game—to gain an edge against losing. They get a lead and sit on it, grimly holding the ball. This is called a "controlled offense," a euphemism that denotes, as euphemisms generally do, something not to be proud of.

A 30-second-shot clock may be needed, but such a change in the game's constitution would suggest an incurable insufficiency of good character and proper values on the part of fans as well as coaches. If fans would bring to their role as much grace as players bring to theirs, they would disdain victories won meanly.

A society is disoriented when proper moral judgment is supplanted by a morally constricted legalism, the notion that whatever is legal—whatever there is a right to do—is morally unobjectionable. There are protected rights to do many things (such as sell pornography, incite hatred) that are wrong. The rules of college basketball permit a stall. But in sports, as in life generally, comportment should be controlled by a morality of aspiration more demanding than a mere morality of duty. A morality of aspiration should elevate people above merely complying with elementary rules.

When a coach orders his team to stall for, say, four minutes (a tenth of a game) without attempting to score, he is doing something even more subversive of good sportsmanship and citizenship than were he teaching his players to break rules. He is teaching them that there is no higher code of conduct than complying with the letter of the law. It is difficult to draw a line between a deliberate style of basketball and a tactic that amounts to not really playing basketball. But it is obtuse or cynical for coaches to say that if the rules are not actually broken, no harm is done. Rules are abused when they are used to frustrate rather than further the essence of the activity that the rules exist to regulate. Fair play, civility and gentlemanliness involve respect for the spirit as well as the letter of the rules or laws that frame particular activities.

In an age short on craftsmanship and long on shoddiness, anything done well—laying bricks, writing poems, playing games—deserves honor. Worked at intelligently, sport is not just compatible with academic purposes, it complements them because it involves striving for excellence, but striving governed by standards of fairness and seemliness. As the ancient Greeks understood, sport is a civic, a moral undertaking because it can teach appreciation of worthy things, such as courage and beauty. A use of the body that is strenuous yet elegant—be it ballet or basketball—can enlarge and express the spirit. Watching a great athlete is, strictly speaking, good for the soul.

Such thoughts are stirred each year when I hear in the recesses of my memory the sound of March in the Middle West, the slap-slap-slap of a cold rubber ball on a cold concrete driveway.

March 15, 1982

Exploring the Racer's Edge

It has been said that someone who cheats in an amateur contest is a cheat, whereas a professional who cheats to feed his family is a competitor. Piffle. All sports should conform to the International Olympic Committee's ban on "the use by a competing athlete of any substance foreign to the body or of any physiological substance taken in abnormal quantity or taken by an abnormal route of entry into the body, with the sole intention of increasing in an artificial and an unfair manner his performance in competition." But even this careful language contains crucial ambiguities—"foreign to the body," "abnormal quantity," "an artificial and unfair manner." Define "fair" and you are home free. Let's start at the fringe of the subject and nibble in.

Seven U.S. Olympic cyclists, including four medal winners, practiced "blood doping." They received infusions of blood from relatives or others with the same blood type, in an attempt—it is not clear this works—to increase their red-cell count and accelerate the transfer of oxygen to muscles during endurance events. An eighth cyclist had a reinfusion of his own blood that had been drawn several weeks earlier. Was his blood (or any blood) "foreign to the body?" Clearly blood doping involves an abnormal quantity of blood entering the body through an abnormal route to increase performance in an artificial (and therefore unfair?) manner.

Steroids can enhance muscle mass. They also can kill you, if they do not just decrease sexual capacity, injure your liver and heart, and do sundry other damages. Some people say: It's the athlete's body, he can mess it up as he pleases—besides, sports often involve injuries. But it is one thing to injure yourself in exertion, another to injure yourself with chemicals in pursuit of the ultimate competitive "edge." And it is surely unfair to force your opponent to choose between similarly risking harm and competing at a disadvantage.

It is said that the improper pursuit of edge derives from valuing winning too much. Actually, it derives from misunderstanding why winning is properly valued.

There is a broad gray area of difficult judgments. For example, what, precisely, is the moral difference between eating energy-giving glucose pills and taking a steroid that increases muscle mass? What is the difference between taking vitamins—or, for that matter, eating spinach—in "abnormal quantities" and taking a drug that deadens the pain of an injured foot or (watch it—we are crossing some kind of line here) a drug that increases aggressiveness?

The science of sports medicine is no longer just about the prevention or treatment of injuries. It uses kinesiology and biomechanics and computer analysis of movement—high-tech stuff that would make even Gary Hart's head swim—to improve performance. Just as the launching of Sputnik 1 aroused American interest in science education, minds were concentrated on sports medicine by another embarrassment—the 1976 Montreal Olympics, where East Germany won more gold medals than the United States. (Of course the phrase "East German amateur athlete" is as much an oxymoron as "married bachelor," and some of those East German, er, ladies probably had interesting concoctions of hormones.)

As sports medicine and related technologies become more sophisticated, there is anxiety about the integrity of sport. This anxiety is an intuition in search of clarifying criteria. When sprinters began using starting blocks (remember in *Chariots of Fire* each runner carried a trowel to dig toeholds in the track at the starting line) the new equipment was available to all competitors and improved performances without altering the performers. When pole vaulters abandoned stiff bamboo and metal poles in favor of flexible fiberglass poles that fling vaulters skyward, the competition remained essentially the same, although at a previously undreamed-of plateau of achievement. Perhaps we are getting close to the key that unlocks the puzzle: Techniques and technologies are unobjectionable when they improve performance without devaluing it. Proper athletics are activities all of us can attempt. The use of certain exotic drugs or techniques alters the character of an activity and devalues it by making it exotic—no longer a shared activity.

We should listen to the promptings of our intuitions about appropriate language. It is one thing to be intense, even obsessive about training, including nutrition. It is different to pursue edge by means of chemical technologies—drugs—that we instinctively speak of as "unnatural" manipulations of the body. Intense training should involve enhancing powers by means of measures or materials that are part of the body's normal functioning, rather than by radical interventions in the body. Interventions are radical when they are designed not just to enhance normal functioning but to cause the body to behave abnormally—not unusually well but unnaturally well.

Illegitimate technologies are subverting the integrity of a sport when we feel inclined to speak of "the body," not "the athlete," performing well. Technologies can blur the sense of the self-involved. We admire people who run fast, not bodies that are made fast by chemical boosters. Some athletes probably are nagged by thoughts like: "My weight-lifting achievement is not mine, it belongs to my medicine cabinet."

The ancient Greeks, who invented the Olympics and political philosophy, believed that sport was a religious and civic—in a word, moral—undertaking. Sport, they said, is morally serious because a noble aim of life is appreciation of worthy things, such as beauty and bravery. By using their bodies beautifully, athletes teach our souls to appreciate beauty. By competing bravely, athletes make bravery vivid and exemplary.

Sport is competition to demonstrate excellence in admired activities. The excellence is most praiseworthy when the activity demands virtues of the spirit—of character—as well as physical prowess. Admirable athletic attainments involve mental mastery of pain and exhaustion—the triumph of character, not chemistry, over adversity. We want sport to reward true grit, not sophisticated science. We do not want a child to ask an athlete, "Can I get the autograph of your pharmacist?"

February 4, 1985

Intrusion by Telephone

The psalmist says that joy cometh in the morning. Fat lot the psalmist knows. Joy comes around noon on Thursday, when the U.S. Postal Service surrenders my copy of *Sports Illustrated*, a splendid journal.

But soon that joy will end, like a dream at daybreak. My subscription is expiring. I am told so by the persons whose telephone calls nagging me to resubscribe have provoked my decision not to.

Those calls transformed me into a John Brown—an abolitionist—concerning commercial solicitation by telephone. Americans should rise in righteous fury against this obnoxious business practice of barging into our homes by telephone to try to sell things.

The first call came when the Will family was enjoying dinner. Well, okay, "enjoying" may be a bit strong, but no two children were exchanging blows or even insults. The caller said it was time to resubscribe. Mrs. Will, who answered the phone, said she would resubscribe. But, ever a lady, she said that if *Sports Illustrated* were a well-brought-up gentlemen, it would know better than to intrude, especially at dinner time.

The second call came an hour later, when father was giving The Phenomenon (Victoria, age two) a bath. The Phenomenon, in her large-spirited way, was giving anyone near the tub a bath as she reenacted the Battle for Leyte Gulf. The *Sports Illustrated* caller said he was calling only to "reconfirm" something. I do not know what the something was. Our conversation was one-sided and short, consisting of nine seconds of robust epithets from me.

When I am aroused, my complexion becomes tomatoesque and I bark like a mastiff. Concerning my bark, the third pestilential caller can testify, when his trauma subsides. He called to explain the second call, and elicted from me a wide-ranging philippic which culminated with a vow never to resubscribe in this world or the next. I will suffer stoically whatever trials God sends to test me and make me a graver, deeper man. But I draw the line at suffering trials sent by lesser authorities, and *Sports Illustrated*, though grand, is lesser.

How did we, the seed of brave Founders and of immigrants who fought Comanche, become a nation of such sheep that we tolerate such intrusions into our homes? Someone has said that the telephone is like a mailman who crashes into your home, thrusts your mail beneath your nose, then stands impatiently at your side and forces you to read it all, immediately. No red-blooded American would stand for that. But we are so cowed by our conveniences, such as telephones, that we accept with bovine docility uses of them that are maddeningly inconvenient.

Perhaps it never enters the jellied mind of a commercial society to set limits to commerce. I note that Boston's commission on landmarks is blocking destruction of a Citgo corporation sign containing 10 miles of neon. The reason? For 40 years the sign has been a, well, landmark. Now, a society that is so reverent about merchandising that it gets gooey and sentimental and invokes the majesty of the law to protect old neon advertisements—such a society is too dotty to resent being assaulted by telephone callers peddling things. If society bristled with irritation about this hectoring extension of the marketplace into the home, the calls would stop.

The broadcasting industry, with the government's agreement, is eliminating the voluntary code that for 30 years has restricted television advertising to one product in each 30-second spot, limited stations to five consecutive commercials and limited commercials to no more than 8½ minutes an hour. A Federal Communications Commission guideline still restricts commercials to 16 minutes per hour, but it is just a guideline. And the FCC's chairman says he wants to deregulate television completely so that broadcasters, like newspaper owners, will be free to advertise what, and as much, as they like. So much for the distinction between printing presses, which can be multiplied at private instigation, and television channels, which, being limited, are allocated as public trusts and regulated by public agencies.

At the Washington Radio Conference of 1922, when the idea of broadcasting advertisements arose, the secretary of commerce said: "It is inconceivable that we should allow so great a possibility for service (radio) to be drowned in advertising chatter." Thus spake Herbert Hoover, whose enthusiasm for commerce was capacious, but not senseless.

Today, most of life's interstices are flooded with merchandising. But surely a dike of commercial ethics can be erected that will keep the flood from trickling through the telephone into our homes.

December 9, 1982

Wilde in Leadville

LEADVILLE, COLO.—Like all Westerners whose fates have been tied to extraction industries, folks here are familiar with booms and busts. This town of 5,000 once was a roughneck boom town. But in 1982, with the molybdenum mine closed by recession, residents of this nicely placed place, facing the front range of the Rockies at 10,200 feet, can enjoy the view and remember better days. One of the best was a century ago, when Leadville was larger than Denver, and the famous aesthete came to lecture the locals about pretty things.

Before the spring of 1860, few—if any—white men had been in this part of the Arkansas River valley. But by July, gold finds had drawn 10,000 adventurers. By 1864 about 300 remained. In the 1890s lead and silver produced a Leadville of between 30,000 and 60,000—no one knows for sure, because in those days people followed wandering stars and did not loiter. However, everyone knows that a red-letter day in Leadville was April 14, 1882, the day a train decanted Oscar Wilde.

He later said that Leadville's miners, in their red shirts, high boots and corduroy trousers, were "the only well-dressed men I have seen in America." What those hearty fellows made of his get-up can be imagined. Told that Leadville rowdies would shoot either him or his manager, he replied that he could not be intimidated by anything done to his manager.

"I read them passages from the autobiography of Benvenuto Cellini and they seemed much delighted. I was reproved by my hearers for not having brought him with me. I explained that he had been dead for some little time, which elicited the inquiry, 'Who shot him?'"

In another letter: "I spoke to them of early Florentines, and they slept. . . . I described to them the pictures of Botticelli, and the name, which seemed to them like a new drink, roused them from their dreams. . . . " Letter writers are not under oath.

What is touching is the ache for refinement and self-improvement that caused communities like Leadville to import the likes of Wilde to proclaim that "life without industry is sin, and industry without art is barbarism." After the lecture, a torchlight parade took Wilde and his host, Horace Tabor, to Tabor's Matchless Mine, into which they descended in a bucket for what Wilde called a banquet: "When I quaffed a cocktail without flinching, they unanimously pronounced me in their grand simple way "a bully boy with no glass eye.""

Tabor was a classic Western figure, a boom-town store owner who made a fortune in silver and land, and became a senator. In the eventful year of 1882, he married a dashing divorcee. A decade later he was bankrupt. The dashing divorcee was found frozen to death in a shack beside the Matchless Mine in 1935.

Before staying a night with Jefferson Davis at his plantation, Wilde passed through St. Joseph, Missouri, where people were paying "the income of an English Bishop" for relics from the house of a recently deceased celebrity, Jesse James. Before that, Wilde had visited a Nebraska prison:

"Poor odd types of humanity in hideous striped dresses making bricks in the sun, and all mean-looking, which consoled me, for I should hate to see a criminal with a noble face. Little whitewashed cells, so tragically tidy, but with books in them. In one I found a translation of Dante. . . . Strange and beautiful it seemed to me that the sorrow of a single Florentine in exile should, hundreds of years afterwards, lighten the sorrow of some common prisoner in a modern gaol. . . ."

Wilde was to read Dante in Reading jail.

When he arrived in America in 1882, Wilde was asked by customs officials if he had anything to declare. He replied: "Only my genius!" Fifteen years later in Reading jail, he wrote (in "De Profundis") that he had been "the spendthrift of my genius. . . . I forgot that every little action of the common day makes or unmakes character."

He died in his 47th year, as a new century was born, in 1900, in the Hôtel d'Alsace in Paris. There, a wit to the end, he said he was dying beyond his means. A monument by Sir Jacob Epstein marks his Paris grave. If, at the end, after a life of boom and bust, he thought of beauty and better days, he may have remembered the rays of the rising sun striking the second highest peak in the continental United States—Mt. Elbert, at Leadville.

August 3, 1982

Making Distinctions and Moccasins

CAMP MINIWANCA, Somewhere in the Trackless Wastes of Michigan—There having been no letters home, the father visited his son's summer camp to ascertain whether his 11-year-old was still in residence or had perhaps moved on to Monte Carlo.

From a distance, the father spotted the son's familiar costume: purple and chartreuse and orange Jams—an unspeakably unshapely brand of shorts—and black Bruce Springsteen "Born in the USA Tour" T-shirt. Children who attend a school that has a strict dress code use the summer for retaliation against aesthetic standards.

The son's skin is a Jackson Pollock canvas of scabs and abrasions that testify to an 11-year-old's refusal to be intimidated by life's sharp edges, and life's refusal to be impressed by 11-year-olds. The tender moment of reunion began with this exchange:

Father: "Hi, Geoffrey, your mother sends her love and says she is going to kill you."

Son: "No, really, dad."

The son's three-word riposte disconcerted dad because it disrupted the familiar rhythm of such exchanges. The "No, really, dad" usually comes at the end of a particularly imaginative fabrication, after dad has rolled his eyes heavenward. This time the sincerity gambit—"no, really, dad"—came even before he launched into his explanation of why he had not written home. The explanation was this:

"I wrote letters but I put them in my fishing-tackle box but I lost my tackle box but fortunately I didn't loose my fishing luros because they were stuck in my towel, I'm not sure why, and I caught an eight-inch large-mouth bass right over there, and you remember those good pants I brought, well, someone left a pen in his clothes and it exploded in the laundry, and don't worry about the books I'm supposed to read for school because I have read one almost, and do you want to go canoeing?"

Camp builds character in campers, but not irreparably. Camp builds character in parents, beginning with the off-to-camp farewell at the airport. When their children show signs of reluctance to leave, and there are flickers of human feelings in the children, the parents learn to their astonishment that their children like them.

Geoffrey was planning a video games orgy at Chicago's O'Hare airport while waiting for the flight to Muskegon. United Airlines had a better idea and clapped him and other minors in a room with a TV and a guard. This, says Geoffrey with a bitterness that time will not assuage, was the summer's foremost airline hostage outrage. He says United is run by Shiites. I do not know where Geoffrey learned the vice, but he is forever editorializing.

He has high regard for the young men who superintend him at camp. One of them, he notes pointedly, "is a halfback and has not broken his neck." This is an oblique editorial comment on father's opposition to son playing football. The leader in another cabin is vastly admired because he has "a Rambo knife and a Rambo bow that can shoot an arrow through two people." I do not ask Geoffrey how he knows that.

Breakfast begins with a sung grace and a short Robert Frost poem, but it is hard to keep the tone so high when tamping food into creatures whose preferred mealtime diversions include one table shouting "Tastes great!" and another responding "Less filling!"

Camp Miniwanca has a liberal parole policy, so I am allowed to whisk Geoffrey down the road to teeming Whitehall, which numbers among its metropolitan pleasures a Pizza Hut. The pepperoni fix is a foretaste of the great coming-home banquet of carbohydrates: Pizzas with a side order of McDonald's french fries. That is just the menu to nourish the metabolism and maintain the emotional equilibrium of my modern American boy who praises Camp Miniwanca for the selection of candy bars in the store.

"The candy," he says with the measured judgment of a fledgling pundit, "is the only contact with the modern world." When his father asks, as any correct thinking father would, "What is so great about the modern world?" the son, who is used to his father's quirkiness, resorts to an unsatisfactory evasion: "Well, okay, not 'the modern world,' but 'civilization.'"

He is learning to make distinctions and moccasins. It is a summer well spent. But the father feels, as fathers will, a pang that is an alloy of pride and regret. It comes with intimations that the world is calling his children, and they are acquiring competencies and independence and are outward bound.

July 18, 1985

Ike Ward, 1862–1982

A doctor says that Ike Ward, who died recently in Florida, died "just of old age." Just? Is old age no longer reason enough for dying in this age of high-technology medicine locked in combat with exotic ailments? Still, it is heartening to know that Ward's promotion to Glory was not due to the back injury he sustained while unloading stumps from a railroad car nine years ago, when he was 110.

Aging, like a lot of other common things (life, love, memory, the existence of the universe, the infield fly rule), remains a mystery. But many gerontologists believe that, absent disease or imprudent living, an individual ages according to his or her genetically controlled "clock." A scientist says that, ideally, we should live fairly healthily and then go "poof" rather than go into slow decline or a nursing home.

Ward, whose genetic clock was one of Nature's better efforts, went "poof" the day after he entered a nursing home where some folks probably were young enough to be his grandchildren. Perhaps he died prematurely. He said he was related to Charles Smith, who was born during the administration of President Tyler, and who was America's oldest citizen when he died in 1979 at age 137.

A smarty-pants once said that no one who has lived to be 110 or more has been remarkable for anything else. But anyone who maneuvers through 110 or more years, including years potholed by such terrors as nuclear weapons and processed cheese, has done something remarkable—foolish, perhaps, but unquestionably remarkable.

Such longevity is a triumph not just of physiology but of the spirit. Ward was black and he set a North American record for understatement when, recalling his youth, he said: "Things were different back then for the Negro race." He was born on Christmas, 1862, in Richmond, Virginia, and in slavery. Persons with unsound views of the Civil War may say that he was born under the presidency of Jefferson Davis. Actually, he was a bouncing baby constituent of Abraham Lincoln. The federal writ did not really run in Richmond at the time, but Virginia never succeeded in seceding.

Ward lived during the administrations of 24 Presidents and— an even more fabulous feat of stoicism—outlived 16 wives. He did not learn to sign his name until he was 85, by which time he probably had figured out how to get along without that particular flourish. But it does him credit, and may help explain his longevity, that he was an 85-year-old still learning new tricks.

He was in his forties in the 1900s, when he was hauling potatoes to Virginia from a large potato field called Staten Island. At the end of his life he weighed 130 pounds and did not use a cane or even wear glasses. When a cousin offered to do his laundry, he told her to buzz off.

According to the Bible, we are allotted three score and ten years, and it has been said that the first 40 years provide the text of life, the last 30 provide the commentary. But Ward was picking up steam—and stumps and things—when he sailed past 70, heading for two score and nine more.

Such longevity can be, in a way, terrible, because it almost invariably involves the burial of many friends, relatives, children (Ward lost three sons during the First World War) and grandchildren. But such longevity can confer perspective on those who experience it, and those who think about it. Such an old person is a powerful reminder that we are a young nation.

He was born before 16 states entered the Union. He lived under most of the Presidents the Union has had. The first presidential election he was old enough to vote in (he probably was prevented from doing so) was in 1884, between Grover Cleveland and James G. Blaine. He saw more social and technological change in every decade of his life than was seen in any previous century. In medical, military, transportation and many other spheres of life, conditions that existed until he was middle-aged were more like those in the Middle Ages than today.

It would be understandable if Ward had died long ago, a victim of historical vertigo. So we must presume that he had considerable competence at the art of living. His life refutes George Bernard Shaw's theory. Shaw said that except during the nine months before birth, no man manages his life as well as a tree does. Ward did.

February 4, 1982

1981: That Depends

Government, like life generally, is an inexact science, and its patron saint should be the stationmaster who, when asked when the train was due, said: "That depends."

"What does it depend on?"

"That, too, depends."

The hostages came home to bizarre "victory" celebrations. What a nation counts as a victory depends, evidently, on how long it has been between victories. Persecuting Congress with charm and cuff links, Ronald Reagan got most of what he wanted and perhaps more than is good for him. That depends on whose economic theories are right, or least wrong.

The first President since Hoover to have had a long, full-time career in the private sector came to town with the first Senate since 1949 to have a majority (54) of members in their first terms. Conservatives are supposed to be bluff, hearty chaps who have no truck with professors; liberals are supposed to be sallow from hours hunched over economic texts. But suddenly, as Pat Moynihan notes, a role reversal occurred. Republicans were spouting the theories of young professors, while Democrats grumbled that as practical men of affairs they knew it was all bosh and a recipe for bloodcurdling deficits.

But some Cassandras were confounded: James Watt has not—yet—put a Burger King on Lincoln's forehead at Mount Rushmore, and Reagan only closed down the government for a few hours in November. Reagan tried to touch the biggest chunk of "big government" (social security) and learned that Americans are less conservative than they talk. Conservatives learned that their agenda costs a bundle—about as much as the liberal agenda—and that they have the nasty task of restoring the government's revenue base. Folks laughed in 1980 when Reagan invoked FDR's name, but in 1981 he began doing for the welfare state what FDR did for capitalism: saving it by tempering its excesses.

A Supreme Court resignation enabled Reagan to make a nomination on a basis exceedingly popular with everyone except anyone who thought clearly about the principle of carving up the Supreme Court into sexual and ethnic entitlements. The air-traffic controllers underestimated Reagan and overestimated their indispensability. They counted on him to behave like a college president and grant amnesty. They also counted on a midair collision. Two Libyan planes awakened American nationalism and stirred up the year's dumbest debate: Should Reagan have been awakened? (Well, the second dumbest. The prize goes to the controversy about the White House china.)

It may have been a setback to radical feminism when a jury told Mrs. Harris that one cannot shoot one's lover even when he is a louse. While radicals tried to rekindle the old passions with a new villain (no, not the Medfly—nuclear power), 72 reactors brought to 650 the number of U.S. reactor-years without detectable injury to anyone. While some antiscientific religious persons were pressuring schools to teach "creationism" (God created man directly, a few—perhaps ten—thousand years ago), astronomers detected four galaxies 10 billion light-years away, the most distant yet discovered. These may be additional evidence for the big-bang theory of the origin of the universe. That theory accords with the essence of the account in Genesis: Man is the result of events set in train by a cataclysm of light and energy.

In this year, probably the 800th anniversary of the birth of Saint Francis of Assisi, the three largest figures on the world stage—Reagan, Sadat and John Paul II—were shot. The year ended with the martyrdom of Europe's most Christian nation, a paradigmatic event to all who are pessimistic about the efficacy of goodness in history. In 1981 the world entered the 37th year of what is called the "postwar" era. During this era 10 million have died in war. To that toll are now added the Poles murdered by the Soviet Union through its instrument, General Jaruzelski, the Pétain of Poland's Vichy regime. Before the first crocuses of spring, Reagan will again be accused of "taking us back to" the cold war.

Iraq and Syria each paid a price for behavior that should exact a price: refusal to make peace. Iraq lost a potential nuclear-weapons facility. Syria lost a small patch of stony ground good only for what it has been repeatedly used for, staging aggression. Israel was called a threat to peace. Margaret Thatcher's refusal to treat terrorists as political prisoners was met by the tragic futility of hunger strikes, and she was called a threat to the peace in Ulster. While the Soviet Union continued its butchery in Afghanistan and its coercion of Poland, a European "peace" movement subsidized by the Soviet Union rent the air with cries that the United States is a threat to peace.

For the first time since the 1930s, the left came to power in

France, and a lot of French money began visiting New York City. But in Spain, where "Eurocommunism" had once been expected to be a wave of the future, an institution from the past, monarchy, continued to show vitality. King Juan Carlos steadied his nation's democracy after a coup attempt, thereby enhancing his eligibility for the Nobel Peace Prize. From a royal wedding in England, a vision of statelinesss trickled down to the occasionally riotous lower orders. And Mother Teresa of Calcutta opened a mission 4 miles from David Stockman's office.

Three famous fighters died: Omar Bradley was the GI's general. Moshe Dayan was a soldier and archeologist (a bit like this year's make-believe hero, Indiana Jones). Joe Louis was a boxer and epigrammatist. (On Billy Conn: "He can run, but he can't hide." On why a black would fight for America in World War II: "Man, whatever is wrong with my country ain't nothing Hitler can fix.")

Finally, in the great American pastime, a team from Canada almost got into the World Series, but was stopped by a Mexican (the people's choice as man of the year, Señor Valenzuela). The worst American scandal since slavery—the designated hitter rule—survived another season, but what can you expect in a year that gave us "designer chocolates"? The Chicago Cubs, the moral equivalent of Soviet agriculture, completed the 36th year of their rebuilding effort. Will next year be better? That depends.

January 4, 1982

1982: Oh, Well . . .

Shedding the wrinkled skin of an old year gives a welcome sense of another chance. Mankind did not distinguish itself in 1982, again. The most it can boast is what the fellow said after the pastor's scathing sermon on the congregation's myriad sins: "Well, at least I haven't made any graven images."

One of the few things that ended right was a war that, even more than most, should not have started. Here is the rationality of history: If Mrs. Thatcher wins reelection and has time to make her economic policies work, it will be partly because of Argentina's economic failures, which led the junta to launch a military distraction. The day after Britain's fleet sailed for the Falklands, *The New York*

Times took time off from criticizing U.S. rearmament and asked, with knowing disparagement: "Once this menacing armada arrives, what precisely is it to do?" The answer was: win.

Half a million persons packed Central Park to "protest nuclear weapons," whatever that means. Bishops searched for a morally comfortable doctrine of statecraft compatible with the political consequences of modern physics and the duty to resist an evil as gross as communism. As Moscow deployed SS-20 missiles aimed at Europe, a "peace" movement protested U.S. plans for a much smaller counterdeployment. The protests were blamed on the bellicosity of Ronald Reagan, who proposed for both sides what NATO now has: zero missiles of that sort. In December, Moscow said that if NATO would stay at zero, it would reduce (perhaps meaning only put in storage, or move east) its SS-20s—but reduce only to a number higher than the number already deployed a year ago when talks began on Reagan's "zero option."

Moscow's quislings returned Poland from martial law to normal law, thereby showing that in Moscow's orbit the distinction is trivial. U.S. allies responded to Poland's agony with toughness . . . againt U.S. attempts to limit subsidies for the Soviet pipeline. The United States became quite cross, and sold Moscow a mountain of grain.

Evidence accumulated that the Kremlin is waging chemical warfare in Afghanistan, and that it orchestrated the attack on the man most responsible for awakening assertiveness in Catholic Eastern Europe. Susan Sontag, her patience exhausted, announced that communism is a bad thing. "Fascism with a human face," she called it, being unable to bring herself to say that communism is bad because it is communism, with a "human face" of gulags and yellow rain.

A bloody war ground on between Iran and Iraq, out of TV range and therefore out of mind. The world stopped deploring terrorism long enough to deplore Israel's dispersal of the worst terrorist organization. The vitality of the Middle East's only democracy was displayed in Israel's relentless investigation of a massacre that Israel did not commit but should have prevented. Syria's regime massacred 5,000 to 10,000 Syrians in a single town, but world opinion execrates Israeli negligence more than murders by Israel's enemies.

Al Haig left the stage and Ted Kennedy stepped back into the chorus, making political life more pastel. This is not an era for primary colors. Ideological grayness stole over government as tax-cutting yielded to . . . er, well, user fees and loophole-closing, compliance-improving revenue-enhancers.

The administration's economic forecasters began to sound like the old Trotskyite who said of his hero: "Proof of Trotsky's farsightedness is that none of his predictions have come true yet." Reagan's legislative victories of 1981 started talk about his ability to conduct "parliamentary government" with party discipline. But 1982 ends with Reagan becoming the first president of the nuclear age to be denied a major-weapons request (MX), and with him about to submit a fiscal 1984 budget that Congress will consider of only historical interest.

Congress passed only 2 of 13 appropriations bills before fiscal 1983 began. The second quarter of that year begins in January, with the government running, for the 29th time in 10 years, on a continuing resolution, a device necessary when government cannot do its elemental duty: pass a budget. Congress vigorously deplored unemployment (there are about as many unemployed Americans as there are illegal aliens) and allowed immigration reform to die.

The country was shocked when someone deranged killed seven people with Tylenol. Drunken drivers killed 26,000, as usual.

Britain's youngest prince has a grandma unruffled by commoners who drop by to chat in her bedroom in the wee small hours. Thanks to the steadying helmsmanship of a king who deserves the Nobel Peace Prize, Spain sailed past another reef, transferring power to the loyal opposition, the moderate left. And Monaco mourned a princess who did something else royalty can do in a democratic age: She exemplified high-mindedness and right action.

Death stilled four unmistakably American voices. Henry Fonda, Archibald MacLeish, John Cheever and Red Smith were craftsmen for the long haul. A television series included a teddy bear named Aloysius, but the republic was infested with cats: Broadway's biggest hit was about them, and at one point 7 of the 15 best-selling paperbacks were about a fat orange cat. Millions of adults seized on E.T.'s going home as an occasion for weeping, which suggests something sad about the emotional aridness of millions of lives. Real men don't eat quiche, but progressive women eat with raised consciousness. About 800,000 readers—well, maybe not exactly readers—shelled out $15 million for Jane Fonda's thin-thighs-through-correct-politics book (or is it the other way around?).

This was a year when medicine, fencing with death, placed

technology in the heart of a man. But it also was a year when science confirmed a fascinating fact first suspected when radar equipment on the space shuttle scanned the surface of the Sahara. The radar spotted the dried beds of a vast system of ancient rivers, some as wide as the Nile. They vanished long ago and were buried by the migrating sands.

So amid the pain and perplexities of mankind's constant companions—wars and economic problems—1982 yielded a fact that puts things in perspective: Even mighty rivers—"roads on the march"—are mortal.

January 3, 1983

1983: Such, Such Were the Joys

This year, like the last 5,000 or so, confirmed the axiom that the only reason God does not send a second flood is that the first was useless.

In the centenary of the birth of a man (Mussolini) who took European politics into the streets, parliamentary processes prevailed. British and German elections preserved NATO, for now. But perhaps more important is the fact that the once-and-future governing parties on the left (Labor and Social Democrat) lurched toward neutralism. The adorable or insufferable (it depends on your geopolitics) Samantha Smith had a jolly time as guest of the grim old men who run the gulag. I hope she gave Andropov the doozy of a cold that has laid him low.

The massacre of Flight 007 provoked only rhetoric, but what rhetoric! A congressman said: "The public revulsion will add starch to the backbones of those who habitually stand on two stools." Actually, it was Grenada, and especially a medical student smooching the tarmac, that transformed lots of people into single-stoolers with backbony starch. The PLO was treated sympathetically in a best-selling novel (*The Little Drummer Girl*) but ended the year riven, dispersed and delegitimized. Terrorists hit military targets, embassies, cherished symbols (the Capitol) and—is nothing sacred?—a temple of bourgeois civilization (Harrods). Truck bombs killed more people in 1983 than ICBMs ever have, and flowers planted in the concrete obstacles outside the White House do not disguise the fact that another casualty may soon be society's sense of well-being, on which many civilities depend.

Diarygate ("Dear Diary: I dream about Danzig . . . ") was followed by Debategate, a molehill in search of a mole. George Brett's pine tar almost let the plague of modern life, lawyers, into the sole redeeming facet of modern life, baseball. The desecration of spring by football accounted for the fact that a large undergraduate runner named Walker decided to do for $8 million what he had hitherto done for the glory and treasury of the University of Georgia.

Speaking of higher education, this is a country in which a university student has asked whether Julius Caesar was annoyed about his characterization by Shakespeare. So this was as good a year as any for politicians to agree that education is a good thing. They know, because a commission said so. We no longer throw money at problems, we throw commissions. Or we throw Alan Greenspan, who presided over 1983's version of the ritual whereby every five years or so we make social security solvent for 50 years.

The nation's second and fourth largest cities got what the third and sixth have had for years: black mayors. Democrats got a black presidential candidate running third in polls and running against "unfairness" (in Reagan's budget and Democratic rules). A conservative GOP president watched the national debt, the product of 19 decades, become 50 percent higher than it was when he took office three years ago. In 1983 it became clear that the president in 1985 may be Reagan but will not be a Reaganite, in this sense: Whoever is president will raise taxes. Reagan made his most important nomination: He renominated Carter's most important nominee, Paul Volcker.

James Watt got into hot water over a black, a woman, two Jews, a cripple and five Beach Boys. His departure dashed the cup of joy from the lips of those, and they are legion, who are happy only when indignant. Washington indignation is, increasingly, moral ostentation, a "more sensitive than thou" (or than Ed Meese) pose.

ABC unleashed Robert Mitchum on Hitler and when the wind of that war passed ABC leveled Lawrence, Kansas, proving twice that war is heaven for network ratings. One war ended: the Korean War. So the 4077th MASH surrendered unconditionally to admiration of its own liberal sentiments. The war between the sexes took some dramatic turns. Barbara Honegger's conscience, and strange voices, told her to resign from the administration to protest Reagan's (yep, you guessed it) insensitivity. The National Organization for Women pondered—wasn't the suspense terrific?—and then endorsed Mondale.

Certain men, or certain parts of them, became calendar pinups. The men are called "hunks." We who cannot aspire to hunkdom salute them. A television anchor woman won, but only temporarily, a sex-discrimination suit charging that she was fired because she was too clever and insufficiently cute. If stations can be required to sacrifice what they are about (ratings) on the altar of equal employment opportunity, then Sally Ride has a right to be an NFL tackle. Fortunately, Ride has a good job.

Someday some people will live longer because in 1983 Barney Clark chose to die as a pioneer. Death claimed many craftsmen and artists, including Scoop Jackson, Jack Dempsey, Bear Bryant, Ira Gershwin, George Balanchine, Eubie Blake. Blake, the son of former slaves, was born when the only way to get from Brooklyn to Manhattan was by boat. He was 100, three months older than the great bridge. Mick Jagger, a creation of contemporary taste, turned 40. An even more durable lad, an emblem of a less, er, *advanced* age, turned 100: happy birthday, Huck Finn.

Five hundred years after the birth of Luther, the pope attended a Lutheran service. A prophet has been defined as someone who hears an octave higher than the rest of us. Luther was one. So may be John Paul II, before whom General Jaruzelski visibly trembled this year.

A scarcity of ugly dolls provoked civil disorder, proving three things. First, Reaganomics works: A nation with money for Cabbage Patch dolls is too prosperous for its own good. Second, we are (ha! you thought you'd get through with without being told) undertaxed: Why tolerate $200 billion deficits when money is chasing those dolls? Third, the United States is not ready for self-government—a sobering thought on the eve of an election year. Thomas Jefferson, call your office, and be quick about it because the telephone company, which ain't broke, is about to be fixed. The next sound you hear may be a busy signal. Forever.

January 2, 1984

1984: God Help Us, Every One!

In 1984 astronomers announced a dismaying discovery—what might be a planet outside our solar system. This supports the premise that there might be life elsewhere. On the evidence of life on this planet this year, the universe should be spared the embarrassment of additional life.

In 1984 the government sitting on 1 billion Chinese had a brainstorm: It declared that the best guide to the 21st century might not be thoughts hatched by a 19th-century German in the reading room of the British Museum. A meticulous Italian prosecutor produced a mountain of evidence connecting Bulgaria (itself a marionette on strings running to Russia) with the 1981 attack on the pope. In Orwell's year the Sakharovs were kidnapped, on the orders of Soviet leaders, one of whom, Gorbachov, visiting Orwell's Britain, so charmed Margaret Thatcher that she seemed to say, "Be still my heart!" His visit stirred more talk about his tailor than about Afghanistan, where the butchery entered the sixth year.

An assassination, an industrial disaster, a movie (*A Passage to India*) and a television masterpiece (*The Jewel in the Crown*) kept India in mind. Once bitten, twice shy: The Miss America Pageant picked a Mormon. The widening gap between medical and moral sophistication was illustrated by the abuse of an infant for an experiment with a baboon's heart. Two young arms—Gooden's and Marino's—rewrote record books. The ridiculous became sublime, sort of: The Chicago Cubs lost their charm by acquiring skill, then lost the playoffs on two ground balls hit directly at Cub infielders. Mozart became a movie star and some unknown works by Bach were discovered at Yale, where a historian published a book demonstrating that the Victorians, those odd ducks, liked sex. This refutes Philip Larkin:

> Sexual intercourse began
> In nineteen sixty-three
> (Which was rather late for me)—
> Between the end of the "Chatterley" ban
> And the Beatles' first L.P.

Yale, a fountain of progressive thoughts, was convulsed by a strike over "comparable worth," but Mickey Mouse went on strike at Disneyland and why should Yale be different?

Progressive thinkers were appalled by Bill Cosby's television show, which portrays a black family happy and—most reactionary of all—middle class. Phil Donahue moved his show from Chicago to New York, improving the cultural life of both cities. That international—nay, intergalactic—bore, Michael Jackson, issued a press release about his hormones and sexual preference. Boy George, thank God, did not. Ah, well, boys will be boys . . . *please.* The range of American popular music was represented in the deaths of Ernest Tubb and Count Basie. An elegant instrument—the voice of Richard Burton—was stilled. Millions of sedentary Americans derived unseemly pleasure from the death of Jim Fixx.

On the 40th anniversary of the Battle of the Bulge, Cap Weinberger won the battle of the bulging budget, preserving the Defense share. But he listed six tests that must be satisfied, and almost never will be, before anyone should use anything Defense is buying. The United States withdrew from UNESCO but continued to fund the larger excrescence, the United Nations itself. Responding to the famine in Ethiopia, the United Nations voted to spend $73.5 million (25 percent of that from American taxpayers) on a grander U.N. building in Ethiopia.

Under Carter one embassy was seized. Under Reagan embassies are blown to smithereens and Americans are methodically beaten and shot in televised terrorism. This year, as usual, the Reagan administration sternly warned that if terrorists keep bombing Americans and grinding lit cigarettes into their faces, then the terrorists had better brace themselves for . . . more stern warnings. (Gunfire from the Libyan Embassy in London killed a woman constable and Margaret [Iron Lady] Thatcher did . . . well, maybe next time.) The Reagan administration reluctantly released a report on the Soviet Union's comprehensive cheating on arms control agreements. The administration said its primary goal is . . . more arms control agreements. Reagan said the United States is back and standing tall. The United States was driven out of Lebanon by the Druse and Shiites.

Like the monk who would eat steak only after baptizing it "cod," General Jaruzelski renamed martial law. So the Reagan administration bowed deeply and stopped blocking Poland from membership in the International Monetary Fund, a source of subsidies from American taxpayers. The great communicator (no, silly, not Reagan—Jeane Kirkpatrick) seemed ready to leave foreign policy entirely in the hands of the boys who are mighty proud of this record.

Presidential campaigns are supposed to be educational and, by cracky, this year Americans learned Gary Hart's names, ages and signatures. They also learned gobs about Mr. Zaccaro's real estate business and the location of the U.S. Embassy in Israel. Jesse Jackson, friend of freedom and of the dictators of Syria, Cuba and Nicaragua, invented the monochrome rainbow. Mondale was rattling on about the "sleaze factor" (you remember—Ed Meese's cuff links) when his campaign was caught laundering hundreds of thousands of labor dollars through phony committees. Mondale and Hart got to know each other well. (Said Oscar Wilde of someone: "Know him? I know him so well that I haven't spoken to him in 10 years.") In the year McDonald's sold its 50 billionth hamburger Mondale won the nomination by asking, "Where's the beef?" But then Reagan said, "It's morning in America and, besides, there's a bear in the forest."

Archeologists unearthed two human skulls 7,000 years old with the brains largely intact and the tissue containing much DNA. Perhaps in 5000 B.C. folks had brains very like we have in 1984, but it would be mean to say that about the folks of 5000 B.C.

December 31, 1984

1985: A Tolerably Adequate Year

'Tis said that folks who live in a golden age complain that everything looks yellow. So let's rate 1985 a tolerably adequate year because the worst disasters were not mankind's fault. Colombia and Mexico City got nature's reminder that life is unfair even without human intervention. Ethiopian starvation showed how a vicious regime can compound nature's cruelties. This year italicized the truth that experience is a good teacher but sends in huge bills.

It was a year of anniversaries: Bach's 300th birthday, the 40th anniversary of the war's end. This coming May will be the first anniversary of the Bitburg visit. Let's let it pass. The United Nations turned 40 run by Third World nations not bashful about noting others' imperfections. A *Washington Post* headline reported Li-

beria's election: PILE OF SMOLDERING BALLOTS TOPS LIST
OF IRREGULARITIES.

As has been usual, a Soviet leader died. His successor as the
most vanguardean proletarian in the vanguard of the proletariat
buys his suits at Gieves & Hawkes, Savile Row. In 1985 espionage
seemed common, in several senses. It has become a tacky transac-
tion, done for cash, not even dignified by political passion. Donald
Regan, an expert at throwing his weight around, but not hitherto
suspected of expertise concerning strategic arms, said women would
not want to trouble their pretty little heads with men's business,
like throw weight. Shultz's anticharisma prevented recognition that
his Feb. 22 speech was epochal. It gave shape to the Reagan Doctrine of supporting insurrection at the fringe of the Soviet empire.

Limousine loads of celebrities were "arrested" but not prose-
cuted for demonstrating too close to South Africa's Embassy in
Washington. Five rabbis went to jail for the same offense at the
Soviet Embassy. South Africa's Nobel Peace Prize winner, Bishop
Tutu, was a constant presence on world television. Another Nobel
winner, Andrei Sakharov, was not. Student denunciations of companies doing business with South Africa (but not of those doing
business with the Soviet Union) were said to be signs of a "rebirth
of conscience." Robert Conquest, the historian, had a good idea:
trade Mandela for Sakharov. Miroslav Medvid plunged into the cold
Mississippi, was dragged screaming back to his ship, again dove
into the river, again was captured, and U.S. officials wondered:
Gosh, what do you suppose he was trying to tell us?

The United States caught four terrorists in spite of Egypt, then
apologized to Egypt. A PLO official announced that Mrs. Klinghoffer killed her husband for the insurance money. That was a revision of the initial PLO position that Mr. Klinghoffer shot himself
and then rolled his wheelchair off the Achille Lauro. It was a hard
year for people who think the PLO has a moral claim on our
attention.

The House passed a 1,379-page tax "simplification" bill that
provides rapid depreciation for rental tuxedos. The bill is a product
of politics conducted according to the principle that any appetite
is its own excuse for existing. Supporters of the Gramm–Rudman
deficit cure are sure it will not cause ring around the collar. That
is all they are sure of. It promises budget cuts without choices (read:
mind) involved. Under it the pursuit of happiness will resemble the

old prayer: *God bless me and me wife, / Me son John and his wife, / Us four: / No more!*

In some countries Chaucer and Dante are classics. Here a soft drink is: "Coke are it!" Bruuuuuuce sold 15 million "Born in the U.S.A." albums and Lee Iacocca, a kind of Springsteen in pinstripes, sold 2.5 million copies of his autobiography, many to groupies in boardrooms. A publisher paid $2.5 million for David Stockman's memoirs of the steamy life at OMB, perhaps soon to be a miniseries starring Joan Collins. The Vatican said Roman Catholics who viewed the pope's Christmas benediction on television would receive release from some punishment for sin. Everyone else could watch Donahue as a penance.

A child prodigy, Dwight Gooden, repealed the last three words of the formula "good pitching beats good hitting, and vice versa." An excruciatingly protracted (two days) strike did not stop some graybeards—Rose, Carew, Seaver, Niekro—from reaching milestones on the road to Cooperstown. After a century of football, a deep thinker in Chicago said: "Hey, down near the other guy's goal line, let's give the ball to the biggest fellow on the field and see what happens." The Refrigerator happened. Texas said high school football players had to be students, too. This was controversial. Grambling's Eddie Robinson became football's winningest coach. Another coach, of sorts, acquired prominence: Dr. Ruth. The emancipation of women achieved the addition of male "rabbits" to the female "bunnies" at Playboy Clubs. In a sex survey, Ann Landers recorded a landslide vote among her female readers in favor of more displays of affection, such as hugging, and less of "the act." Male readers asked for a recount.

Voyagers not seen for more than 70 years were spotted: Halley's comet and the *Titanic*. In this decade AIDS has killed Rock Hudson and more than 8,000 others. In 1985 it was called the No. 1 public-health problem, and cancer killed nearly 500,000. It was disappointing to learn that Mengele no longer knew the fear of the hunted. Death released Karen Ann Quinlan from a coma and ended the reign of the King of Siam after 4,625 performances. Death claimed Robert Todd Lincoln Beckwith, 81, Lincoln's great-grandson and last direct descendant. The Constitution, age 198, lost a friend, Sam Ervin, 88. As a sage has said, time is a great teacher, but it kills all its pupils.

The year opened echoing with arguments about Bernhard

Goetz and closed to the roar of Rambo, and a bear died of a cocaine overdose when it snacked on a knapsack dropped by a smuggler. No wonder many Americans migrated in their minds to Lake Wobegon, Minnesota, the town that time forgot.

January 6, 1986

PART **2**

*Skirmishes
on the
Home Front*

In Defense of the Mother Tongue

On the Fourth of July the corn, rhetorical as well as agricultural, should be as high as an elephant's eye. But while enjoying the rhetoric of liberty, consider the connection between the English language and American liberty.

A proposed amendment to the Constitution would declare "the English language shall be the official language of the United States" and "neither the United States nor any state shall require . . . the use in the United States of any language other than English." It would prohibit governments from mandating multilingual publications and from establishing bilingual education as a general entitlement. It would end the pernicious practice of providing bilingual ballots, a practice that denies the link between citizenship and shared culture. Bilingual ballots, says Richard Rodriguez, proclaim that people can exercise the most public of rights while keeping apart from public life.

Rodriguez's autobiography, *Hunger of Memory*, is an elegant and eloquent evocation of the modern immigrant's experience. A son of Mexican immigrants, he grew up in Sacramento in the 1950s. He was so "cloistered" by family sounds, so long "poised at the edge of language" that he was timid in public—too timid to be at home outside his home, in his community. Language is an instrument of intimacy, and Rodriguez's book is a hymn to the poignant bravery of immigrant parents. Such parents often launch children toward a cultural divide the parents cannot cross, the passage into linguistic fluency and social ease.

Rodriguez's intelligent and unsentimental opposition to bilingual education makes his opposition to the constitutional amendment interesting. Writing today, he notes that bilingualism became part of the agenda of the left in the late 1960s, when there was "a romantic surrender to the mystique of the outsider." Those people who considered the culture diseased naturally thought the culture should be shunned. Bilingualism is an urgent issue because so much of current immigration comes from the Spanish-speaking Western Hemisphere and because the availability of Spanish-language news and entertainment broadcasting encourages the notion that English is merely a marginally important option.

"Those who have the most to lose in a bilingual America," Rodriguez says, "are the foreign-speaking poor, who are being lured into a linguistic nursery." However, he considers the constitutional amendment divisive because many Hispanics will regard it as aimed "against" them. Such sensitivity should not be decisive, especially given the reasons, which Rodriguez gives, why bilingualism is injurious to Hispanics.

"Our government," he says, "has no business elevating one language above all others, no business implying the supremacy of Anglo culture." He is wrong, twice. The government has a constitutional duty to promote the general welfare, which Rodriguez himself says is linked to a single shared language. Government should not be neutral regarding something as important as language is to the evolution of the culture. Furthermore, it should not be bashful about affirming the virtues of "Anglo culture"—including the political arrangements bequeathed by the men of July 4, 1776, a distinctly Anglo group. The promise of America is bound up with the virtues and achievements of "Anglo culture," which is bound up with English. Immigrants, all of whom come here voluntarily, have a responsibility to reciprocate the nation's welcome by acquiring the language that is essential for citizenship, properly understood.

Citizenship involves participation in public affairs, in the governance and hence the conversation of the community. In ancient Greece, from which the political philosophy of "Anglo culture" directly descends, such participation was considered natural and hence essential to normal life. When government nurtures a shared language it is nurturing a natural right—the ability to live in the manner that is right for human nature.

Nowadays this nation is addicted to a different rhetoric of rights—including, for a few specially entitled minorities, the right to a publicly assisted dispensation from learning the language of public life. This age defines self-fulfillment apart from, even against, the community. The idea of citizenship has become attenuated and now is defined almost exclusively in terms of entitlements, not responsibilities. Bilingualism, by suggesting that there is no duty to acquire the primary instrument of public discourse, further dilutes the idea of citizenship.

Rodriguez wants America to "risk uncertainty" and "remain vulnerable," "between fixity and change." Obviously America cannot freeze its culture. But another way of saying that human beings are social animals is to say they are language-users. To be sociable they must share a language. America has always been (in Rodriguez's nifty phrase) "a marinade of sounds." But it would be wrong to make a romance of linguistic diversity. Americans should say diverse things, but in a language that allows universal participation in the discussion. Acceptance of considerable pluralism is a precondition of a free society; but so, too, is a limit to pluralism. Yes, *e pluribus unum*. But also: One national language is a prerequisite for the sort of pluralism that is compatible with shared national identity.

Teddy Roosevelt's life was one long Fourth of July, a symphony of fireworks and flamboyant rhetoric. He embodied the vigor of the nation during the flood tide of immigration. He said: "We have room for but one language here and that is the English language, for we intend to see that the crucible turns our people out as Americans, of American nationality, and not as dwellers in a polyglot boarding house." American life, with its atomizing emphasis on individualism, increasingly resembles life in a centrifuge. Bilingualism is a gratuitous intensification of disintegrative forces. It imprisons immigrants in their origins and encourages what Jacques Barzun, a supporter of the constitutional amendment, calls "cultural solipsism."

On the Fourth of July, when we are full of filial piety toward the Founding Fathers, we should not lightly contemplate tampering with their Constitution. But a change may be necessary to preserve the linguistic unity that is as important as the Constitution to a harmonious national life.

July 8, 1985

Academic License

Amidst cries of alarm about the rise of censorship and the decline of academic freedom, a California professor has bowed to public pressure and dropped certain homework options in a course he teaches. The controversy is a case study of how the absence of a private citizen's self-restraint subverts healthy traditions of public restraint.

The professor at Cal State Long Beach had hitherto allowed students in his course on the "psychology of sex" to fulfill homework requirements by engaging in group sex, extramarital sex or homosexual sex. His prior permission had been required for that option. It is unclear—but fascinating to speculate—by what criteria permission had been granted or withheld. Some taxpayers are not amused and are not apt to be mollified by the remaining list of homework options, which include dressing in drag for a day, or taking "field trips" to homosexual bars and bathhouses, and nudist camps.

The *Los Angeles Times* reports—and by golly, I believe it—that the professor "is under attack by evangelical Christians." But surely broad church pagans and nondenominational atheists and everyone else should be incensed about the degradation of higher education. Everyone loses when sensible people begin to ask about higher education, "What, pray tell, is it higher than?"

Speaking of his now abandoned homework options, the professor says: "The idea is not to go out and do some kinky things just to see what they're like, but to see a change in your behavior and your feelings." He says: "It can be a very powerful growth and learning experience."

Well, yes. New sexual behavior is, indeed, apt to involve new feelings. But by the same logic, getting drunk, or getting mugged, can be a "learning experience." If feeling something is, by definition, learning something, then indigestion is educational (and perhaps the stuff of college credits at Cal State Long Beach).

The Long Beach professor has offered a peculiarly lurid manifestation of premises that are more prevalent than most persons realize. Those premises make sense if, but only if, there's no higher imperative than pleasure, and no authority higher than the individual for reckoning the value of particular pleasures. According to those premises, the idea of learning should be unmoored from the traditional sense—indeed, from any sense—that among the universe of things that can be experienced, there is a hierarchy of things eligible to be part of higher learning, properly understood.

Any idea of hierarchy is nowadays vulnerable to derogation as a sign of "elitism." That word did not even appear in the *American Heritage Dictionary* published just 13 years ago. But it is now part of America's cultural baggage. Anti-elitism makes education incoherent, because education is inherently elitist, in the defining of it and the delivering of it.

The world is divided, by no means evenly, between those who believe, as I do, that the proper aim of education is primarily to put something—learning—into students, and others who believe that the primary aim of education is to let something—"feelings," or "the self," or "authenticity," or something—out of students. If the task is "putting in," putting in a legacy of learning refined over the centuries, the legacy must be sifted and selected from. That is an aristrocratic task; it is the business of intellectual authority, not political democracy.

The American genius for tempering democracy, for embanking its passions within institutional restraints, for preventing arbitrary mass willfulness, is nowhere more impressively demonstrated than in the protestations extended to academic institutions. The depredations of the McCarthy era were sporadic, random, short-lived, and represented no systematic government policy. The broadest and most comprehensive infringements of academic autonomy have been inflicted recently, and by liberal political forces. The intrusion of political values into sensitive, core academic decisions, such as faculty hiring and tenure decisions, has been justified in the name of "affirmative action" for government-approved minorities.

As a former professor, and the son of a former professor, I appreciate the value of academic freedom. As a student of politics I fear the intrusion of popular passion into academic settings. But when a respected liberty is arrogantly debased into taunting license, lacerating the feelings of the community that pays the bills, the community will, one way or another, find its voice.

Vox populi, vox dei? Not likely. When incensed about ignorant abuses of academic privileges, the populace is not apt to be temperate or discriminating. Extremism outside the academy will mirror that within.

May 25, 1982

A Doctrine of the High Priests

As the idea of "comparable worth" sinks beneath the weight of its implausibility, note how far it leaps beyond the principle that people should receive equal pay for equal work—for performing identical jobs. The idea of comparable worth is that jobs traditionally filled by women should receive pay equal to different but "comparable" jobs traditionally filled by men. Comparable worth might have the retrograde effect of reinforcing a "pink collar" ghetto of jobs considered "women's work." Advocates of comparable worth say comparable jobs are of comparable worth to employers. Advocates are not content to let employers say what that worth is.

Instead, the idea of "worth" is to be moralized, surreptitiously, in the guise of objective social science. A proponent of comparable worth devised a formula to assign different amounts of "worth points" to particular jobs on the basis of an assessment of jobs in terms of four criteria.

One is the amount of "knowledge and skills" required, meaning the "total amount of information or dexterity" involved. This requires yet another problematic assessment of comparability. It requires an assessment of the comparable "worths" of mental and manual capabilities—of information relative to dexterity. The second criterion is "mental demands." Hmmmm. What, precisely (and if this is science, let the precision flow), is the distinction between the "knowledge" requirements of the first criterion and the "mental demands" of the second? Here is a heretical thought: Perhaps a job that is dull because it is simple and repetitious should be considered a job that makes especially difficult mental demands. Dull jobs can be difficult because attention and zest are difficult to maintain.

A third criterion is "accountability," meaning the amount of supervision the job involves. A fourth criterion is "working conditions." But is supervision a chore or a pleasure? A job performed outside would, presumably, get special "worth points" because working outside is less pleasant than working inside. Unless, of course, the worker prefers working outside. But, then, who asked the worker? It is the manufacturers of criteria—the social scientists formulating formulas—who will be asked.

Michael Barone is content to work indoors at *The Washington Post*, where he produces writings of incomparable worth. He notes that the formula outlined above was devised for applying comparable worth to jobs in a state government. Civil service jobs often are graded similarly. That is the problem. Advocates of comparable worth seem to think that public sector jobs, in which productivity is often difficult to measure, are the typical jobs in late-20th-century America. That assumption says much about the statist leanings of comparable-worth advocates. Furthermore, comparable worth, says Barone, is the product of a mentality that focuses on questions of distribution and takes production for granted. It thinks of most Americans as working for giant bureaucracies, with tasks that can be readily quantified. It assumes that the crucial question is whether at the end of the workday an employee has gone through every item on his or her checklist.

Comparable worth looks like part of the not-very-hidden agenda of the left. It serves the goal of giving control of almost everything—in this case, everyone's wages or salary—to a small priestly class of "experts." Computing the comparable worth of every activity would inevitably be the work—the profitable work—of a particular class. Comparable worth would be a jobs program for an articulate, theorizing class of intellectuals. Not surprisingly, a member of that class devised the formula outlined above.

And not surprisingly, that formula gives special value—extra "worth points"—to the kind of work done by the kind of person who devises such formulas, work involving "knowledge" skills. Surprise! The formula enhances the economic value of formula makers. And, of course, it lowers the relative "worth," moral and monetary, of the labor performed by the neediest women.

When society's least pleasant work is considered, someone might ask a really radical question: Should not nurses be paid *more* than doctors? Doctors have the psychic income of intellectual stimulation and social prestige. Nurses have bedpans and subordination. Surely nurses should have more money. Michael Walzer, a political philosopher, goes a step farther: Perhaps citizens should be conscripted to collect the garbage.

Walzer says we place limits on the power of money to allocate things in society. It is illegal to sell your vote. There was riotous disgust with the 1863 conscription act that allowed men to buy their way out of the civic duty to serve in the Civil War. Some work, such as military service in wartime, is necessary but extremely unpleasant. Most people feel, intuitively, that such work should not fall only upon those who cannot avoid it—persons driven to it by economic necessity. Many societies have decided to share the burdens of soldiering through conscription, at least among young men. Walzer asks: Why just soldiering?

There are other jobs that must be done but are onerous. Garbage collection is one. Caring for the very aged is another. Such jobs often are filled by people of whom Walzer says, felicitously, this: "When they were growing up, they dreamed of doing something else." Anything else. Walzer argues that "negative" but necessary jobs should not be allotted by economic forces to "negative" categories of people such as the poor or recent immigrants. Walzer is not saying that collecting the garbage is work without dignity. He says there is no such thing as undignified work that is socially necessary. He says the physical nature of such unpleasant work cannot be changed, but its moral nature can be. It can be accorded due dignity by distributing it as a duty of citizenship, rather than leaving it for those at the bottom of society's status system.

When next you hear someone who fancies himself or herself a radical saying that the market is not an adequate measure of the "worth" of jobs, bring up Walzer's argument about garbage collection. You will see how swiftly people change the subject.

September 30, 1985

The Perils of Urban Planning

NEW YORK—Two sections of this city are especially fascinating to students of urban pathologies. The South Bronx looks as though it has been bombed, and Times Square looks as though it should be. Times Square may soon be, according to the many people who consider urban renewal to be the moral equivalent of what the allies did to Dresden in 1945.

The argument about the plan to cleanse Times Square illustrates some truths about urban life and the perils of urban planning. It also illustrates a process of political education. The trajectory of postwar liberalism follows the path of soaring and then crashing hopes associated with urban renewal.

It used to be said that if you stood long enough in Times Square, the "crossroads of the world," you would meet everyone you know. Nowadays if you stand there for long, you will meet lots of people you would rather not get to know. It is given over to the satisfaction of the sort of appetites that got Gomorrah into such hot water.

There are movies and live, er, performances that are called "explicit." The sidewalks are planted thick with entrepreneurs renting themselves or selling what are called, but barely are, "controlled substances." The air congeals with the mingled aromas of foods that should not be taken internally. The *New York Times* reports fears that the renewal plan "would mute the liveliness."

Muting is surely an aim of the $1.6 billion plan that would do a lot of demolishing and would put four office towers, a merchandise mart, a hotel and nine refurbished theaters on 13 acres. Mayor Ed Koch, a believer in unminced words, calls people "idiots" who "say they like 42d Street the way it is." But that is not the point. True, there are the usual people who live at a comfortable distance from 42d Street and would not go there on a dare but who, to advertise their broadmindedness, say Times Square has soul. However, the interesting objection to the big plan is simply that it is a big plan.

As such it is apt to fall victim to the law of unintended effects. That law is: The unintended effects of an ambitious act of social engineering are apt to be more important than the intended effects. Already, for example, people associated with Broadway theaters are concerned, reasonably, that the renewal project will drive up land values, causing theater owners to sell to developers.

My desk groans beneath the weight of an "environmental impact statement" on the Times Square project, a statement thicker than the Manhattan telephone directory. It says, with a nice sense of nuance, that the area has "a strange and disturbing street life" and "a menacing, even assaultive atmosphere." It asks: Where will the area's "special uses and street crowd go?"

The question has a healthy anti-Utopian cast. It assumes that the seamy side of life will always be with us. If it is suppressed in one place, it will pop up in another. After all, Times Square is not a "slum" where people are forced by economic factors to live in unhygienic and unsafe conditions. Times Square is a place where people freely congregate for unsavory purposes.

The term "urban renewal" came into common currency 30 years ago, with the 1954 enlargement of the Housing Act of 1949. The 1949 Act had been sponsored by Mr. Conservative, Senator Robert Taft, who envisioned only "spot removal" of the worst slums. The 1954 enlargement infused hubris into that modest measure. People began talking about the redevelopment of entire city centers. Such urban renewal was never a conservative cause, but it helped cause conservatism.

Urban renewal—which often has atomized cohesive communities, reduced the stock of low-income housing and erected highrise instant slums—contributed to the growth of populist conservatism: the belief that government is a blunt instrument wielded by overbearing bureaucracy. The rise of an intellectual conservatism has been partially a reaction against a governmental impulse to treat all problems as solvable, and to define as a problem anything unpleasant, untidy or unreasonable.

The Times Square project should proceed as it is proceeding—under the skeptical gaze of people who say that sterility might be preferable to squalor, but it is not worth $1.6 billion. The argument about the project suggests that many people who would never consent to be called conservative have internalized this truth of conservatism:

A community is not a Tinker Toy that can be pulled apart and reassembled by acts of will. A community is a living organism, like a flower (or, in this case, a weed). It can be delicately pruned, but pulling it apart means death.

April 5, 1984

A Word for the Wilderness

It is said that any stigma will do to beat a dogma with, and environmentalism is often stigmatized as an "elitist" cause. It is odd to say that removing lead from gasoline or from paint in tenements concerns Palm Beach more than Baltimore, or that regulating chemical wastes benefits only one class. It is less obviously wrong, but still wrong, to say that preservation of wilderness is elitist in any awful way.

Colorado's Maroon Bells wilderness area is one of the brightest jewels in the nation's diadem. More than 50,000 persons visit it annually, more than visit most wilderness areas but fewer than half the number that watch the average Michigan Wolverine home football game. And no wilderness area is as heavily used as most national parks are. (Yosemite has an indispensable institution of civilization: a jail.)

In 1964 Congress created the wilderness system, "where man is a visitor but does not remain." A 20-year "window" was left open for leases for oil, gas and mineral claims. As the Dec. 31, 1983, deadline approaches, there is developing a dash for applications. More than 1,000 are pending against 3 million acres in 200 wilderness areas, including 30,000 acres of the Bells. Previous administrations routinely rejected virtually all applications, but the current Interior secretary, James Watt, wants to open up wilderness areas. This week Congress considers a bill that would close the window, imposing an immediate ban on leases except in cases of urgent need affirmed by Congress.

There are 80 million acres of designated wilderness, 56 million of them in Alaska. Only 1.2 percent of the "lower 48" states is wilderness; only 4 percent could ever be so designated. Surely the nation's vitality and security are not so marginal as to depend on that 4 percent. According to one study, wilderness contains just 1 percent of the nation's onshore oil and gas. It would be a pity to damage an irreplaceable asset for a few weeks' worth of oil. Particular wilderness designations may have to be reconsidered, eventually. For example, one area (the Sawtooth Range in Idaho) contains perhaps $1 billion worth of minerals, including cobalt. The United States imports 97 percent of the cobalt it uses.

Opposition to wilderness designations comes not only from industry. It also comes from individuals whose recreation preferences are at stake. This conflict may have a class dimension, pitting plain folks in their station wagons and motorboats against backpackers who are suspected of packing Brie rather than Blue Ribbon and of going to earth in winter at Radcliffe or Grosse Point. Pristine wilderness is an acquired taste and is incompatible with the enjoyment of some popular tastes such as dirt bikes, snowmobiles and other off-road vehicles. But surely there is no shortage of space in America for persons whose play must involve internal-combustion engines.

All gains involve pains. Environmental protection has an economic price. Wilderness designation can raise the cost of many things, from minerals to lumber, affecting many things, from job creation to the cost of housing. Environmentalism that is careless about cost will be regressive in effect and will discredit itself by seeming to be a luxury of persons affluent and callous. But the current danger is that Watt will discredit economic analysis by seeming sympathetic only to economic considerations.

Part of the Watt problem is the Watt manner: He acts like a machine in the garden. When he testifies beneath bright television lights, his high, glistening forehead, his electric smile and his eyes flashing behind metal-rimmed glasses call to mind a 1955 Buick, a convention of chrome. When he speaks, you half expect to hear gears grind, and you sort of do. He has no patience for the toing-and-froing practiced by persons who understand that in politics the straightest line between two points is rarely the easiest route. He speaks almost too clearly, indifferent to the bureaucratic art of constructing whole paragraphs perfectly devoid of substance.

His cocksureness, his thirst for conflict, his tone-deafness regarding his own shrillness in the nuances of a subtle city—have invigorated environmental groups and have caused Congress to say (as a Michigan state legislator once said), "From now on, I'm watching everything you do with a fine-toothed comb." He has made it easy to caricature conservatism as philistine, as hostile to all but commercial values. He sometimes seems unreconciled to government's stewardship concerning community assets. Some assets, such as wilderness areas, cannot survive if unprotected from the morals of the marketplace.

It is a law of politics: Extreme political intensity begets equal and opposite intensity. Watt is partly a cause and partly an effect of persons for whom environmentalism is political romanticism masquerading as science, a doctrine for putting sand in the gears of industrialism and for expressing root and branch rejection of America's commercial civilization. Their liking of chipmunks expresses primarily a dislike of human beings, creatures of nasty despoiling rationality. Such environmentalists value wilderness areas primarily as refuges from all reminders that they share the planet with other human beings.

This nation began as an "errand into the wilderness." The first task was to tame that wilderness, but as Wallace Stegner says, we need to preserve some of it "because it was the challenge against which our character as a people was formed."

Most Americans will never care a fig about wilderness. Perhaps that means it is an elitist concern. But so what? Edith Hamilton, the classicist, once said to Ezra Pound: "I have heard of a great Confucian who wrote a letter so difficult there was only one other man in all China who could understand it. That is not very democratic, I'm afraid. That is aristrocratic, like you, Mr. Pound." Pound replied: "It is democratic insofar as it provides that anyone may have the opportunity to learn enough to read that letter." Enjoyment of wilderness may not be spontaneous and "natural." It may be a learned process, inviting and even requiring reflection. But it is nonetheless valuable for being an aristrocratic pleasure, democratically open to all.

August 16, 1982

Bearbaiting and Boxing

For 150 years people have been savoring Macaulay's judgment that the Puritans hated bearbaiting not because it gave pain to the bear but because it gave pleasure to the spectators. However, there are moments, and this is one, for blurting out the truth: The Puritans were right. The pain to the bear was not a matter of moral indifference, but the pleasure of the spectators was sufficient reason for abolishing that entertainment.

Now another boxer has been beaten to death. The brain injury he suffered was worse than the injury the loser in a boxing match is supposed to suffer. It is hard to calibrate such things—how hard an opponent's brain should be banged against the inside of his cranium—in the heat of battle.

From time immemorial, in immemorial ways, men have been fighting for the entertainment of other men. Perhaps in a serene, temperate society boxing would be banned along with other blood sports—if, in such a society, the question would even arise. But a step toward the extinction of boxing is understanding why that is desirable. One reason is the physical injury done to young men. But a sufficient reason is the quality of the pleasure boxing often gives to spectators.

There is no denying that boxing like other, better sports, can exemplify excellence. Boxing demands bravery and, when done well, is beautiful in the way that any exercise of finely honed physical talents is. Furthermore, many sports are dangerous. But boxing is the sport that has as its object the infliction of pain and injury. Its crowning achievement is the infliction of serious trauma on the brain. The euphemism for boxing is "the art of self-defense." No. A rose is a rose is a rose, and a user fee is a revenue enhancer is a tax increase, and boxing is aggression.

It is probable that there will be a rising rate of spinal cord injuries and deaths in football. The force of defensive players (a function of weight and speed) is increasing even faster than the force of ball carriers and receivers. As a coach once said, football is not a contact sport—dancing is a contact sport—football is a collision sport. The human body, especially the knee and spine, is not suited to that. But football can be made safer by equipment improvements and rules changes such as those proscribing certain kinds of blocks. Boxing is fundamentally impervious to reform.

It will be said that if two consenting adults want to batter each other for the amusement of paying adults, the essential niceties have been satisfied, "consent" being almost the only nicety of a liberal society. But from Plato on, political philosophers have taken entertainments seriously, and have believed the law should, too. They have because a society is judged by the kind of citizens it produces, and some entertainments are coarsening. Good government and the good life depend on good values and passions, and some entertainments are inimical to these.

Such an argument cuts no ice in a society where the decayed public philosophy teaches that the pursuit of happiness is a right sovereign over all other considerations; that "happiness" and "pleasure" are synonyms, and that there is no hierarchy of values against which to measure particular appetites. Besides, some persons will say, with reason, that a society in which the entertainment menu includes topless lady mud wrestlers is a society past worrying about.

Some sports besides boxing attract persons who want their unworthy passions stirred, including a lust for blood. I remember Memorial Day in the Middle West in the 1950s, when all roads led to the Indianapolis Speedway, where too many fans went to drink Falstaff beer and hope for a crash. But boxing is in a class by itself.

Richard Hoffer of the *Los Angeles Times* remembers the death of Johnny Owen, a young 118-pound bantamweight who died before he had fulfilled his modest ambition of buying a hardware store back home in Wales. Hoffer remembers that "Owen was put in a coma by a single punch, carried out of the Olympic (arena) under a hail of beer cups, some of which were filled with urine."

The law can not prudently move far in advance of mass taste, so boxing can not be outlawed. But in a world in which many barbarities are unavoidable, perhaps it is not too much to hope that some of the optional sorts will be outgrown.

November 21, 1982

Violence as a Communicable Disease

With his beard and armor-piercing gaze, Dr. C. Everett Koop resembles an Old Testament prophet who has discovered his neighbors making graven images. Actually, he is not fierce, but is determined to be heard, which is good because that is his job. He is Surgeon General of the United States.

The Surgeon General's job includes monitoring the health of the American people, publicizing significant findings, and using information to change behavior, as has been done with several reports on smoking. Having saved millions of lives and billions of dollars, the Surgeon General's office has done more good per dollar spent than any other federal office.

Recently Koop expanded slightly the scope of his office's monitoring. Speaking to the American Academy of Pediatrics, Koop, a pediatrician, urged physicians generally but pediatricians especially to consider violence as a treatable public health problem. Statistics show that there are periods when there are striking changes in the incidence of violence. We now are in one, which began in the late 1960s. Koop thinks it unlikely that mortality rates from violent acts will return to the levels of the early 1960s.

For example, for 15- to 24-year-olds, the homicide rate went from 5.9 per 100,000 in 1960 to 11.7 in 1970 to 13.2 in 1978. For black males, the rates were 46.4 in 1960, 102.5 in 1970, 72.5 in 1978.

Among all 15- to 24-year olds, the suicide rate rose from 5.2 per 100,000 in 1960 to 12.4 in 1978. For white males, that rate went from 8.2 to 20.8.

We have neither the historical distance nor, perhaps, the analytic capability to say what has happened to cause the increased violence. But Koop believes that violence is "treatable" in this sense: We know enough about the symptoms of violent personality in children and parents to make diagnostic, predictive and preventative decisions. Clues include the fact that homicidal children tend to have histories of attempted suicides and of psychomotor seizures. Many have seen or been victims of family violence. Many have mothers who have had inpatient psychiatric care. High-risk families tend to be socially isolated, lacking strong friendships and subject to stress from even such common social transactions as shopping and using public transportation.

Koop wants physicians to be sensitive to the signals of personal and family stress, and to master the growing literature about the predisposition to violence. He believes there should be "the same kind of counseling or referral service as if the patient showed a predisposition to cardiovascular disease, obesity or diabetes." Physicians, he notes, do not hesitate to counsel patients with hypertension to avoid salt or certain sugars. "Similarly, if we have a patient with a predisposition for violent behavior, especially against family members, I think we need to advise that patient to get some professional counseling and also suggest that he or she monitor their entertainment 'menu' and avoid the kinds of television or motion picture fare that stimulates and contributes to the violence in their personalities."

There is controversy about "desensitization"—about what is known or knowable about the effect of entertainment that depicts violence short of murder as a common, semi-acceptable response to frustration, insult or injury. Koop believes the evidence "strongly suggests that physicians ought to recognize that a diet of violent entertainment for the violence-prone individual is as unhealthy as a diet of sugar and starch is for the obesity-prone individual."

But it is one thing for a doctor practicing physical medicine to diagnose and treat a proneness that is, say, metabolic; it is quite different and more problematic for him even just to diagnose a predisposition that is part of the patient's disposition. Such dispositions may reflect metabolic or other physical disorders, but our understanding is currently slight.

Violence is, unquestionably, a health problem, and there is much more to enhancing health than practicing medicine. But many physicians are inclined, by temperament and training, to confine themselves to administering medicine. They understandably resist being pulled into the periphery of social problems. But Koop understandably wants to expand somewhat the physicians' sense of what the practice of medicine should encompass.

He argues that medicine and the social services have similar ethical imperatives and that pediatricians, especially, have special relationships with, and insights about, the irreducible social units that shape citizens—families. He may have a misplaced confidence in research about the causes—biological, psychological, social—of violence. But a Surgeon General, like an Old Testament prophet, cannot do his job without starting an occasional argument.

November 14, 1982

Ideology Masquerading As Medicine

The verdict on Hinckley—not guilty by reason of insanity—is the last reverberation of the shots he fired at the President. The verdict illustrates three perversities: The most morally indefensible crimes are becoming the most legally defendable. The idea of the individual is being obliterated in order to maximize the rights of the individual. And the quest for the chimera of perfect justice is subordinating the social good, including the rule of law, to the quicksilver axioms of a "science" that is long on pretenses and short on testable assertions.

Seated atop a ramshackle scaffolding of superstitions, merrily minting nouns that denote nothing, many psychiatrists are today condescending to the American people, chiding them for not comprehending the intellectual marvelousness of the Hinckley verdict. But the verdict will serve the social good only if it generates disgust with the incompatible marriage of psychiatry and law. To that end, Americans should read *The Killing of Bonnie Garland*, Willard Gaylin's meditation on another trial featuring an insanity defense.

Gaylin, a practicing psychiatrist, argues that the premises and purposes of law and psychiatry are in tension. The premise of the law is that the self is autonomous. The premise of psychiatry is that the self is a cauldron of impulses that determine behavior. The purposes of the law include protecting the social order and expressing its moral sentiments. The purpose of psychology is to explain an individual's behavior. An explanation may facilitate a "cure," but any explanation can be made to seem exculpatory, by diluting to the point of disappearance the idea of responsibility.

The insanity defense is many centuries old and is indispensable to justice. What is incompatible with justice is the proliferation of categories and gradations of diminished capacity. The old, workable questions were: Did the accused know the nature of his act (that he was, for example, shooting a person, not a poltergeist) and did he know it was wrong? Those questions, which do invite psychiatrists' baroque speculations, lead to this conclusion: Hinckley is a very strange, very guilty individual.

Law must assign responsibility. All of psychiatry's permutations of determinism locate "responsibility" somewhere other than with an autonomous "self"—whatever "self" can mean after enough acts and attributes are explained in terms of a yeasty subconscious.

153

The rule of law requires predictability and regularity: treating like cases alike. But a judicial system that is deferential to psychiatric storytellers invites extreme individuation: No two cases can be alike, because each defendant is determined by—or perhaps just is—his idiosyncratic jumble of impulses.

Did a killer act in a rage? If so, "he"—whatever pudding of neuroses that pronoun denotes—was sick. Did he kill without passion? Even sicker. He shows no remorse? That clinches it: He is no more "guilty" of his behavior than he would be of appendicitis.

It is an old joke: A person kills his parents and demands mercy because he is an orphan. The joke is now the jurisprudence of "compassion." A crime becomes the ground for evading punishment for the crime. The more odious the crime—premeditated ("How inhuman!") or spontaneous ("An irresistible impulse!")—the more "reasonable doubt" there is about the person's sanity at the time.

Today Americans have an admirable but unconsummated desire to see the law express, through commensurate punishment, the doctrine of individual responsibility and the wickedness of political assassination. The law performs an expressive function. It teaches—ineluctably, for good or ill. The Hinckley verdict does not teach the idea of responsibility on which habits of restraint and moderation depend.

Now the absurdity will be compounded. The trial allowed—indeed, required—a jury to pick between numerous flatly incompatible theories spun by credentialed "experts," theories purporting to divine Hinckley's mental state on one day 15 months ago. Now the same wonderful psychiatric "profession" (the word is barely applicable) that produced a cacophony of loopiness in court, and cannot even define its perishable terms, will dazzle the world by predicting Hinckley's future behavior.

Is he dangerous? The trial verdict means the jury thought it had a reasonable doubt about Hinckley's sanity·last year. Surely there can be as much uncertainty about his dangerousness. So let him loose—that is the logic of the process.

Some alarmed lawyers propose restricting psychiatric testimony to statements of "fact"—what psychiatrists see or hear—and forbidding conclusory statements. But psychiatrists often are hired to put an acre of embroidery around a pinhead of "fact." So they bandy diagnostic categories that are as evanescent as snowflakes, swapping bald assertions with the serenity of philistines operating far from serious intellectual criteria.

Psychiatric "defense" of the individual often obliterates the individual. The "compassionate" treatment of Hinckley causes him to disappear, leaving only a residue of traits that may or may not be symptoms of this or that "disturbance." Psychiatry as practiced by some of today's itinerant experts-for-hire is this century's alchemy. No, that is unfair to alchemists, who were confused but honest chemists. Some of today's rent-a-psychiatry is charlatanism laced with cynicism.

Much psychiatry is ideology masquerading as medicine. In Aldous Huxley's nightmare of determinism, *Brave New World* when someone commits a crime the normal response is: "I did not know he was ill." We are not yet in that mental world, but you can see its suburbs from here.

June 24, 1982

The Value of Punishment

Last February Jimmy Lee Smith walked out of Soledad Prison. His partner in murder nineteen years ago, Gregory Powell, is scheduled for release from another California institution June 18. These and other parole cases, including Sirhan Sirhan's, have stirred proper fury.

On March 9, 1963, Ian Campbell and Carl Hettinger, young Los Angeles policemen, stopped a car that had made a suspicious U-turn. The occupants, Powell and Smith, pulled guns, disarmed the officers, drove to an onion field near Bakersfield and murdered Campbell. Hettinger escaped. The day Campbell was buried, a kidnapper and rapist named Miranda was arrested. Miranda's case generated one of the Warren Court expansions of defendants' rights. It became the basis of one of the blizzard of motions that caused the Powell–Smith case to consume almost seven years and fill 159 volumes—45,000 pages. The harrowing story is in Joseph Wambaugh's superb book (and movie) *The Onion Field*.

Smith and Powell were sentenced to death. Retried, Smith was sentenced to life, Powell to death again. In 1972 California's capital punishment law was declared unconstitutional, sparing Powell and 101 others, including Sirhan, who now says he should be paroled because his victim, Robert Kennedy, were he alive, would agree that he, Sirhan, has suffered enough.

It is grotesque for Sirhan to put words into the mouth of the man he silenced. And it is grotesque that in 1975—just seven years after his crime—the parole board set a 1986 release date, now moved up to Sept. 1, 1984. The board acted without knowledge of two letters he has written threatening to kill three people. To his lawyer he wrote concerning an author: "Hey Punk . . . if he [the author] gets his brains splattered—he will have asked for it like Robert Kennedy did . . . neither of you is beyond my reach." These threats may be a sufficient reason, but are not the best reason, for denying him parole. The best reason is that fifteen years in jail is not a punishment that fits his crime.

Sirhan has mastered the buzzwords of the playacting that is a normal part of parole processes. He promises to work "to improve the quality of life" if he gets the parole that he says is dictated by "equal treatment under the laws." Actually, the parole board has treated him as it does other murderers. But he did not just murder a man, he assaulted and maimed the democratic system that so many have died defending.

Punishment always involves a judgment of proportionateness. Of the 102 men who in 1972 were sentenced to die in San Quentin's apple-green gas chamber, 29 have been paroled and 25 have release dates. Steve Grogan, 30, was convicted with Charles Manson (another man saved in 1972). A witness to Grogan's crime quoted him saying: "So I had this big machete and I chopped his head off and it went bloop, bloop and rolled out of the way." Grogan has a 1987 release date. Another murderer, who was paroled after 1972, committed a second murder and is back on death row under a new capital punishment law. Of the 2,173 men serving life sentences for murder in California, only two have been in prison more than twenty years. Increasingly, a life sentence is seen as a fraud that mocks the dead and jeopardizes the living by trivializing the crime of murder and diluting the indignation society needs for self-defense.

William Fain, 36, has twice had his parole from San Quentin blocked by public pressure. In 1967 he flagged a passing car, shotgunned a 17-year-old student and raped two young women. The murder victim's family has gathered 62,500 signatures protesting parole. A court has held that "awareness of the public hostility" is a legitimate reason for denying parole.

It may be unfortunate that parole decisions have become political issues. And it may be unconstitutional for them to be influenced by mass pressure tactics. However, a legitimate function of the political process is to serve as a safety valve when judges or bureaucracies lacerate the public's sensibilities. Furthermore, law has an expressive function, expressing and thereby sustaining certain values. There also is a cathartic function of expressive state action. The Nuremberg tribunals, however problematic they were jurisprudentially, performed the vital function of civilizing the vengeance that was going to be expressed, one way or another.

In 1952 Justice Hugo Black wrote: "Retribution is no longer the dominant objective of criminal law. Reformation and rehabilitation of offenders have become important goals of criminal jurisprudence." Today, after 30 years of rising crime and recidivism, we at least know what we do not know—how to reform and rehabilitate. In 1972 Justice Thurgood Marshall, wrote that "punishment for the sake of retribution is not permissible under the Eighth Amendment." That is absurd. The element of retribution—vengeance, if you will—does not make punishment cruel and unusual, it makes punishment intelligible. It distinguishes punishment from therapy. Rehabilitation may be an ancillary result of punishment, but we punish to serve justice, by giving people what they deserve.

From plea bargaining through sentencing through paroling, the criminal justice system is riddled with exercises of discretion that are unjustified by sufficient knowledge, and unrationalized by coherent theories. This is especially true at the parole stage, where judgments often presuppose—rashly—knowledge of rehabilitation and individual predictability.

In penology, as in other fields of social reform, the millennium has been indefinitely postponed. For now, we should do what we know how to do, for reasons we can explicate. We should use the criminal justice system to isolate and punish—that is, to protect society from physical danger—and to strengthen society by administering condign punishments that express and nourish, through controlled indignation, the vigor of our values. We should be ashamed and alarmed to live in a society that does not intelligently express through its institutions the public's proper sense of proportionate punishment for the likes of Smith, Powell and Sirhan. We are in danger of becoming demoralized—literally, de-moralized.

May 24, 1982

Punishment and "Official Straighteners"

When a South Carolina judge sentenced three especially brutal rapists to a choice—30 years in prison or castration—he stirred a visceral reaction of revulsion. But it was a reaction in search of reasons.

The important point is not constitutional—that such a sentence violates the ban on cruel and unusual punishments. Castration may be cruel even if chosen in preference to 30 years in prison (actually, less than half that time, given good behavior and normal parole procedures). And the important point is not that castration would be somehow medieval. Actually, the sentence reflects a modern turn of mind.

Leave aside the problem of medical ethics: What becomes of the doctor's oath to "do no harm" when his skills are put in the service of what purports to be punishment? Leave aside the fact that this sentence is another instance of a judge improvising intolerably with sentences. Leave aside the fact that the sentence flows from the false assumption that rape is a crime of sex rather than of violence. And leave aside the fact that castration, when administered after puberty, may not be sexually incapacitating.

Sexuality is thoroughly woven into the notion of personality, and the sense of personhood. That is one reason why a mastectomy can be so emotionally traumatic. When the state undertakes to tamper, surgically or chemically, with sexuality, it is touching personal identity in an alarming way.

The fundamental wrong in the sentence of castration is present also in what many people consider an untroubling, even "progressive," sentence: requiring rapists to undergo drug treatments that reduce the body's production of testosterone, and hence the sex drive. Such drugs, in conjunction with psychotherapy, reduce recidivism dramatically. But that fact does not suffice to establish such treatment as an acceptable substitute for incarceration. It is not satisfactory in terms of the rights of society, or of the criminal.

Consider a hypothetical case. It is possible to identify many persons who have a tendency to steal. One way to prevent them from stealing might be "monetary therapy": Give each an annual income of $30,000—which might be less than the cost of catching, convicting and incarcerating them. Suppose that this would "work" in this narrow utilitarian sense: It would be a cost-effective way to reduce stealing. The idea brings us face-to-face with a fact: Non-utilitarian values must intrude in the matter of punishment. Therapy can not substitute for punishment—for the expression of retribution, of "paying back"—unless all crime is considered a manifestation of sickness.

Suppose the expressive role is discounted and the only justification for punishment is the prevention of crime. Suppose it were possible to implant, surgically, small monitoring devices in the bodies of persons after, say, a third conviction for a crime. Suppose the device would enable the police to monitor the movements of such persons, much as naturalists keep track of the migrations of animals.

If prevention of crime is the only purpose of punishment, such monitoring might be an alternative to incarceration. But this punishment—deprivation of privacy—would license the state to exercise an ominous talent.

Some people will say: What is the difference? If we can (and in some sense we can) implant ideas that help control behavior, what is wrong with implanting mechanical devices or chemicals? After all, devices and chemicals are easier to remove than ideas.

There are two differences. Ideas that are intended to regulate behavior through moral appeal (including the idea implicit in real punishment: What we are doing to you "fits" what you did to society.) involve taking seriously the self-determination of the individual. Therapy sometimes denies that self-determination. Second, it is not just superstition that causes us to feel that the skin is in some way the boundary of the self. When the state may violate an individual's integument, it may disregard his individuality.

It may seem odd to speak of a person having a right to be punished rather than treated as a patient needing therapy. But a criminal has a right to be dealt with in a way that respects the integrity of his personality. It is a right to be dealt with in a way that says the wrongdoer is a self-determining creature responsible for his acts.

The alternative is to cast the criminal into a terrifying limbo where he has no status as a moral agent, and becomes raw material for what C. S. Lewis called "official straighteners." When a society that is squeamish about punishment goes looking for alternatives to incarceration, it is apt to get the penology of scalpels and chemicals.

December 29, 1983

Beyond Civil Rights

The week that began with the first national observance of Martin Luther King's birthday ends with a stunning demonstration of the general irrelevance of the civil-rights era to the calamity currently engulfing much of black America. The demonstration will be on CBS for two hours Saturday night (January 25) in Bill Moyers's "The Vanishing Family—Crisis in Black America."

The honors accorded King are proportional to his accomplishment, and nostalgia for the clarities of his day is understandable. But the struggles of the 1950s and 1960s, against institutional barriers to blacks and for material assistance, are almost irrelevant to the catastrophe of the 1980s.

Government programs on behalf of access and amelioration for blacks are necessary. But such programs are barely germane to the growing crisis of personal behavior by millions of inner-city blacks. All other value-generating institutions—schools, churches, youth organizations—are unavailing if the primary institution, the family, fails.

Today nearly 60 percent of all black children are born out of wedlock. Imagine the astronomic percentages in many inner cities. Black girls between ages of 15 and 19 are the most fertile population of that age group in the industrialized world. Half of all black teenage girls become pregnant. The resulting "families" rarely are self-supporting. Almost half of all black children are partially supported by government payments.

As a result, social pathologies multiply. More than half of all black pupils in primary and secondary schools are in the 12 largest central-city school districts, where schools are inadequate and only one-quarter of the students are white. Blacks are about 11 percent of the population, but about 50 percent of imprisoned felons. The principal cause of death among blacks aged 15 to 24 is murder by blacks. Approximately 40 percent of murder victims are black men killed by black men. The yearly total approximates the total number of black deaths in the entire Vietnam War.

Young blacks, whose sexual recklessness produces oceans of misery, feel little of the kind of guilt that changes behavior. One reason for this is that they have been taught by reflexive "civil rights" rhetoric that they are mere victims, absolved from responsibility by the all-purpose alibi of "white racism."

When next you hear a "civil-rights leader" (probably a middle-class black selected from a small and self-selected pool of middle-class blacks important as brokers of government benefits) say that the big problem is, say, "failure to enforce the Voting Rights Act," try this:

Suppose that the Act is now imperfectly enforced. Also imagine perfect enforcement. Then ask yourself: What would that accomplish?

The problem of black America is not an insufficiency of elected officials prepared to regard blacks, alone among American groups, as permanent wards of government compassion. The problem is that millions of blacks are victims of many irresponsible blacks.

Moyers begins asking a young unwed mother if she does not need a man's help. She replies, "Not really. I didn't have a father." Today most black families are headed by women. Most black children are growing up without fathers. Moyers talks with a Timothy, unmarried father of six children (not counting the abortion and the stillborn baby) by four women:

"I ain't thinking about holding up as far as no sex, my man, you know. If a girl, you know, she's having a baby, carryin' a baby, that's on her, you know. I'm not going to stop my pleasures because of another woman."

Moyers: "How did it feel to have those. . . . "

Timothy: "Women?"

Moyers: "No, kids. Kids."

Try to concentrate, Timothy. The subject is kids. He laughingly says, "I'm highly sexed" and "I just got strong sperm," and he had "a lovely time begetting the children. But he says, "I'm old-fashioned" about marriage. And he means he wants "a big wedding" with the men in tuxedos.

Moyers: "When?"

Timothy: "Whenever."

The Timothys are more of a menace to black progress than the Bull Connors ever were.

There is much heroism in the ghettos. Moyers interviews a black man, a Newark detective, who tries to be a caring father for some fatherless children. He says that with Medicaid, welfare and food stamps, "a lot of the women are more married to welfare than to the guys layin' in the bed next to 'em. 'Cause he's just a physical thing. The whole backbone of the family is coming out of downtown or out of uptown offices."

Wrong. Such backbone can not come from offices or any other mere physical thing. The detective really knows that. He says: "Freedom is a lot of times destruction [to fatherless children]. . . . So I try to, you know, keep 'em in a little cage . . . keep 'em in my arms."

That is the voice of a real father. Nothing—not laws propounding "rights," not rhetoric deploring "racism"—can do what such a loving, protective cage can do.

January 23, 1986

"Compassion" that Dehumanizes

At the risk of reigniting some highly flammable people, I herewith recur to the subject of the black family, because some of my critics are practicing a perverse form of "compassion." Their "kindness" has a severe cost. It dehumanizes some blacks by denying that they have the capacity for responsibility, and hence for moral choice. In depicting them "compassionately," as toys of fate, it causes their personhood to disappear.

Recently I wrote to praise Bill Moyers's CBS documentary, "The Vanishing Family—Crisis in Black America," which deals with the causes of statistics like these: Nearly 60 percent of all black children are born out of wedlock. Half of all black teenage girls become pregnant. Many of the resulting "families" are hardly families and rarely are self-supporting. About half of all black children are partially supported by government payments.

I said: Civil-rights struggles of the 1950s and 1960s, struggles against institutional barriers to blacks and for material amelioration for blacks, are largely irrelevant to today's catastrophe. Ameliorative programs are necessary but are doomed to be overwhelmed if the family, the primary value-generating institution, collapses. Such alleged government failures as "failure to enforce the Voting Rights Act" are peripheral to the point of inconsequence regarding the social pathologies Moyers discussed.

Moyers highlighted a person named Timothy, the unmarried and unconcerned father of many children. I said, and say: Timothy is not a mere anecdote, he is a paradigm of those persons whose sexual irresponsibility produces misery but who feels little of the guilt that changes behavior. One reason they feel little such guilt is that they have been taught by reflexive "civil rights" rhetoric that they are mere passive victims, absolved by the all-purpose alibi of "white racism" from all responsibility for their behavior.

Now come two columnists who buttress my argument with their objections to it. Ray Jenkins is white. Carl Rowan is black. Both ask: Why such lack of compassion for Timothy from George Will who has a son, Jonathan, with Down's syndrome? Have Jenkins and Rowan considered the logic of their "compassion"?

Down's syndrome is a genetic defect, present from conception, involving varying degrees of mental retardation and physical abnormalities. Jenkins says Timothy "is as much a victim of fate as Jonathan." Rowan says I am compassionate when commenting about afflictions like Down's syndrome, "but Will's compassion and knowledge turn to meanness and ignorance"—the light touch is not Carl's specialty—"when he writes about another handicapped youngster, a ghetto lad. . . . "

Hold it right there.

"Youngster"? "Lad"? Rowan's exquisite sensitivity to racial insults would cause him to have an apoplectic seizure were any white person to refer to any black man as a "boy." Yet Rowan calls Timothy a "youngster," a "lad"—Timothy who is 26 years old, who in the eight years he has been eligible to vote has caused eight pregnancies and says he had "a lovely time" doing so.

"Youngster"? "Lad"? A more apposite noun is: "man."

The great proclamation on placards in civil-rights demonstrations 20 years ago was: "I am a man." It cut to the heart of the matter, the denial of the full personhood of blacks. Today people who think like Jenkins and Rowan demonstrate, unwittingly, and in the name of "compassion," that there are many ways to deny personhood. The essence of personhood is an irreducible element of responsibility for one's choices and deeds.

Timothy, having grown up in a social setting of material deprivation and moral underdevelopment and narrow horizons, is indeed somewhat a product—a victim, if you prefer—of bad circumstances. But consider the damage done by thinking of him, and telling him to think of himself, as just as much a "victim of fate" and "handicapped" as a child with a retarding genetic defect. Is it not obvious the harm such "compassion" does to the thinking of whites and self-esteem of blacks?

I say again: The Timothys are more of a menace to black progress than the Bull Connors were because only political will was required to remove the Connors. I now add: Another menace to black progress is the "compassionate" portrayal of such black men as utterly passive victims, as no more to be judged than infants—as less than men.

Again, the dignity of personhood is related to the capacity for responsibility in making moral choices. Persons with Down's syndrome do not lack that capacity.

Some people who advertise their "compassion" should suspend their self-congratulations long enough to consider this: Black Americans should be spared the condescending "compassion" that portrays irresponsible black men as not really responsible because they are not really men.

February 13, 1986

First Amendment Follies

On page 15 of a 27-page Supreme Court opinion, this thought appears: "The value of permitting live performances and photographic reproduction of children engaged in lewd sexual conduct is exceedingly modest. . . . " Scrambling farther out on a constitutional limb, the Court adds:

"We consider it unlikely that visual depiction of children performing sexual acts or lewdly exhibiting their genitals would often constitute an important and necessary part of a literary performance or scientific work."

The Court complains mightily about its work load. But it has only itself to blame for the fact that it churns 36 pages of hairsplitting opinion and concurrences, just to rule—unanimously—that New York did not act unconstitutionally when it prohibited distribution of materials depicting children in "actual or simulated sexual intercourse, deviate sexual intercourse, sexual bestiality, masturbation, sado-masochistic abuse, or lewd exhibits of the genitals."

I will not give readers migraines by detailing the intricate arguments by which the Court lumbered to a common sense conclusion. Even when the Court rules sensibly in free speech cases, it does so for a chef's salad of wrong reasons. In this case it furrowed its collective brow to devise a justification for banning child pornography that is not (I'm not making this up) legally obscene. One justice mused: New York has an interest in protecting its children from exploitation, but what of a pornographic movie "if the child actor resided abroad"?

A state court, conscientiously struggling to comply with previous Supreme Court decisions, denied the constitutionality of a law banning an extraordinarily repellent and exploitative form of filth. Then the Supreme Court labored nervously and with ludicrous complexity to justify pulling such pornography out from under First Amendment protection. How did we get to such a situation?

We got here by a series of Court decisions that are beads without a string—opinions without a coherent constitutional theory of the scope of the free speech guarantee. We got here by sleepwalking down a path strewn with irrational and grandstanding rhetoric, such as the idea that the First Amendment is an "absolute" (Hugo Black), that "even a reasonable regulation of the right of free speech is not compatible with the First Amendment" (William Douglas), that "one man's vulgarity is another's lyric" (John Harlan).

Regarding free speech, the Court has acted as though a multiplicity of distinctions and criteria can make up for an absence of serious constitutional analysis. The Court has set itself and other courts such tasks as: detecting a "dominant theme" of pornography; measuring appeals to "prurient interest"; determining when offensiveness is "patent"; announcing when pornography is "utterly" without redeeming social value; gauging affronts to "contemporary standards."

Were the Court to go back to basics, it would begin by saying that free speech serves three basic values: individual development, individual enjoyment, and the discovery and dissemination of political truths. The first two are important private rights deserving broad scope, but are not the concern of the First Amendment. That amendment is an instrument of government. It concerns the democratic disposition of public power. Hence, its protections extend only to political speech.

A Court that accepted this premise would have quite enough to do monitoring the distinction between political and nonpolitical speech. It could find uses for the hours hitherto spent watching pornographic movies and pondering the "expressive" value of nude dancing.

The First Amendment, properly understood, protects not "expression" but speech. As part of a political instrument, the amendment protects political speech—language addressed to other persons with a view to persuading them about political matters. Speech, unlike "expression," is intrinsically connected with the distinctive human capacity: reason. It is by reason that the individual governs his or her self; it is by reason that groups achieve self-government.

The Court took a radically wrong turn when it "incorporated" the First Amendment into the 14th Amendment, thereby imposing on states the restrictions that the authors of that amendment clearly intended to apply only to Congress. It is, of course, arguable that, absent "incorporation," state governments would impose, and democratic processes would not correct, intolerably foolish censorship. And it is arguable that trusting democratic discretion would produce a worse situation than we have: unstanchable pollution by pornography, and courts improvising antic theories about how this and that "expression" involves constitutional—that is, political—values.

All that is, as I say, arguable. But it is rarely argued. Many people cite their libertarian interpretation of the First Amendment as evidence of their brave receptivity to all thoughts, but have minds sealed against more rational interpretations of the First Amendment.

July 11, 1982

Abortion and Fetal Pain

In the eight years since the Supreme Court nationalized the abortion controversy, one facet of that subject has been neglected: pain. Abortion is painful for the aborted.

The neglect is explainable. To opponents of abortion, death, not pain, is the paramount issue. And proponents of abortion need (emotionally or logically, or both) to deny the possibility of fetal pain.

In its 1973 decision legislating abortion on demand, the Supreme Court announced that fetal life is not alive. At least that is what the Court seems to have meant (if it can be said to have meant anything) when it described the fetus as "potential life." Those who support the 1973 decision are committed to the idea that a fetus, being only "potential" life, cannot feel pain, pain being an attribute of actual life.

Thus does a legal absurdity breed a biological falsehood. This intellectual train wreck is the subject of an essay in *The Human Life Review* by Professor John Noonan of the University of California (Berkeley) Law School. There are, he notes, four principal means of abortion.

Sharp curettage involves a knife killing the fetus (if the amateur embryologists on the Court will allow us to speak of "killing" life that is merely "potential"). In suction curettage, a vacuum pump sucks out the fetus in bits (and a knife cleans out any remnants). In second trimester and later abortions, a saline solution is injected into the amniotic fluid. The salt seems to act as a poison; the skin of the fetus, when delivered, resembles skin soaked in acid. If by accident the solution leaks into the body of the mother, she experiences pain that is described as "severe." The fetus can be in this solution for two hours before its heart (a stubborn bit of "potential" life) stops beating. Alternatively, the mother can be given a dosage of a chemical sufficient to impair the circulation and cardiac functioning of the fetus, which will be delivered dead or dying.

A fetus, like an infant or an animal, has no language in which to express pain. But we infer, and empathize with, the pain of creatures, such as baby seals, which lack language to express pain.

There are uncertainties about the precise points in fetal development at which particular kinds of sensations are experienced. But observations of development and behavior indicate that by the 56th day, a fetus can move. Discomfort may occasion the movement. Tactile stimulation of the mouth produces reflex action about day 59 or 60. By day 77 the fetus develops sensitivity to touch on hands, feet, genital and anal areas, and begins to swallow. Noonan believes that the physiological literature teaches that "beginning with the presence of sense receptors and spinal responses, there is as much reason to believe that the unborn are capable of pain as that they are capable of sensation."

Americans are proud of their humane feelings and are moved by empathy. Thus, we regulate the ways animals can be killed. Certain kinds of traps are banned. Cattle cannot be slaughtered in ways deemed careless about pain. Stray dogs and cats must be killed in certain humane ways.

But no laws regulate the suffering of the aborted. Indeed, Planned Parenthood, the most extreme pro-abortion lobby, won a

Supreme Court ruling that it is unconstitutional to ban the saline abortion technique. That's right: The Court discovered that the "privacy" right to abortion, which right the framers of the Constitution neglected to mention, even confers a right to particular abortion trechniques.

Most pro-abortion persons have a deeply felt and understandable need to keep the discussion of abortion as abstract as possible. They become bitter when opponents use photographs to document early fetal development. The sight of something that looks so much like a child complicates the task of trying to believe that there is nothing there but "potential" life. And if fetal pain is acknowledged, America has a problem: Its easy conscience about 1.6 million abortions a year depends on the supposition that such pain is impossible.

Magda Denes, in her book, *In Necessity and Sorrow: Life and Death in an Abortion Hospital*, brought to her subject not anti-abortion convictions but a reporter's eye for concrete detail. Examining the body of an aborted child, she described the face as showing "the agonized tautness of one forced to die too soon." That is a description to bear in mind this day, as many thousands of abortions occur.

November 5, 1981

Abortion: The Court's Intellectual Scandal

Last Tuesday, the day before the Supreme Court compounded the travesty it has made of abortion law, a California court convicted a former sheriff's deputy of murder in the shooting death, during an unauthorized drug raid, of a fetus in a woman who survived the wound. Because of the Supreme Court's 1973 abortion ruling, no state could forbid the woman to kill the child by abortion, even though it was in the third trimester. But how can anyone "murder" something the Supreme Court says is only "potentially" human and has the legal status of hamburger in the woman's stomach?

In last week's decisions, the Court discovered that the Constitution forbids Akron's requirement that other than first trimester abortions be performed in a hospital; forbids Akron's requirement that physicians perform abortions on unmarried women under 15 only with certain parental permission or court orders; forbids Akron's requirement that physicians tell women seeking abortions the developmental status of their fetuses, the date of viability, physical and emotional complications that can result from abortion, and alternatives to abortion; forbids Akron's requirement of a 24-hour interval between a request for and performance of an abortion; forbids Akron's requirement that abortionists dispose of aborted fetuses in a "humane and sanitary manner."

To see the intellectual scandal of the Court's position in 1983, consider Wednesday's ruling that Missouri can require the presence of a second physician during an abortion performed after "viability."

With 1.6 million abortions annually, it regularly happens that an abortion procedure results in a live birth and the inconvenient life is "terminated" by suffocation or aggressive neglect. However, Missouri requires (when the requirement does not increase the woman's risk) a late abortion to be performed by the method most likely to preserve fetal life—that is, the method most likely to fail, least likely to kill the fetus, which is the aim. Now the Court says Missouri can require the presence of a second physician because if the fetus survives the attempt to kill it, the state "may" protect "the lives of viable fetuses," meaning "a fetus born alive."

Well.

The "viable fetuses" whom the second physicians serve are often called, quaintly, "children." A "fetus born alive" is, in the vernacular, a "baby."

Concerning abortion, the justices use words and categories the way babies use forks and spoons: with gusto, but sloppily. In 1973 the Court made much—or thought it did—of "trimesters." But regarding pregnancy a trimester is a demarcation without moral or medical significance, and without much legal significance, in spite of the Court's attempt to give it such. The Court, which does not yet seem to know what it did in 1973, said then that no state can prevent even a third trimester abortion that any physician says is necessary for a woman's health. And "distress" (which can be caused by denial of an abortion) can be a health hazard.

In 1973 the Court thought it made much of "viability," the point at which a fetus can lead a "meaningful" life outside the womb. Actually, viability made no significant difference concerning permissible regulation of abortion. The Court gave no meaning to the word "meaningful." And the point at which a fetus could survive outside the womb was unclear then and has moved since, thereby demonstrating the folly of linking constitutional law to a dynamic science.

Two years ago a Georgia court in effect took custody of a fetus, holding that an unwilling woman must undergo a caesarean section for the fetus's safety. Evidently, the fetus had a right to protection.

In Baltimore, a pregnant drug abuser has been placed under court jurisdiction to protect the health of the fetus. She may not injure the fetus with drugs. Of course, she retains a right to kill it with an abortion.

In Maryland, a fetus has a right to inherit property if the fetus is conceived before the death of the person from whom the property will be inherited. Prenatal medicine can perform wonders for fetuses that can be aborted at any stage. Malpractice cases are establishing that a child born injured as a result of negligent prenatal medicine can claim violation of rights it had as a fetus.

Fetuses, it seems, have various rights—but no right to life.

Cut adrift by its 1973 decision from constitutional and biomedical realism, the Court manufacturers ever finer distinctions from never relevant categories. The justices should pray—not in a public building, of course—for Senator Orrin Hatch's amendment ("A right to abortion is not secured by this Constitution"). That would restore the *status quo ante* 1973, thereby restoring to the states responsibility for dealing with an issue that clearly is beyond the Court's competence.

June 19, 1983

Noticing the Differences Between Boys and Girls

The young man's sexual ethics were unrefined, but his lawyer was not. So the Supreme Court was given another occasion for adding a brick to the rising edifice of law about when and how government can notice the differences between boys and girls.

A 17-year-old California male had sexual intercourse with a 16-year-old and was convicted of statutory rape under a statute that makes it unlawful for a male, but not for a female, to have intercourse with a minor. The California Supreme Court rejected his contention that the law violated the "equal protection" clause of the 14th Amendment. The court held that the law's unequal treatment of the sexes is reasonably related to a legitimate aim: the prevention of teenage pregnancies.

By a 5–4 vote, the U.S. Supreme Court (Justice William Rehnquist speaking for the majority) has sensibly agreed, holding that the law "realistically reflects the fact that the sexes are not similarly situated in certain circumstances." The risk of pregnancy can be a deterrent to promiscuity among females; a criminal sanction imposed solely on males "serves to roughly 'equalize' the deterrents on the sexes." Furthermore, California believes that if females were punishable under the statute, enforcement would be frustrated because a female would be less likely to report violations.

Justice William Brennan argued in dissent that California had failed to show that its objective could not be achieved with a "gender-neutral" law. But more interesting is that Brennan makes much of the fact that the statutory rape law did not originally have the objective that California says it now has. Brennan says the law was originally designed not to prevent pregnancies but to "further" some "sexual stereotypes" that are now, he announces, "outmoded."

There may be a non sequitur lurking in Brennan's argument: the idea that if the original purpose of a law was X rather than Y, it is impermissible to defend the law, years later, as reasonably related to purpose Y. And there is in Brennan's argument a trace of a constricting theory about the legitimate uses of law.

He says the law "had its origins" in King Edward I's 13th-century statute that stipulated 12 as the age of sexual consent for females. In 1576 the law was amended to lower the age to 10. The English common law was imported into America, and California's first statutes proscribed sexual intercourse with females under 10. That age was raised to 14 in 1889, 16 in 1897, and 18 in 1913.

Brennan says that the only legislative history of California's statutory rape law dates from 1872 and indicates that the legislature's intention was not pregnancy prevention but protection of those girls (aged 9 and under) presumed incapable of giving true consent to sexual intercourse. Brennan cites California court decisions that indicate that the original purpose of the law was to protect "young girls from their own uninformed decisionmaking."

An 1895 decision held that "the obvious purpose" of the law was "the protection of society by protecting from violation the virtue of young and unsophisticated girls." It was designed to prevent "the insidious approaches and vile tampering with their persons that primarily undermines the virtue of young girls." As recently as 1964 a California court held that the law's aim is to prevent the young female from making "an unwise disposition of her sexual favor" which would be harmful to "herself and the social mores by which the community's conduct patterns are established."

That language from just 17 years ago has an anachronistic ring. Increasingly, the cultural assumptions that shape the minds of those who shape the law suggest that it is at least quaint, is almost certainly quixotic, and probably is wrong to try to use law to promote virtue. After all (or so the reasoning runs), it is "natural" for particular virtues, "social mores" and "conduct patterns" to become "outmoded," because it is natural for them to change, and proof that something is "outmoded" is that it is changing.

The epidemic of teenage pregnancy has coincided with the increasing availability of contraception, sex education and abortion, and it is perhaps unlikely that anything a state legislature is apt to do will make teenagers less sexually ardent or more careful about their ardor. When a society's values, habits, dispositions and mores begin to dissolve quickly, trying to arrest the dissolution with law can be like trying to stop a stallion with a cob-web.

But law need not passively reflect social change; it need not regard the evolution of society's spirit as an entirely autonomous process, immune to the influence of thoughtful interventions. One function of law is expressive; it expresses the community's core values, and by so doing it can ratify them, and can resist and retard the dissolution. Unfortunately, recent changes in law, changes regarding pornography, abortion, and parental authority, have actually helped the stallion gain speed.

March 29, 1981

The Decline of Liberalism: A Case Study

When Georgetown University, a Catholic institution, denied a certain status to two groups of homosexual students, the groups sued, citing the District of Columbia's Human Rights Act, which bans discrimination based on "sexual orientation." The homosexuals' lawyer said that unless Georgetown were compelled to yield, it "would mean that a corporation—that's all Georgetown is, a business—could say, 'I'm religiously affiliated, thus I don't have to abide by your human rights act.' "

That assertion—that a university is just a business like any other—expresses a political agenda for breaking all private institutions to the saddle of government. It is an assault on pluralism, waged with the rhetoric of pluralism. It is an example of how the proliferation of "rights" threatens freedom.

The two groups were granted "student body endorsement" but denied "university recognition." The former, conferred by the student government, gives access to university facilities, student advertising, the comptroller's services, and the right to apply for lecture funds. "University recognition" involves approval by Georgetown's administration. It involves a few additional privileges, but is important because the university considers the recognition an "endorsement" of a group's activities.

Roman Catholic teaching is that no person affiliated with the Church may be neutral about homosexual orientation or acts; an individual has a moral obligation to try to change his or her homosexual orientation; homosexual activities are morally wrong. Georgetown concluded, reasonably, that the homosexual groups' philosophy, goals and activities—promoting the doctrine that homosexuality is an equally moral alternative to heterosexuality— were contrary to Church teaching, and "university recognition" would be construed as endorsement and would undermine Church teaching.

The issue, said Georgetown, is its constitutionally protected right to the "free exercise" of religion. The D.C. Superior Court has now agreed.

The suit was part of the campaign to legitimize homosexuality—legitimize it in the sense of establishing public policy that seems to endorse the idea that homosexuality is a matter of moral indifference. The D.C. Human Rights Act is nothing if not comprehensive. It bans discrimination "including, but not limited to, discrimination by reason of race, color, religion, national origin, sex, age, marital status, personal appearance"—I am not making this up— "sexual orientation, family responsibilities, matriculation, political affiliation, physical handicap, source of income, and place of residence or business."

("Personal appearance" refers to "bodily condition" and manner or style of dress. But the D.C. government says there can be a "requirement of cleanliness." The American Civil Liberties Union probably sees in such a requirement the mailed fist of fascism.)

The homosexual groups employed the rhetoric of academic freedom: "If ideas cannot be freely discussed. . . . " But it is absurd to say that homosexual "ideas" are suppressed by withholding the university's imprimatur from homosexual groups. Anyway, the groups sought to strip Georgetown of its freedom to define its educational mission. That mission is fundamentally incompatible with an idea the groups embody, the idea (in the words of Father Timothy Healy, Georgetown's president) "that human beings should be identified and their essential nature classified in terms of their sexual orientation."

Although it reflected current liberal values and used the familiar rhetoric of rights, this was a bullying suit. It was an attempt to use government power to compel an institution of learning to endorse a particular opinion.

The homosexual groups argued that by applying for federal grants, loans and contracts, Georgetown had, necessarily, presented itself as essentially secular, and so had forfeited the right to assert religious rights in this way. The fact that the groups were mistaken about what the law requires is less important than what their interpretation of the law says about their aim: They want the receipt of any government aid by a private institution to make that private institution thoroughly subordinate to public dictates.

If the groups had prevailed, their victory would have meant that all values, even those given "preferred" national status in the First Amendment (values such as the "free exercise" of religion), would be subordinate to whatever values are promoted by local agencies such as the D.C. City Council.

Forty years ago liberals were pleased when, in a famous case, the Supreme Court held that West Virginia could not abridge the right to "free exercise" of religion by compelling children to salute the flag in a manner contrary to their religious beliefs. Today many liberals favor attempts such as that by the Georgetown groups to force that First Amendment value, and an academic institution, to yield to the commands of a city council. This change of attitude should bother liberals who are bothered by the fact that liberalism has lost its ascendancy in American politics.

October 30, 1983

Against Prefabricated Prayer

I stand foursquare with the English ethicist who declared: "I am fully convinced that the highest life can only be lived on a foundation of Christian belief—or some substitute for it." But President Reagan's constitutional amendment concerning prayer in public schools is a mistake.

His proposal reads: "Nothing in this Constitution shall be construed to prohibit individual or group prayer in public schools or other public institutions. No person shall be required by the United States or by any state to participate in prayer." This would restore the *status quo ante* the 1962 Supreme Court ruling that public school prayers violate the ban on "establishment" of religion. The amendment would not settle the argument about prayer; it would relocate the argument. All 50 states, or perhaps all 3,041 county governments, or all 16,214 school districts would have to decide whether to have "voluntary" prayers. But the issue is not really voluntary prayers for individuals. The issue is organized prayers for groups of pupils subject to compulsory school attendance laws. In a 1980 resolution opposing "government authored or sponsored religious exercises in public schools," the Southern Baptist Convention noted that "the Supreme Court has not held that it is illegal for any individual to pray or read his or her Bible in public schools."

This nation is even more litigious than religious, and the school prayer issue has prompted more, and more sophisticated, arguments about constitutional law than about the nature of prayer. But fortunately Senator Jack Danforth is an ordained Episcopal priest and is the only person ever to receive degrees from the Yale Law School and the Yale Divinity School on the same day. Danforth is too polite to pose the question quite this pointedly, but the question is: Is public school prayer apt to serve authentic religion, or is it apt to be mere attitudinizing, a thin gruel of vague religious vocabulary? Religious exercises should arise from a rich tradition, and reflect that richness. Prayer, properly understood, arises from the context of the praying person's particular faith. So, Danforth argues, "for those within a religious tradition, it simply is not true that one prayer is as good as any other."

One person's prayer may not be any sort of prayer to another person whose devotion is to a different tradition. To children from certain kinds of Christian families, a "nondenominational" prayer

175

that makes no mention of Jesus Christ would be incoherent. The differences between Christian and Jewish expressions of piety are obvious; the differences between Protestants and Roman Catholics regarding, for example, Mary and the saints are less obvious, but they are not trivial to serious religious sensibilities. And as Danforth says, a lowest-common-denominator prayer would offend all devout persons. "Prayer that is so general and so diluted as not to offend those of most faiths is not prayer at all. True prayer is robust prayer. It is bold prayer. It is almost by definition sectarian prayer."

Liturgical reform in the Roman Catholic and Episcopal churches has occasioned fierce controversies that seem disproportionate, if not unintelligible, to persons who are ignorant of or indifferent about those particular religious traditions. But liturgy is a high art and a serious business because it is designed to help turn minds from worldly distractions, toward transcendent things. Collective prayer should express a shared inner state, one that does not occur easily and spontaneously. A homogenized religious recitation, perfunctorily rendered by children who have just tumbled in from a bus or playground, is not apt to arise from the individual wills, as real prayer must.

Buddhists are among the almost 90 religious organizations in America that have at least 50,000 members. Imagine, Danforth urges, the Vietnamese Buddhist in a fourth-grade class in, say, Mississippi. How does that child deal with a "voluntary" prayer that is satisfactory to the local Baptists? Or imagine a child from America's growing number of Muslims, for whom prayer involves turning toward Mecca and prostrating oneself. Muslim prayer is adoration of Allah; it involves no requests and asks no blessing, as most Christian prayers do. Reagan says: "No one will ever convince me that a moment of voluntary prayer will harm a child . . . " Danforth asks: How is America—or religion—served by the embarrassment of children who must choose between insincere compliance with, or conscientious abstention from, a ritual?

In a nation where millions of adults (biologically speaking) affect the Jordache look or whatever designer's whim is *de rigueur*, peer pressure on children is not a trivial matter. Supporters of Reagan's amendment argue that a nine-year-old is "free" to absent himself or otherwise abstain from a "voluntary" prayer—an activity involving his classmates and led by that formidable authority figure, his teacher. But that argument is akin to one heard a century ago from persons who said child labor laws infringed the precious freedom of children to contract to work 10-hour days in coal mines.

To combat the trivializing of religion and the coercion of children who take their own religious traditions seriously, Danforth suggests enacting the following distinction: "The term 'voluntary prayer' shall not include any prayer composed, prescribed, directed, supervised, or organized by an official or employee of a state or local government agency, including public school principals and teachers." When religion suffers the direct assistance of nervous politicians, the result is apt to confirm the judgment of the child who prayed not to God but for God because "if anything happens to Him, we're properly sunk."

It is, to say no more, curious that, according to some polls, more Americans favor prayers in schools than regularly pray in church. Supermarkets sell processed cheese and instant mashed potatoes, so many Americans must like bland substitutes for real things. But it is one thing for the nation's palate to tolerate frozen waffles; it is another and more serious thing for the nation's soul to be satisfied with add-water-and-stir instant religiosity. When government acts as liturgist for a pluralistic society, the result is bound to be a purée that is tasteless, in several senses.

June 7, 1982

Unconstitutional Silence

The U.S. Constitution has, according to a New Jersey judge and the American Civil Liberties Union, been ravished. The instrument of this outrage is a New Jersey law which the judge says "is unconstitutional on its face and as applied, in that it violates the First and Fourteenth Amendments . . . and that immediate and irreparable injury will result to plaintiffs. . . . "

Whoa! The law that is pregnant with such awfulness says:

"Principals and teachers in each public elementary and secondary school . . . shall permit students to observe a one-minute period of silence to be used solely at the discretion of the individual student, before the opening exercises of each school day, for quiet and private contemplation or introspection."

But according to the ACLU, that violates the constitutional guarantee against "establishment" of religion. What is the injury—the irreparable injury—that a minute of silence will cause to anyone? No doubt a few children and parents will find it offensive that someone may use the minute for prayer. But since when is it an "injury" to be offended by what might be going on in someone's head? Such chaos is what a society comes to when it believes that every grievance should be expressed as a conflict of individual rights, and that every conflict should be adjudicated.

The ACLU's bullying litigation is designed not to protect the plaintiff (a student) but to compel others to behave as the plaintiff prefers. A lawyer for New Jersey's legislature argues that the law is constitutional because it is "neutral with respect to any religious content." The legislator who sponsored it says: "All we did was provide the opportunity for contemplation," and regarding the possibility that someone might silently pray, he says: "Who has the right, in this day and age, to determine that any thoughts someone has could violate the Constitution?"

An ACLU lawyer says New Jersey must "prove that nowhere among the purposes of the law is the opportunity for prayer." Opportunity? Perhaps the ACLU will soon say that a state "establishes" religion unless its schools make contemplation impossible for even a minute. (Many schools do make it difficult.) But even today, after some bizarre Supreme Court rulings, the ACLU lawyer may be correct about what New Jersey must prove.

The authors of the "establishment" clause wanted to guarantee that government action would be impartial among religions. They did not intend to require that it be neutral between religion and secularism. Still less did they intend what the Supreme Court has mandated—that any law must have "a secular legislative purpose and a primary effect that neither advances nor inhibits religion."

Such fine-spun formulations result when the Court tortures the Constitution to yield particular social policies. Consider, for example, the abortion decision of 10 years ago this week.

That decision is generally conceded to be intellectual train wrecks of carelessly assembled language—"potential life" before "viability," and "the capability of meaningful life." Pro-abortion extremists—those who favor unlimited abortion on demand, achieved by incoherent judicial fiat—are reduced to arguing that "no one knows" when life begins, but that the Court knows when "meaningful life" begins. That is, biology is unfathomable, but philosophy and theology are simple.

The reverse is true: The justices cannot know when "meaningful" life begins, but every high school biology student knows that life begins at conception. The argument is about when legal protections accorded to persons should be extended to that life.

Such confusions and insincerities are produced by result-oriented judges who labor to wring particular social policies from broad constitutional language, and who produce rococo rationalizations. The ACLU is a political organization pursuing its agenda primarily through litigation rather than legislation—often an authoritarian shortcut around the democratic process. It construes the Constitution the way a few religious extremists construe scripture. It is impatient with ambiguity, and defends as a merely literal reading of the document various policies that bear no discernible relation to the intention of the authors.

I oppose "voluntary" school prayer for two reasons: The collective speaking of words cannot be truly voluntary, and if the words are to be inoffensively ecumenical, they must be mere mush. But the ACLU is fanatical when it finds silence a menace to constitutional values.

Heaven (if the ACLU's thought police will pardon the word) forbid, but perhaps the ACLU's real worry is this: Getting adolescents quiet for even 60 seconds is a miracle, and miracles can arouse religious sentiments. There are precedents.

January 20, 1983

The ACLU and Sobriety

There is this to be said for the American Civil Liberties Union: It provides perfect examples of how not to argue about public policy. Consider its complaint about Maryland's "sobriety checkpoints."

Maryland police set up checkpoints, announced by large signs, at places where there are reasons for suspecting a high incidence of drunken driving, such as where there have been many alcohol-related accidents. Maryland's attorney general says:

"Vehicles are not stopped at random or on whim . . . *all* vehicles must stop. Motorists are given written information about the checkpoint program and the debilitating effects of alcohol. The stop lasts from 15 to 30 seconds. No search of the vehicle or its occupants occurs. No driver is asked, or required, to take any sort of test. A driver may be further detained only if the trooper's observations during the brief encounter reveal tell-tale signs of intoxication or impairment."

The Supreme Court struck down a Delaware practice of stopping cars at random to check drivers' licenses and registrations. The court held that Delaware was violating the Fourth Amendment ban on "unreasonable searches and seizures," in part because police selecting cars at random exercise unconstrained discretion. The court suggested that halting all oncoming traffic might be permissible. Still, the ACLU says Maryland's checkpoints constitute an "unreasonable" seizure. The dispute is about reasonableness. The attorney general says the amendment protects against "arbitrary, capricious, unbridled" police intrusion. He says the contact between the citizen and the state at a checkpoint is comparable to that at a toll booth. The intrusion is "minimal," and far less than what we submit to at airports. An ACLU lawyer says:

"If you refuse to stop or roll down your window or be properly sheeplike, you'll discover how 'minimal' the police consider the matter . . . of course, drunken driving is awful, and, of course, roadblocks may 'work.' But there are dozens of offenses as vile as drunken driving. It would 'work' to allow the police to search everyone entering a schoolhouse for drugs, alcohol or weapons; to demand, in a crackdown against shoplifting, that everyone carrying bags of merchandise during the Christmas season show the police proof of purchase; or periodically to search homes in selected neighborhoods for heroin, pistols, stolen goods or escaped prisoners. We disposed of these alternatives a couple of hundred years ago, when we decided not to be an authoritarian society of snarling mercenaries and sniveling peasants. . . . "

Gracious! We are, I guess, "sheeplike" when we stop at red lights. By ACLU reasoning, red lights are not "minimal" state intrusion in our lives because if we do not stop, the consequences will be serious. The ACLU lawyer puts disparaging quotation marks around the word "work." Let us be clear: if checkpoints work— and they do—many thousands of lives can be saved. Are there "dozens" of offenses "as vile as" drunken driving? None causes suffering on the scale of drunken driving—a quarter of a million dead in a decade.

If drugs, alcohol and weapons were killing 26,000 a year in schools, we would search everyone entering a school at least as thoroughly as we search airline passengers. Searching a house is hardly comparable to stopping a car for 30 seconds. Yes, a suffocating police presence would be a disproportionate response to shoplifting: The "reasonableness" of a government action is, to some extent, a function of the importance of the public interest served. But drunken driving is terrible and demonstrably deterrable behavior. The ACLU would sacrifice lives on the theory that tyranny lies down the road from the checkpoints.

Checkpoints are the thin end of the wedge of authoritarianism, a step toward a society of snarling mercenaries and sniveling peasants? Such hysteria is a product of "slippery slope" reasoning. Yes, police measures could become disproportionate. But any police force "could" (in the sense that it is imaginable) become a Gestapo. Taxation "could" become confiscation. But prudence does not dictate doing without police and taxation.

The ACLU thinks Maryland is on a slippery slope—how will Maryland stop from sliding into tyranny? But all government takes place on a slippery slope. Anything can be imagined carried to unreasonable lengths. That is why the most important four words in politics are: up to a point. Are we for liberty, equality, military strength, high employment, low inflation, environmental protection? Sure—up to a point. The point is where the cost to other values is disproportionate to the incremental gain.

The Founding Fathers, in proscribing "unreasonable" searches and seizures, allowed for reasonable ones. Sensible government is impossible when the citizenry succumbs to the corrosive suspicion that governors are incapable of reasonable distinctions. It is mindless to insist that any practice that conceivably could be carried to extremes is, for that reason, intolerable even when carefully circumscribed. As Woodrow Wilson said, a clear principle of representative government is that "somebody must be trusted."

Some self-styled "conservatives" express a feckless hostility to government (the Defense Department exempted, of course). The ACLU has a liberal variant of that attitude. Of course many ACLU members are complacent about expanding government power in education, culture, racial entitlements ("affirmative action") and other areas requiring sensitive distinctions.

Certain restraints as well as certain rights are part of a sensible society. Drivers have a right to be free from unreasonable intrusion from the police—and a right not to have drunks hurtling a ton of steel at them. But enough about rights. Driving is a privilege. It is conferred by the state that certifies competence. It is revokable when certain duties are not fulfilled. Every driver has a duty to cooperate with reasonable efforts to reduce drunken driving, which is taking American lives about four times faster than the Vietnam War did. Unfortunately, Americans speak so constantly—and truculently—the language of rights that "duty" is one of the less frequently heard four-letter words.

January 31, 1983

The ACLU's Second Thoughts on Freedom

CHICAGO—In this city, wonderfully lumpy with unmelted ethnic neighborhoods, in Ukrainian restaurants, on October 3, glasses will be raised to celebrate Walter Polovchak's birthday. The littlest defector is not so little now. He will be 18 and secure from the Soviet regime and the American Civil Liberties Union.

Walter was born in the Ukraine. When he was 12, his parents were allowed, inexplicably, to emigrate to the United States. Walter's father indicated his intention to return: Instead of selling his home, he "lent" it to a neighbor and gave other possessions to a KGB official. The Soviet Embassy in Washington pressured the father to require Walter and his sister to return with him. The sister soon turned 18 and was safe. Walter, having seen what makes America great—freedom and the Chicago Cubs—sought asylum. The ACLU sided tenaciously with the father. It is deplorable that only the calendar—Walter's birthday—not America's courts gave Walter a decisive victory.

The closing of Walter's case coincides with the publication of a book (*The Politics of the ACLU* by William Donahue) that shows how the ACLU has become a lobby for the left's agenda. The ACLU's support for the right to distribute child pornography or use heroin is less illuminating than this: Racial quota systems, once vigorously opposed, now are as vigorously supported. This illustrates the ACLU's result-oriented approach to constitutional rights.

Aaron Wildavsky, political scientist at Berkeley and a former ACLU member, says the ACLU has reversed traditional American thinking about equality. The traditional sequence has been: Equality of rights guarantees equality of opportunity, which will produce satisfactory equality of conditions. The ACLU reverses the sequence: Equality of condition is a prerequisite for equality of opportunity in the exercise of equal rights.

The contradiction in the ACLU program is that a government promoting equality must be powerful, but the critique of society implicit in the ACLU's ideology undermines governmental authority. It does so by defining government as the keystone of the "system" that sustains unequal conditions and therefore makes a mockery of rights and opportunity. Another glaring ACLU contradiction concerns children.

Children once were chattel of their parents, but intelligent laws have limited parental discretion—regarding the employment, schooling and medical care of children. No one, least of all the ACLU, says the law should not abridge parental sovereignty or take cognizance of children's rights.

The ACLU believes the civil rights of a child under 18 include the right to have an abortion even when both parents are opposed. Indeed, the ACLU believes a minor's civil rights are violated if her parents are even notified when she acquires contraceptives from a federally funded clinic. The ACLU has detected civil-rights ravishments in school dress codes.

Fifty states would remove Walter from the custody of parents who abused him. But the ACLU supports the right of Walter's father to commit the ultimate and unappealable abuse of consigning him forever to a prison society.

Alan Dershowitz is a professor at Harvard Law School and a hyperkinetic litigant on behalf of civil liberties. He says the ACLU's behavior regarding Walter, seen in the light of policies regarding children's rights to abortions and other matters, can be understood only in terms of "an unwillingness to criticize communism."

ACLU advocates say that those judicial and other government actions that helped Walter were "political" in that they took cognizance of the nature of the Soviet regime. But of course. The problem would have been different had Walter been resisting return to, say, Denmark, where he would have been free to decide his future. Suppose Walter were black and resisting return to South Africa. Who believes the ACLU would have opposed him? While the ACLU was opposing him, the New Jersey ACLU was defending a child in a case similar except for the fact he was resisting return to Chile.

Walter's case involved ludicrous governmental brooding about whether, were he returned, he would face persecution. The Soviet regime, which tortures its most distinguished citizen, Andrei Sakharov, would take up where it left off with Walter who, as punishment for his Catholicism, was kept at school on Christmas Eve to chant Leninist slogans. Ten years of comprehensive noncompliance with the Helsinki Accords demonstrates that the Soviet regime persecutes everyone guilty of an appetite for freedom.

Walter's case is a splendid and timely embarrassment for the various Washington bureaucracies that are toiling to produce an atmosphere of false cordiality for the summit. The cordiality is supposed to facilitate the achievement at the summit of . . . more accords.

September 26, 1985

Tactile Government

BALTIMORE—On a recent visit here, I saw two stirring sights. One was a wisp of a child, a severely handicapped four-year-old, seated in a wheelchair, his arms in slings, maneuvering a fork with his mouth, exhausting his body but not his chirpy spirit in a desperately difficult struggle to feed himself a bit of cheese sandwich. The other was the face of a man watching the boy.

Mayor William Donald Schaefer has a large head, like Franklin Roosevelt. FDR's face seemed made for that famous smile, but Schaefer's countenance, although not exactly woeful, is creased like that of a basset hound. While Schaefer was visiting the John F. Kennedy Institute for Handicapped Children, where briskly matter-of-fact professionals do their unsung work healing bodies and unlocking minds, a change, a slight tautness, came over his face, a change that was the more striking for being so controlled that it was barely discernible.

At the national level, government is a matter of abstractions and formulas. At the local level, government is elemental, even tactile. The sort of human feelings visible on Schaefer's face are a reward, sometimes a risk, of government on a human scale.

The Kennedy Institute performs social services as well as basic research. It is the last hope for some children and the primary hope for some scientists, and it is all of this on a budget of just $11 million a year. Now federal cuts may cost it $3 million. It is up to Baltimore, the community as well as the government, to patch and caulk and keep things afloat.

Fortunately, Schaefer embodies his community more completely than even Richard Daley or Fiorello LaGuardia embodied Chicago and New York. Baltimoreans are only human, so when approached by someone asking them to do good works, their instinct is to take evasive action. But when galvanizing Baltimore's public-spirited sector, Schaefer resembles a German shepherd that has been to finishing school: He is quiet, but you'd better do what he says.

At almost exactly the moment Schaefer was watching the boy struggle to feed himself, Texas A & M University, casting about for some way to augment its near-perfection, signed a new football coach to a contract worth $1.7 million over six years. We are a nation that spares no expense on behalf of the strongest bodies.

On the great contemporary question of whether Atari or Intelevision makes the best video games by which the nation can further drug itself, I remain agnostic. But of this I am sure: It is disgusting for the limbs and minds of children to remain unmended because of a shortage of money in a nation where television commercials, aimed at mass audiences of millions, advertise video disc machines for "under $500." Whatever else can be said—and few adjectives are pungent enough—to describe a society characterized by million-dollar college football coaches and expensive adult toys, it is not a society that has any excuse for neglecting its needy.

I shall make myself tiresome by saying again and again and again that America is undertaxed. That conclusion is compelled by considerations of equity as well as national security. President Reagan was right to cut marginal tax rates, which were having irrational disincentive effects. But especially in older cities like Baltimore, there is an inverse relationship between equity problems and revenue sources for dealing with them. So national revenue measures (such as a value-added tax, or a $1 tax on a gallon of gasoline) are needed.

On the other hand, Schaefer's record supports some of Reagan's essential points. They are that local communities can rise to local challenges more than they realize; that enlarged responsibilities will attract larger persons into local politics; and that $1 raised and spent by someone like Schaefer is apt to do more good than $10 dispersed by the federal bureaucracy 40 miles down the road.

When Reagan became America's most important political figure, Schaefer and others similarly situated became almost as important, not least to Reagan. The moral correctness of Reagan's policy of dispersing responsibilities depends on the ability of Schaefer and others to elicit new material and spiritual resources from their communities. Schaefer must practice what Reagan preaches. By this division of labor, the Democrat can vindicate the Republican.

The 1930s called for an FDR—a great energizer and mobilizer—at the national level. The 1980s call for FDRs at the local level. Of course, something called for need not come forth. But in Baltimore it has.

January 24, 1982

Phillip Becker: A Boy

The Supreme Court's refusal to hear California's appeal means Phillip Becker's parents have successfully asserted a right to block lifesaving surgery. So Phillip, 13, will die prematurely, probably slowly and painfully, perhaps suddenly, drowning in his blood from bleeding into his lungs. Surely, the reason his parents have promoted, and the law has allowed, this is: He is retarded.

He has Down's syndrome (Mongolism), a chromosomal defect that involves varying degrees of retardation and physical abnormalities. He has a common heart defect, correctable by standard surgery. Uncorrected, it probably will kill him by 30. The pattern is progressive debilitation until reduced to a torturous bed-to-chair existence, with headaches, chest pains and fainting spells during which the sufferer turns a terrifying blue-black. Already Phillip suffers attacks of weakness and bluishness. His heart must work three times harder than a normal heart. Blood is pumped into his lungs under dangerously high pressure, damaging the lungs' thin vessels.

Already he may have passed the threshold of dangerous harm; soon his condition may be inoperable, his decline irreversible.

California, which would have paid, called the surgery a "necessity of life." The Beckers responded with three inharmonious arguments. They said the operation was too risky. There are special risks in surgery with Down's children, but the risk of death in Phillip's case was well within conscionable range, even when not weighed against the awful alternative certainty. Anyway, the Beckers simultaneously argued against surgery because of fear it would succeed. They said they feared he would survive them and, bereft of their attention, might someday receive care so poor that life would not be worth living.

Although they assert a right to make it probable that Phillip will predecease them, they never considered allowing him to live at home. They say he "is an integral part of our family," but only claim to visit him six times a year. The home for handicapped children says the visits are even fewer, that "Phillip doesn't know who his parents are," and that he calls many men "Dad." For years his parents have fought a partial and temporary severance of their autonomy over a child they never even brought home from the hospital and rarely see. What might have been accomplished if the energy devoted to abbreviating Phillip's future had been devoted to providing for it?

However that may be, the Beckers' argument against surgery on the ground that it might mean Phillip might someday lead a life not worth living was superseded by their third argument: That his life is inherently not worth living. They solicited a letter from a pediatrician who said that Phillip leads "a life that I consider devoid of those qualities which give it human dignity." He said Phillip's "simple and innocent nature" makes him a "natural victim" of people bent on "taking his money." Phillip might not "fit into modern suburban society."

A man who talks like that should not announce that someone else is deficient in dignity. I yield to no one in my reverence for pediatricians when the subject is tonsils and the like, but is pediatric medicine definitive on the subject of human worth? I will not speculate about the worth of those who presume to deprecate Phillip's worth, or about the quality of life in a society that, on "quality of life" grounds, truncates a life like Phillip's. But this is tiresome: Just when society is beginning to acknowledge an obligation to nurture the significant fulfillment of even the limited potentialities of retarded citizens, the Becker case works to cast those citizens into legal limbo as less than persons with a full right to life.

My aim is not to demonstrate the demonstrable: that respect for parental sovereignty has here been carried to absurd, not to mention lethal, lengths, unthinkable were Phillip not retarded. (There even has been court-ordered treatment, against parents' wishes, of deformities that threatened not the lives but only the psychological well-being of normal children.) My aim is to stress this: The idea that the value of human life varies with intelligence is an idea at war with our civilization's core belief in the intrinsic and equal value of lives.

Down's newborns have been allowed to starve to death in hospitals by parents who refused consent for surgery to correct intestinal blockages. In *The Making of a Surgeon*, William Nolan recalls a surgeon saying to a pediatrician that he wouldn't worry if a particular patient died during upcoming surgery. The pediatrician replied, "Oh, now I get it. You're doing a Mongoloid." The Beckers testified that one reason they never considered allowing Phillip to live with them is that they did not want him to be a "burden" to his brothers. One reason they blocked the operation was fear that his two brothers might have to be their brother's keeper.

It is often said that someone "suffers from" Down's syndrome. But Down's people lead happy lives when parents and other friends allow their own lives to be enriched by loving and being loved by them. The suffering Phillip faces is premeditated and preventable, so let there be no mincing euphemisms about "passive euthanasia." Euthanasia means "pleasant death," a release from suffering. Phillips's *life* is pleasant.

People ignorant about retardation, or eager to believe the worst, often produce or seize upon excessively pessimistic prognoses about retarded children's potentialities. Those prognoses become self-fulfilling, even fatal, when used to justify neglect. Those who know Phillip best consider him gentle and promising. His teacher says that he is "working at a very high level" for any retarded child. He assembles Legos and operates a recorder. If allowed to live, he could work in a sheltered workshop and live in a supervised group home with other retarded adults. He is in a Boy Scout troop. He makes his bed, feeds the cat and does other chores where he lives. His taste in TV shows runs to *Six Million Dollar Man*.

The Down's child I know best is 7. He is learning to read but prefers *Happy Days*, the Washington Bullets and the Baltimore Orioles. These impeccable tastes help explain why neighborhood children treat him as what he, like Phillip, is: a boy.

April 14, 1980

"A Trip Toward Death"

Who is Phillip Becker that so many have been so mindful of him? I wrote about him when his parents successfully asserted a right to block life-prolonging surgery to correct his heart defect. Without the surgery he probably will die prematurely, slowly and painfully, possibly drowning from blood in his lungs. Now a California court has given Phillip to the custody of another couple. Surgery may occur if his biological parents do not erect yet another legal impediment. But it now may be too late for surgery.

Phillip, 14, has Down's syndrome, a chromosomal defect involving retardation and physical abnormalities. The Beckers opposed surgery on two grounds: It might fail, and it might not. Doctors testified to a 90 to 97 per cent chance of success, but the Beckers said it was too risky. And they said it might succeed and Phillip, surviving them, might receive care so poor his life would not be worth living. But they cited a pediatrician who said Phillip's life *now* is devoid of "all qualities of human dignity," he is "so innocent" he would be a "natural victim" of people bent on "taking his money" and is unsuited for modern society. And his father said it would be best for everyone, including Phillip, if he were dead.

Does the constitutional guarantee of equal protection of the law allow the right to life to vary with intelligence? Mr. Becker has said he would not deny such surgery to one of his normal sons. Would any court have allowed the denial were Phillip not retarded? A court did say the Beckers could exercise absolute discretion regarding medical care for a child who might become a "burden." The sovereignty that the court gave the Beckers over Phillip seems especially grotesque considering testimony about the sort of responsibility they have exercised.

Until Pat and Herb Heath filed their action for guardianship, the Beckers never allowed Phillip, who has been institutionalized since birth, a single night in their home. They claimed to visit him six times a year; others said the visits were even fewer. The Beckers say he would be better off dead than surviving them and being without their vigilance. Vigilance? A court has now asked: "Why was he still in diapers at age 6? Why did all his teeth rot? Why didn't he have pre-school?" Why was it necessary for another adult to call the Beckers' attention to the care deficiency at one place they institutionalized him?

The judge who supported the Beckers emphasized their fear that Phillip would be a "burden" to their other sons, who might have to be their brother's keeper. Apparently the judge was ignorant of the fact that the Heaths were eager to adopt Phillip. They had been visiting Phillip and bringing him to their home (and Cub Scout pack) until the Beckers forbade contact with the Heaths, causing attested injury to his health. Pat Heath told *60 Minutes:* "I can handle Phillip being dead, because we believe in heaven and we believe he'll be in a much better place. What I can't handle is for him to spend two years dying an agonizing death while adult people sit around and fight about who has the right. That's killing." The Heaths went to superior court.

The earlier case involved California against the Beckers, who benefited from the presumption in favor of parental rather than state judgment regarding a child. But the Heaths' action in Judge William Fernandez's superior court posed a choice between two sets of parents, the "psychological" and "biological" parents. It turned not on the narrow issue of who should make a particular decision affecting Phillip, not on a parental right to assess medical risk. It turned on who should make decisions affecting the rest of Phillip's life. It turned on the detriment already inflicted by "the great parenting fault of the Beckers," and the detriment that would be inflicted by severing Phillip from his "de facto" parents, the Heaths.

Fernandez said children have rights and courts must seek the "least detrimental alternative" for those like Phillip. He said Phillip's parents felt "he should never be close to anyone." Although "ripe for affection and love," he never received from his parents "nurturing" or "constancy of affection and love." Each is a "sine qua non of parenting." A true parental relationship exists between Phillip and the Heaths. Phillip "suffered harm by the parenting of the Beckers"—physical, medical and severe emotional harm, and "stigmatization." And he can "never receive any benefit from custody with the Beckers because they have no expectations for him and will therefore do nothing to allow him to win a place into our society."

It is reprehensible that the Beckers continue to judge their son even though by all accounts, except their own, they barely know Phillip. They say he is an ineducable "low Down's" who cannot talk, communicate, write his name, draw, cook or form loving attachments. But Fernandez says: "Whenever the Becker side claimed he couldn't do something, the witnesses for Phillip Becker proved the counter."

Fernandez says Phillip has been denied his right to "habilitation," which includes training. Phillip is "emancipatable" and should have a right to choose, through the "substitute judgment" of the court, between being "warehoused" or living "bathed in the love and affection" of the Heaths.

Fernandez described Phillip's case as a wonderful and irrational tragedy. Wonderful because so many have worked for Phillip, braving "a storm of parental indignation including scathing cross-examination and a multimillion-dollar lawsuit." Tragic because "I weep uncontrollably" when reading evidence of Phillip's strangling illness, evidence that he is "beginning on his trip toward death," and knows it. (By years of delay the Beckers may have so raised the risks of surgery that his premature death has begun.) The tragedy is irrational because the case has consumed so much time and money that could have been used "to make the last part of Phillip Becker's life happier than the earlier part."

I conclude by mentioning two things, only the second of which is really relevant. I am being sued by the Beckers, who think that what I have reported injures their reputations, and who mistakenly think they have been libeled. Jonathan Will, 9, trout fisherman and Orioles fan, has Down's syndrome.

August 31, 1981

Reagan's Expansion of Civil Rights

Civil rights "activists," so active denouncing President Reagan, have not noticed, or will not acknowledge, that he is significantly expanding civil rights protections. That is the importance of cases like that of "Baby Jane Doe" in New York.

The government is seeking medical records in the case of the infant born with spina bifida and excessive brain fluid. Without surgery the baby is expected to die within two years. The parents oppose surgery. Doctors say—guess, really—that the child would be "severely" retarded and would die as a young adult. The federal government may seek treatment the parents oppose.

The administration is not acting on an ideological quirk. It is giving a reasonable interpretation to a civil rights law, Section 504 of the Rehabilitation Act of 1973. Section 504 prohibits discrimination solely on the basis of handicap. The administration is not trying to sever Section 504 from medical judgment. There is no notion of an obligation for futile treatment that merely prolongs dying or extends life a short span. But treatment should not be withheld to cause the death of a newborn because parents decide, on the basis of doctors' guesses, that the child's life would be inconvenient, disappointing or without acceptable "quality."

After parents and doctors agreed in Indiana in 1982 to starve a Down's syndrome baby rather than perform routine surgery, Reagan ordered regulations requiring the posting in hospitals of notices that discriminatory denial of care to handicapped infants is prohibited. A hotline was established for reporting violations.

The *New York Times*, which favors aggressive federal action to protect the right to vote or to a safe work place, denounces the government as "Big Brother" when it moves to protect an infant's right to life. If a parent and an employer decided to employ the parents' healthy child at less than the minimum wage, the *Times* would demand a federal posse. But when the government considers intervening to prevent parents and doctors from causing death by withholding treatment, the *Times* champions parental sovereignty.

Such sovereignty is highly conditioned. Parents cannot abuse or neglect their children, or keep them from schooling, or prevent them from receiving certain vital medical care, such as transfusions, on religious grounds.

The *Wall Street Journal*, which at least has a crazy consistency (it doesn't much like government, the Pentagon excepted) denounces the administration for "harassment" of parents and doctors and for expanding "the role of Washington in our lives." The *Journal* wants the rights of handicapped newborns allocated by the private sector, by parents and doctors. But surely even conservatives of the *Journal*'s stripe can concede that the federal government, in addition to running the Navy, can legitimately protect babies from being condemned because of imperfections.

Many editorialists insist on deference toward doctors' judgments. In the Indiana case, a doctor testified that the baby should die because the baby would never achieve a "minimally accepta- ble" quality of life. The doctor decreed that "some" Down's syn- drome persons are "mere blobs"; and that he had never known a Down's syndrome person "able to be gainfully employed in any- thing other than a sheltered workshop . . . that could be self- supporting. . . . These children are quite incapable of telling us what they feel, and what they sense. . . . "

The moral squalor of that statement (should lifesaving treat- ment be denied to all economically marginal persons?) is exceeded by its ignorance: I'll introduce the doctor to Down's syndrome cit- izens—sorry, doctor, that's what they are—who work outside shel- tered workshops and who can tell what they feel and sense about people like him. Clearly, some doctors claim authority concerning matters that are in no sense medical. Note the doctor's opinion about the "acceptable"—to whom? the AMA?—quality of life.

A person who calls the police to protect a child that is being abused next door is called a good citizen. A nurse who tells the government that a baby is suffering the ultimate abuse is de- nounced by editorialists as a "spy" or "police informant" or "busy- body." A professor writes that the hospital notice and hotline "in- sult" all doctors as potential child abusers. But do child abuse laws insult all parents? Editorialists who have favored sending civil-rights enforcers, even the Army, into the South now express horror about "Baby Doe squads" descending on hospitals.

Why the hysteria? Perhaps it is because editorial writers con- sider doctors as peers—fellow professionals and equally infallible. It is one thing to urge federal enforcers on businessmen, but re- stricting the discretion of professionals like us is an affront. Fur- thermore, many members of the social stratum from which edito- rial writers come cannot cope with the fact of permanent defects, especially in children, defects that neither a new law nor a new antibiotic nor a new curriculum can cure. Parents who conjugate French verbs for their superbabies are unnerved by what they think is the meaninglessness of a life that will not include reading *New York Times* editorials.

But American history is a story of progressive inclusiveness as rights have been extended beyond healthy, white, property-holding males. America today is on the threshold of another great inclusion, that of handicapped, and especially mentally handicapped, per- sons. This is Ronald Reagan's doing, and he is getting neither help nor credit from the self-appointed custodians of the nation's conscience regarding civil rights.

November 13, 1983

The Short Life and Long Dying of Infant Doe

The baby was born in Bloomington, Indiana, the sort of academic community where medical facilities are more apt to be excellent than moral judgments are. Like one of every 700 or so babies, this one had Down's syndrome, a genetic defect involving varying degrees of retardation and, sometimes, serious physical defects. The baby needed serious but feasible surgery to enable food to reach its stomach. The parents refused the surgery, and presumably refused to yield custody to any of the couples eager to become the baby's guardians. The parents chose to starve their baby to death.

Their lawyer concocted an Orwellian euphemism for this refusal of potentially lifesaving treatment—"Treatment to do nothing." It is an old story: Language must be mutilated when a perfumed rationalization of an act is incompatible with a straightforward description of the act.

Indiana courts, accommodating the law to the Zeitgeist, refused to order surgery, and thus sanctioned the homicide. Common sense and common usage require use of the word "homicide." The law usually encompasses homicides by negligence. The Indiana killing was worse. It was the result of premeditated, aggressive, tenacious action, in the hospital and in courts.

Such homicides can no longer be considered aberrations, or culturally incongruous. They are part of a social program to serve the convenience of adults by authorizing adults to destroy inconvenient young life. The parents' legal arguments, conducted in private, reportedly emphasized—what else?—"freedom of choice." The freedom to choose to kill inconvenient life is being extended, precisely as predicted, beyond fetal life to categories of inconvenient infants, such as Down's syndrome babies.

There is no reason—none—to doubt that if the baby had not had Down's syndrome the operation would have been ordered without hesitation, almost certainly, by the parents or, if not by them, by the courts. Therefore the baby was killed because it was retarded. I defy the parents and their medical and legal accomplices to explain why, by the principles affirmed in this case, parents do not have a right to kill by calculated neglect any Down's syndrome child—regardless of any medical need—or any other baby that parents decide would be inconvenient.

Indeed, the parents' lawyer implied as much when, justifying the starvation, he emphasized that even if successful the surgery would not have corrected the retardation. That is, the Down's syndrome was sufficient reason for starving the baby. But the broader message of this case is that being an unwanted baby is a capital offense.

In 1973 the Supreme Court created a virtually unrestrictable right to kill fetuses. Critics of the ruling were alarmed because the Court failed to dispatch the burden of saying why the fetus, which unquestionably is alive, is not protectable life. Critics were alarmed also because the Court, having incoherently emphasized "viability," offered no intelligible, let alone serious, reason why birth should be the point at which discretionary killing stops. Critics feared what the Indiana homicide demonstrates: The killing will not stop.

The values and passions, as well as the logic of some portions of the "abortion rights" movement, have always pointed beyond abortion, toward something like the Indiana outcome, which affirms a broader right to kill. Some people have used the silly argument that it is impossible to know when life begins. (The serious argument is about when a "person" protectable by law should be said to exist.) So what could be done about the awkward fact that a newborn, even a retarded newborn, is so incontestably alive?

The trick is to argue that the lives of certain kinds of newborns, like the lives of fetuses, are not sufficiently "meaningful"—a word that figured in the 1973 ruling—to merit any protection that inconveniences an adult's freedom of choice.

The Indiana parents consulted with doctors about the "treatment" they chose. But this was not at any point, in any sense, a medical decision. Such homicides in hospitals are common and will become more so now that a state's courts have given them an imprimatur. There should be interesting litigation now that Indiana courts—whether they understand this or not—are going to decide which categories of newborns (besides Down's syndrome children) can be killed by mandatory neglect.

Hours after the baby died, the parents' lawyer was on the *CBS Morning News* praising his clients' "courage." He said, "The easiest thing would have been to defer, let somebody else make that decision." Oh? Someone had to deliberate about whether or not to starve the baby? When did it become natural, even necessary, in Indiana for parents to sit around debating whether to love or starve their newborns?

The lawyer said it was a "no-win situation" because "there would have been horrific trauma—trauma to the child who would never have enjoyed a—a quality of life of—of any sort, trauma to the family, trauma to society." In this "no-win" situation, the parents won: The county was prevented from ordering surgery; prospective adopters were frustrated; the baby is dead. Furthermore, how is society traumatized whenever a Down's syndrome baby is not killed? It was, I believe, George Orwell who warned that insincerity is the enemy of sensible language.

Someone should counsel the counselor to stop babbling about Down's syndrome children not having "any sort" of quality of life. The task of convincing communities to provide services and human sympathy for the retarded is difficult enough without incoherent lawyers laying down the law about whose life does and whose does not have "meaning."

The *Washington Post* headlined its report: "The Demise of 'Infant Doe' " (the name used in court). "Demise," indeed. That suggests an event unplanned, even perhaps unexplained. ("The Demise of Abraham Lincoln"?) The *Post*'s story began:

"An Indiana couple, backed by the state's highest court and the family doctor, allowed their severely retarded newborn baby to die last Thursday night. . . . "

But "severely retarded" is a misjudgment (also appearing in the *New York Times*) that is both a cause and an effect of cases like the one in Indiana. There is no way of knowing, and no reason to believe, that the baby would have been "severely retarded." A small fraction of Down's syndrome children are severely retarded. The degree of retardation cannot be known at birth. Furthermore, such children are dramatically responsive to infant stimulation and other early interventions. But, like other children, they need to eat.

When a commentator has a direct personal interest in an issue, it behooves him to say so. Some of my best friends are Down's syndrome citizens. (Citizens is what Down's syndrome children are if they avoid being homicide victims in hospitals.)

Jonathan Will, 10, fourth grader and Orioles fan (and the best Wiffle-ball hitter in southern Maryland), has Down's syndrome. He does not "suffer from" (as newspapers are wont to say) Down's syndrome. He suffers from nothing, except anxiety about the Orioles' lousy start.

He is doing nicely, thank you. But he is bound to have quite enough problems dealing with society—receiving rights, let alone empathy. He can do without people like Infant Doe's parents, and courts like Indiana's asserting by their actions the principle that people like him are less than fully human. On the evidence, Down's syndrome citizens have little to learn about being human from the people responsible for the death of Infant Doe.

April 22, 1982

Reagan's Two Carnegieisms

The nation's long underestimation of Ronald Reagan ended recently with the swift apotheosis of him, but soon the assessment of him will turn on the success of his policies rather than on his success in enacting them. Already there is a striking contrast between the affection for him and the skepticism about his policies.

Stock and bond prices are sagging and administration criticism of the markets resembles Mayor Beame's criticism of New York banks in 1975 for refusing to buy city bonds. The banks were right. Markets respect mathematics and they say Reagan's sums don't tally. They think he adopted optimistic projections (of growth, interest rates, spending, inflation), and they doubt that he can cut the budget enough to hold down deficits. Interest rates are the core of the contradiction in economic policy: The tax cuts are stimulating consumption but interest rates are depressing investment. And the country's problem remains the high ratio of consumption to investment. Today's interest rates do not reflect short-term demand for money. They are a prophecy embodied as a premium in the price of money, an anticipation of long-term upward pressure on inflation by Federal borrowing.

What Reagan has done so far has been relatively small and easy. Many budget cuts came from enrichments added in the 1970s to programs that didn't even exist in 1960. Most of the cuts came from the poor and the cities, constituencies of few Republicans or "boll weevil" Democrats. Even so, the President, then in his honeymoon-and-hero stage, barely won the cuts. And they were a piece of cake compared with cuts that might touch the thin skin of the middle class, which received the bulk of the benefits of social programs. Middle-class people would not be middle-class people were they not gifted at organizing and complaining. So the administration is retreating from its proposed defense spending—spending which still would have left the nation devoting a significantly smaller percentage of its GNP to defense than it did under Eisenhower.

In July, Democratic Representative Patricia Schroeder of Colorado, an implacable foe of defense spending, proposed cutting $8 billion from Reagan's defense proposals. Now some of Reagan's senior aides, who are not bashful about anticipating and perhaps forcing his decisions, say he will go much further than Schroeder proposed to go.

Regarding defense, unlike domestic policy, Reagan campaigned candidly and received a mandate for substantial spending. Domestic spending cuts were not, shall we say, stressed. The theory was that the tax cuts would be basically self-financing, stimulating the economy to produce higher revenues from lower rates.

Given the tax cuts, and the assumed unwillingness of Reagan to raise new revenues, the markets can only be assuaged by cuts of a size that must come from social security or defense. Even when Reagan was bestriding Washington's narrow world like a colossus, Congress reacted vehemently against his tentative ideas about touching social security (96–0 in the Senate, 405–13 in the House). So the knife will drift toward defense. That will please liberals who think all other spending is more important than defense spending, and won't deeply distress conservatives who think nothing is more important than reducing government spending. The public is eager to believe that everything, including security, can be had cheaply. So the public wants to believe that only "will," not costly matériel is required to restore American power. Maybe a one-minute scrap with Libya makes everything all right.

Reagan's election did not solve problems, it just made some solutions possible. But the great question of the twentieth century remains: Has the United States the stamina for what JFK called a "long twilight struggle" with the totalitarians? Reagan's retreat on defense is disheartening.

What is intended as a small retreat may become a rout as Congress seizes on defense cuts as alternatives to painful cuts in domestic spending. The political climate has changed a lot in two months. Legislators have returned from a recess during which they met many elderly persons afraid of social-security cuts, and almost everyone else was anxious about interest rates. Few people were demanding more spending on defense. Obviously, there is waste in defense; obviously, an accumulation of budget authority cannot be equated with enhanced defense. But by retreating from its defense program so soon, the administration sends a signal: Rebuilding defense is less important than reducing government spending.

Reagan's philosophy of Carnegieism—half Andrew and half Dale; 1890s capitalism and 1950s charm—will not suffice. The fact that his tax cuts were wise does not alter the fact that America is undertaxed—especially in light of the conservatives' agenda. The tax cuts were actually tax-limitation measures, counteracting tax increases imposed by inflation. By 1984 income and social security taxes will be, as a portion of personal income, about where they were in 1978. But the conservatives correct agenda for national security, and concern for social equity and prudence (billions for prisons, courts and the crumbling infrastructures—roads, bridges—of major cities), compel this conclusion: The public sector needs more resources than the revenue system currently will provide.

Many conservatives are obsessed by a crude measurement—the percentage of GNP taken by taxes. (By that measure, Britain has been much better off than Germany.) But more important is the incidence of taxes—where they fall across society and how they affect particular behavior. Today, considerations of social policy as well as fiscal needs may call for a change in the deductibility of consumer credit and mortgage interest payments. And it may be time for a value-added tax—in effect, a national sales tax. Conservatives should favor a tax on consumption, one that would reduce the progressiveness of the tax system while moving the budget toward balance.

What will history say of those who sacrifice everything, including defense, to shrink the public sector's portion of GNP? In 1950 a man was arrested for creating a public disturbance. One witness said: "He was using abusive language, calling people conservatives and all that." Such a day could come again.

September 14, 1981

Grading the President

Journalists are justly famous for impartiality in dispensing criticism to the deserving and undeserving alike. And now that a year has passed since the election of Ronald Reagan, it is time to give him a first-semester grade. When asked "How's your wife?" a wit replied, "Compared to what?" Compared to Nixon, Ford and Carter (F, C-minus and D-minus, respectively), Reagan's grade (B-minus) is a considerable improvement. But it leaves room for improvement. His domestic policy is a bit too Reaganite, and his foreign policy is not nearly Reaganite enough.

Foreign policy depends on material assets and political will. Reagan's rearmament proposals address the crisis of military capability. But his preoccupation with shrinking the government's revenue base, and budget, is cracking the consensus for rearmament. Regarding political will, the United States remains a good customer for Kaddafi's oil and a good supplier of grain and technology to the U.S.S.R. And in response to indications of continuing Soviet violations of two test-ban treaties, Reagan's administration has made only the sort of limp démarches that Carter's made.

Reagan is splendidly immune to the sort of penitential feelings Carter had about American wealth and power. He knows that people are not hungry in Bombay because people are well-fed in Boston. He has neither Nixon's nor Ford's delusions about détente. He knows that Soviet capabilities and intentions are as ominous as they were said to be by the general who was fired from the NSC staff for saying so.

Reestablishing stable deterrence is a military and diplomatic task, so two talented dynamos—Weinberger and Haig—are involved. But as has been said: One bad general is better than two good ones. Reagan must become the one general, and a good one, which means no more ad libs—even true ones—about limited nuclear war. They stimulate Europe's appeasement reflex. So far there has been a discouraging deficiency in what should be, for Reagan, a piece of cake: articulation of this country's case. By focusing so tightly on domestic policy, he seems more alarmed about OSHA than the U.S.S.R.

With AWACS opponents speaking of having "48 to 53 firm votes," it did not require magic for Reagan to make some senators seem like trained fleas. He did wield Presidential power with admirable assurance, and more impressively than any President since LBJ (a comparison that may make Reagan wince). But on a second-rate issue, Reagan lost 3 to 1 in the House and barely won in the GOP-controlled Senate. Foreign powers will draw their own conclusions about the likelihood of Congressional support for, say, the use of force to preserve the Saudi regime, or for other difficult tasks.

Domestically, Reagan has forced an overdue debate on the allocation of public and private responsibilities. In the process, middle-class people have been taught a puncturing truth: They are the big beneficiaries of the "big government" they grouse about. Conservatives have had to face a disconcerting fact: Their agenda (rearmament, prisons, tuition tax credits, etc.) is as costly as the liberal agenda. So now comes a debate about "revenue enhancements" (tax increases). Remember when bombing raids in Vietnam became "protective reaction strikes"? That is how folks talk when they are uneasy about what they are doing.

Like a child touching a hot stove, Reagan found touching social security a learning experience. It taught him that the biggest component of big government is not just popular, it expresses a cherished dimension of citizenship, a bond between generations, and Americans' acceptance of an ethic of common provision. Reagan must convince Americans that his conservatism is compatible with that ethic—that there can be conservatism with a kindly face. The federal government is a mirror in which Americans see themselves reflected. They do not want to see in it a flinty face. They feel as Simone Weil did: "One must always be ready to change sides with justice, that fugitive from the winning camp."

Until Reagan, liberals were the proponents of a plebiscitary Presidency in the Andrew Jackson and FDR style, arousing "the people" against "the interests." But Reagan keeps quoting Tom Paine's statement: "We have it in our power to begin the world over again." Oh, no we don't, and it would be hard to find a less conservative notion. Perhaps because Reagan finds the public so responsive to his plebiscitary appeals, he commits the liberals' error of exaggerating the plasticity of the world. Perhaps that is why his economic program seems to involve unrealistic assumptions about rapid changes of American behavior.

His program is still being forged on the anvil of controversy, and the controversy outside the administration is nothing compared with that within. He must choose between—he dare not split the differences between—monetarists and supply-siders, who sometimes make his administration resemble a graduate school seminar. A President cannot control the budget. (Congress can but won't.) He cannot control the Fed. (It can barely measure, let alone control, the money supply.) What a President can do is instill in the country a creative, meaning confident, orientation toward the future. Capitalism is a confidence game. Reagan's foremost achievement has been in convincing the country not that he knows the future but that he knows his own mind. (I shall be ill if I see one more photo of Mondale or some other middle-aged Democrat staring into the middle distance, "rethinking" his convictions.)

The country has many shortages (of capital, of revenues, of batters who can hit Goose Gossage), but none as serious as the shortage of patience. Without it, electoral cycles overwhelm policy cycles. But a President as serene and steadfast as Reagan is about his essential program can lengthen the public's patience. In James Gould Cozzens's wartime novel "Guard of Honor," an officer tells his wife how much he admires a general who has decided "they would do what they had to do." "What's so remarkable about that?" she asks. He replies: "It may not seem remarkable, but you'd be surprised at how many people avoid coming to that conclusion." The country thinks Reagan rather enjoys coming to that conclusion.

November 9, 1981

A Need for Simple Arithmetic

Once, H. G. Wells wrote that the upper and lower classes would someday be so different that one would eat the other. Later he changed his mind, saying the middle class is the coming thing. G. K. Chesterton praised Wells for telling a truth even though it is unexciting: "It is only the last and wildest kind of courage that can stand on a tower before 10,000 people and tell them that twice two is four." From Sacramento to Washington, America now needs leaders with the courage to do simple arithmetic in public.

Last week California got a new Republican governor and, moments later, got a new nuance. In his inaugural address, George Deukmejian, who campaigned on balancing the budget without new taxes, said California's budget could be balanced "without a net tax increase." What is that cute little word "net" doing there? Creative semantics is the key to contemporary government: It consists of talking in strange tongues lest the public learn the inevitable inconveniently early. Last fall I asked Deukmejian how he could fulfill the state constitution's requirement to balance the budget, yet not raise taxes if, as he said, the state faced a deficit of $1 billion. By cutting spending, he said. Where? I asked. Pause. He said he would abolish the coastal commission.

Well, now. That commission had better have a budget of at least $1.5 billion (larger than 19 states) because that is now the low estimate of the deficit. Last year about half the states voted tax increases to sustain services. Wisconsin's new governor is talking about an income tax surcharge. Ohio's new governor is talking about tax increases for individuals and corporations. California is not going to cut spending $1.5 billion and Deukmejian now is suggesting that his campaign rhetoric will be effectively buried before his administration is a fortnight old. Perhaps his word "net" means that new taxes will be "temporary," lasting only until recovery drives up revenues. Good news! You had no "net" increase in weight from holiday feasting because you will lose weight at the beach in August.

Verbal flinching about taxes was recently ridiculed by former Congressman Henry Reuss, who jokingly spoke of a higher "user fee on incomes." However, Washington recently heard semi-crisp language when Senator Paul Laxalt called the projected deficits "a little terrifying." A little? Each of the next three deficits is apt to be around 5 percent of GNP, requiring the government to borrow one-half to two-thirds of net private savings. That would cut investment, depress productivity and push up interest rates. Republicans almost have to hope that if, as some administration advisers say, there will be a $300 billion deficit by 1988, awful things will happen. If not, Republicans have wasted the 20th-century warning about deficits.

For two years I have been taxing the patience of readers, including one in the White House, by saying this nation is undertaxed. I shall now say it again, and then drop the subject, at least until the fields are white with daisies.

Given existing domestic programs, defense plans and revenue provisions, we face a gap between revenues and outlays of more than $200 billion, even assuming a rate of economic growth more rapid than can be assumed. The administration's forecast is for only 1.4 percent growth in 1983. Ms. Rosy Scenario, the administration's mistress in 1981, has been sent packing. The political will to cut domestic spending was never strong. (Quick: Name even one social program Reagan campaigned on cutting.) That will is now negligible. Reagan's most important task is to lead regarding defense—to get people to do what prudence dictates but appetites discourage. When Congress sees how much of the defense budget goes for pay, retirement, readiness and operations, only antidefense extremists will think defense cuts can take the country far toward a balanced budget.

Reagan can try to balance the budget by waiting for recovery, passing the time scrapping with Congress—including most of his own party—over niggling cuts in domestic spending, cuts for which he never sought a mandate. But he will lose, often; he will multiply the intense constituencies arrayed against him, and he will keep the "fairness" issue paramount. But the "terrifying" deficit projections will not be substantially altered by nickel-and-dime cuts, so waiting for recovery will be like waiting for Godot.

Once upon a time two conservatives became governors of neighboring states. Both faced large deficits, and a choice. They could subject their states to the torture of a thousand tiny cuts, spending four years allocating disappointment. Or they could increase taxes sufficiently to pay the bills their constituents were determined to run up. Both did the latter, and they and their states prospered. The year was 1967 and the governors were Nevada's Laxalt and his California friend.

The Californian raised income taxes and sales, liquor, cigarette, bank, insurance and corporation taxes—the whoppingest increase in his state's history. He was not hurt politically. The hard right was angry, but it always is, and that anger helped him with everyone else. Most people liked him but worried that his ideology would render him unable to improvise. They were relieved when he said arithmetic, not ideology, must prevail: Twice two is four.

Today the country is ready for Reagan to show that he still respects arithmetic. And it is time for him to say: Whatever else conservatism consists of, it includes the belief that we must pay our bills.

What could Reagan say to those who would charge that a deficit-reducing tax increase is an inconsistency? He could say: Yep, sure is—sorry about that, but so what? Reagan is, or was, fond of quoting FDR. Well, FDR once said he was like a quarterback: Don't ask what play I will call three downs from now—I have to see how the next two plays work.

Game plans concocted on Tuesday are all very well, but Sunday's heroes are quarterbacks who can rethink things in the heat of action, even reading defenses at the line of scrimmage. It is now the second half, the Gipper is behind and has his back to his goal line. We shall see if he is, as he was 15 years ago, able to modify a game plan and go for a big gainer.

January 17, 1983

America the Undertaxed

Ah, July: the fields are white with daisies. In January I promised that not "until the fields are white with daisies" would I again mention that we are, as a nation, undertaxed. I now return to that topic because the inescapable need to raise taxes raises this question: Can Ronald Reagan really want to be reelected? If he faces facts—if he reads the numbers rather than the *Wall Street Journal*—he knows that in 1985 the President must hurry to restore the government's revenue base. Reagan cannot be a Reaganite after 1984.

The conclusion that the country is undertaxed derives not from social masochism but from political realism. The point is not that higher taxes are inherently good for us. The point is that without higher taxes to pay for the spending the government clearly is going to do, the amount of government borrowing will be extremely bad for the country. The government is collecting only $75 for every $100 it spends, and in 1984 it will spend $100 8 billion times, and then some. We can pay taxes sufficient to pay our bills, or we can pay the price of inflation, or stagnation, or both. One way or another, we shall pay.

The principal variables—defense and nondefense spending, and economic growth—are not going to vary enough to solve the problem. The contours of future spending are clear. Given today's Swiss-cheeselike tax code, no attainable rate of economic growth can generate revenues sufficient to eliminate twelve-digit deficits. Congress's budget revolution alters Reagan's proposed mixture of spending. But the three-year total approximates the real (inflation-adjusted) size of government in the 1983 budget. Congress has ratified the status quo. Reagan's effect—slowed growth of domestic spending—is not negligible. But ruinous deficits remain and there is no possibility that they will be adequately reduced by spending cuts.

Two summers ago, when Reagan was at the peak of his power, a small episode revealed how little appetite Congress has for cutting middle-class benefits that compose the bulk of domestic spending. The administration proposed changing eligibility for subsidized student loans. It would have made it harder (although not impossible) for affluent families to qualify. It would have affected primarily upper-middle-class families. But Congress, busy cutting means-tested entitlement programs serving the poor, made only cosmetic changes to this middle-class subsidy. Odd, is it not: When you cut a welfare mother's food stamps she does not bark at her secretary, "Take a letter"; but try to tamper with the welfare programs of the attentive, articulate middle class and you will be buried beneath letters—forcefully phrased letters neatly typed on prettily engraved stationery.

Almost absent-mindedly the government has all but abolished corporate taxation. It has cut personal income taxes. It has virtually exhausted the capacity of the payroll tax—on the eve of a hair-curling Medicare crisis. (The Reagan administration reports that the Medicare hospital insurance trust fund faces "complete exhaustion" by 1990, so "either outlays will have to be reduced by 30 percent or income increased by 43 percent.") The government loses $83 billion in revenues by granting tax-exempt status for fringe benefits, primarily for members of strong unions and other middle-class persons. If the government taxed employer-paid health insurance as what it is—as compensation, a form of income—it would raise $21 billion in 1984, $36 billion in 1988. If employees paid income and social security taxes on employer contributions to pension plans (and income earned by pension funds were taxed), government would raise $56 billion in 1984, $109 billion in 1988. Since 1981, 45 states have raised taxes, but have raised less than one-tenth the sum of the federal decreases.

It sometimes seems that the government consists of 16 persons—nine Supreme Court justices handling all the issues Congress dodges and seven members of the Federal Reserve Board trying to hold the economy together. Today, regarding taxes, the elected government is taking a walk, leaving the Fed to keep things afloat.

Conservatives whose ideology has not immunized them against evidence can face fiscal facts. Ideologues can bury their heads in the *Wall Street Journal,* which is grimly excommunicating heretics from the Church of True Conservatism. Last week the *Journal* cast Martin Feldstein into outer darkness. Feldstein, the deeply conservative chairman of Reagan's Council of Economic Advisers, is guilty of empiricism—allowing facts to influence his thinking. He thinks that even robust economic growth will leave huge deficits— deficits incompatible with robust growth over the long term.

So if Reagan runs and wins, he will find his second term taxing, in several senses. Had he quickly extinguished inflation, achieved full employment, begun rearmament, balanced the budget and, for good measure, restored teenage chastity, he might have said: "I *told* you this stuff is easy. Now I'm going home to ride the range." Unemployment, the budget and teenagers remain recalcitrant. But the recovery may be strong enough long enough to allow him to say that Reaganism—tax cuts and spending restraints—has been vindicated. And if he cannot bear the idea of raising taxes in 1985 he may want to ride into the sunset on the 20th day of that year.

Today he hates the House–Senate proposal to take $12 billion more in taxes next year from our $3 trillion economy (with a budget of $849 billion and a deficit approaching $200 billion). The $12 billion is less than would be raised by a compliance measure—withholding of taxes on interest and dividends—that Congress wants to repeal. Reagan's treasury secretary says tax increases will be needed in the middle of this decade to prevent government borrowing from crowding private borrowers out of the capital market and aborting the recovery. Some Reagan aides say his reelection is especially crucial because he would raise taxes less destructively than a Democrat would—he would tax consumption, whereas any Democrat would tax income and savings. That argument may or may not be valid. The fact that aides are making it proves that for Reagan, as for 39 previous presidents, inertia and events, not his preferences, are setting the agenda.

July 18, 1983

That Shocking David Stockman

Baked in the oven of controversy, a public official becomes hard as cement or brittle as a pretzel. David Stockman is not half-baked, or brittle.

The history of Washington hypocrisy was enriched last week by Congressional democrats professing themselves scandalized by what they are pleased to characterize as Stockman's "cynicism." Actually, the magazine article illustrated—in addition to his intelligence—his innocence, the opposite of cynicism.

He thought he had an agreement with the journalist that nothing would be published yet, and that there would be no direct quotes he did not authorize. He has negotiated hundreds of agreements with politicians in the past year and can be presumed to know when he has struck a bargain. But the journalist says Stockman did not understand the agreement. No one who knows Stockman believes he talked with such absence of inhibition except on the assumption that he would not be quoted. He spoke with the sense of release that one relishes if one is, like Stockman, required constantly to speak in public, often in confrontational settings, always weighing every word.

Someday, perhaps, a Trollope of our politics will do justice in literature to the grinding down of the best people in highly visible appointive offices. Only a fine novelist's gift for nuance can convey the difficulty of working, as Stockman has, to the edge of exhaustion while maintaining, as Stockman has, intellectual vitality and honesty. It is hard to keep the private self nourished and balanced behind the public self. Private talk, venting frustrations and doubts, is necessary. Bottling it up and living an entirely public life eats the spirit the way rust eats iron. But before Stockman said all those things to that particular journalist, he should have remembered Calvin Coolidge's insight: "You don't have to explain something you never said."

Now, at the risk of dampening all the jolly indignation in which some folks are luxuriating, let me ask: What, precisely, did Stockman say that is supposed to cause the mind to reel and civilization to totter? The complaint seems to be that Stockman said that policy has been to some extent formulated in a rushed and confused process. Furthermore, some numbers were adjusted to fit theories, and some theories were bent to accommodate politics.

This is a news bulletin? Not to anyone who has been looking at the economic numbers, or listening to the economic testimony, for the last nine months. Not, indeed, to anyone who has paid attention to government during recent decades. Democrats have controlled Congress, which means taxing and spending powers, for nearly three decades. Given their lamentable record, I would think they would welcome Stockman's candid admission that the government's economic instruments (the budget, the Fed) are blunt, and current economic theories are unhelpful—in short, that confusion, guesswork and surprises are unavoidable.

Stockman's critics, some of whom are strangers to candor, feign dismay about his acknowledgment that economic policy is improvised while a dozen important variables are varying unpredictably. Are the critics saying that they were never before surprised by economic events? If so, are they saying that the previous administration *planned* to triple inflation and interest rates?

Finding President Reagan disinclined to govern as though they had won the election, Democrats have now resorted to a theatrical display of amazement about the unamazing fact that his alternative to their status quo—change—is, as change always is, fraught with uncertainties and bumps. P. G. Wodehouse described a maiden who was so unworldly she thought that "every time a fairy blows its wee nose a baby is born." She should be the patron saint of those who are sincerely saying: "Oh my, Stockman was—heaven forfend—more confident in public than in private."

The fair criticism of Stockman and those who assigned him his mission is that they had an unconservative faith in the ability of government to alter substantially, quickly and neatly the working of a social mechanism as complicated as this $3 trillion economy. They abandoned conservative skepticism about the ability of one election and a passing mood to alter political habits developed over several generations. And they ignored the central tenet of conservative prudence, as taught by recent liberal practice: The unintended effects of any policy are apt to be larger and more lasting than the intended effects. They forgot what conservative analysis shows: Almost everything, from the cost of kidney dialysis to the effects of urban renewal, has involved unpleasant surprises for government.

One reason government is a brutal business is that Cabinet officers are so utterly another person's instruments. In our government, unlike in a parliamentary form, Cabinet officers derive all their power from the President. They serve "during the pleasure of the President of the United States." Two ways they serve his pleasure are by not getting into unnecessary public trouble and by not involving him in their trouble. Reagan, whose secretary of state recently embroiled him with a newspaper columnist, now finds his administration buffeted by a magazine, for Pete's sake. Reagan knows what the person meant who said that life is not one damn thing after another, it is the same damn thing over and over.

Stockman has caused his President trouble and has been rewarded by a glimpse of something the public has yet to see, a scowl on Reagan's visage. But in the (unlikely) event that many people actually read the magazine article, Stockman may even be, when the dust settles, an enhanced asset to the administration. The country, and especially the financial community (on the confidence of which so much depends), will welcome the proof that there is in Washington one person who knows when a fact has wounded a theory.

Stockman read the magazine article the day he turned 35, just halfway through his biblically allotted threescore and ten. In the testing days that followed, his manly comportment contrasted nicely with the clamorousness of his critics, who, collectively, are not apt to compile a record of public service that matches what he already has done. And he has just begun.

November 23, 1981

Will's Doctrine of Double Meaning

Suddenly, in the nick of time, there are three astonishing breakthroughs in the science of economics: Will's Law, Will's Doctrine of Double Meaning and Will's Equilibrium Hypothesis. The Law is: All economic news is bad, and all news is economic news. The Doctrine is: Every economic fact means what it means, and the opposite. I will come to the Hypothesis in a moment. When you understand all this you will understand why everything is incomprehensible.

The United States is about to become what a lot of Third World nations are, a debtor nation. More money will be lent and invested here by foreigners than Americans will be lending and investing abroad. That is absolutely, positively bad. And good. It is happening because the United States is the most vigorous remnant of capitalism, and because of policies that are certain to sap that vigor. A key reason for the inflow of capital is that the federal deficit contributes to high interest rates that attract foreign buyers of U.S. government and corporate bonds. Thank God, or Reagan, or Keynes or someone. Without the inflow, Americans would have to pay the actual cost of their standard of living—a revolting idea. Foreigners, bless their hearts, are lending Americans enough to allow Americans to spend much more than they earn (which means consume much more wealth than they produce). Foreigners like the strong dollar.

A riddle: Why is economic analysis like modern art? Answer: because it is impossible to do it wrong. Or right. Consider the following. You say the dollar is standing tall and that must be good? You must be daft. The dollar's strength reduces the costs of imports and raises the prices of U.S. exports. This contributes to today's huge trade imbalance which is costing lots of American jobs. That increases the federal budget deficit, which puts upward pressure on interest rates, which helps make the dollar strong.

On the other hand (warning: Economic analysis can give you intellectual whiplash) a strong dollar creates jobs precisely because it increases imports. They provide anti-inflationary price competition for U.S. goods, and low inflation encourages job creation. Besides, if the dollar weakens significantly, the inflow of money may stop or even become an outrush causing a severe credit shortage. (U.S. personal savings are not sufficient to finance the federal deficit.) Interest rates would jump. I told you so: Whatever the news about the dollar is going to be, it is going to be bad.

A quiz: The United States is bailing out irresponsible, shortsighted, undisciplined, etc., etc., Third World nations, lending them billions to pay the interest they cannot pay on the billions they have borrowed and cannot pay back. These nations have been living beyond their means, financing consumption with credit from abroad, credit attracted by overvalued currencies. Question: What North American nation's economy is embarrassingly similar?

The economy is sprinting along above the 4.2 percent growth path the administration projects through 1989. That is encouraging—and, of course, alarming. If real GNP does not grow at least that fast, the five-year deficits will be even worse than the $1 trillion that many economists expect. But if growth is going to remain fast, the administration is almost certainly wrong to project declining inflation and interest rates. Rising inflation and interest rates could bring on a contraction that would produce deficits huge enough to make a $200 billion deficit seem as innocuous as Carter's projected fiscal 1981 deficit of $16 billion now seems. (Carter's projection knocked Wall Street on its ear and forced him to submit a new budget.)

Well, at least inflation is down, right? And that is good, right? The answers are: yes and no, and yes and no. Inflation is down from the dizzying heights of four years ago. But even when it is down, as it now is, to 5 percent it is about triple the rate in the 1950s and early 1960s. And even at just 5 percent the price level would increase almost two-thirds in a decade. Is the fact that inflation is down but up good or bad? Both, of course. Stable prices are nice, but high inflation has its charms for a nation bent on piling up huge deficits and debt. Inflation reduces the real value of the national debt and the size of the debt relative to GNP. Indeed, inflation is, as Herb Stein says, slow-motion repudiation of the debt.

But at least interest rates are down from the levels of the Carter days, right? Wrong. The real interest rate—the difference between the interest rate and the inflation rate—is higher. So, you surmise, that makes it especially awful that rates are edging up. No, silly, your surmise is a mess. You should be doing buck-and-wing dances of joy because rates are rising. Rising rates are, in part, signs of health. Corporations are demanding more capital because returns on investments are rising (because energy costs are down and because of the 1981 enactment of accelerated depreciation and the investment tax credit).

Deregulation of the financial system also has raised rates. Elimination of most interest rate ceilings on bank deposits has forced financial institutions to compete to attract funds, raising the cost of money to them. The old limits on what banks could pay small depositors made those depositors subsidize the biggest customers for credit. The multiplication of depositors' options has drained money from the mortgage market, so mortgages have become more expensive, which is bad. And good. More funds probably are going into more productive capital investments.

But surely the enhanced position of the average saver has caused Americans to save more? Surely not. The savings rate, which in 1980 was a miserable 6 percent of disposable income, is now worse. In 1982 and 1983 it was 5.3 percent, the lowest for a two-year period in almost four decades. No wonder we need foreign credit to finance, directly or indirectly, about 40 percent of the federal deficit. Therefore we need high interest rates to attract the foreign funds. Therefore large deficits are helpful because they keep interest rates high. So (you have been patient, gentle reader) here is Will's Hypothesis: Economic analysis always demonstrates that what is is necessary, and that all things are in equilibrium, even when everything is going to hell in a handcart.

April 23, 1984

The Grandfathered Society

The day David Stockman's resignation was announced was an important day for him and perhaps for the nation. It was a momentous day for Rachel Stockman. It was her 67th day and the day she discovered her hands. It is a magnificent moment when a baby looks up and sees those splendid things, and it dawns on her that they are attached to her and under her control, and she thinks: Look out, world, what fun I can have with these. Rachel, who weighs about as much as the federal budget and is even more complicated, is David and Jennifer's first child and is a sufficient reason for David to want to leave one of the government's most time-consuming jobs.

In the summer of 1981, when the steam might have gone out of the new President's push for tax and budget cuts, his guardian angel was sitting up late working up blisters manufacturing good luck. Justice Potter Stewart resigned from the Supreme Court, enabling Reagan to gain fresh élan by nominating a woman. The air traffic controllers' union led with its glass chin, enabling Reagan to look like Jack Dempsey. The Libyans sent up two rattletrap fighter planes over the Gulf of Sidra, giving Reagan a chance to wave the "don't tread on me" flag.

The administration had (in the phrase of the day) "hit the ground running." It had been able to do that, and to keep going through the summer, because of Stockman, who was both tortoise and hare—a meticulous sprinter. Reagan was going from triumph to triumph because Stockman was going from line to line in the labyrinth of the budget. His mastery of the substance was as important as Reagan's mastery of public communications in maintaining through the summer the unprecedented unity of congressional Republicans and their Democratic boll-weevil allies.

Stockman's mastery gave rise to the Stockman jokes. "If the air conditioning fails, we'll get Stockman's heart to cool the room." "At the airport Stockman's heart set off the metal detector." Ho, ho. The jokes derived, in part, from the anti-intellectual assumption that in any individual, intellect and sensitivity must be inversely apportioned.

In a city clogged with people who fancy themselves indispensable, or at least consequential, Stockman actually has made a big difference. If he had not been in the Executive Office Building, that stone wedding cake next door to the White House, Reagan would have hit the ground just loping. Not even his guardian angel, a workaholic on a Stockman-like scale, could have ginned up enough luck to provide the legislative triumphs.

Furthermore, in a city where ideas are used primarily as camouflage for interests, Stockman's interest has been in ideas. Most people in government are oral and audio people: They are most comfortable talking or listening. By the end of the day they have had a surfeit of words. Stockman has done his share of talking and being talked at, but he also is a reader and writer.

Ten years ago, when his 30th birthday was still over the horizon, he came to the attention of the cardinals of the church of neoconservatism. He did this with an article in *The Public Interest,* the official journal for church encyclicals. In his 1975 article on "the social pork barrel," he said domestic spending had become "a political maintenance system," a system maintained by—and maintaining—congressmen and senators who consider themselves "constituency ombudsmen and grant brokers." He has spent half of the subsequent decade learning how dreadfully right he was. He has diagnosed the enervating dispersal of authority in government, but has made the position of OMB director a concentration of power unrivaled outside the Oval Office.

Stockman already is writing a book about all this. It will not be just, or even primarily, a memoir. When Pétain was asked why he was not writing his memoirs, he said: I have nothing to hide. Stockman has little to hide, having been so frequently, not to say promiscuously, public in his thinking. His book will be short on the sort of stuff people seem to want in Washington books—tangy details about who spilled tapioca on whose taffeta at what party, or what beastly thing Al said to Cap about Jeane. Instead, the book will be about how we learned the answers to the two "how much" questions about Reagan's program when the dice were rolled with the 1981 tax cuts.

How much would the cuts stimulate the economy? How much could spending be cut? It is now clear that the answer to both is: not enough. The tax cuts are not self-financing. They are not fueling so much growth that the deficits are shrinking. The deficits are not producing pressure sufficient to compel spending cuts large enough to shrink the deficits.

Rachel's father has tuckered himself out in the coils of the "grandfathered society." Government has so threaded itself through the lives and expectations of so many people that it cannot, and arguably should not, pull out the thread quickly. The groups whose expectations have been shaped by government perhaps should be, and probably will be, "grandfathered." That is, policy changes will exempt and protect those who would be adversely affected because they have come to count on continuity in the structure that government action has given to their expectations. But almost everyone is in a grandfathered group, and the grandfather agreements get renewed, perpetually.

So, the political limits of domestic budget cutting have been reached, as have the prudential limits of defense cuts. Given the limits to reasonable assumptions about economic growth, the task for a responsible director of OMB is to convince the crucial 537 people (those who are in Washington because they won elections) that they should simultaneously cut spending and raise taxes more than they have ever done either. Before they are so convinced Stockman will be—Rachel willing—grandfathered.

July 22, 1985

The Economy of Leadership

Are your children better than they were four years ago—more studious, tidy, obedient, polite? Neither are mine. But if any children are, their parents should thank Ronald Reagan, according to the Republican platform. It says that suddenly "young people have turned away from the rebellion of the 1960s and the pessimism of the 1970s." The suggestion is that this is because Republicans are at the wheel. You thought Republicans did not believe Washington can produce useful change? Fiddlesticks. If your kids are eating their broccoli and picking up their socks, thank the leader of the free world.

The most conspicuous word in the Democrats' platform is "fair." The Republicans repeat the phrase "Carter–Mondale" 57 times. Subtlety is not the point of platforms. Sincerity is. Platforms are not reliable maps of the future, but they are touchingly, painfully sincere. Consider the much-masticated subject of taxes.

America's historic battles include Antietam, Iwo Jima, Inchon. They now pale. 'Twas a famous victory conservatives won over the almost-as-conservatives in Dallas in the Battle of the Comma. A comma was inserted between the words "taxes" and "which" in a sentence proclaiming Republicans opposed to "any attempts to increase taxes, which would harm the recovery." Well, conservatives should occasionally resemble medieval thinkers arguing about whether the sky was made of bell metal or angels' wings.

Nasty reality, not a comma, will settle the tax dispute. Reagan has not proposed a balanced budget or pelted Congress with vetoes. There will be a tax increase, unless conservatives are right. The only logical explanation—not that logic explains such things—of their position is that they think Reagan has repealed the business cycle and there will be uninterrupted and unprecedentedly rapid economic growth evermore. Meanwhile, there are many Republicans who, when asked what they think about Republican tax policy, feel like the Peter de Vries character who, asked what he thought of Western civilization, said he thought that would be a good idea.

The tax issue bothers Reagan because it threatens to blur the sharp outline of his political profile. It has been well said that the way to get across an idea is to wrap it up in a person. Reagan became a political force by embodying clear, elemental ideas. He will be judged primarily on his leadership of the economy, but what he understands best is the economy of leadership. He understands how presidential effectiveness depends on minimizing the audible clutter in politics, keeping priorities few and clear—priorities like tax cuts. Unfortunately, governing—the culprit, again, is reality—requires accommodations that mute the strongest messages and mix pastels in among the primary colors of a political profile. That is why it is most fun to run against, not as, an incumbent.

Reagan has run four previous campaigns, two for governor (1966, 1970), one against Gerald Ford (1976) and one against Jimmy Carter (1980). Only in 1970 was he an incumbent. He ran against an underfinanced, mistake-prone opponent (Jess Unruh), yet his 1966 majority was halved. This was, in part, because he is at his best on the attack against persons mired in the ambiguities of office. He is like a lot of professional basketball players: His heart is not really in playing defense. Give him the ball so he can run and gun. But, then, many politicians understand what one of Trollope's politicians meant: "The delight of political life is altogether in opposition. . . . The very inaccuracy which is permitted to opposition is in itself a charm."

Reagan won in 1980 because by that July one of Carter's aides bluntly, and correctly, told him in a memo: "The public is now convinced that Jimmy Carter is an inept man. . . . He is weak and indecisive—in over his head. *We have to change people's minds.*" They failed. In one commercial Carter said, "I think I'll be a better President in the next four years"—surely the limpest appeal ever made. An aide called this "a roundabout *mea culpa.*" It was not very roundabout. It could not help Carter persuade the country to steer clear of the "inexperienced" Reagan. Carter's second theme—that Reagan was dangerous and divisive—only earned Carter a reputation for "meanness."

Carter's difficulties dealing with Reagan illuminate some of Mondale's problems. Even when Reagan was without Washington experience, Carter could not make stick the charge that Reagan would be out of his depth as President. Mondale says Reagan does not know that he is doing, but Mondale's real message is that Reagan is alarmingly effective at turning the country in a direction that he, Mondale, disapproves. And being beastly to the Gipper can earn Mondale a meanness problem. Mondale can talk about deficits. But Carter ran an ad noting that Governor Reagan "increased state spending by 120 percent; he brought three tax increases to the state; he added 34,000 employees to the state payroll." That may just have seemed to say: In spite of what I have been saying about Reagan being a radical outside the mainstream, actually he is just like the rest of us.

But aside from the fact that both Reagan and Mondale are accomplished professionals, representing the mainstream of two mainstream parties, they are not alike. They represent significantly different views of the nation and the world, views that have enormous constituencies. At the end of the day—in September and October, quadrennially—American politics is, although hardly solemn, quite serious. That is, the outcome turns on substantial concerns—national security, economic growth and the candidates' abilities to communicate an energizing hopefulness (which—who knows?—may even cause the kids to do their chores).

August 27, 1984

The Senate: Not Suited for Prime Time

Outside Interstate 495, Washington's beltway, there is no detectable sense of deprivation arising from the fact that senators, who are televised in hearings and elsewhere, are not also televised on the Senate floor. But, understandably, many senators want more opportunities to be seen by vast audiences. And journalists naturally want to extend the domain of all facets of their craft.

The case for putting cameras in the Senate is often couched in rhetoric about "the public's right to know." Of all the rights that have recently blossomed in tropical luxuriance, that right is, to me, the most ill-defined. But whatever it means, the "right to know" about the Senate is not in jeopardy or at issue. It is, to be polite, terminologically inexact to say, as some do, that the Senate today is "closed." Most of the work of the Senate occurs in hearings open to cameras. The floor is observed from the press gallery, and the Senate has provided itself television facilities a short walk from the floor. Many senators citing the "right to know" deserve to be hoist by their own petard. Actually, they want a carefully circumscribed right to know about the chamber. They want cameras restricted to covering only the person speaking. Cameras free to scan the chamber would frequently reveal 94 empty chairs, and five senators paying no attention. But if the public has a sovereign right to "know," should not the cameras scan?

Some journalists seem to think that those governmental policies are best that make their profession most fun. So we can expect demands to intrude journalism's myriad technologies into every recess of government. Some courtrooms already welcome electronic journalism. Why not the Supreme Court? The court's conferences? All meetings of the Federal Reserve Board? But government exists to produce good government, not entertaining journalism. And it is not axiomatic that "openness" always conduces to better government. Homer nods and so does Howard Baker. Normally wise, he has announced that the Founding Fathers, were they among us, would want television in the Senate. But in the steamy Philadelphia summer of 1787, they closed the doors and even the windows so they could draft the Constitution in an atmosphere conducive to statesmanship. The Senate met behind closed doors for its first seven years.

Some persons advocate television because they think it will change the Senate substantially. One senator professes to believe that cameras would draw a majority of senators to the chamber for great debates about great issues. Never mind the assumption that great debates occur whenever many senators gather. And disregard the danger that senators will use the floor as a stage for making campaign commercials. But remember, because of time constraints (22 minutes of news in the evening newscast), television coverage of political controversies consists almost entirely of short snippets of talk, called "sound bites." The only significant use of cameras in the Senate would be to provide the networks with such bites. Bites? Nibbles, really. Twenty seconds is a big bite. Imagine the incoherence of the Lincoln–Douglas debates reduced to such bites between denture adhesive commercials.

Anyway, if television altered senators' behavior by luring them to the floor, when would the Senate's work get done? All senators believe, rightly, that they are maddeningly overburdened already. More than half of this fiscal year is past and fewer than half the appropriations bills have been passed. Senators do not need cameras tempting or coercing them to make cameo appearances on the floor to convince the folks back home that their senator is diligent.

Many senators favor television only because they are sure the effect on behavior will be negligible. They say, rightly, that the introduction of television into the House in 1979 did not significantly change the House. But they wrongly argue that television is as suitable for one body as the other.

Scientists know that observing a phenomenon can change the phenomenon. Enlarging the Senate's audience from a few hundred in gallery seats to millions of viewers would mean qualitative change wrought by quantitative change. It would further diminish the Senate's ability to function as intended by the Founders, who designed it as a mitigation of popular government, somewhat insulated from popular pressures.

Both the House and the Senate embody the defining principle

of republican government, which is the principle of representation: The people do not decide issues, they decide who shall decide. But the Senate is much smaller. Its members are insulated by six-year terms (and were insulated by the Founders from popular election). The Senate has permissive rules allowing extensive debate and substantial blocking power for intense minorities. The Senate exemplifies the fact that in America the people are sovereign, but popular sovereignty is mediated and qualified.

I worked on the Senate staff for three years. Since then I have watched the Senate with affection and interest for a decade. I do not think senators feel too isolated from clamorous pressures. They certainly are not insufficiently attentive to the eddies of public opinion. What the government, and especially the Senate, needs is more, not less, insulation from the importunings of the immediate. The Senate is supposed to be a haven for independent judgment. It needs less, not more, pressure to focus on the country's short-term concerns. Televising the Senate would make it even more tumultuous and plebiscitary than it already has become. George Washington said the Senate is the saucer into which we pour controversies to cool. Television would turn up the temperature.

The healthy working of representative government requires a residuum of detachment, distance, aloofness, even mystery. This truth is intellectually difficult to formulate and politically dangerous to express. But this truth is important, as is the process of nurturing an elevating ambience anywhere in the passionate business of politics. The Senate, perhaps more than any of the world's great institutions of representation, has had such an ambience. Television would further subvert that, and the Senate's assigned role in our system.

April 25, 1983

The Architecture of Democracy

Many senators are so impatient for the rectification of the world's ills that they have not taken time to notice that the Senate itself needs some attention. However, Dan Quayle has noticed, and has some proposals, to which I add this one: Rearrange the furniture on the Senate floor.

Quayle is in the fifth year of what will be, if God is willing and Indiana is wise, many terms in the Senate. A lissome young Republican of 37, he looks 27, and during his 1980 campaign he was accused—yes, accused—of looking unfairly like Robert Redford. (When will the Federal Election Commission issue regulations to correct the unfairness of candidates not looking equally splendid?)

Quayle has a number of ideas to improve two things: the conduct of business on the Senate floor and the committee system in which most Senate business is done. He would reform the rules governing the Senate floor to make it more difficult—it is now simple—for one member to bring the Senate to a standstill by dilatory devices (frivolous amendments, filibusters, etc.). And he would reduce the size of committees and the number of subcommittees.

If the Senate is to be what it is pleased to be called—"world's greatest deliberative body"—it must be disposed to, and able to, deliberate. But deliberation takes time, and a certain rhythm of institutional life. Deliberative senators can not live like dray horses in harness, driven by staff from one hearing to another. But for 30 years the number of senators has remained constant, as has the number of hours in the day. Neither number is apt to change soon. The number of committees and especially subcommittees has grown rapidly as senators have sought new opportunities to hire staff and make news.

When Jim Buckley left the Senate after one term representing New York (1971–76), he said the work load had doubled during his six years. One reason the load is so heavy is the proliferation of subcommittees. That has multiplied the burdens of the executive branch. When William Ruckelshaus first served as head of the Environmental Protection Agency 15 years ago, he had to report to 15 committees and subcommittees. When he returned to that job in 1983, the number was 44.

Quayle's ideas are sound, but not sufficient. The Senate should rearrange its desks and chairs, for Churchillian reasons. When a German bomb destroyed the House of Commons, the chamber could have been rebuilt along various lines. But Churchill insisted that its traditional physical features be reproduced because they sustain particular political principles.

He wanted the chamber to be oblong, with benches on two sides, facing each other, rather than with individual seats arranged in a semicircle. And he was adamant that the chamber be only big enough to seat about two-thirds of the members. He warned against "semicircular assemblies with buildings that give to every member not only a seat to sit in, but often a desk to write at, with a lid to bang"—a description of the U.S. Senate.

Churchill believed that the oblong shape was "a very potent factor in our political life" because it buttresses the rule of two durable and disciplined parties. Semicircular assemblies, he said, encourage loose assemblages of lesser groups in constantly shifting coalitions of weak principles. He said the semicircular assembly encourages "the group system" because it does nothing to encourage party identification, party discipline and clarity of principle. He said a strong two-party system, and a government capable of vigorous action, is nurtured by an oblong chamber. The physical fact of confrontation concentrates minds on the reality of two competing blocs, and the act of voting with the other side becomes more momentous.

Churchill thought a legislative chamber should be so small that it cannot contain all its members without overcrowding. Otherwise almost all debates will be conducted in the dispiriting, trivializing atmosphere of an almost empty chamber. He thought good legislative rhetoric should be conversational, not haranguing, and that conversational style requires a small space. Furthermore, on great occasions crowding gives a sense of urgency.

It will be said that Americans should not want the Senate to sit in a smaller chamber (with, say, 50 chairs—25 to a side) because party cohesion and conversational, cut-and-thrust rhetoric are not important to American goals. But perhaps they should be. And Churchill's theory—call it architectural determinism, or the Seating Arrangement Theory of History—is easier to ridicule than refute.

January 27, 1985

Martin Luther, Founding Father

Ask 20 thoughtful persons to list the 20 historical figures most important as makers of the modern world and you may get a hundred names. But a few names would be on every list: Einstein. Freud. And the man born half a millennium ago, November 10, 1483.

Arguably, the modern world began when Martin Luther, appearing at an inquiry into his thought, reportedly said: "Hier steh' ich, ich kann nicht anders." "I can do no other." It seems an odd cry of freedom. It foreshadowed societies based on recognition of "unalienable" rights.

Luther's words announced the ascendance of private judgment—of conscience. But he was speaking the language—"ich kann nicht"—of restriction, compulsion. The life of this driven man demonstrated that the modern notion of freedom—freedom from external restraints imposed by others—can mean submission to a hard master, one's conscience. Alternatively, it can mean the soft tyranny of conformity to opinion. That, however, is an option that never occurred to Luther. He was perhaps the most potent opinion-shaper since Christ.

Luther was a conservative and a revolutionary. He supported forceful, sometimes brutal, defense of the social status quo while actually subverting with his ideas the established order in every particular. An Italian contemporary, Machiavelli, was secularizing politics, orienting it toward man's passions rather than God's laws. Luther was peeling politics off religion, in a quest for religion's essence.

Of course Luther's theology had political consequences. You, reader, are living in a country that is, in no small measure, a consequence.

His dispute with Rome was cast, unavoidably, in categories of political thought: "authority" within the Church, the Church's "power" in society, the "right" of the faithful to "participate" in certain arrangements. He thought the State legitimately could be, and probably must be, powerful and sometimes ruthless. By his reckoning, the State is of less dignity than it was when Church and State were thoroughly melded. The State, he thought, is responsible only for order, and is barely relevant to the serious business of life, salvation.

It is said that someone seeking a purpose in life should see a bishop, not a politician—but today's bishops talk like politicians. Someone seeking to extract political agendas from Christianity gets little help from Luther.

Christianity's assessment of man, at once high and severe, is about right for political philosophy: Man can be magnificent, but is magnificent rarely, and never spontaneously—without help from nurturing institutions. Luther had a haunting sense of the utter fallenness of mankind, and of mankind's total dependence on God's grace for even the slightest amelioration of the consequences of sin. This insulated him from the political temptation to believe in the perfectability of man through the improvement of social arrangements. In the endless argument about which dominates, nature or nurture, Luther knew: nature.

His quest for purity in religious experience—an anticipation of the modern quest for "authenticity"—led him to scant the institutional help necessary to mankind's quest for religious satisfaction and social fulfillment. But the radical individualism implicit in his thought was tempered by his celebration of the family as society's molecular unit.

The former monk started a family at age 41. Although never without a piercing sense of sinfulness, this most human of outsized heroes overflowed with enjoyment—of beer and sex and music. (His chorales and hymns earn him a significant place in the history of music.)

Luther's career was made possible by another German's career, Johann Gutenberg's. Luther's was the first great life bound up with mass communication—printing with movable type. He was the most prolific serious writer in history. One edition of his works exceeds 100 volumes. More than 2,500 of his letters survive.

Charles V, Luther's antagonist, said the German language was suited only for speaking to horses. Luther made it speak to God. His translation of the Bible into German virtually invented the German language. It also showed how the tangible (a new technology, printing) can shape the intangible (the idea of an institutional church). When laymen could read scripture, priests were challenged in their role as mediators between laymen and God.

Luther's doctrine of salvation by faith alone rather than by good works expressed his belief that salvation derives from God's gift of unmerited grace. This doctrine challenged the role of priests as deliverers of grace through sacraments.

He was no democrat, but with seven words—"each and all of us are priests"—he asserted an idea of equality that evolved into an underpinning of popular sovereignty. So this Republic, 207 years old, should honor a Founding Father born 500 years ago.

November 6, 1983

Democracy's Foot Soldiers

BETHESDA, MD.—Many Americans believe that on an average day, the average congressman joins a lobbyist for what is, between them, a six-martini lunch in furtherance of some conspiracy against the average American. If the average American thinks legislators should lead lives of travail, asceticism and insecurity, the average American should rejoice about the kind of days that Howard Denis, lives. Welcome to the world of the state legislator: one-Coke lunches, heavy on tunafish.

His 1974 Chevrolet has gone 96,000 miles and acquired that many dents and scratches carrying him to and from Annapolis and around his suburban Washington district. The district contains 56,506 registered voters. Two years ago he won by 211 votes out of 26,905 cast. Before his two-year campaign is over he will have knocked on about 30,000 doors. In his six years as a state senator he has been bitten by five dogs, threatened with a shotgun, and had his literature thrown in his face.

Politicians know better than to wantonly aggravate the electorate, so they smile until their cheeks ache, especially during the cruelest month—October. About now, a candidate feels that he or she is a toy in the hands of Fate—a fragile toy in the hands of an ill-behaved Fate that should be sent to its room without dinner. Denis's salary as senator ($18,500) is a lot less than the fees (he's a lawyer) he must pass up for the pleasure of campaigning.

He looks 42, which he is. He should look dreadful but doesn't. You would, if you were a Republican running in a district liberally stocked with federal workers who were not generally Republicans even before the Reagan administration arrived with its "RIF" (reduction-in-force) program for slimming the government. There are just seven Republicans among Maryland's 47 senators. The ratio is even worse in the House of Delegates, where only 15 of the 141 delegates are Republicans.

Denis's campaign will spend about $20,000, most of it for mailings. Madeleine Will, who is what Boss Tweed would have been if he had really meant business, lobbies for the Maryland Association of Retarded Citizens and has held a fundraiser for Denis, who has been helpful to her cause.

He distributes a four-page newspaper listing numerous achievements, such as his support for community placements for the retarded and better street lights to combat crime at the University of Maryland. He stresses the common issues of state government: education, the struggle with the big city—in this case, Baltimore—over funds. He also stresses seniority. Such is the wear-and-tear of the legislator's life, if elected to a third term he will be among the top ten senators in seniority.

Thomas Jefferson's tombstone lists his three proudest achievements: Author of the Declaration of Independence and Virginia's statute for religious freedom, and father of the University of Virginia. Denis's tombstone can announce:

Here sleeps the author of the truck cover bill.

Maryland truckers are not required to cover cargoes such as gravel, to the detriment of Maryland windshields. The truckers have an argument (costs) and so does Denis (other costs, such as for windshields), and of such arguments the fabric of politics is woven.

Denis's chores are not contemptible for being of less than Jeffersonian grandeur. Whose chores are consistently grand? Anyway, this nation cannot do without the profession of state legislator, which is more than can be said of, say, the columnist's profession.

Maybe it is because of the proximity of his district to the nation's capital, but Denis gets questioned about the Middle East as well as about Maryland. Many people are, to put it politely, vague about what state legislators are. They are the infantry lieutenants of American government. Many more Americans are reverent about states' rights than are ready to join, or support, or even notice the infantry.

Between the policeman on the corner and the President on television, not much of government is tangible, concrete, even visible. But the quality of roads, schools, parks, prisons—among other things—depend on state government, where the ratio of work required to prestige received is awfully high.

When night spreads its mantle over America, when the nation puts its feet up and loosens its belt a notch, the nation can take its ease, and can take many good things for granted, in part because thousands of persons like Denis are putting their blistered feet in hot solutions of Epsom salts. Morning comes early for democracy's foot soldiers.

October 3, 1982

A Devil of a Town

Mayor Harold Washington is a master of the pregnant pause. Would he care to characterize "Fast Eddie" Vrdolyak, chairman of Chicago's Democratic Party and leader of the anti-Washington majority in the city council? Vrdolyak, says His Honor, is intelligent. And hard-working. Pause. "*And vicious.*" Actually, Washington is dialed-back today. Sometimes he calls Vrdolyak a "scurrilous low-life." When asked if he has really abolished patronage, Washington says, Oh, gracious yes. Pause. "But we draw a line between patronage and reasonable discretion." Love that line. In Chicago the limits on discretion do not chafe. The ethic packed into the phrase "reasonable discretion" is, in duller cities, something that keeps grand juries busy.

Chicago, Chicago, where Fred (Peanuts) Roti, son of Bruno (The Bomber) Roti, smiled when a fan suggested the slogan "Vote for Roti—and NO ONE GETS HURT." Compared to the spicy curry of Chicago politics, national politics is just cornflakes. When Carl Sandburg said Chicago was "coarse and strong and cunning," he was paying it a compliment. The description fits Mayor Washington, and I mean that as a compliment. His critics complain that he is indolent. The charge is strange as a complaint, because the complainers are folks who you would think would pray: If Washington must exercise power, please, God, make him do it indolently.

Like Richard Daley, Washington is built like a beer keg. But Daley radiated the will to dominate. Washington seems at pains to appear passive. He was content as a congressman, which need not be an exacting job. Daley could think big. (He proposed constructing an airport on the bottom of Lake Michigan, behind a gargantuan dam.) But what made Daley big was thinking small. There were 40,000 jobs for the boys (and, occasionally, girls), and he decided who got them. Washington promised to abolish patronage, which would have been a rotten thing to do. Blacks deserve their time at the trough. Chicago should not come down with a fever of morality at the moment when blacks have a mayor who made no bones about what the 1983 election was about: "It's our turn."

Some court decisions have limited the right to fire people for political reasons, but weep not for the mayor. He had thousands of jobs to dispense even before the 1984 budget put 1,400 more at his disposal. Vrdolyak's lads also did well, getting eight new committees to manufacture jobs for the aldermen to allocate. James Winters, a splendid Chicago-ologist, says that Vrdolyak's secret meeting with some Reagan aides (presumably he was plotting vengeance against national democrats who helped elect Washington) made Vrdolyak look like "a cross between Machiavelli and Monty Hall." Washington, who has his own way with words, says of Fast Eddie: "He has a very jaded past." So does the city.

Politics were, er, *colorful* under "Bathhouse John" Coughlin and Michael (Hinky Dink) Kenna, but politics became science under "Pushcart Tony" Cermak, elected in 1931. He perfected the policy that everybody gets something. Or, in the concise political philosophy of his successor: "You win by addition." But Washington won by division: Two white rivals divided the white vote. He won the 1983 Democratic primary with 37 percent of the vote (Jane Byrne 33 percent, Daley *fils* 30 percent). He won the general election by a whisker against a Republican who had all that a lot of white voters demanded: White skin and a pulse beat. But Washington is a product of powerful social forces. Between 1950 and 1970 Chicago's black population doubled. In the 1960s half a million middle-class whites moved out. By 1970 Chicago had elected more black officials than any other city.

Little things, like a piddling tax on tea, can get white folks riled up. A medium-size thing put a match to the political kindling in Chicago's black community. During the snows of January 1979, Mayor Bilandic (another rhetorician: He compared criticism of his snow-removal effort to the crucifixion of Jesus and the Nazi persecution of the Jews) allowed el trains packed with whites from the outskirts to save time by whizzing past stops in black neighborhoods. Blacks rallied round Jane Byrne's campaign against "sinister apostles of self-aggrandizement." The apostles included Fast Eddie, who responded, more in sorrow than in anger, that she was deranged by menopause. He called her "Hot Flash" Jane.

She won. Her four years—a newspaper said Chicago was run by Bonnie and a bunch of Clydes, and one of her advisers called it "management by hysteria"—made Washington's checkered past seem no worse than, well, jaded. (When he made a campaign stop at the jail where he served 40 days for forgetting to file tax returns, a television station called it "a homecoming," and another broadcast his mug shots.)

Washington has considerable charm. I asked: Did Jesse Jackson decide to run for president because he, Washington, became

Chicago's most important black person? Washington let the question hang in the air like a Cub pitcher's curve ball. Then he said: "Let's just say I raised his sights a bit." He, unlike Daley, can be droll.

The city of America's first saint (Mother Cabrini) is a tad short of saints at the moment. Daley did give Chicago government that was (in his words) "better than you never had it before." But he governed the way the White Sox won last year—"Winning ugly." (Only in Chicago would a team adopt such a slogan.) Is Harold Washington worse? I asked a student of Chicago politics. Toying with a sliver of turbot in the Cape Cod Room at the Drake Hotel, Saul Bellow said: "Do you want the facts, rumors or apocrypha?" The winner of the Nobel Prize in Literature knows that art cannot compete with lurid reality in a city where, at the city council session when Fast Eddie questioned the mayor's "gender" and the mayor threatened to give Fast Eddie "a mouthful of something you don't want," the aldermen voted to study bulletproofing the chamber.

You expect fragrant politics in a city named after an onion (Indians called the onion *Checagou*). And it would be sad were Chicago to get lathered up about civic hygiene. Chicago is America's museum, where old ways are on display.

February 13, 1984

In Defense of Nonvoting

Here comes another campaign to encourage voting, alas. Last weekend ABC News and Harvard's Kennedy School of Government sponsored a symposium on "the problem of declining voter participation." Problem? As more people are nagged to the polls, the caliber of the electorate declines. The reasonable assumption about electorates is: Smaller is smarter.

Voting has been declining since 1960, when almost 64 percent of those eligible voted. In 1980, when 53.9 percent voted, almost twice as many citizens stayed home as voted for Reagan. In 1982, 38 percent voted for House members. Voting has declined as impediments to voting (poll taxes, literacy tests, burdensome registration and residency requirements) have declined, as the populace has become more affluent and better educated, and as government has become more central to American life. Voting has declined as politics has become a television enterprise, delivered to even the most passive people in their living rooms.

Twenty-four-hour voting might increase turnout a bit, as might Sunday voting, if only because voting would be distributed round the clock, and there would be fewer discouraging lines at polls. Registration could be even easier than it is, but it is not a serious burden anywhere. In some democracies (Australia, New Zealand, Belgium) nonvoting is penalized; in others, registration is automatic; in others, registration is done by government canvass. The United States is the only major democracy where satisfying eligibility requirements is entirely up to the voter. In 1980, 29 percent of the electorate (47 million people) were not registered. In 1982 it was 36 percent (60 million). As Gary Orren of the Kennedy School notes, in this country voting has been linked to individual initiative, and even mild registration requirements are effective "filters" screening citizens on the basis of motivation.

It is assumed that higher turnouts would be bonanzas for Democrats because certain groups, such as blacks and Hispanics, are "underrepresented" in election turnouts. But Austin Ranney of the American Enterprise Institute says that the level of cynicism and the distribution of policy preferences seem to be almost the same among voters and nonvoters. A study of the groups with the lowest voting rates in 1980 (blacks, Hispanics, whites earning less than $5,000, whites with less than high school education, working-class white Roman Catholics) concluded that if they had voted as much as the whole electorate did, the Carter share would have increased just 1.5 percentage points.

The symposium was told that in measuring a government's legitimacy, "the criterion"—note the definite article: "the" criterion—"is how many people vote." Not how many are eligible, but how many choose to vote. That odd theory of legitimacy is related to the even odder theory that high turnouts are an index of social health. In two presidential ballotings in Germany in 1932, 86.2 and 83.5 percent of the electorate voted. In 1933, 88.8 percent voted in the Assembly election swept by the Nazis. Did the high 1933 turnout make the Nazi regime especially legitimate? Were the 1932 turnouts a sign of the health of the Weimar Republic? The turnouts reflected the unhealthy stakes of politics then: Elections determined which mobs ruled the streets and who went to concentration camps.

The fundamental human right is to good government. The

fundamental problem of democracy is to get people to consent to that, not just to swell the flood of ballots. In democracy, legitimacy derives from consent, but nonvoting often is a form of passive consent. It often is an expression not of alienation but contentment, or at least the belief that things will be tolerable no matter who wins. People may not feel that way in Venezuela, where there are 94 percent turnouts. But the glory of our politics, as conducted by two parties with low ideological flames, is that the stakes of our elections, as they affect the day-to-day life of the average American, are agreeably low.

Besides, under the U.S. Electoral College, not voting in a presidential election often is understandable as an economy of effort. If polls make clear that the outcome in a particular state is not in doubt, the value of voting is the emotional reward. If voting is not cathartic or otherwise satisfying, people will stay at home. Might as well curl up with a good book. Casting a vote is not inherently virtuous. The quality of the infrequent act of voting depends on the constant thoughtfulness of the citizens's life.

In Morgantown, North Carolina, a wise 87-year-old says: "I'd be happy if nobody in the United States votes except for the people who thought about the issues and made up their minds and wanted to vote. No one else who votes is going to contribute anything but statistics, and I don't care that much for statistics." Sam Ervin, we miss you.

October 10, 1983

Gary Hart: Jay Gatsby in Politics

On New Hampshire primary night, television viewers saw something called Boy George accept a Grammy Award by saying: "You know a good drag queen when you see one." Prime-time America certainly is open to new, er, *ideas.* The second biggest winner of the night, Michael Jackson, has made a Pepsi commercial that says: "You're a whole new generation." And that night's biggest winner, Gary Hart, says he is the voice of a new generation.

Hart is Jay Gatsby in politics: He is his own work of art. His cowboy boots are nutty. This Yalie from Kansas is now from the Denver–Colorado Springs corridor, which is more like Connecticut than old Colorado. Denver, a city of rapid risers (buildings, people), is Western primarily in the go-for-it spirit associated with extraction industries (oil, mining). Hart is running as the fourth Kennedy brother, one hand in the suit-jacket pocket, the other sweeping his forelock off his forehead. But McGovern's former campaign manager is also projecting the image of a Howard Baker Democrat, a cool professional. He may be what Mo Udall was in 1976, the fellow who chases the winner all the way to the convention. But Udall is Mr. Congeniality. Hart, whose ambition is more consuming and whose attacks are more acid, may be more wounding than Udall was.

Or Hart could be what Carter was in 1976. He says he knows how to win a nomination, as he showed with McGovern in 1972. (Can you name the other campaign manager who ran for president? Bobby Kennedy.) Carter, too, was a loner who ran a theme campaign that distanced him from his party's big battalions. Certainly, Mondale's people feel the way LBJ's people felt in 1960 when JFK would not wait his turn.

He has JFK's "generational" theme but with this difference: Nothing in nature is infinite, but one thing comes close—the narcissism of the "Vietnam generation." It is convinced that its experiences have been uniquely deepening. But the *New Republic's* Charles Krauthammer, 33, says that what distinguishes whippersnappers like Hart from codgers like Mondale and Reagan "is not what the younger guys *did* experience, but what they *didn't:* the Depression, World War II, the early nuclear years. They claim that having missed the great trials and triumphs of the century is some special qualification for the presidency."

Gene McCarthy once said that an "issues candidate" is one who constantly says "issues." So far, that is the sense in which Hart is the "candidate of ideas." Since Aristotle there have been precious few political ideas that are both new and true, but Hart understands that if you run to the left or right you offend the right or left, so he is running foursquare for "the future." Hart's theme— the "new"—is a damp squib, but Mondale's theme—"I am ready"— is positively soggy.

The Democratic establishment, as an act of penance for the Carter presidency and to help Carter's vice president, compressed the early delegate selection season. The theory was that no dark horse would have time to gather strength. But fads, which is what Hart is at the moment, are fast movers, like prairie fires. Mondale may wind up wishing there had been more dead time after New Hampshire for Hart's heat to dissipate. New Hampshire also may have done for Mondale what Iowa did for Reagan in 1980: "Hello, this is your wake-up call . . . "

Had Mondale mashed everyone by March 1, he might have seemed untested. For a variety of reasons—his voice, his withdrawal from the race for the 1976 nomination, his history of rising (to the Senate and vice presidency) by others' initiatives, his association with Carter–Mondale strikes many people as a weak guy fronting for tough guys, such as labor leaders. New Hampshire's sock in the nose may make him become mean. He must say: "Gary is a nice boy but we are all growing old waiting for his first new idea. Gary's second favorite word, after 'new' (which he used five times in one clause the other day), is 'fundamental.' OK, what is so *fundamentally* wrong with the party of Roosevelt, Kennedy and Humphrey?"

If on March 13 Mondale beats Hart by even a whisker in Massachusetts, much air will escape form Hart's balloon. If Hart wins there, he can say: Democrats cannot nominate anyone who consistently loses Northeastern primaries. Down South, a tong war is brewing. Labor has plighted its troth early, and may campaign against Hart as a McGovernite, eager to get U.S. forces out of Oklahoma and prepared to sacrifice economic growth for the convenience of lesbian snail darters. Hart may respond by bashing labor, and the venom may reach 1972 levels. It is unclear which is more unpopular in the South, labor or McGovernism. This is clear: A Democrat who cannot carry five Southern states is unlikely to become president. Carrying five would be hard for the survivor of a nasty fight.

There is still life in John Glenn. He wanted to be a halfback but became a pulling guard. His negative campaign against Mondale's labor ties opened a hole that Hart scampered through. Now Glenn might benefit from the chaos Hart has created. Chaos raises thoughts of a brokered convention. When Democrats are out of power and unable to fiddle with the country, they fiddle compulsively with their rules, and in 1984 delegates will be free to follow their "consciences"—a terrifying idea, but perhaps an entertaining event.

However, this prize will be settled in the primaries. If Hart is still in the thick of things by April 1, he probably will win, and Reagan will have his hands full. Hart will have no baggage: After

12 years the statute of limitations has run out on the crime of managing McGovern, and Hart cannot be tied to the Carter calamity. Also he can pick a big-state, Eastern, Catholic running mate from an ethnic group that is politically ascending and normally casts many GOP votes: Italian-Americans. Reagan gets lots of blue-collar votes? Hart's running mate can be Archie Bunker's representative. The film footage introducing Bunker's show looks exactly like New York's Ninth District in Queens. It is a battleground: In 1980 it favored Kennedy in the primary and Reagan in November. It is the home of a former prosecutor, who ran on the slogan "finally . . . a tough Democrat," Representative Geraldine Ferraro.

March 12, 1984

The Art of Invective

A political campaign is not expected to be a flow of soul or a feast of reason, but the one featuring Messrs. Mondale and Hart is not even interestingly rude. Indeed, it demonstrates that the art of political invective is, like most things, in decline.

To hear Mondale and Hart tell it—and they tell it with fawnlike eyes filled with hurt—the other fellow is being unbearably mean. Their idea of beastliness is a statement like "Warmonger Mondale will leave four jeeps in Honduras!" or "Heartless Hart would not bail when water was coming over Chrysler's gunwales!" This is rough stuff? If these guys were desserts, they would be crème caramel.

When this Republic was brimming with youthful vigor, John Randolph said of a rival, "He shines and stinks like rotten mackerel by moonlight." Ulysses Grant said James Garfield had the backbone of an angleworm. Teddy Roosevelt said William McKinley had no more backbone than a chocolate eclair and he said of Oliver Wendell Holmes that he, Roosevelt, could carve a judge with more backbone from a banana. Harold Ickes, FDR's interior secretary and holder of the indoor record for tartness, said that Senator Huey Long suffered from "halitosis of the intellect."

Even recently American public life has known barbed wit as well as rhetorical barbed wire. Justice Hugo Black, attending the funeral of an enemy, was asked by a late arriver how far the service had gone. Black whispered, "They just opened the defense." Dean Acheson said you should trust J. Edgar Hoover as much as you would a rattlesnake with a silencer on its tail. Adlai Stevenson said of Norman Vincent Peale, "I find Paul appealing but Peale appalling." Gene McCarthy said Walter Mondale has the soul of a vice president. When George Romney said U.S. officials in Vietnam had brainwashed him, McCarthy said he thought a light rinse would have sufficed.

And in 1980, what passes for brutality? This does: "Where's the beef?" Where's the wit?

My interest in invective was whetted in 1963 when living in England, which was luxuriating in the Profumo–Christine Keeler sex-and-espionage scandal. In Parliament, a Labor member, annoyed by Lord Hailsham's moralizing, exclaimed: "When self-indulgence has reduced a man to the shape of Lord Hailsham, sexual continence involves no more than a sense of the ridiculous."

British political comment still can be as sharp as the best British cheddar. A recent editorial in *The Economist* said: "As for Mr. Hart, the primaries have shown him to be not much more than a loofah—abrasive but without much solidity." (A loofah is a bath sponge.) But even the British are now more restrained than they were when Disraeli said of Lord John Russell: "If a traveler were informed that such a man was leader of the House of Commons, he may well begin to comprehend how the Egyptians worshiped an insect."

Perhaps the tang of British political rhetoric owes something to the acidity of British literary criticism. Remember the critic who said of Tennyson's "Maud" that the title contains one too many vowels and that it is a matter of indifference which one is removed. Or Samuel Butler, who said of the Thoms Carlyles, "It was very good of God to let Carlyle and Mrs. Carlyle marry one another and so make only two people miserable instead of four."

When British political and literary wit mix, the result can be wonderful. When Evelyn Waugh heard that a growth removed from Randolph Churchill was benign, he said the surgeon had removed the only part of Churchill that was not malignant. When George Bernard Shaw offered Winston Churchill two tickets to the opening night of a Shaw play, saying, "Bring a friend—if you have one," Churchill reportedly responded, "I can not come opening night but can come the second night—if there is one."

Bear these brickbats in mind the next time Hart or Mondale

gets sulky because the other guy has said something naughty. The naughtiness is apt to be one of them disputing the other's claim to have been the first to do something foolish (such as endorse a nuclear freeze) or to have done something impenetrably obscure (such as voting to table a perfecting amendment to an amendment to a bill to accelerate the depreciation of something).

The campaign is about to tumble into a abyss of blandness-no more sizzlers like "Nyah, nyah, Hart opposed the Trade Amendment Assistance Act!" So Simon & Schuster should rush Hart and Mondale galleys of the forthcoming book *Whatever It Is I'm Against It*. This book is a compendium of negative thoughts, my favorite being Baudelaire's suggested epitaph for Belgium: "At last!"

April 15, 1984

Jesse Jackson, Political Pilgrim

Jesse Jackson shows no symptoms of shyness. He is frequently and piercingly audible about almost everything, and is especially boisterous when expressing scathing disapproval of social arrangements. Thus it is an occasion for astonishment when his indignation flags, as it did in Cuba and Nicaragua.

Jackson—him with the red-hot impatience for human rights—got "good vibrations" from Fidel Castro, who gave him a few political prisoners as campaign props. (Castro has a bountiful supply of such prisoners.) Jackson, whose moral grandeur is a subject introduced by him with indefatigable energy, found in Nicaragua a regime he considers a flower of creation. The regime has never permitted an election, boasts of exporting war to El Salvador and has concentration camps for persons who are unreconciled to it. Jackson praised it for marching toward "democracy, peace and reconciliation."

Jackson's propensity for historical parallels is always entertaining, and never more so than when, on ABC's *This Week with David Brinkley*, he explained that Nicaragua's Sandinista dictators are doing better than America's Founding Fathers did. The Sandinistas have wielded dictatorial power for only five years, whereas "the gap between American independence, a revolution from Britain in 1776, and a President being elected in 1789 was 13 years."

For America, as for the Sandinistas, "the transition between coming into power militarily and moving toward full-scale democracy" was a "slow process."

Even if you assume, as Jackson does, that independence was achieved, not just declared, in 1776 (what does he think happened at Yorktown in 1781?), it is peculiar to think, as he does, that there was a military dictatorship until 1789. Actually, the Constitutional Convention of 1787 was called because there was too little central authority over the 13 robust constitutional democracies that were loosely linked under the Articles of Confederation.

What is interesting about Jackson's argument is not that it is stupid but that it is willfully, almost painstakingly, so. Obviously he and his deepest thinkers sat down and asked: How can we concoct an apology for Sandinista tyranny? So the problem is not that Jackson is as inane as is any child whose supply of convictions is disproportionate to his supply of information. The problem is that he seems to relish the challenge of defending the indefensible for the benefit of leftist dictators.

Jackson was asked whether he told Castro that a quarter of a century of dictatorship should suffice and that it is time for an election. His answer—no—came swaddled in philosophic babble: "I had to respect the sovereignty of his nation, his territorial integrity, and the right of their government to operate as they see fit." When you hear from Jackson such unwonted deference toward authority, you can be sure that he is enjoying the hospitality of a communist or Arab tyrant.

It is one of the familiar farces of this century: A political pilgrim from a democracy, exercising his right to leave his country, travels to a nation suffocating beneath a regime that denies that right and most others. There, by the intensity of his raptures, the pilgrim makes of himself a perfect ninny. But never before have American taxpayers helped fund such a pilgrimage for a politician. (Part of Jackson's bills were paid by the communist regimes.) And never before has a pilgrimage had as its real destination a major party's convention.

If America is, as Jackson seems to think, a nation that esteems people in proportion to their ability to create telegenic uproars, then the public may come to endorse Jackson's immense appreciation of himself. (He is, he constantly says, rather like Jesus.) If, however, this is, as Democrats have reason to think, a nation that punishes extremism, Democrat's toleration of Jackson is going to be costly.

Since the 1968 convention and the 1972 McGovernite take-over, the Democratic Party has been trying to expunge the taint of extremism. That taint is one reason for the steady defection of the moderate Democrats who gave Ronald Reagan his margin of victory. Jackson is the latest example of Reagan luck.

Jackson's collaboration with dictators who loath his country has given some Democrats the following nightmare. In October Republicans run a television commercial with no spoken words, only six photographs flashed on the screen: Jackson hugging the terrorist Arafat. Jackson grinning with Syria's Assad, killer of Marines. Jackson fawning over Castro. Jackson being jolly with Ortega, leader of the Sandinistas, whose anthem refers to the United States as "the enemy of humanity." Jackson hugging the anti-Semite Farrakhan. ("I respect him very much," says Jackson.) And Jackson hugging a nervously grinning Mondale. Does Mondale have anything—anything at all—to say about Jackson's travels?

Last Sunday found Jackson on the Mexican border, leading a demonstration that, naturally enough, featured detestation of what Jackson calls U.S. "arrogance." When some of his fans burned an effigy of Uncle Sam holding a swastika in one hand and a club in the other, Jackson said of his campaign, "That's not what we're about." Oh yes it is.

July 5, 1984

Ronald Reagan's Paradoxes

Ronald Reagan's reelection campaign is stepping so high, wide and plentiful that the mind reels off into paradoxes, including these two: Reagan is soaring because he has restored trust in that which he distrusts—government. And he is exactly in tune with the mood of the moment, which is liberal.

One must take the bitter with the sweet, but it must be bitter indeed for Reagan to note that fate has played him the scurvy trick of causing him, the scourge of government, to rehabilitate it. The ugly truth must be faced: When folks feel good about their country, some of the feeling spills over and attaches to the institutions of community life, the expression of collective effort—the government. There are 80,000 governmental units in this Republic, but one sets the tone—the one Reagan has. And—"drat!" he may say—contentment with the presidency is spreading and contaminating all of public life.

It was especially reckless of him to reduce inflation. In the last decade inflation became considered the principal domestic problem, and government was considered the principal cause of inflation. Inflation was the main reason why, just two years ago, three-quarters of those questioned in one reliable poll said government causes more problems than it solves. The taming of inflation, for now, has removed the irritant in the public's eye regarding government.

The public's liberalism, and Reagan's benefit from it, is less apparent but even more important, and explains why the Reverend Jerry Falwell's favorite candidate is overwhelmingly the favorite candidate of voters aged 18–26. Eighty years ago, Henry James defined journalism as the science of beating the sense out of words. It certainly has done so to political labels. But it is no mere semantic quibble to insist that the essential aim of liberalism, and the central liberal value, is the maximization of individual choice. And that is the feeling—the aura—produced by the President's achievement, rapid economic growth.

The illiberal aspects of the President's program—opposition to abortion, and perhaps support for school prayer—have received attention disproportionate to their importance to the electorate. The Supreme Court, not the executive branch, has, for the foreseeable future, custody of issues concerning abortion and church–state relations. With five justices in their late seventies, a President can make a profound difference on the Court, but that is a contingency too remote to be controlling on the minds of many voters.

The conservative temperament is, at bottom, incorrigibly skeptical of the ability of human plans to eliminate the rattling bumps from the road of life. But Reagan is infectiously serene about the evaporation of deficits and all other limiting facts, painlessly, under the heat of economic growth. This, because he seems easily to imagine that business cycles have been banished.

Recently Reagan told an audience that Americans should avoid "hedonism." It was an enchanting moment, involving a word not usually featured in American politics. Arguably Reagan, by denouncing the incontinent pursuit of pleasure, was striking at the

American Way of Life. Certainly Reagan coming on as Cotton Mather is singularly unconvincing. He is our President Monroe— the man for the era of good feelings.

September 23, 1984

A Lovely Disregard of Logic

Jim Wacker, professor of football at Texas Christian University, may have the finest sense of nuance in language since Flaubert, or at least since Woody Hayes. Wacker says his team, the Horned Frogs, plays "smash-mouth football." He means that his lads are (as less poetic coaches are wont to say) "physical," meaning vigorous. As the clock—the merciful clock—runs out in this final quarter of what feels like a 27-quarter presidential game, Messrs. Mondale and Reagan are playing smash-mouth politics. Vigorous, they are.

Last week Mondale was merrily reading a letter Reagan sent to Nixon in 1960 comparing Kennedy's economic program to Marx's and Hitler's. Reagan says he meant that Kennedy was a statist and statism leads, inexorably, to totalitarianism. When Reagan plucks up the large ideas of Western civilization, all hell breaks loose and a Latin phrase comes to mind: *"Ne puero gladium"* ("Do not give a child a sword"). But, 25 years later, Reagan is more mature about such things and, anyway, he is not running for a professorship of intellectual history.

For his part, Reagan is giving public readings of something more relevant than old letters—Mondale's Senate voting record on defense issues. This gives Reagan an opportunity to say the magic word: "McGovern!" "Crazylegs" Mondale (as he was known with the Elmore, Minnesota, high school Wildcats) says Reagan is a dunce. Reagan, a plucky lineman for the Eureka, Illinois, Golden Tornadoes, says Mondale is a McGovernite. If the voters believed both, Reagan would win in a walk.

In politics, as in football, there is a fine line between permissible and impermissible ferocity. Against Army in 1946 Notre Dame's Bob Livingstone missed a tackle, and his teammate Johnny Lujack screamed, "Livingstone, you son of a bitch!" Coach Frank Leahy said, "Another sacrilege like that, Jonathan Lujack, and you will be disassociated from our fine Catholic university." Then Livingstone missed another tackle and Leahy addressed his bench: "Lads, Jonathan Lujack was right about Robert Livingstone." In politics, the trick is to play like TCU while talking like Cicero.

The burned child fears the fire and when dawn breaks next Tuesday voters may pull the covers over their ringing heads and refuse to get out of bed. The painter Whistler once shot a dog because the brute (the dog, not Whistler) had, Whistler said, "placed itself badly in relation to the landscape." You may feel that way about this campaign, which has been almost lovely in its disregard of logic, and never more so than in the use by certain Reaganites of the slogan "Let Reagan be Reagan!" Who is stopping him? The White House staff? If the likes of them can manipulate, inhibit, deflect, dilute, suffocate and sidetrack Reagan, then what, exactly, is this Reagan who is yearning to breathe free, and how hard is he yearning?

Try this experiment. In a loud voice say: "Let Teddy Roosevelt be Teddy Roosevelt!" If you have even a sliver of a sense of the absurd, you will burst out laughing. If Teddy's White House staff had been foolhardy enough to try to "manage" him, the staff would have been reduced to a cinder by the flame of his temper. But, then, he hardly had a staff: one secretary, one assistant secretary, 13 clerks, one telegrapher, seven messengers. "Let FDR be FDR"? More laughter. Harry Hopkins should "let" Roosevelt be Rooseveltian? It is odd for a leader's supporters to demand that his subordinates "let" his leadership flow forth.

Reaganites who say "Let Reagan be Reagan!" are expressing lack of confidence in, and disrespect for, Reagan. He is a finished product. He is what he has been, a man who has the staff he has chosen to have, and who has chosen to give them the discretion they exercise. He is a temperamentally moderate man, comfortable about the confinements of a modern state and a large party. Moderates almost always are the people who win American elections. And only moderates win electoral-vote landslides.

Reagan's second landslide may be in the offing, judging by Mondale's upside-down campaign. Last week he was in Ohio wooing steelworkers. If they still need wooing in October, why was he wooing Mississippi in August? In presidential politics you first secure your base, and then you go looking for swing states. This year what should be Mondale's base—most of the industrial Northeast and Midwest—has been, at best, a potential swing region, and he has had trouble finding swing states elsewhere. Mondale has hoped for a "Humphrey style" fast finish. In Humphrey's rush at Nixon in 1968, he was switching hundreds of thousands of votes a day. But Humphrey finished with just 42.7 percent of the vote. (Nixon got 43.4, but most of Wallace's 13.5 would have been Nixon's.)

It is a common failing to see inevitability where there really are contingencies. Republican success this year was not inevitable. Consider. Republicans use Tip O'Neill's name to scare their children into eating broccoli. "Eat, or Tip O'Neill will getcha." But if Tip had not agreed to a bipartisan commission to fix social security, the Reagan administration would have had to commit the unpleasantness on its own. That would have exacerbated the GOP's gravest vulnerability, with incalculable consequences.

The most important contingency—the outcome of the Democratic primaries—calls into question God's wisdom in giving free will to people who do not live in Dixville Notch, N.H. At 12:01 A.M. on primary day, Dixville Notchers tumbled out from beneath their covers to vote as soon as possible. That community has peculiar habits but impeccable taste: It produced a landslide for Fritz Hollings (8 for Fritz, 4 for everyone else). Alas, the axiom is not that as Dixville Notch goes, so goes the nation. Were it, the competition this fall would have been more fun, and maybe even closer.

Now, on election eve, it is well for all competitors, and the public, to put matters in perspective. One Friday before a game, Notre Dame's Leahy was informed that a coach's father had died. "Well," said Leahy solemnly, "at least that man won't have to undergo the humiliation of being defeated by Pittsburgh tomorrow." In politics, at least, there is life after an election, even—sometimes especially—for the losers.

November 5, 1984

Mondale: Bullied and Buried

In his 1980 concession statement, Vice President Walter Mondale said: "The people have peacefully wielded their staggering power." No one has been as blasted as Mondale by that power. Adlai Stevenson lost twice by a cumulative electoral vote total of 899 to 162. In Mondale's last two times on a national ticket he has lost 1,014 to 62.

Often after elections the sluice gates of criticism open as leaders in the losing candidate's party say, with an air of slighted genius, "If only he had listened to me." Not this time.

Mondale might have made it slightly closer with a more plausible (and a Southern) running mate, and a serious idea, such as radical tax simplification. Instead, the campaign that began with the appearance of him being bullied by women's groups ended with him promising to appoint a Hispanic to his Cabinet. Ye gods.

The traditional edifice of Democratic politics has been razed to the ground, the rubble has been plowed and salt has been sown. There should be no nonsense about the 1984 outcome being caused by tactical miscalculations. The Democratic Party is a refractory mule, but surely this third landslide in four elections will get its attention.

On election eve, Mondale told a crowd that Republicans never use the word "decent." Democrats would do well to quit using it. Mondale frequently said, "I would rather lose an election about decency than win one about self-interest." Such rhetoric, implying that Republicans are not just wrong but indecent, is the extreme moralizing of a party out of the habit of thinking and even arguing, and in the habit of asserting a moral monopoly.

The 1982 recession was bad for Democrats because it allowed them to think that they did not need to think—that they could coast, counting on the hammer blows of economic hardship to reassemble the old coalition. But by now it is bizarre, if common, for otherwise rational people to ask, "Are we on the verge of a 'realignment' in favor of the Republican Party?" Suppose Noah, in the 34th day of the 40 days of rain, had asked his wife, "Do you think we may get some rain?" At the presidential level, realignment is a fact.

Republicans have won four of the last five presidential elections. In the last four they have won 82.4 percent of the electoral votes, approaching Franklin Roosevelt's four-election achievement of 88.3 percent. And the Republicans have done it with three candidates, not just one political giant.

The nation was moderately conservative when it chose Eisenhower over Stevenson twice. Next it barely preferred Kennedy, a moderate Democrat, over Nixon. Johnson, the only post-Truman President with a Rooseveltian, liberal domestic agenda, was an accident of assassination and the perceived radicalism of his Republican opponent, Goldwater. Two years later Republicans gained 47 House and three Senate seats. In 1968 the combined Nixon and George Wallace vote was 57 percent. In 1972 Nixon got 61 percent against McGovern. In 1976 the Democrat perceived as the most conservative in the nomination contest, Carter, was nominated and narrowly defeated a conservative Republican, Ford. Then came two conservative landslides.

Tuesday's election buried the most ideologically uniform and liberal ticket in American history. The ticket was a quixotic offering to an electorate even more conservative than the electorate has been at any point since 1952.

Many Democrats will say that the Republican run of successes is a fluke compounded of weak Democratic nominees and the unreasonably charming Reagan personality. But in four elections the Democratic Party has tried to sell the country McGovern, Carter twice and Mondale. Four such "aberrations" consecutively are not aberrations. They constitute a single propensity. It is the Democratic Party's propensity to disregard the public's thoughts—not thoughts about Reagan's smile, but about the issues.

Reagan has a right to feel as though he is sitting on a pink cloud over an ocean of joy with a rainbow draped around his shoulders. But Reagan will rightly insist that Democrats are deluding themselves when they say this was a rout produced by his smile rather than by his party's positions.

In the 19th century, an exasperated (and probably jealous) critic said: "Horatio Alger wrote the same novel 135 times and never lost his audience." In Reagan's long career he has demonstrated that in a democracy you build an audience by saying a few clear and convincing things 135,000 times. The lesson of Tuesday—a lesson so stark that it may be missed by persons in hot pursuit of subtleties—is that both Mondale and Reagan spoke clearly, but Reagan convinced.

November 8, 1984

The Great 49-State "Non-Mandate"

The Democratic nominee lost 49 states but, in the aftermath, his party has won the John Jacob Astor trophy for displaying fortitude and phlegm in the face of disaster. According to legend, Astor was having a drink when the *Titantic* struck the iceberg. He quipped: "I sent for ice, but this is ridiculous." If you admire savoir-faire amidst falling ceilings, listen to Democrats solemnly saying that Reagan won no mandate. Watch them curvet around the awkward fact that Reagan won 40 times more electoral votes than their man won.

Mondale was shifting into second gear the summer of 1982 when the "nuclear freeze" rally filled Central Park's Sheep Meadow. Mondale made the freeze the centerpiece of his campaign, evidently on the theory that "as the Sheep Meadow goes, so goes the country." That theory, though bizarre, is no more so than the theory behind the denial that Reagan got a mandate: "As Minnesota and the District of Columbia think, so thinks the country."

The Democrats' thesis is that Reagan's victory was "merely personal"—whatever that means. Presumably the voters stood with their hands hovering over their ballots and thought: "Mondale is right on the issues. Reagan is going to impoverish me and then incinerate me. But, shucks, he is sweet and will do it sincerely." Mondale people spent the autumn convincing a small and gullible group (themselves) that the electorate "really" agreed with Mondale, but . . . but what? Such talk carries the loud implication that the voters are ninnies.

Like Lady Macbeth exclaiming, "Out, damned spot!" the Democrats asking, "Mandate? What mandate?" are trying to talk away an embarrassment. A facet of the current denial of a mandate, and the disparagement of the electorate, is the television alibi. Mondale says he never "warmed" to television. There is truth in that, but not much explanation. Suppose Mondale were as at ease on television as Reagan is, and suppose Reagan were as handicapped on television as Mondale believes he is. The result of the 1984 election would have been . . . a Reagan landslide. When a Mondale speechwriter was asked who could have beaten Reagan this year, he said: "Robert Redford. Maybe Walter Cronkite." Oh? Democrats have no serious political problems, just image-tuning problems? Where do these Democrats live, in Tennyson's valley where falls not hail, or rain, or any snow, nor ever wind blows loudly?

The politics-as-cosmetics people should try something. They should get Redford or Cronkite or even Laurence Olivier, invest him with the majesty of the Democratic nomination, put him on a podium in San Francisco and have him say in the most polished way, "Mr. Reagan will raise taxes, and so will I. He won't tell you. I just did." The nation will say: "That handsome fellow sure talks well." Then the nation will give that fellow's opponent about 49 states.

Perhaps if, say, picklemakers were as talkative and as given to hanging around with each other as journalists are, we would have a pickle theory of this election. The picklemakers, being human and hence self-absorbed, would come to the conclusion that, somehow, pickles and their makers are the movers and shakers of the universe and the shapers of large events. The intellectuals among them would concoct a full-blown pickle theory of history, demonstrating the centrality of pickles in the rise of Cromwell and the Italian *Risorgimento*.

And so it is with many journalists. They tend to think that what they deal in—communication—is not just the business of explaining, it is the explanation. They think the means of communication are decisive, that mastery of the media makes any message palatable. This is a comforting doctrine for Democrats eager to believe that Mondale's message did not get out. Alternatively, they can believe that Mondale's message got out but his delivery was awkward, and voters—the dolts—care only about graceful delivery. Again, it seems, the public has let down the Democrats, who have a new slogan: "Blame the electorate first."

Democrats might want to dissolve the electorate and elect a new one. But before condescending to the electorate, Democrats should note a fact from this election. Democrats tried to use Geraldine Ferraro to get half the electorate to act from frivolous motives. The selection of her was condescending toward women, an attempt to trigger collective, reflexive voting by women on something other than serious issues. Judy Goldsmith and other strategic thinkers of the National Organization for Women are dusting themselves off after their tumble into Gender Gap. Even they must by now understand what the gap is. It is not the difference between Reagan's substantial defeat of Mondale among women (57–42) and his shellacking of Mondale among men (61–37). The real gap is this: White males compose 45 percent of the electorate, and Mondale lost 68 percent of that group. Ferraro was, from the start, a disaster for the Democrats. She mounted a campaign to secure the nomination and, by winning, made Mondale seem, yet again, bullied. On the issues, her liberalism underscored Mondale's at a moment when just one-fifth of Democrats described themselves as liberals.

The crux of the case for denying that Reagan received a mandate is this: Republicans gained only 14 seats in the House. But few if any Democrats took the risk of endorsing Ferraro's opposition to the Grenada operation. Virtually every Democrat who won backpedaled away from Mondale's promise to increase taxes. Every Democrat elected in the South, and many Democrats elected elsewhere, knows that if he votes against Reagan on an important issue, his opponent in the next election will say: "In 1984 the people of this district endorsed Reagan's record and values and his promise of four more years of the same. Yet my opponent has voted to frustrate the will of this district."

There was merriment—outright laughter—in the White House mess two days after the election when the *Washington Post* carried this eight-column headline: DEMOCRATS CHALLENGE PRESIDENT'S LANDSLIDE AS A MANDATE. The people in the mess saw in the headline a Democratic flight from reality, and the seeds of a 1988 landslide large enough to be called a mandate.

November 19, 1984

Reagan's Small Republican Renaissance

The campaign that ground into high gear 12 months ago now has hollow echoes in the form of fat books that preserve, like insects in amber, all the political details that seemed trivial at the time and seem more so today. An insect in amber is still just an insect. No matter how high political trivia is piled between hard covers, it does not explain events. For that, thought is required, because American politics involves, to an extent unsuspected by some journalists, ideas. Journalists too proudly "factual" to pay attention to anything but the nuts and bolts of campaigning miss the element of mind that is more important than the machinery. They know everything about events—everything except why they happen, what they mean and why they matter.

For example, Jack Germond and Jules Witcover have perpetrated a 552-page tome composed of coagulated trivia titled *Wake Us When It's Over*. They say the campaign was "devoid of content." And clearly they found it tedious. But people are apt to be bored by what is, to them, unfathomable. Readers will learn more from an essay 534 pages shorter. It is William A. Schambra's "Progressive Liberalism and American 'Community'" in *The Public Interest*. His deft dissection lays bare the skeletons of ideas within the Reagan and Mondale compaigns. He demonstrates that the contest was morally serious, intellectually interesting and expressive of ideas with long pedigrees. Schambra says the election involved conflicting notions of community.

Mondale's notion of community was Lyndon Johnson's. Johnson's aim was to "perfect the unity of the people." The people would be prodded by the central government into a "national" community. Without the prodding, the people would be a lonely crowd, an atomized aggregation of individuals. Johnson's idea of "national" community was as old as the century, as old as the progressive impulse in American politics. It envisioned a degree of national cohesion and central direction known only in wartime. Hence the martial metaphors, such as the "war on poverty" and, later, Jimmy Carter's energy program as "the moral equivalent of war."

Paul Johnson argues that the "war corporatism" Woodrow Wilson imposed on the nation in 1917 began one of America's "great continuities," a collectivist impulse extending through the New Deal and Great Society. Certainly liberals have often seemed nostalgic for the domestic effects of war. After World War I John Dewey applauded the "social possibilities of war." Walter Lippmann said war had given Americans "a new instinct for order, purpose and discipline" and had drawn them "out of their local, group and ethnic loyalties to a greater American citizenship." In his first Inaugural, FDR, who first came to Washington during the war, said: "We must move as a trained and loyal army."

In his address to the 1984 convention, Mario Cuomo applied to the nation, as he has to New York, the collective noun denoting the most intimate association: "family." Mondale said: "Let us be a community, a family . . . Let us end this selfishness." Mondale said Reagan was leading America into callous, greedy individualism. He seemed unaware of the tension between his populist celebration of "the people" and his evident belief that they were easily corrupted by Reagan. Did he wonder why faith in "national" community had withered since its apogee in 1965, the year he came to Washington?

The faith withered because the federal government, while advertising itself as an engine of unity, became a divisive force, a hammer pounding local communities. It used bureaucratic edicts and judicial fiats to launch what Schambra calls "an assault against the traditional prerogatives of locality and neighborhood to define and preserve their own ways of life." In the name of the national community, liberalism tried to break smaller communities to the saddle of the national government.

Local communities were told they could not enforce standards of sexual conduct or protect themselves against pornography. They were told that all their laws expressing community values regarding the regulation of abortion were illegitimate infringements of a freshly minted national right. They felt their neighborhoods becoming less safe as their police forces and courts became more regulated by national edicts. Local unions' seniority systems were overturned. Local communities were told their children could no longer pray in school and often must be bused away from neighborhood schools.

Such bullying of communities was the work of liberals like Mondale. By 1984 they were bewildered by the public's scorn for liberal rhetoric in praise of "community." In August 1985 a judge ended a decade of fine-tuning the "integration" of Boston Schools. The result of his 414 court orders is a shrunken, less integrated system. Enrollment is down from 93,000 to 57,000; a system that was 65 percent white and 35 percent minority now is 28 percent white, 72 percent minority. Thus another community has been ground to powder by power wielded in the name of the "progressive" vision of national community.

Mondale said, "Reagan's strategy has been to divide us into two Americas"—rich and poor. Schambra says Reagan's message has been more complex than the "rugged individualism" of simple-minded conservatism. Reagan has "spoken the new language of the small republic renaissance." In 1976 he called for "an end to gigantism, for a return to the human scale . . . the scale of the local fraternal lodge, the church organization, the block club, the farm bureau." He said "activity on a small, human scale creates the fabric of community." Schambra says Reagan does not see America as Mondale does, as a single national community, or as Mondale says Reagan sees it, as a mob of disconnected individualists. Rather, Reagan sees a community of communities—what he has called "an archipelago of prospering communities and divergent institutions.

Mondale, says Schambra, tied his campaign to an 80-year-old idea of community, one that has been declining for years. Reagan tied his to an older, Jeffersonian idea, and 49 state communities endorsed it in an election that turned on ideas.

September 2, 1985

A Roman Candle Called Iacocca

In the spirit of this season, in which it is more blessed to give than receive, Lee Iacocca is being urged to make of himself a gift to the nation. He does not find the idea of being President either tiresome or disproportionate to his capacities, but although he is flattered by the attention he is repelled by the prospect. So he says. Now.

In the auto industry, the key word recently has been "downsize." Iacocca is in no way scaled down—not in physical presence or energy or certitude. If confidence were chrome, he would be the human equivalent of a mid-Fifties Chrysler Imperial. He wears worsted the way roughnecks used to wear chain mail, and he brandishes a cigar like a lance.

He is the conspicuous star of ubiquitous television commercials that may incidentally sell cars and certainly solve every politician's first problem: name recognition. As director of fundraising for the restoration project, he is going steady with the Statue of Liberty, a romance sufficient to cause the most hardened political consultant to swoon. And then there is The Book.

It is breathtakingly successful and as breathtakingly awful. There are 2.5 million hardback copies in print, and it does not even tell you Princess Di's path to thin thighs. What it does tell you is stuff like this: "John Ricardo and his wife, Thelma, were two of the finest people I've ever met. Unfortunately, the crisis at Chrysler was so severe I never really got to know them."

Lots of people—none of them literary critics—are beating a path to his door to try to seduce him into politics. Some people think that is like seducing Catherine the Great, such is the strength of the tendency. But he combines canniness with an oddly engaging ingenuousness, and he knows that politics "is not my business."

Martin Van Buren was described, not admiringly, as one who approached power with muffled oars. People like Iacocca because nothing is muffled as he approaches anything. People like his off-the-cuff pugnacity and they think they would like that attribute in a presidential candidate. But his say-it-and-see-what-happens spirit is what causes some professional politicians to say that the only way he could be elected is to nominate him in Barbados in the middle of October and keep him there for the next three weeks.

However, the professionals are speaking from vocational vanity. They probably are right, but it would be amusing for him to see if the nomination marathon can be, just once, an amateur's hour. People like his cantankerousness, so he could make it his tactic, even his platform. He could say: No way am I going to Iowa in winter. Or New Hampshire. My campaign will be part McKinley, part McLuhan. I will come out on my porch every day or so and snap at Sam Donaldson.

Detroit perfected "dynamic obsolescence," the steady alteration of fashion to keep consumers itching for the latest model. It is said that models of men, like models of cars, come to seem dated. Iacocca is both up-to-date and dated.

He is in tune with the times in that he resembles Ronald Reagan, in one particular: He has erased the line between public and private personas. That is all very well if you are, like Reagan, a placid lagoon. If you are, like Iacocca, a human emery board, you have to wonder whether you will wear well over the long haul.

Iacocca seems, if not dated, certainly sailing against the wind in his thinking about public policy. Most politicians economize ideas the way some farmers economize water, knowing the supply is not plentiful. Iacocca is a Roman candle of ideas for things Washington should do. Lots of them involve taxes—a value-added tax, a gasoline tax. On those he is probably right, but in politics that is no excuse. He also is hot for an "industrial policy."

The country, however, is skeptical about agenda-setting in Washington. And the decline of liberalism is directly related to the perception that it has embraced what a critic calls the Quantity Theory of Policy—the more policy the better. Furthermore, in spite of all the oceans of malarkey in his book about "motivation" ("The only way you can motivate people is to communicate with them"), a chairman of a corporation is in a command position. A President is in a persuasion position. Persuasion is for the patient.

So, Iacocca for President? The answer probably is: Good man, wrong job. But, then, that is what Sam Rayburn said about another political newcomer—Dwight D. Eisenhower.

December 22, 1985

Mario Cuomo Takes Batting Practice

It is spring training time in Brooklyn, and the phenom is taking batting practice, smacking line drives off the fences. Mario Cuomo, a former minor league centerfielder, currently is a major league governor and (according to the boys in the press box) is a can't-miss candidate for the politicians' Cooperstown.

Today he is in the Brooklyn Supreme Court building, seated beneath a sign that says "Vox Populi." Evidently Latin is big in Brooklyn. Cuomo certainly is.

He is taking questions from the bleachers, and the natives are not restless. The questions are what baseball people call meatballs—soft tosses grooved over the heart of the plate, letter-high. Such questions ("I want to begin by thanking you, governor, for all you have done for . . . ") do not give Cuomo a chance to be impressive, but the questions say something impressive about his governance.

Ebbets Field, home of the Brooklyn Dodgers before Los Angeles's larceny, was never a garden of shrinking violets. Brooklynites, even more than normal New Yorkers, are vocal about their grievances. But the only serious grievance voiced in two and a half hours of Cuomo's open meeting is that Brooklyn deserves a new stadium and a team to romp in it.

The main argument between Cuomo and New York Republicans is how big the tax cut should be. Republicans want it bigger than Cuomo's proposal. They say he is underestimating revenues. Cuomo promises that the cut in personal income taxes is just the start of a "pattern" of cuts that will include business taxes. This, in the Peoples Republic of New York? Yep, and it is like many other states: The two most popular politicians are the President, a Republican, and the governor, a Democrat.

Cuomo came to the nation's attention at the 1984 Democratic National Convention with the keynote speech that proclaimed: "We can do it again." The antecedent of the pronoun "it" was approximately this: We can use energetic government to engineer a more egalitarian society.

But William Schneider, a fellow at the American Enterprise Institute, understands the Democrats' problem. Their ambitious social agenda depends, he says, on sustained and rapid economic growth to produce the economic surplus for egalitarian social engineering. However, such growth dilutes the sense of urgency for redistributive policies.

It is possible that—God and national journalism willing—Americans can come to find governors interesting. Governors have many more direct responsibilities than legislators have, and inevitably have more interesting records. It is hard to be ideologically monochrome when administering education and health systems, settling strikes and prison riots, and balancing budgets—as governors are required to do.

Schneider notes that recent Democratic nomination contests have not been left-versus-right contests, or young-versus-old contests. Rather, they have been "insiders" versus "outsiders."

The modern history (and the decline) of the Democratic Party began in 1968, in Chicago. There, Hubert Humphrey (assisted by a protégé named Walter Mondale) defeated forces outside the party establishment—actually outside the convention hall, in the streets. In 1972 and 1976, the nominations went to outsiders—George McGovern over Ed Muskie and others, Jimmy Carter over Scoop Jackson and others. In 1984 Mondale, the insiders' revenge, defeated Gary Hart, whose new idea was that insiders are burnt-out cases.

A governor, especially of New York, is an interesting blend, being outside the federal publicity machine but inside the game of governance. But Cuomo does not give the impression of wanting a presidential nomination in the consuming way that one must want it if one is going to get it. He says that the wrong question, constantly asked, is: Are you going to run for President in 1988? The correct question is: Are you going to seek re-election in 1986? He says that if his answer to the latter is "yes" (and it almost certainly will be), then the answer to the former must be "no." It must be, because he could not, practically or properly, begin, simultaneously, a second term as governor and a presidential campaign.

He often rises early, sometimes to write his diary, and occasionally he tunes in C-Span. He watches—can you imagine?—reruns of congressional proceedings. Is he inoculating himself against Potomac fever or measuring the opposition? Whichever, he has been warned.

When a New York reporter at the Brooklyn meeting asks Cuomo about the presidency, Cuomo groans. He is required to do that. The audience also groans. This is optional and interesting. They like him where he is, and will become more like New Yorkers—surly—if he starts acting like a presidential candidate. When he arrived in Brooklyn for his batting practice, a female constituent semiswooned: "You're not as ugly in person as on TV." That was a New Yorker trying to be nice.

March 7, 1985

Arf

The optimistic statement "George Bush is not as silly as he frequently seems" now seems comparable to Mark Twain's statement that Wagner's music is better than it sounds. Bush's recent New York performance suggests that although the 1988 nomination is his to lose, he has a gift for doing things like that.

Before his New York debacle, his most recent splash was in the waning days of the 1984 campaign when he had debates with Geraldine Ferraro and himself, winning only the former, and only sort of winning it. His performance earned—yes, earned—him the *Washington Post*'s designation as "the Cliff Barnes of American politics," a reference to the *Dallas* character whom the *Post* characterized as "blustering, opportunistic, craven and hopelessly ineffective all at once." Kinder critics referred to Bush's "hyperkinesis."

After the debate, he bragged about how he had "kicked a little ass." Actually, he had applied his foot firmly to the inside of his mouth as when he claimed Mondale and Ferraro had said the Marines killed by the Beirut truck bomb had "died in shame." His charge was flatly false, and if it was not initially a lie it quickly became one as he refused to retract it.

That rancid episode is relevant to Bush's New York shambles because, yet again, the question of his intention arises: Did he intend to talk rot? It is hard to believe that premeditation was involved in what he said about Mario Cuomo but, alas, he was not improvising, he was reading from a prepared text. Does he read such texts before rising to speak?

A few days before Bush addressed the New York State Conservative Party, Cuomo, no slouch in the silliness sweepstakes, said he might run for President to disprove ethnic "slurs," by which he means speculation that an Italian-American can not win. That is among the silliest reasons ever offered for trying to become leader of the Free World. Besides, speculation about the consequences of a particular ethnicity hardly constitutes a "slur."

Cuomo is right to raise the matter of the sort of thinking that I have heard phrased this way: "If Cuomo looked like Bush, he would be the odds-on favorite for the Democratic nomination." Ah, but what if Cuomo had the handicap of sounding like Bush? This is how Bush sounded when characterizing Cuomo's thought in New York:

"He's telling us to ignore the millions of blacks, Jews, Irish, Italians, Latins, and Poles who shattered the bonds of discrimination and built this great land. . . . "

You blew it, Bush—you blew the American–Samoan vote by neglecting to pander to them, too. But, unwilling to leave wretched enough alone, Bush slogged on:

"Worst of all, he's telling us to be ashamed to stand up and be proud of this great land. . . . "

There he goes again, dishonestly tossing around the idea of shame. What Bush said is gibberish, but not just gibberish. It is a lie. And it suggests how bare Bush's mental cupboard is of themes. He began by accusing Cuomo of "divisiveness," another echo of the Ferraro debate, in which Bush accused Mondale of "telling the American people to divide [by] class—rich and poor." Bush's syntax was as muddled as his thought.

But Bush's low point came with his smarmy sentence: "I can tell you one thing about the difference between a liberal politician and a conservative one: Governor Ronald Reagan kept cop-killers in jail." That was a ten-thumbed attempt to squeeze political advantage from a complicated case in which Cuomo recommended clemency for a man who has spent 18 years in jail and who may— but who never was found to—have directly killed a policeman. Among those who have campaigned for clemency is William Buckley, not hitherto famous as a coddler of "cop-killers." Anyway, anyone can tell Bush one difference between a real conservative and a charlatan: A real conservative does not consider an office like the vice presidency a license to meddle in a state's system of criminal justice.

The unpleasant sound Bush is emitting as he traipses from one conservative gathering to another is a thin, tinny "arf"—the sound of a lapdog. He is panting along Mondale's path to the presidency.

When Norman Mailer published a particularly dreadful novel, a critic—an optimist—titled his review "Mailer Hits Bottom." Realists replied: Not unless he (Mailer) never again gets near a type-writer. Concerning Bush, optimists say: Well, er, perhaps in New York he got the demagoguery out of his system. Realists say: That was not a momentary dereliction of taste; that was part of a pattern.

January 30, 1986

PART 3

The World So Much with Us

Defeat in Berlin

It can be as important to contemplate defeats as it is to celebrate victories. So consider the monument to an American defeat two decades ago: the Berlin Wall.

On July 25, 1961, President Kennedy said that West Berlin was "the great testing place of Western courage and will." It was stirring talk. Nineteen days later it was revealed as just talk.

Berlin was the hole in the Iron Curtain, the city in which you could take a taxi (or subway, or elevated, or a walk) to freedom. On August 12, a 24-hour record was set as more than 3,000 East Germans arrived at a West Berlin reception center. At midnight, August 13, the Communists began sealing off East Berlin.

The afternoon of the day that a million people were annexed into a Soviet satellite, the U.S. secretary of state went to a baseball game. Kennedy was, if not actually relieved by the Communist action, inclined to see it as opening the way to a Berlin settlement.

Berlin is one of the emblematic cities of this unfortunate century. It was the symbol of the unified Germany that upset Europe's balance of power and precipitated World War I, and hence Europe's lingering sickness. In the 1920s, Berlin, even more than Paris, was the capital of the avant-garde. It was hospitable to all the arts celebrating dissolution of forms and overthrow of inhibitions. The fiercely antibourgeois cultural climate was as destructive of middle-class confidence as was the political violence from the right.

In the 1930s, Berlin displayed the dreadful compatibility between advanced devices and primitive purposes. In Berlin, barbarians made effective use of modern bureaucracy and technologies of mass communication (radio, cinema). After the war Berlin became the scene, and then the symbol, of the Cold War.

I feel for Berlin the affection one feels for a place where one has had a kind of epiphany, and where one has done foolish things but emerged unscathed. When I first saw the wall in December 1962, I first saw the stakes of politics in our time. I idiotically risked years in East German jails by smuggling newspapers and novels (such as Gunter Grass's *The Tin Drum*) to a student I had met in East Berlin. He escaped, with a little help from his friend, in 1964.

History invites hypotheticals: "What if . . . ?" What if the blockade begun in 1947 had been smashed by force? What if the allies had used force to unseal East Berlin at dawn, August 13, 1961?

In 1947 the Soviet Union was a shattered nation, having just lost 20 million people. The United States had a nuclear monopoly. But the allies flinched from using force to protect their rights, opting instead for an airlift to supply the city. The Kremlin got the message: The West was so eager to avoid the use of force that its material strength was substantially nullified by its weakness of will. This judgment probably influenced Soviet calculations about attacking Korea.

Korea, at best a tie, was followed by Vietnam, a defeat. The "breaking" of the Berlin blockade is today remembered as one of two postwar American victories. It was no victory. The other supposed victory was the Cuban missile crisis, a "victory" in which, in exchange for the removal of some missiles, we accepted Cuba as a Soviet base for everything else, thereby nullifying the Monroe Doctrine.

The Soviet Union began building a wall across Berlin just a year before it put nuclear missiles in Cuba. The Soviet Union might not have done the latter if it had not got away with the former.

In 1961, the United States had what it subsequently forfeited—an enormous power advantage. In Berlin it had legality on its side. If on August 13 the United States had swept aside the barbed wire (the stone and mortar came only after the United States had shown surprising—to the Communists—passivity), the Soviet Union would have had to concede Berlin to the West. It would have had to stop the hemorrhaging of East Germany's population by sealing East Germany off from East as well as West Berlin. Instead, we acquiesced. It was another installment in a series of lessons whereby we taught the Soviet Union to have contempt for our resolve.

Today, for the first time since the early 1960s, the United States has a rhetorically gifted President who uses his gifts for tough talk toward the Soviet Union. His task is to convince the Soviet Union that unlike in the Berlin crisis 20 years ago, America's President means what he says.

August 6, 1981

"Victory" in Cuba

We are waist deep in muddy analyses celebrating the famous victory in the Cuban missile crisis 20 years ago, and extracting "lessons" from it. Evidently many Americans would not recognize a success if it were served on a platter surrounded by parsley. The crisis began with a failure of U.S. intelligence—in several senses. It ended with Cuba secured as a Soviet outpost. U.S. diplomacy was so slipshod no one could say what had been agreed to. Yet U.S. leadership was inebriated by the wine of self-approval, and foreign policy became saturated with hubris and complacency.

On August 31, 1962, Senator Keating, Republican of New York, trusting leaked intelligence reports from agents and refugees, charged that offensive missiles were going into Cuba. Gulled by Soviet lies, Kennedy's administration repeatedly denied this. On October 14, on ABC's *Issues and Answers*, McGeorge Bundy, Kennedy's national security adviser, denied it again. Photos taken from a U-2 that day proved Keating right.

The crisis ended with withdrawal of the missiles, and of bombers less menacing than those now in Cuba. In addition, the Soviets agreed to . . . well, not much. Kennedy failed to stipulate what offensive weapons the Soviets could not deploy in Cuba. In 1970, when the Soviets began building a submarine base there, Kissinger sent for the record of the Kennedy–Khrushchev understandings. "It emerged," he writes, "that there was no formal understanding in the sense of an agreement, either oral or in writing." Anyway, the Soviets had not agreed in 1962 to a verification system—"because of Castro's opposition," says Kissinger (which is like saying Charlie McCarthy opposed Edgar Bergen).

Why is Finland "Finlandized" but Cuba not "Cubanized"? Why must Finland take care not to offend its Soviet neighbor, while Cuba exports subversion and expeditionary forces in this hemisphere and Africa? Because in 1962 the United States, which had might and right on its side, failed to achieve the only success worthy of the name—a severing of the Soviet military connection with Cuba. Castro had seized Havana less than four years before the crisis. His relationship with Moscow was widely resented in this hemisphere. During the crisis, Brazil's president—a leftist—suggested a solution based on neutralization of Cuba. But Kennedy did not try to condition Cuba's status, and hence he legitimized its status as a Soviet ally. The United States even made a no-invasion pledge, in exchange for Soviet assurances that . . . oh, never mind.

In 1978 MiG-23s arrived in Cuba. We do not know if they have nuclear arming and fusing boxes—which, in any case, can be quickly installed. This much we know: The MiG-23s are offensive weapons—nuclear delivery systems—in wartime. The Soviets are giving Cuba excellent new frigates and new diesel-electric submarines. Cuba already has 25 missile-attack boats, 21 torpedo boats, 10 subchasers—a formidable interdiction force for the Straits of Florida, through which 85 percent of resupplies for the U.S. Army must pass in wartime. The Soviets are completing testing on cruise missiles with 1,500-mile ranges. They are small and do not require silos or large launch platforms. It will be difficult for U.S. intelligence to know if they are sent to Cuba.

Writing in *Commentary* magazine, Peter W. Rodman, diplomat and scholar, provides a counterpoint to complacency about the outcome of the missile crisis. "In the intellectual aftermath of Cuba," he writes, "can be found the seeds of much of the history of the next 20 years." Early in 1963 Bundy said the crisis had "extraordinary pedagogical importance." Soon, Rodman says, four "lessons" became conventional wisdom: The United States succeeded because it limited its objective to restoration of the *status quo ante:* success vindicated crisis management by carefully calibrated escalations of force; the crisis demonstrated the relative unimportance of strategic weapons, and the crisis presaged a Soviet turn toward peace. These lessons were, as Rodman says, "mutually reinforcing." They also were flattering to those who drew the lessons, and lulling to the nation.

By limiting its objective to removal of the missiles, the United States left Cuba free to serve Soviet military aims in many ways. The idea that delicate bargaining had won a splendid victory coincided—not coincidentally—with the Kennedy men's pose as cool pianists improvising at the world's keyboard. Having been "successful" using intimations of latent force, we soon tried using minute gradations of force to send "signals" to Hanoi. It read our signals—correctly—as evidence of a reluctance to press advantages. This reluctance was apparent in the missile crisis, when the U.S. made the least of its moral and military advantages.

In 1965 Ted Sorensen wrote that the crisis had provoked a Soviet decision to "forgo trying to win the arms race" and to "implicitly accept" U.S. strategic superiority. In 1965 Robert Mc-

Namara said the Soviets "have decided that they have lost the quantitative race . . . There is no indication that the Soviets are seeking to develop a strategic nuclear force as large as ours." But by 1970 the Soviets had numerical parity—and raced ahead.

Last month Sorensen, McNamara, Bundy are three other participants in the crisis declared that a lesson of the crisis was the "insignificance" of nuclear superiority when an adversary has a survivable retaliatory capability. (In 1962 U.S. superiority was overwhelming—3 to 1 in long-range bombers, 6 to 1 in long-range missiles.) Alas, the Soviets decline to learn the "lessons" we prefer.

Inevitably, the idea soon spread that (as a Kennedy aide put it) "Khrushchev must have been under very heavy pressure, to take the risk he took." As Rodman says, "The theory of 'moderates' under pressure from 'hard-liners' in the Kremlin is a hardy perennial." Twenty Octobers ago it helped rationalize limiting U.S. objectives—which could hardly have been more limited. When Brezhnev dies there will be calls for the United States to do something forthcoming, lest his successor fall victim to the "hawks" in the Kremlin closets. More dangerous than the missile crisis were—and are—the lessons learned from it.

October 11, 1982

Vietnam: Choosing Defeat

Six years after the last American was evacuated from the roof of the American Embassy in Saigon, a new article adds to the evidence that the military defeat that was sealed April 30, 1975, need not have happened.

The article is in *The Washington Quarterly*, published by the Georgetown University Center for Strategic and International Studies. It is an excerpt from a forthcoming memoir by John Colvin, who was consul general at the British Mission in Hanoi during 1966 and 1967. Colvin has a writer's eye for detail, is unfailingly fascinating, occasionally scalding and, in the end, moving. His thesis is that America had the war won in September 1967, and then renounced victory. He recalls:

"[E]very morning since I reached Hanoi, the streets of the quarter had been lined with war matériel brought in from China across the Paul Daumer Bridge, amphibious vehicles, artillery, armored fighting vehicles, Sergeant surface-to-air missiles on flatbeds, saucily parked even outside the British and Canadian missions. By August and September [1967] there were none at all. . . . "

When Colvin left for England in September, North Vietnam "was no longer capable of maintaining itself as an economic unit nor of mounting aggressive war against its neighbor." This judgment, he says, is not refuted by the strength of the Tet offensive five months later, because "most of that equipment had been in South Vietnam or en route there before the summer air offensive in the north had even begun."

The key to the effectiveness of the 1967 bombing was its consistency, which "for the first time, allowed the North Vietnamese no time to repair war-making facilities. [Their] ingenuity had been defeated . . . their will eroded to near-extinction." Their capacity to wage a major war had been broken by continually cutting the rail lines from China and Haiphong to Hanoi and by putting the ports out of action.

Colvin believes that prompt use of air power against North Vietnam's northeast quadrant would have won the war in 1965 and would have spared both sides the agonizingly higher costs of "gradualism." But after September 1967, the bombing of the northeast quadrant was greatly reduced and frequently interrupted by "peace initiatives" that had no other purpose, from Hanoi's point of view, than to paralyze U.S. operations. Thus the persistence of the campaign that "had sapped North Vietnam's endurance was discarded. And at the end of March 1968, all bombing of North Vietnam north of the 20th parallel was discontinued. Victory—by September 1967, in America's hands—was not so much thrown away as shunned with prim, averted eyes."

Colvin says that "even now, this renunciation is difficult to understand," but he understands it perfectly. It was the sort of prosecution of war that should be expected from a nation in which a significant portion of the intelligentsia was eager to think ill of its country and eager to think kindly of its country's enemy (as "put-upon nationalist Social Democrats").

An oddity of liberalism at the time was its selective skepticism about the competence of government. Liberals believed that government had the skill, if it could just summon the will, to build a "Great Society" adorned by "Model Cities" and skillfully administered "Head Starts." But it was allegedly beyond the capacity of the American government to pound the capacity for aggressive war out of a tin-pot country like North Vietnam.

By 1981, some liberal wreckers ("revisionist" critics of America's post-1945 internationalism) and some conservative wreckers (dogmatic denigrators of social programs), working from opposite directions and from diametrically opposed motives, have had the combined effect of wrecking public confidence in the capacity of government to accomplish anything. Colvin's corrective appraisal of American air power in Vietnam comes, usefully, at the beginning of a decade in which Americans must have confidence in their government's ability, if necessary, to use military assets effectively.

Colvin believes that America's military effort in Vietnam "held the line long enough to permit the secure establishment of a democratic market economy outside Indochina." He may generously overstate matters, but there is truth in his assertion that such liberty and independence as there is in the region springs "from the United States resistance to tyranny in Vietnam. They are living monuments to the American dead in Indochina and to all those men of the United States armed forces whose presence in Vietnam gave the rest of Asia the time to grow, unharassed and at peace. The war was not in vain."

Colvin has provided something Americans too rarely hear, and almost never hear regarding Vietnam: a friendly—and brave—foreign voice.

May 10, 1981

Grenada and the Price of Power

Grenada, although small, is 15 times the size of Iwo Jima and of large symbolic value. U.S. soldiers' boot prints on Grenada's soil have done more than the MX will do to make U.S. power credible and peace secure. President Reagan's defense budgets are not, by themselves, a fully effective signal to the Soviet Union of U.S. seriousness. The boot prints prove that the United States will not only procure sophisticated weapons systems but also has recovered the will to use the weapon on which its security rests: the man with a rifle.

Napoleon's axiom about resorting to force was: "If you start to take Vienna—take Vienna." The Grenada and Lebanon missions demonstrate right and wrong ways of using military forces. In Grenada there is a force sufficient for a clearly defined mission; in Lebanon the mission is ill-defined and, hence, the force is not tailored to it.

Paratroopers had just dropped on Grenada's airfields when Pat Moynihan dropped into the Senate press gallery to charge that we may have violated the U.N. Charter. But it is bad enough we pay for the United Nations; surely we do not have to pay attention to it. In the United Nations' 38 years there have been many hundreds of uses of force by members for territorial aggrandizement or religious, ideological or ethnic advantage. If the United Nations, which condemned Zionism as racism and would not condemn the Korean Air Line massacre, condemns the United States, it should be told that the world needs more uses of force such as the Grenada invasion. The invasion thwarted persons (they can hardly be called a government) who were about to rivet in place a regime allied with the mortal enemy of all open societies, the Soviet Union.

America's legalistic turn of mind reflects its liberal temper, its belief that the world can be tamed and rendered tidy by codifying everything. One consequence is that America is a lawyer's paradise. Another is that Americans take an inappropriately juridical approach to problems with other nations. After something like the invasion of Grenada, Americans tend to ask not "Was that the right thing to do?" but rather, "Did we have a right to do that?" Americans seek to locate "a right"—a license to act—in particular laws, charters, conventions, treaties. Hence the administration made much of what is legally unconvincing and morally unnecessary—the fact that eastern Caribbean nations urged us to act.

But even if there had not been a single American on Grenada, and even if every nation in the world disapproved, an invasion to overturn an indecent regime would have been justified by the security needs of our decent society. Two Cubas—Cuba and Nicaragua—are enough. If the United States were too paralyzed to prevent the planting next door, near vulnerable nations and crucial shipping lanes, of another Soviet outpost with ports and airstrips designed for military use, then nations such as Saudi Arabia would correctly conclude that the United States is irrelevant to their security. If Cuba cannot be "Finlandized" by the United States, Western Europe eventually will be by the Soviet Union.

The Grenadians who wanted to rule Grenada with Soviet and

Cuban help had no more right to do so than Vidkun Quisling, a Norwegian, had to rule Norway with German help. But the window of opportunity for frustrating these Caribbean quislings was closing fast. MacArthur said that all military failure can be explained, in the end, in two words: too late—too late in discerning danger, too late in preparing to meet it. This time the United States acted in time.

When certain senators say they support the use of force only to rescue Americans, their defense votes become understandable: they favor a military suited only to conduct evacuations. When many Americans say we should not use force because communists do, they compound political and intellectual irresponsibility: To equate the invasions of Grenada and Afghanistan is to ignore the fact that a nation's aims must be considered when assessing a nation's actions.

Walter Mondale laments that the invasion undermines "our ability to effectively criticize" Soviet actions in Afghanistan, Poland and elsewhere. That is nonsense squared, first because our criticism is utterly ineffective as a restraint on Soviet power, and second because the validity of our criticism is undiminished. The logic of Mondale's position is that all uses of force, by Castro or Reagan, Hitler or Lincoln, are censorable, regardless of the aims or outcomes. Slogans about nonintervention, and solemn disavowals of force, might allow Americans to seize the rhetorical high ground. The Soviet Union and its surrogates would continue to occupy more and more real ground.

The day editors were in full cry about a "secret war," the front pages of the *New York Times* and the *Washington Post* each contained five stories about the war. People can reasonably differ about when journalists should have been allowed into Grenada. But journalists have earned a certain coolness from officials making life- and-death decisions. Many journalists advocate an "adversary" stance toward their government, denying any duty to weigh the consequences of what they print or broadcast. But incantation of the words "the public's right to know" is no substitute for thinking. Someone must make judgments. Many journalists assert a moral as well as constitutional right to the status of—strictly speaking—irresponsibility. Commanders responsible for soldiers' safety will understandably reciprocate the "adversary" feelings of such journalists.

The first journalists sent overseas in times like these should be those who specialize in shoving cameras at grief-stricken parents. This is the pornography of suffering, making public what should be private, to satisfy a voyeuristic curiosity. It shapes, and I suspect is sometimes intentionally used to shape, the political climate: It promotes national flinching.

So do the sights of war. As I have argued here before, if there had been television cameras at Gettysburg, this would be two countries: The carnage would have caused the North to let the South go. It is an unanswered question whether, given modern communications technologies and modern sensibilities, a democracy can pay the price of remaining a great power.

November 7, 1983

The Perils of Legalism

Pat Moynihan is a traditionalist, but a liberal traditionalist, a keeper of Woodrow Wilson's flame. His loyalty, as elegantly explained in his fine new book *Loyalties*, is to the idea of the rule of law in international affairs. He believes the United States pays too little attention to international law. I believe it pays too much.

Decrying what he calls the "Sovietization" of U.S. policy, he says recent administrations have accepted normlessness, meaning policy insufficiently oriented toward standards of international legality. The role of law, says Moynihan, is to provide proportionate responses to violations of norms. But the very idea of international law is problematic, partly because there is no international consensus about norms. Besides, can there be law among sovereign nations—law where there is no sovereign to adjudicate and enforce judgments?

When the United States invaded Grenada to replace a government, Moynihan said the United States had no "right" to do so and indeed had a "positive obligation not to" because the charter of the Organization of American States declares that no state has a right to intervene, for any reason, in another state's internal affairs. When he said we also had violated the United Nations Charter, I wrote in this space that "it is bad enough we pay for the United Nations; surely we do not have to pay attention to it." Moynihan now rejoins: "Paying attention to the U.N. Charter is paying attention to *our* understanding of the law of nations." Oh? Says who? Moynihan says the charter imposes a dual obligation on governments "to be law-abiding in their relations with one another" and to protect " 'fundamental human rights' as these were understood by British and American constitutional lawyers in 1944." But the charter was a mockery from the moment in 1945 when Stalin's government subscribed to "our understanding" of the law of nations.

It would have been mere right-mindedness—a moral pose rendered immoral by its consequences—to have allowed our values to be extinguished in Grenada so that we could be said to be "paying attention" to our understanding of "the law of nations." Had there been no invasion, Grenadians would be groaning beneath a dictatorship imposed with the indispensable help of Cuba, which cares not a fig for the OAS Charter, and the Soviet Union, which is in violation of virtually every clause of the U.N. Charter. In order to seem to be conforming to the forms of international law, Reagan talked rubbish about the invasion being a rescue mission for medical students. The lie reflected misplaced respect for a codification of national obligations that makes no sense in a world menaced by regimes like those in Havana and Moscow. Reagan should have said: International law, such as it is, in an intramural code, useful among nations that share common values but not germane to dealings with totalitarian or gangster regimes.

Moynihan wishes the Reagan administration had approached the Korean airline massacre "as a violation of a treaty, specifically the Chicago Civil Aviation Convention of 1944," which obligates signatories, including the Soviet Union, to help a lost plane, not shoot it down. Well, OK: It is useful to remind Westerners how little such obligations mean to the Soviet Union. But that is a use of the modalities of law to improve the Western mind, not Soviet behavior. And the Western mind is itself at risk because of certain uses of international law.

The "Helsinki process" might seem to be a use of law, or at least its forms, to do what Moynihan favors. That ongoing process asserts norms in relations between nations and between governments and citizens. But, as Moynihan says, in doing so it fosters a "denial of reality." The 1975 Helsinki accords on human rights were frauds because there was no accord about anything, from the meaning of freedom to the definition of a trade union. In 1976 Moynihan declared that "it has become unmistakably clear that the West was utterly deceived." Surely not. No one thought the Soviet regime had agreed to dismantle itself and its empire, which it would have had to do to comply with the accords. This was détente, the willful suspension of disbelief.

Moynihan cites the International Labor Organization as "the largest single initiative" extending Western, liberal ideas into international law. Well. In 1948 the ILO adopted a convention protecting labor's right to organize free unions. Ninety-four countries have ratified it. Perhaps half of them are not violating it. Many members forbid unions, within the Western meaning of the term. But Western meanings are casualties of participation with communist regimes in things like Helsinki and the ILO. The West seems to agree that there are two diametrically opposed but equally eligible meanings for the crucial words in the political lexicon.

It is said that even organizations like the ILO (the very name is a lie: many member regimes deny representation to labor) and "agreements" reflecting no real agreement are useful as mechanisms for indicting the Soviets. But that sterile exercise does not change Soviet behavior. Signing documents that one side violates in every particular de-moralizes—literally, demoralizes—the West. The public is desensitized by a minuet of diplomacy that fosters the delusion that the two sides share a frame of reference. It is said: "But we have to talk to them." Yes, but not at the cost of eviscerating the language of politics.

Many people who are incensed by Reagan's obviously accurate description of the "evil empire" applaud the charade of the Helsinki process, which is meretriciousness institutionalized. Reagan was elected, in part, to restore realism to the language of East–West relations. But he has been too respectful of corruptions perpetrated in the name of international law. At last year's Madrid event in the Helsinki process, all participants, including the Soviet Union and Poland, solemnly vowed respect for workers' rights to free unions and to "the prerogatives that are recognized by international law." Consider the denial of reality required for participation in such a burlesque—a charade conducted in the name of law. The real danger is not the Sovietization of U.S. policy but of the world's vocabulary, and hence its mind.

February 27, 1984

Why Arms Control Is Harmful

Today's arms control controversy is remarkable for the virtual absence of the most important argument. It is that the arms control process is injurious to U.S. interests. That argument offends conventional wisdom and (what is much the same thing) wishful thinking. It has the redeeming merit of being true, as Seymour Weiss knows. In a paper presented at the Lehrman Institute, Weiss, retired ambassador and State Department director of political and military affairs from 1960–67, argues that enthusiasm for the arms control process—a process barren of achievements—reflects misapprehensions about the usefulness of that process in slowing the arms race, saving money and taming the Soviet Union.

The idea of an arms "race"—often described as "spiraling"—is odd. The U.S. nuclear weapons inventory has been sharply reduced. It contains 8,000 fewer warheads and 25 percent less megatonnage than in the 1960s. This is the result not of arms agreements but of modernization programs that produced safer, more effective weapons—modernizations of the sort that arms control advocates try to block with agreements.

During the era of détente and arms control the Soviet nuclear arsenal has grown quantitatively and qualitatively. A study commissioned during the Carter administration compared 41 categories of nuclear capabilities (warheads, megatonnage, delivery systems, etc.) in the period beginning with the Cuban missile crisis. It concluded that the United States had been well ahead in every category in 1962 and was behind in all but two by the late 1970s. Since SALT II was signed in 1979 the Soviet Union has added more than 3,400 warheads. Does anyone think the world is safer than it was when the SALT process began in 1969?

The achievement most celebrated by arms control enthusiasts is the 1972 treaty effectively banning antiballistic missiles. True, we saved the cost of ABMs. But partly as a result of that decision we will spend many more billions on MX missiles, an unsatisfactory response to the fact that our undefended land-based ICBMs are vulnerable. Because MX is unsatisfactory, billions more may be spent on smaller, mobile "midgetman" missiles. Why is MX so unsatisfactory? Because of an arms agreement.

SALT I limited the number and size of launchers—basically, holes in the ground—rather than numbers or megatonnage of war-

heads. Limits on those would be hard to verify, given Soviet secrecy. So SALT I drove arms planning toward big missiles packing
maximum megatonnage. SALT I did what arms agreements usually
do: It did not restrain competition, it turned it in a new direction.
It was a direction in which the Soviet Union, with its huge SS-18s,
had a lead. SALT I ratified a Soviet advantage and, by giving rise
to the inherently vulnerable MX, reduced the stability of deterrence.

This republic overflows with laws, lawyers and faith that the
world can be tamed by words on parchment. Americans see arms
control as a way of freezing the status quo; the Soviets see it as one
arena in a comprehensive, unending competition. Furthermore,
Weiss says, persons who think arms control should be the "centerpiece" of U.S.–Soviet relations ignore the fundamental incompatibility of U.S. and Soviet objectives. The configuration of the Soviet
buildup in the arms control era is unambiguous. The arms are not
designed for defense but for producing a world pliant to Soviet de-
signs. Weiss says there is no reason to expect the Soviets to negotiate
away advantages, and ample reason to expect the Soviets to exploit
the American thirst for agreements.

In addition to sowing discord among U.S. allies and paralyzing
U.S. procurements, Soviet negotiators have, Weiss says, five aims.
First, limit the wrong things (e.g., launchers). Second, make sure
the limits on important things are ambiguous. (SALT I limited but
did not define "heavy" missiles.) Third, accept specific limits only
if they are unverifiable (e.g., the ban on biological weapons or the
SALT II limits on cruise missile ranges). Fourth, evade even strict,
verifiable limits by claiming they do not apply to this or that program. (The Soviets claim their ABM system is just a defense against
bombers.) Fifth, get the treaty to legitimize violations of the treaty.
(SALT II's flimsy verification terms forbid encryption of data from
missile tests—except when encryption is not intended to evade arms
control limits. But given that it is encrypted, how are we to tell?)

Because ours is an open society, our government cannot cheat
on agreements, and because our society invests such hope in arms
control, even an administration as starchy as Reagan's is apt to forgive Soviet cheating or mute even required reports of it. When,
complying with a Senate demand, the administration submitted a
list of Soviet violations, the *New York Times* denounced the—you
guessed it—administration for "initiating this damaging laundry
list."

The arms control era has coincided with unparalleled Soviet

aggression and threats, from Indochina through Afghanistan. Try to tell victims of "yellow rain" about the wonders of arms control. Biological weapons are controlled—on paper. What has violation of the controls produced? A U.S. clamor for yet more agreements. And arms control enthusiasts, their enthusiasm impervious to evidence, continue to use slogans that were threadbare when Dean Acheson refuted them.

Acheson demolished the bromide that "as long as the Russians are talking they are not fighting." Acheson said that Americans are so wedded to the belief that negotiations are means of ending conflicts that they are blind to the fact that negotiations are equally suited to continuing conflicts. Of the slogan "There is no alternative to negotiations with the Russians," Acheson said: "This is, of course, silly. For if there is no alternative, and if the Russians will only negotiate, as is now the case, on their own terms, then there is no alternative to surrender."

For that reason someone should tell Ronald Reagan to quit saying that nothing is more important than "development of a better working relationship with the Soviet Union." Such talk worsens the asymmetry in U.S.–Soviet negotiations by building pressure on the U.S. government for concessions to produce "movement." An immoderate and unempirical belief in arms control produces a policy of apologetic retreats.

June 18, 1984

Nuclear Morality

Among the sundry and manifold changes in the world (the words are from the prayer book; a theological tone is apposite this week) is a political message from portions of the clergy, especially the Roman Catholic clergy.

The bishop of Corpus Christi has protested the naming of a submarine for that city. This has drawn from the Navy Secretary (a Catholic) a starchy letter rejecting the implication that "naval ships and even military service are somehow profane." He says church teachings recognize the need for deterrent systems for the virtuous task of peace-keeping. "To maintain peace within the natural order of men," Augustine said, "rulers require the power and decision to declare war." They must, Aquinas said, "defend the state against external war weapons."

Do nuclear weapons invalidate that? When an Indianapolis parish votes to protest nuclear arms spending by withholding half the $50 tax on its yearly phone bill, it is just confusing right-mindedness with moral seriousness. But when the bishop of Amarillo urges workers at a nuclear weapons assembly plant to consider seeking other jobs, is he saying that deterrence is possible without nuclear weapons? That deterrence is not a great enough good to justify involvement with nuclear weapons because they are inherently immoral? It is morally incoherent to will an end without willing the means to that end. If the bishop desires a free Europe and America, and also desires unilateral nuclear disarmament, can he say how he thinks his desires are compatible?

Seattle's archbishop urges people to consider refusing to pay half their Federal taxes to protest spending on nuclear arms. (Such spending accounts for about 2 cents of every tax dollar.) He says: "We have to refuse to give our incense—in our day, tax dollars— to the nuclear idol. Some would call what I am urging 'civil disobedience.' I prefer to see it as obedience to God." The archbishop is hardly the first person to put his political objectives above the law and to think he hears God's applause for doing so. He says, "When crimes are being prepared in our name, we must speak plainly." Moralists, especially, must speak carefully, which the archbishop is not doing when he uses words like "idol" and "crimes."

A coherent position, consistent with traditional church teaching, can turn on the distinction between what is tolerated and what is approved. Instruments of mass destruction, which for reasons of accuracy or controllability cannot be or are not apt to be used in ways that discriminate between military and civilian targets, cannot be approved. But they can be tolerated if the unilateral renunciation of them would bring on an intolerable evil (such as subjugation to an evil regime), and if the nation strives to reduce and end reliance on them.

Unless the bishops, including the Bishop of Rome, think and speak about this, clearly and soon, the church's reputation for rigorousness in moral reasoning will be jeopardized, and they will forfeit their rightfully important role in the Western world's debate about practical policy options. Already a growing number of clergymen assert that any use of nuclear forces, against any target, even in response to a Soviet use, is immoral, and so is the threat to use them under certain conditions, which is the basis of deterrence. As a practical matter in today's world, this amounts to asserting a moral duty to eschew effective resistance to a gross evil, Soviet tyranny.

Any of the wide variety of possible uses of nuclear weapons would be dreadful. However, it is reckless to decree that any use, even any possession for deterrence purposes, is necessarily a larger evil than the long night of centuries that would follow the extinguishing of Western cultural values by armed totalitarianism.

The idea that nuclear weapons require such radical revision of all rules about the use of force derives, in part, from the idea that those weapons make possible devastation on a scale hitherto unimaginable. But it is well to remember that wolves roamed through deserted villages at the end of the Thirty Years War, when weapons were primitive. In the 1950s John Courtney Murray wrote that "the whole concept of force has undergone a rapid and radical transformation, right in the midst of history's most acute political crisis."

The technology of nuclear weapons and delivery systems has driven us to a deterrence policy based on a practice that was once universally condemned: holding enemy civilian populations as hostages. But even before August 6, 1945, injuries inflicted on noncombatants were not just unintended collateral effects of war; they were deliberate results, on a vast scale, of tactics tailored to conventional weapons.

What was done to Dresden and other cities does not make the use of nuclear weapons any less dreadful. But our thinking should not be controlled by the mistaken notion that any use of a nuclear weapon, of any size, would involve violence vaster and less discriminating than anything mankind has experienced.

The tone of this century (as it has been experienced by Cambodians, Biafrans, Russian kulaks, European Jews, among others) was set by the Turkish massacres of Armenians (1914–15), which followed the Bulgarian massacres of Armenians (1894–95). They did not require sophisticated technology. Sixty thousand people died in a single day in the first world war, half a million died at Verdun, without the use of missiles, nuclear weapons or even bombing.

Between 1914 and 1918 not a single photograph of a corpse appeared in a French, German or British newspaper. Perhaps that is one reason why the carnage continued so long that our civilization suffered wounds that may yet prove terminal. Clearly, societies should face facts, and the facts about nuclear weapons are so appalling they can numb any imagination not already numbed by modern history, and can provoke unreasonable responses. That is why when the subject is nuclear weapons, everyone, and especially persons propounding radical and dubious new religious duties inimical to deterrence, should remember the duty to be clear in their own minds about where their logic leads, and to be candid with others about the probable real-world consequences of the behavior they favor.

December 21, 1982

Giving Peace a Bad Name

Senator Jennings Randolph, a West Virginia Democrat, is an affable slab of a man who looks like a piece of Stonehenge that walked away. He first came to Congress 50 years ago. He is leaving next year, and many colleagues want to honor him by fulfilling his fondest desire, establishment of a United States Academy of Peace. Unfortunately, that is another idea that could give peace a bad name.

The proposal for a peace academy is as American as, well, the Kellogg–Briand Pact, which outlawed war many dozens of wars ago. A peace office was proposed for the government in 1793. In 1945 a young congressman from Pekin, Illinois—et tu, Everett Dirksen?—proposed a division of peace within the State Department. Today the lobby for the peace academy claims 30,000 supporters. Its list of advisers begins with Ed Asner. A fundraising letter begins, "Dear Fellow Human." I never learn how letters that begin that way end.

A peace academy would be part graduate school, part think tank. It would sponsor research about the causes of conflict, and techniques of conflict resolution, duplicating work done at many universities. If it were just a slice of pork for the academic lobby, it would not matter. It matters because it illustrates odd ideas about peace.

Peace is so desirable that, if an academy were relevant to it, it would be worth paying the terrible price of having yet more graduate students. But the idea of a peace academy flows from many premises, all mistaken. One is that mankind's "natural" condition is peace, the breakdown of which results from remediable "mistakes" and "misunderstandings." Another premise is that peace can be taught as a discrete subject, like dentistry. A third premise is that conflicts between individuals, and domestic social discords, are closely analogous to, and pregnant with lessons about, conflicts between nations. Hence conflicts are opportunities for applying clear, teachable techniques of "conflict resolution." A fundraising letter for the peace academy lobby proclaims: "There is now a science—tested and proved in actual practice—that can help make war obsolete."

Supporters speak of learning to "wage peace." They say, "peacemaking is as much an art to be learned as war." But it is not. War is the intense focusing of will and matériel, of leadership and technique, to achieve clearly definable political aims. War is a profession; peace is a condition.

The words "war" and "peace" are misleading when used in ways that suggest a clean, clear distinction. At different times and places the words have denoted quite different things. Gen. Sir John Hackett says that when Britain and France were engaged in the Seven Years' War (1756–1763) most citizens of both countries were unaffected by it and many never even heard about it. Today in the continuum between peace and war lies a broad terrain of troubles such as terrorism, subversion and ideological aggression. Hackett says that weapons of mass destruction have made the prevention of war rather than the waging of it the principal purpose of armed forces. But he also notes that in the less than 40 years since peace (of sorts) came to Europe, outside Europe there have been at least 40 wars with more than 40 million dead.

And now add the population of Kansas City to the casualty list. ABC is about to treat the nation to a prime-time entertainment movie, *The Day After,* portraying the reduction of that city to a cinder. The movie is this month's—they come about one a month—original discovery that nuclear war would be awful. It is safe to assume that some of the persons who made the movie consider it a political act. It will have the predictable and intended effect of stirring recruits for the "peace movement." One thought behind movies like this is that it is morally frivolous for anyone to go through life other than weighed down by woe about living in dangerous times. A related and equally dumb thought is that if everyone can just be scared witless, everyone will act constructively to make a less scary world.

In the current climate, the last thing the nation needs is a peace academy staffed by people stuffed full of the ideas you would expect in people attracted to a peace academy. All that an academy could usefully do is what every liberal arts school does: teach history. Taught properly, history refutes the idea that there is some social or scientific key to peace.

However, the academy bill has 55 Senate and 158 House co-sponsors. It is a double temptation. Peace is a good thing, and Americans believe in academies because they believe that any unpleasant fact is a "problem" solvable by good will backed by education.

Besides, an important tactic in contemporary politics is semantic hijacking: Factions make certain words their private property. The agreeable adjective "gay" has been ruined. Let's see: "Environmentalists" want a nice environment, so the people environmentalists oppose must be opposed to that. Then there is the "peace movement," which has cornered the market on "concern" about war. (Some people want to ban the bomb. I want to ban the word "concern" as used by groups calling themselves Clergy and Laity Concerned About This or That.) A peace academy is another instrument for moral posing: Everyone who loves peace, line up behind our latest peace-promoting scheme (the League of Nations, the Oxford Resolution, the United Nations, SALT I, SALT II, cultural exchange, East–West trade, nuclear freeze, peace academy); everyone who doesn't care a fig if Kansas City goes poof, line up over there. Of course there are all sorts of ways of loving peace. As Clausewitz said, "The conqueror is always peace-loving; he wishes to make his way into territory unopposed."

Peace is made possible by many factors, but not least by (in words Herman Wouk once spoke at West Point) "the willingness of an able few to give up personal freedom in the necessary discipline of a military arm. On a planet which is mostly not free, a free society can only live by such a sacrifice of this able few." So, if I can attempt a counter-hijacking: We already have three peace academies. One is on the eastern slope of the Rockies, one is on Chesapeake Bay and one is where Wouk spoke.

November 21, 1983

A License to Lie

Jack Lemmon, star of *Missing,* insists that the virulently anti-American movie says things "I happen to agree with," but that he would have taken the part even if he disagreed with the movie's message. It's "like playing Richard II."

Not quite.

Charles Horman, 30, an American left-wing journalist living in Chile during the 1973 overthrow of Salvador Allende, disappeared and was killed. *Missing* charges that the U.S. government assisted the coup and the murder of Horman, who "knew too much." The movie does not suggest why Horman's friend, who knew all that he knew, was unharmed. But, then, the movie, a tissue of tendentiousness, alleges, on the basis of wild inferences, that Horman and others "knew" many things that, in fact, are untrue.

The movie begins portentously, and fraudulently: "This film is based on a true story. The incidents and facts are documented." "Based on" is a weasel phrase. Journalists and lawyers eager to find evidence of U.S. complicity in the coup have ransacked the documents without finding evidence. A Senate committee that would not have been sad to find evidence said it found "no evidence." Horman's father's suit charging U.S. complicity in the death of his son was dismissed for lack of evidence. To paranoiacs that is especially sinister: The utter absence of evidence, as testified to by Secretary of State Muskie, proves how comprehensive and diabolical the conspiracy was—and is.

Challenged about the movie's truthfulness, Costa-Gavras, the Greek director, says he did not try to prove the truthfulness "of anything and practiced poetic license," but is "convinced" that America "had something to do" with Allende's overthrow. By way of alibi he says, "Don't ask a film director to be a political technician"—whatever that means. Don't ask him to be truthful when he is busy tutoring America in ethics.

His movie is one of the hit-and-run acts of cowardice called "docu-dramas," a label that is a license to lie and smear, using references to real people and events to give a patina of authenticity to innuendos and fabrications. Universal's president announces himself proud of this "totally true story," which is showing in 600 theaters, grossing millions. The wages of anti-Americanism are handsome.

William Wolf, movie critic of *New York* magazine, welcomes this "tough, outspoken" movie as evidence that Hollywood is "developing a taste for controversy." Tough, outspoken Joe McCarthy should have made movies: He, too, had a taste for controversy. Vincent Canby of the *New York Times* says that in spite of its "unsubstantiated conclusions" the movie is "healthily provocative." It was made by and for the sort of people who consider themselves virtuous because they are not Richard Nixon. He never lied as smoothly as this movie does, and he was not considered "healthily provocative."

Stanley Kaufman of *The New Republic* is not at home in the intellectuals' slum inhabited by persons who are tolerant of lies from the left. He says of Costa-Gavras:

"His picture is a mixture of caution and irresponsibility. He cautiously names nothing and no one precisely; he glibly implies deep guilt, making empty heroic gestures of protest without foundation and without risk. It's thus a perfect Hollywood liberal picture, playing to a gallery of trained seals and to another gallery of the gullible, for the happiest kind of Hollywood profit—big returns plus big ego-satisfactions. . . . "

Only once does the movie hint at what Allende did that provoked the military coup. One of Costa-Gavras's cloying young idealists says: "They (Allende's forces) were trying to do something new here." That "something" would not have struck Eastern Europeans as novel.

In 1970 Allende came to power with a 39,000 vote plurality out of nearly three million votes: 62.7 percent voted against him. With no mandate he began attacking what he disdainfully called "bourgeois" democracy—elections, pluralism and all that. Chile's congress refused to confirm him as president until he subscribed to a bill of rights. He did so, he assured a colleague, only as a "tactical necessity" en route to the "overthrow" of the "bourgeois state" and its replacement by "total, scientific, Marxist socialism." He harassed rival newspapers and parties, imported thousands of revolutionaries, imported arms through Cuba's embassy, and ran inflation up to 350 percent. After the coup, Eduardo Frei, a former president and one of Latin America's most distinguished democrats, said:

"The military have saved Chile. . . . A civil war was being

well prepared by the Marxists. And that is what the world does not know, refuses to know."

This information and all other traces of truthfulness are missing in *Missing*.

March 11, 1982

Henry Kissinger's Craft

Henry Kissinger's second volume of memoirs is like a mountain hike, both exhausting and exhilarating. It is exhausting not because of its length, but because a reader gets a numbing sense of the relentless pressure on statesmen, the pressure of too many variables varying, too little time to think. The book is exhilarating because of the author's craftsmanship in teaching a great truth: the contingency and impermanency of everything. He writes most admiringly of the Chinese, "scientists of equilibrium, artists of relativity." He understands that all political structures are sand castles standing too close to the tides of time.

The most eventful year of the postwar period, 1973, punctuated the quarter-century that began with the Marshall plan. An ephemeral Vietnam "peace" was concluded, a President's authority disintegrated, the Yom Kippur war triggered a revolution in energy prices. By the end of the decade slow economic growth would alter politics in the West's welfare states that were built when revenues came easily.

Kissinger's book is published at a propitious moment for him. In 1976 Reagan ran against Kissingerism, and in 1981 he became President committed to sterner policies. But Reagan's response to the Polish crisis retroactively discredits his criticism of Kissinger. By 1976 Kissinger was accused of historical pessimism about the West's staying power. But publication of his book coincides with developments that make him seem too sanguine.

Kissinger's détente was at least delimited by some strong actions, such as mining Haiphong on the eve of the 1972 summit and the alert during the Yom Kippur war. Reagan has abandoned linkage regarding Poland and, what is worse, may be drawing the Soviets into Central American diplomacy. The unraveling there could make him the President who really loses the Panama Canal.

Reagan's policy is détente without intellect, détente shorn of a strategy for exploiting Soviet vulnerabilities. Kissinger refutes the criticism that his version of détente derived from naïveté about the Soviet system. However, he seems more ambivalent about a more subtle criticism. It is that his attempt to make cooperation with the Soviets serve containment of the Soviets was bound to disorient democracies. Kissinger did not exaggerate the Soviet desire for things the West could give. He exaggerated the West's willingness to exact a cost. It is ironic: The Soviet economy is a shambles because it cannot set rational prices. The West's diplomacy is a shambles for the same reason.

Three decades ago the West decided to trust its survival to technological virtuosity rather than civic virtue—to weapons of mass destruction rather than the sacrifices (higher defense spending, more conscription) required for heavier reliance on conventional forces and regional defenses. Western nations put their trust in nuclear superiority and their social resources into welfare states. Soon, however, Soviet science erased the West's nuclear advantage, and the balance of power began to reflect the Soviet Union's conventional-force predominance and geographical proximity to America's principal allies. Today, the West's accelerating loss of nerve is reflected in the growth of European neutralism and American illusions of escaping from history on the cheap, with a quick fix like a nuclear "freeze."

Kissinger understands that "in a democracy, the prerequisite for effective prolonged struggle is a continued demonstration of the willingness to end it." But such demonstrations disorient the public they are supposed to keep reassured and steadfast. The rhetoric and policies of flexibility blunt the West's ideological keenness and dilute its sense of purpose. Such blunting and diluting may be necessary if democratic government is to pursue the relaxed East–West relations demanded by its public, which is dispirited by the prospect of unending tension. But such blunting and diluting diminish the public's stamina for a foreign policy of permanent exertion. Thus détente tends to destroy its prerequisite: It dissolves the clarity of purpose that alone can prevent a desire for peace from becoming an overmastering impulse toward accommodation. Détente is always possible; perhaps safe détente never is.

Kissinger saw that two problems—the West's weariness and Soviet aggressiveness—must be treated simultaneously. He hoped détente could be the compatible marriage of two treatments, psychotherapy for Western publics and a geopolitical strategy against the Soviet regime. It was therapy for the nervous exhaustion and impatience of the West. It also was a strategy of rewards and punishments, a strategy for inhibiting the Soviets by shaping their calculations and intentions. The atmospherics of détente, including increased trade and multiplying agreements, were to be balm for Western publics worn down by what John Kennedy called the "long twilight struggle." And détente was supposed to foster a climate sufficiently hopeful that Western publics would tolerate the rigors of the twilight struggle. Instead it fostered a predisposition to consider rigorous Western measures either inexplicable or provocative. Détente could tranquilize the West. But a tranquilized West cannot contain the Soviet Union.

If Kissinger errs, he errs generously, in favor of faith in democracy. He considered his statecraft a way of teaching his country the science of equilibrium, the art of relativity, patience with contingency and fortitude in the face of impermanency. His memoirs are statecraft carried on by other means, a contribution to building a domestic base for farsighted action. Political wisdom begins with taking this seriously: Nothing lasts. The continents themselves drift; mountains only seem eternal because they wear away slower than we do—although rapidly as timed by the universe's clock. Creative politics involves buying time and improving the odds for what we value.

Nothing lasts forever, but in the world of letters we find many enduring works. Many generations hence, Kissinger's memoirs will be read as Machiavelli's "discourses" are, for literary elegance, lapidary axioms about governance, the savor of the author's personality and the flavor of a wine that travels well through time: patriotism.

March 29, 1982

The Un-American Jeane Kirkpatrick

The maxim "the more cooks, the worse the broth" does not apply to the making of U.S. foreign policy. Too few cooks produce the bland cuisine of the State Department's policy cafeteria. That department has an unreasonably high ratio of interests to ideas, which is why the Reagan administration needs to be leavened by Jeane Kirkpatrick.

She has served a four-year sentence as ambassador to the United Nations. She would like to pass back through the looking glass, to a more reasonable world and a better office.

However, until such an office—secretary of state or national security adviser—becomes vacant, she should stay at the United Nations. Otherwise, she will relinquish her "seat at the table." It is the table where the President, Vice President, chairman of the joint chiefs, CIA director, secretaries of state and defense and—gloriously—Kirkpatrick deliberate about policy. The fact that she must, for now, sit amidst irrationality in New York in order to retain a role in Washington's reasoning is just one paradox in Kirkpatrick's public life, a life rich in paradoxes.

Here are two more: She is indispensable to American policymaking because she is somewhat un-American. And although her temperament is said to tax the patience of Secretary of State Shultz, his temperament is why she should stay at "the table."

Ronald Reagan is no intellectual, but he first insisted on meeting Kirkpatrick because he had read one of her articles. Then he employed this woman whose intellectual gifts and attainments at least match those of Dean Acheson and Henry Kissinger.

Reagan is an elemental political force because he is utterly at one with his countrymen. He is pure American, to the center of all his cells. But that means he is inclined to indiscriminate optimism. In foreign policy, that produces a reluctance, even an inability, to understand that problems will not be dissolved by better communication, that the Cold War is not just a misunderstanding, that all human beings are not "basically alike."

Most citizens of tranquil, liberal democracies have difficulty understanding different national characters and the radically different motives and goals of the world's governing elites. Kirkpatrick does not. Churchill said, sincerely and truly, "The Almighty in his infinite wisdom has not seen fit to create Frenchmen in the image of Englishmen." Kirkpatrick has a deeper understanding than anyone in government of the fact that Soviet leaders are not "like us."

Reagan, unlike FDR, does not relish conflict among subordinates. But for an intellectual of Kirkpatrick's stripe, conflict—civil but sharp—is like oxygen: essential to life. The sainted Edmund Burke said that antagonists are helpers because they strengthen our nerves and sharpen our skills. At the United Nations, Kirkpatrick has been surrounded by antagonists. She went there with strong nerves and sharp skills, and today they are stronger and sharper.

Perhaps that is why many other foreign policy officials in the administration are reportedly not eager to see more of her. Why? Why does butter avoid a sword? Secretary Shultz is not butter. He is a mature, experienced man. But she is a necessary complement to him. He has had a "British" career, moving through a succession of quite different high offices. (He has been head of what now is the Office of Management and Budget, and secretary of labor, then of treasury, then of state.) But "British" careers are apt to require, as they do in Britain, the departmental head to become habituated to dependence on the "permanent government."

This is the bureaucracy, with its inertia and conventional thinking. Shultz, the quintessential "government man," is necessarily dependent on the State Department bureaucracy that is the part of the permanent government most ill-attuned to the President's professed vision of the world.

Futhermore, Irving Kristol argues that economists, businessmen and lawyers are ill-suited to diplomacy. Shultz is an economist and businessman surrounded by lawyers.

Economists think in terms of rational behavior models. But in international relations, cost-benefit analyses often are difficult, and such calculations often are rendered irrelevant by animal spirits, national atavisms and ideological frenzies. Businessmen live in a world of ordered, regulated, almost decorous competition. Nations do not.

For lawyers, a negotiated outcome is normally presupposed, and winning is measured in adjustments at the margins of a dispute. Relations between superpower adversaries are not so mild. A capitalist country, where one person's gain can also profit another, is apt to underestimate the extent to which the game of nations is a zero-sum game, where one nation's gain is an adversary's symmetrical loss.

Kirkpatrick is a precious commodity precisely because she is not like economists, businessmen or lawyers.

November 25, 1984

Dissipating an Asset

The public mind, like wax, is easiest to shape when heated. President Reagan has not just missed an opportunity to shape it, he has labored to minimize the opportunity.

The Korean airliner atrocity raised the public's temperature to a healthy degree. But Reagan has squandered the moment, using it to solve what he evidently thinks is one of his political problems— a perception that he is not as peace-loving as the editors of the *New York Times*. In the process he has dissipated a national asset: the Kremlin's anxiety that he just might mean what he says.

It would be one thing—unconvincing and unbecoming but at least intelligible—for him to cite reasons why he should not do any of the many things he could do to strengthen U.S. policy toward the Soviet Union. It is something else for him to deny the existence of options other than rhetoric or war.

Senator William Armstrong (R-Colo.) and others have made him a list. It includes declaring Poland in default on debts owed to the Commodity Credit Corporation.

Last summer, saying there must be "deeds not just words" in Poland, Reagan said: "The Soviets should not be afforded the additional security of a new long-term [grain] agreement as long as repression continues in Poland." Evidently he thinks repression no longer continues in Poland—perhaps because the regime, using words to disguise deeds, took features of martial law and put them in the normal law. Anyway, Reagan also said the Soviet Union would not be guaranteed minimum grain sales if it engaged in "heinous" acts.

Reagan obviously did not mean what he said. He has made a serious case against the usefulness of grain embargoes. But why are we subsidizing Poland?

Armstrong and others want Reagan to report on Soviet violations of existing arms control agreements. Reagan has talked not at all to the American people and only flaccidly to the Soviet Union about violations.

The *Wall Street Journal* predicts that when Pershing missiles are deployed in Europe, Moscow will deploy antiballistic missiles (some necessary radars are already deployed, in violation of SALT

I) and will say it is not violating the ABM ban because these ABMs are for use against theater, not strategic, weapons. The *Journal* asks: "What will we do then?" Well, what are we doing about violations of other agreements? Consider.

The Soviet Union has in excess of four million persons (including half a million Vietnamese) in 2,000 forced labor camps. In at least 40 extermination camps, the work inevitably causes leukemia or other fatal effects as a result of such things as exposure to radioactivity in uranium mining, or cleaning exhaust tubes of nuclear submarines, or polishing glass without ventilation. According to Mikhail Makarenko, who spent eight years in Soviet camps, the diet for "heavy labor" prisoners is 2,000 calories a day. For "strict regime" prisoners, it is 1,300. In Auschwitz it was 2,050.

The Soviet Union has subscribed to and is violating the U.N. Charter, the Universal Declaration of Human Rights, the Anti-Slavery Convention of 1926, and the Forced Labor Convention of 1930. Furthermore, U.S. law forbids the importing of goods "manufactured wholly or in part by convict labor or/and forced labor." The law has never been enforced. The Customs Service has no enforcement mechanism. Armstrong has a list of the goods that would be barred. Reagan should read it. Armstrong has a corrective bill. Reagan should demand it.

Here is an option Armstrong has overlooked: revising U.S. relations with the United Nations.

After wasting her valuable energies wheedling and cajoling, Jeane J. Kirkpatrick, U.S. Representative to the U.N., rounded up just enough votes to get the Security Council to "deplore" (it refused to condemn) the airline massacre. There are 157 "nations" (counting, of course, the Ukraine and Byelorussia) in the United Nations. We pay approximately one-quarter of the U.N.'s bills. If we paid one-eighth, we would pay more than the Soviet Union, which, unlike the United States, benefits from the U.N.'s existence. We should radically reduce our payments. The savings should be invested in substantially more—and more technologically sophisticated— broadcasting into the "evil empire" (a.k.a. "world's most lucrative grain market").

The airline atrocity is not the reason for such measures. Rather, it is an occasion that, properly handled by a leader, would make clear why such measures are reasonable, and overdue. If Reagan continues to say that he has done all that he can do, short of going to war, he will vindicate those who say that American conservatives care more about containing the Occupational Safety and Health Administration than containing the Soviet Union.

September 18, 1983

A Third World Kleptocracy

Just in time for Christmas comes a publication from the United Nations Educational, Scientific and Cultural Organization. Entitled *The Communication Tree*, it contains photographs of communication devices, from drums to electronic marvels, and it has words from UNESCO's chief, M. M'Bow, who announces:

"It is time that the promise held out to us by the convergence of our distinctive characteristics prevailed over the enticements of selfishness rooted in our long-standing ignorance of each other."

That exquisite sample of U.N.-speak is an example of your tax dollars at work, America. You pay 25 percent of UNESCO's bills. For that, the better restaurants and boutiques of Paris thank you. They are beneficiaries of the handsome salaries paid to the elephantine bureaucracy at UNESCO's headquarters. But on January 1, black crepe will go up in the boutiques, because that's when the United States withdraws from UNESCO. Happy New Year.

Last year the United States gave the required one-year notice of its intention to withdraw. Now Britain has done likewise. Drape more black crepe around UNESCO's army of chauffeurs and gardeners: Britain pays 5 percent of UNESCO's bills. (Eighty of the 161 countries contribute the minimum of .01 percent of the budget; 72 others contribute between .02 and 1.55 percent.)

An opponent of U.S. withdrawal blames "radical conservatives" who believe that "willingness to debate as equals amounts to defeatism." But members of UNESCO are not equals. They are not equally civilized. Only a tiny minority of member nations have preserved admirable traditions of education, science and culture. Why should they "debate" as equals, which they are not? Anyway, who thinks that what UNESCO does is "debate"? It is an echo chamber for Third World slogans about the "North–South dialogue" and "redistribution" of almost everything.

But UNESCO is primarily a jobs program for word merchants.

An opponent of U.S. withdrawal says it is significant that "virtually every American organization that works with UNESCO, including federal agencies, has come to its defense." Well, yes, of course. Threaten the trough where the intelligentsia feeds and folks will fly to their typewriters.

UNESCO regards U.S. wealth as a scandal, except, of course, when that wealth is subsidizing Third World circuses like UNESCO. UNESCO does share its wealth with some Americans, many of whom are innocent of the sin of "ethnocentrism." (That is the belief that the West knows a thing or two the Third World could stand to learn.) Here is a thought from something called the U.S. Commission for UNESCO: "UNESCO is more than an institution, it is a work of art still being thought out and worked on, therefore fascinating by reason of its very incompleteness and unresolved 'enigmas.'"

Say what?

A British commentator with a flair for the perfect phrase calls UNESCO "a Third World kleptocracy." It is that, but also is more, and worse. A few days before the British Government announced its intention to withdraw, the editors of *Encounter*, the indispensable journal, sent to Prime Minister Thatcher an article that must have stiffened her resolve. The author, Gordon Crovitz, notes that UNESCO churns out propaganda for state control of economic life and for "people's rights" rather than human rights. People's rights include such things as "the right of solidarity" and "the right to cultural identity." Such "rights" rationalize the use of power by totalitarian governments to suppress the individual in the name of the collective.

UNESCO perfectly reflects the United Nations itself, and therefore all the reasons for leaving UNESCO are some of, but not all of, the reasons for leaving the United Nations. Crovitz says UNESCO has met one goal: It has contributed to international understanding. Every observant person now understands that most nations in the "one nation, one vote" United Nations are hostile to democratic values. They are hostile because those values are subversive of those nations' dictators.

But the mere fact that UNESCO has engaged in an unrelenting assault on the moral foundations of the West was not sufficient to get it into hot water. No, its wide-ranging attack on democratic decencies went on without hindrance, indeed with democracies feeling obliged to foot the bill, until it committed the tactical blunder of suggesting a "new world information and communication order." It had in mind the regulation of journalists.

At last, the rascals had gone too far. UNESCO has been tolerable when attacking everything else. Tolerable? UNESCO had been a church of progressive thought. It was one thing to revile the United States. But to be disrespectful of journalists . . . well! I mean, the nerve!

December 16, 1984

The President Tunes the Atmosphere

The celebration (yes, that word is used) of the United Nations' 40th birthday has caused much traveling to and fro. So has the presummit minuet. One wishes world leaders, especially our leader, could be more like Macon Leary.

Leary, a character in Anne Tyler's wonderful new novel *The Accidental Tourist*, hates traveling and writes guidebooks for people who feel as he does. The books tell people who would rather be at home where to find a Taco Bell in Mexico City, a Rome restaurant that serves Chef Boy-ar-dee ravioli, a Madrid hotel with Beautyrest mattresses. "Generally food in Britain is not as jarring as in other countries."

Consider the confusion sown by recent and anticipated travel:

Because the President is to travel to Geneva, he traveled to the United Nations to say, sensibly, there are summit issues other than arms control. But this attempt to lower expectations was vitiated by the proclamation of a utopian expectation: U.S.–Soviet "differences" can be "resolved" through "dialogue." Because the Geneva trip now drives all policy, the administration succumbs to the sentimentality of democracy.

A few days before announcing yet another Soviet violation of SALT limits on offensive weapons (deployment of the SS-25, a new mobile ballistic missile), the administration made an announcement. Under the pressure of pre-Geneva maneuvering, it said that it would bind itself with an unnecessarily restrictive reading of the treaty concerning defenses against ballistic missiles. Why this irrational decision to embrace what the administration says is a misreading of a treaty the Soviet Union is flagrantly violating?

Were the President not trying to tune the atmosphere for the trip to Geneva, he would not have said this: The correct reading of the ABM treaty allows development and testing of space-based defenses against ballistic missiles, but we shall abide by an incorrect reading that forbids even development of an integrated system. If Reagan thinks this is an innocuous concession to nervous allies and domestic opponents, he understands neither the sociology of a large scientific undertaking nor the politics of an expensive military procurement.

The Strategic Defense Initiative (SDI) will require many scientists to devote their prime years to it. If the administration's commitment seems tenuous, they will find other devotions. Furthermore, Congress always is reluctant to diminish discretionary spending opportunities by committing vast sums to weapons systems. Congress confronts, simultaneously, a future barren of discretionary spending and full of SDI, the most expensive public project in history.

Reagan says SDI is morally urgent—but less urgent than pacifying critics who make a fetish of a misreading of the ABM treaty. Congress will not fund an SDI system that is subordinated to the ABM treaty in any way that prevents all except inconclusive tests of subcomponents. So the wounding, perhaps mortal wounding, of SDI is one result of the maneuvering for the Geneva trip.

Nancy Reagan traveled to the United Nations to give a lunch for the wives of world leaders, for the purpose of discussing drug abuse. Her guests included the wife of Nicaragua's dictator, who said she hoped our nations would improve relations. Mrs. Reagan, polite to a fault, did not ask the dictator's wife to autograph a photograph—the one showing Sandinista soldiers loading a plane with drugs bound for America.

Nicaragua's first couple taped *The Donahue Show*, where the host asked, plaintively: Many of us abhor the Reagan administration's hostilities toward your regime. Why do you embarrass us by suppressing civil liberties? (Nicaragua has finally gone too far. It has annoyed Donahue by making Reagan look correct.)

In a ten-minute session with a representative of Solidarity, Poland's outlawed trade union, Reagan, who has raised optimism to a philosophy and has severed philosophy from evidence, said he has "high hopes" for happiness in Poland, happiness from "dialogue." An administration climatologist explained the mushiness of Reagan's remarks in terms of the "East–West climate." That is, the problem is travel—the trip to Geneva. The President who believes in dialogue between communists and their victims should read the forthcoming *Reader's Digest* account of the murder of Father Jerzy Popieluszko by the regime:

"His eyes and forehead had been beaten till black. His jaw, nose, mouth and skull were smashed, his fingers and toes dark red and brown from repeated clubbing. Part of his scalp and large strips of skin on his legs had been torn off. . . . His muscles had been pounded again and again until limp. . . . The teeth were found completely smashed. In place of his eloquent tongue, there was only mush."

A tongue like that makes dialogue difficult. But an early arrival at the U.N.'s birthday bash, General Jaruzelski, asphyxiator of Poland, was given a dinner by the Council on Foreign Relations. Well, a traveler must eat. And at the council, the general found neither the food nor the talk jarring.

October 27, 1985

Mitterrand Kills Socialism

The French, who politicize everything from industry to poetry, suddenly are having a lot of backaches, and socialism may be to blame. Polls show that since 1981 the percentage of people who say they are increasingly irritable has risen from 26 to 42 percent, the prevalence of backaches has increased substantially, as has the number of people who say they expect to be in an automobile accident. A decline in the nation's sense of well-being has coincided with the floundering of the first Socialist government under the Fifth Republic.

Four years ago this month, France elected François Mitterrand president and embarked on a historic journey in Europe's experience, a journey to the end of the line for socialism. Mitterrand, who once criticized Sweden's socialists for not dealing capitalism "a mortal blow," has dealt one to socialism.

In the 1981 campaign, he promised stimulative spending through expanded entitlements, a shorter work week with no cut in pay, job creation through public works spending, steeper taxes on the wealthy, sweeping nationalization of many industries and banks, and an attack on the independence of Catholic schools. Then he rounded on the country and began keeping his promises.

Because France listens intently to intellectuals, it often is late learning the obvious. It has now learned that much of the money pumped into the pockets of people who are working less was spent on imports. So while productivity fell, demand rose and the franc fell, unemployment rose, the purchasing power of the employed fell, and so did Mitterrand in the polls, to a point lower than any postwar leader.

His biggest blunder was a bill to break Catholic schools to the state's saddle. The bill embodied traditional socialist thinking about conquering reactionary tendencies by nationalizing consciousness, and liberating children from the dead hand of the past, including parents. This brought a million protesters into Paris streets in the largest demonstration since Liberation.

Mitterrand promised radicalism and in two years he has delivered perhaps the most radical reversal in recent European history, imposing budgetary austerity more severe than Reagan has proposed. Candidate Mitterrand exhorted, "Let's break with the logic of profitability," and under his policies many businesses, alas, did. President Mitterrand now says, "We can no longer keep on crushing those who create wealth in France with taxes and social contributions."

He insists his conversion to tax cuts and spending restraints is just a "parenthesis" in the story of French socialism. But the parenthesis was preceded by failure so complete that the intellectual cupboard is barren of ideas about what can come next that will resemble socialism.

His semi-Reaganism has been called "supply-side socialism," but that is an oxymoron. The crux of supply-side economics is tax cutting to lighten the weight of the state on entrepreneurship, and the essence of socialism is the use of the state as the central directing source of entrepreneurial energy. Mitterrand lamely says that socialism just means a "mixed economy." If so, France has had socialism since 1945. Mitterrand's predecessor, Giscard d'Estaing, warned that when the combination of taxes and social security contributions exceeds 40 percent, "we're in socialism." If so, socialism arrived under Giscard, when the combination neared 43 percent.

France has more politics than probably is good for it. With 468,000 municipal councillors, 2 percent of the electorate is in elective office. But what unquestionably is good about French politics today is that the political label with cachet is "liberalism." Here liberalism retains its traditional connotations, which are unlike those of American liberalism. Here it means an antistatist emphasis on personal initiative and market mechanisms.

Mitterrand's personal initiative has been a hyperactive foreign policy, searching for what some European politicians, envious of Mrs. Thatcher, call a "Falklands effect." But the principal effect of foreign events during the last decade has been to speed the collapse of confidence among French intellectuals on the left, who have abominable records of communist affiliation or fellow traveling.

Only intellectuals inordinately fond of abstractions (like the three great incompatibles, "Liberty, Equality, Fraternity") would take until 1975 to learn (from a book, of course: Solzhenitsyn's, which had its strongest impact here) about the concrete reality of the Gulag. Also instructive were Vietnam boat people, Cambodian genocide, Afghanistan atrocities and the suppression of Poland, a nation about which France has long been sentimental. Today French intellectuals, writing with the vigor of people making up for lost time, are robustly anticommunist on their flight toward the right.

One fine day in 1953, the front page of the communist newspaper *L'Humanite* had a black border and this headline: "Dreadful News: Stalin is Dead." One fine day a headline may say: "Socialism, too."

May 9, 1985

The Last 19th-Century War?

After wondering if the Falkland Islands crisis—the last 19th-century war? an operetta looking for a Gilbert and Sullivan?—is a case of carrying the nostalgia craze too far . . .

After remembering the axiom that the average citizen is no more capable of a grand passion than of a grand opera, and wishing that William James were here to see the roaring crowds in Argentina, and those cheering the British fleet at Portsmouth . . . ("Man lives by habits indeed," wrote James, "but what he lives for is thrills and excitements. The only relief from habit's tediousness is periodical excitement. From time immemorial wars have been, especially for noncombatants, the supremely thrilling excitement.")

After being pleased that this episode will further discredit the moralizing majority at the United Nations (where Spain—which has a restive army and covets Gibraltar—abstained from the call for Argentina to withdraw) . . .

After wondering when Senator Kennedy or some similar keeper of the peace will seek legislation requiring the Reagan administration to get congressional permission before "becoming involved in" the Falkland Islands . . . (There is a slogan for the next Kennedy campaign: "He kept our boys out of Port Stanley.")

After marking this down as another example of the strength of the weak and the weakness of the sort-of-strong . . . (Argentina was not deterred by Britain's nuclear deterrent—or by anything else. Lord Wigg, a Kiplingesque soul, laments that Britain has spent "111 billion pounds on defense since the end of the last war and we can't knock the skin off a rice pudding." Welcome, your Lordship, to the Iranian hostage experience.)

After hoping that this episode will call American attention to this truism: That when your political will and military assets are perceived to be insufficient to sustain your commitments and pretenses, other nations begin acting rudely . . . (Britain's task force is led by the aircraft carrier *Invincible*, which Britain is selling to Australia for budgetary reasons.)

After recovering from astonishment at the principle that dictated the resignation of Lord Carrington, Britain's foreign secretary . . . (The principle is that a minister is responsible for what goes on in his area of responsibility, and that when something goes smash, he resigns. America has "no fault" government: Not even a military fiasco like the rescue mission to Iran produces resignations.)

After savoring this paradox: A nation at the eastern end of the Mediterranean may benefit from the crisis in the South Atlantic . . . (Israel considered Carrington a nemesis. And if Third World diplomats are capable of feeling embarrassed, they will blush when, having been "understanding" about Argentina's aggression, they return to denouncing Israel. Israel is occupying the West Bank only because Jordan launched aggression from there.)

After fainting from shock at the impudence of Argentina's occupying force, which, with tanks rumbling through the sheep, decrees imprisonment for any Falkland Islander who commits "actions that disturb community normality" . . . (The Islanders are, to say no more, happier about life under British sovereignty than most Argentinians are about life under the current government of Argentina.)

After fainting again from the thought that a number of governments which, like Argentina's, project internal tensions toward external foes, may someday have nuclear weapons . . .

After noting that this crisis underscores the wrongheadedness of American liberals who insist that the world is made safer by decreasing American power . . . (In 1956 American disapproval was sufficient to halt an invasion of Egypt by Britain, France, Israel; in 1982 American disapproval is disregarded by Argentina.)

After all such thoughts, comes this one: Little crises have ways of growing, faster than you can say "Sarajevo." Every little bit hurts: Every little injury done to the forms of international law lowers more than the tone of life on the planet. It also lowers, perhaps imperceptibly but not innocuously, the threshold at which disputes become violent.

And what a stimulating lot of disputes there can be if Argentina's "repossession" principle becomes an infectious precedent. Here is a mental game to play in the silent watches of the night: Count the number of borders and other political arrangements around the world that can be considered merely provisional, pending arbitration by force, if Argentina's action is not reversed.

Argentina has declared, in effect, that there is no statute of limitations on historical grievances, or at least none on grievances that are only 149 years old. So dust off a 19th-century globe and let's reopen every dispute, from Schleswig-Holstein through . . . well, Heads Up, Texas. Manifest Destiny had its messy aspects.

April 8, 1982

Taking Sides in the Falklands

When Margaret Thatcher nailed her colors to the mast, Ronald Reagan nailed his to the fence on which the United States sat while Alexander Haig ricocheted around the Atlantic. When James Byrnes was Secretary of State, someone said: "Truman fiddles while Byrnes roams." Argentines say: *"Dios arregla de noche la macana que los Argentinos hacen de día*" ("God puts right at night the mess the Argentines make by day"). Haig is playing God's part. At last, a role spacious enough.

Conservatives are supposed to be like the Bourbons, forgetting nothing and learning nothing. British Conservatives remember Suez, when the United States scuttled the British-French-Israeli attack on Egypt. And this Tory government has learned how to circumscribe the U.S. role, by quickly getting the fleet out onto the bounding main and demanding restoration of the *status quo ante*. Haig's task was confined to fashioning a face-saving solution that would be universally called that, yet would save the face, and hence the life, of the Argentine regime.

It is hard, without an anesthetic, to contemplate that regime, so why save it? Consider a parable. A young preacher came to his first church the day of a funeral and, not having known the deceased, asked if anyone would care to offer a eulogy. From a back pew a voice called: "His brother was even worse." The alternative to Argentina's junta—the Peronists—would be worse.

They would fill the jails with different victims and empty the Treasury for different beneficiaries. It has been said that Argentines have no causes, only enemies. The Peronists' enemies include "American imperialism," Zionism and rich people. Peronism has perhaps the world's highest ratio of jargon to thought. "Violence," said Juan Perón, "in the hands of the people, isn't violence: It is justice." A Peronist says about torture: "*Depende de quien sea torturado*" ("It depends on who is tortured"). Eva Perón said that the existence of poor people caused her less pain than did the knowledge that "there were people who were rich." She warned, "We mustn't pay too much attention to people who talk to us of prudence." The Falkland debacle shows that the junta, which fancies itself a dam against the Peronist tide, is Peronist regarding prudence.

There is a theatrical element in all politics, but there seem to be few other elements in Argentina's. When General Galtieri became President Galtieri in December, he said Argentina suffered from "lethargy, apathy and lack of confidence." Perhaps the Falkland adventure is intended as a stimulant to provoke one of what Argentines call "*esos instantes magníficos en que todo recomienza*" ("those magnificent moments in which everything is remade"). Certainly Argentina does not need the Falklands for Lebensraum. Argentina, with a population of 27 million, is almost as large as India, which has a population of 667 million.

As V. S. Naipaul sees Argentina—so much of it, so little of it—it has the artificiality of a society based on mimicry of Europe, a civilization bought up, not thought out. He says: " . . . Argentine political life is like the life of an ant community or an African forest tribe: full of events, full of crises and deaths, but life is only cyclical, and the year ends as it begins." The military has toppled elected presidents five times since 1930.

Many Argentines are, or are descended from, immigrants from Spain and Italy. According to an American statesman who likes them, they combine Spanish pride with an Italian sense of the state. Even by the standards of 20th-century dictatorships, the Argentine state devotes an unusually large portion of its energies just to maintaining itself. But the junta's anticommunism seems entirely internal. In 1980 it shattered the U.S. grain embargo against the Soviet Union, which now buys 80 percent of Argentina's grain exports. Argentina has just agreed to buy an enormous amount of Soviet oil equipment and to conduct joint operations for oil exploration and shrimp harvesting.

Many Argentines are Anglophiles. Buenos Aires has a replica of Big Ben and a store called Harrods—another replica—where high tea is served. But the junta's aggression expresses contempt for Britain. Perhaps because of the notorious Argentine *machismo*, the junta has misjudged Thatcher. She thinks as Admiral Nelson did: "It matters not at all in what way I lay this poker on the floor. But if Bonaparte should say it *must* be placed in this direction, we must instantly insist upon its being laid in some other one." But it remains to be seen if Thatcher can hold her country if the crisis becomes bloody, or even just boring. A Labor Party spokesman calls Galtieri "a bargain-basement Mussolini," but Labor is today, as the Conservative Party was when Mussolini was active, a party of instinctive appeasement. In this it may soon represent the country. Today, liberal democracies generally have only one goal—commodious living—and only two convictions: Anything is negotiable and force is an anachronism. So opinion is apt to change quickly from "Up, boys, and at 'em!" to something like this:

> I was playing golf the day
> That the Germans landed.
> All our soldiers ran away,
> All our ships were stranded,
> And the thought of England's shame
> Nearly put me off my game.

An unequal struggle is raging within many Labor breasts, between the desire to bring down the junta and the desire to bring down Thatcher. But some Laborites worry that if she goes, her successor will have two years to burnish the Tory image. Laborites, too, remember Suez: Harold Macmillan replaced Anthony Eden and the Tories prospered.

A 19th-century divine, in a sermon giving thanks for some good outcome, said: "We owe this to Providence, and a series of happy accidents." It is time to give Providence a hand lest we suffer the kind of unhappy accidents that occur when intentions are left unclear. The junta probably is unsavable in the long run—whatever *that* means in Argentina. Thatcher, an indispensable friend, needs help, and the United States needs an opportunity to demonstrate reliability. Some U.S. ships sailing south would concentrate the junta's mind on the fact that the United States intends to guarantee the success of its NATO ally.

April 26, 1982

Woodrow Wilson's Ghost

Strange, is it not, how different persons are haunted by different specters. Concerning Central America, some persons say they see the ghost of Vietnam. I see the thin, austere ghost of Woodrow Wilson. However, come to think about it, that ghost, too, seems like a ghost from Vietnam.

Wilson was an exceptionally complex tangle of admirable and disagreeable qualities. Certainly he was not at his best regarding hemispheric problems, which in his day meant, primarily, Mexico.

Mexico today is governed by an oligarchy so secure that it can export its overflowing moral energies, principally in the form of disapproval of the United States. In Wilson's day, Mexico was barely governed at all.

Announcing that "my passion is for the submerged 85 percent who are struggling to be free," Wilson said he was "seeking to counsel Mexico for her own good." Lord Bryce, Britain's learned ambassador to Washington, warned that "the best thing that can happen is to get as soon as possible a dictator who will keep order and give a chance for material and educational progress." But Wilson said: "I am going to teach the Latin American republics to elect good men!"

Wilson had a secretary of state, William Jennings Bryan, who thought Pancho Villa was an "idealist" because he neither smoked nor drank. (Villa was, however, a live wire. Barbara Tuchman writes: "On one occasion, angered by the yells of a drunken soldier while he was being interviewed by an American journalist, Villa casually pulled his pistol and killed the man from the window, without interrupting the conversation.") And for Wilson, problems with Mexico were serious. They spilled into the American Southwest. And the "Zimmerman telegram," revealing German meddling in Mexico, helped pull the United States into World War I.

Eventually Wilson quit preaching and sent General Pershing into Mexico. But the Wilsonian dimension of today's events concerning Central America is not the sending of the fleet. Rather, it is the universal and ritualistic insistence that the primary U.S. aim is to spread democracy and prosperity. In the Vietnam era, this Wilsonian aspiration was called "nation-building."

In Central America, as it was in Vietnam, U.S. policy is like a Lionel electric train. It is a "three-track policy." It is to deal with the military problem, negotiate, and build free institutions and economic vitality. Lionel trains have one too many tracks. U.S. policy may have two too many.

Of course, the United States must be ready to negotiate—ready, but not eager. Eagerness produces a willingness to treat a guerrilla force as a party on an equal footing with the legitimate government. Eagerness produces a willingness to negotiate absurd arrangements, such as "power-sharing" among mortal enemies.

"Power-sharing" is the standard proposal made by movements that believe in a monopoly of power but are out of power. In the United States it is considered daring when a President includes a member of the other party in his Cabinet. Yet many Americans casually suggest that foreigners who have been shooting each other should form coalition governments. Experiences in Eastern Europe between 1945 and 1948 are forgotten.

Furthermore, eagerness for negotiations makes the United States susceptible to what the Sandinistas are doing. They are using rhetoric about negotiations the way the Soviet Union uses arms control negotiations: to buy time and sow irresolution in U.S. policymaking. Of course the United States should—to the extent that it is consistent with security objectives—use what leverage it has to nudge friendly nations toward democratic values. But in this "age of democracy"—since the late 18th century—there have been relatively few democracies. And almost all the durable ones have been durable because traditions of civility have made economic growth possible, and because economic growth has moderated disputes about distributive justice.

Yet many Americans—and sometimes American policies—seem to suppose that democracy is the natural condition for all societies, and can be planted even in the soil of economic backwardness, even during the social monsoon of war.

In Britain during the Second World War, when not a single enemy soldier was on the island, the electoral process was suspended cooperatively, by the parties in Parliament. Yet with a war raging in El Salvador, the regime is expected, and coerced, to hold various elections and impose fundamental social reforms. This may be necessary to rally support in El Salvador and in the U.S. Congress. But it will be worse than futile if it is considered a substitute for military success.

The United States force-fed elections and other reforms on Saigon. Saigon is now Ho Chi Minh City.

July 31, 1983

South Africa: Dismounting from a Tiger

Just (yes, "just") 125 years ago the United States began solving a racial problem significantly less difficult than the one afflicting South Africa. The process began with four years of civil war and was followed by a century of intermittent litigation and legislation. All this was needed to open American society to a racial minority that was regionally concentrated.

Writing in *The Public Interest*, Glenn C. Loury notes that "in little more than a generation we have advanced from a circumstance in which the great majority of Americans were indifferent or actively hostile to blacks' quest for full citizenship rights, to one in which racial equality of opportunity is a value staunchly upheld by the law and universally embraced in our politics." Now, what of the prospects for change in South Africa?

John Buchan, in his magnificent autobiography *Pilgrim's Way,* published in 1940, recalled serving as an aide to Lord Milner in South Africa in the first decade of the century. When read today, this passage leaps off the page: "The hope of breaking down the racial barrier between town and country was always very near to Milner's heart. He wanted to see the Dutch share in the urban industries and men of British stock farming beside the Boers in the veldt." South Africa's blacks were invisible then.

Today they are omnipresent in the global circuitry of journalism. A crucial fact about South Africa's turmoil is its presence in American living rooms.

South Africa is far from being an open society but so, too, is it far from being as closed as any communist society, or many African despotisms. Bishop Tutu holds press conferences; he regales white students with witty and withering ridicule of government policy. South Africa is an opening society. Changes in laws touching matters as varied and vital as trade unions, interracial sex and marriage can not be dismissed as cosmetic.

There are two certainties about South African change: It is coming; it will occur behind a fusillade of bluster designed to deny foreign critics the satisfaction of thinking they are forcing any change.

On a planet where narrow creeks can create canyons and even the continents drift, nothing lasts, least of all social arrangements. But it is said there are three lost tribes in today's world—the Protestants in Ulster, the Israelis in the Middle East and the white (especially Dutch) South Africans. These three groups are not going to go home. They are home. As Chief Buthelezi, leader of the Zulus, says, South Africa may avoid the calamity that has befallen so much of postcolonial Africa (one man, one vote—once) because blacks and whites are "a community of Africans. . . . The whites have become indigenous and the interdependence between blacks and whites doesn't exist anywhere else in Africa."

South Africa's foreign minister says, tendentiously, "There is no clear-cut majority" in South Africa because there is no "homogeneous" black majority. There are, he says, "differences of opinion" among blacks. Well, do tell. Imagine: Blacks do not all think alike. Next thing you know, they won't all look alike. There certainly is a clear-cut minority: It is white and it, too, is not homogeneous.

Buthelezi says the minimal demand is for the government to

acknowledge "that we are one people in one country." The government is closer to doing that than even it may realize. Its ambassador in Washington says the government is committed to a process of change that should end in a federal structure with whites not in a privileged position in the central government.

Whether or not the people in Pretoria actually feel so committed, the crucial point in President Botha's otherwise barren speech last week was the offer to negotiate with blacks. Negotiation presupposes human beings on both sides of the table. It is too late for a South African "Dred Scott decision." In America, that 1857 decision lit the short fuse to war by declaring a constitutional principle that blacks could not be complete citizens, and hence, inferentially, were not completely human.

To pass from authoritarianism to popular government without falling into anarchy and more authoritarianism is difficult. King Juan Carlos of Spain deserves the Nobel Peace Prize for his indispensable role in making Spain the only European nation to move from fascism to democracy without being conquered. The problem in Spain—a relatively homogeneous nation with a majority in favor of the change—was less demanding than South Africa's problem.

Foreign critics are demanding that South Africa's regime dismount from a tiger. Perhaps the regime is to blame for being on the tiger. Perhaps the tiger is only angry because it has been ridden so long, so recklessly. Perhaps. But critics should consider this: Telling a rider of a tiger that he deserves to be devoured is no way to persuade him to dismount.

August 22, 1985

Right-mindedness About South Africa

The United Nations, which is largely run by and for the benefit of tyrannical regimes, is divesting its pension of South African assets. Various European governments that are purchasing gas pumped through a Soviet pipeline built by slave labor are suddenly stern about South Africa. And the music of American moralism has reached fortissimo regarding South Africa, with a brisk staccato of demands for disinvestment and other gestures involving no noticeable risk or even inconvenience for those doing the demanding.

Clearly some of the current campaigning against South Africa is a fad, a moral Hula Hoop, fun for a while. Regarding interest in a foreign crisis, even altruism is not fuel for the long haul. For a foreign crisis to preoccupy a relatively content society such as ours, it must affect a vital interest of a majority on a continuing basis. Injustice in Africa does not. Not even the very vocal spokesmen for black Americans are audible often about the tyranny of black despots over the majority of the 400 million black Africans.

The *New York Times* recently carried this melancholy headline: "Uganda Regains Uneasy Normalcy." In South Africa in the last year more than 600 persons have died in political violence, some of them blacks and Indians killed by blacks. Six hundred has been the average weekly death toll during the last decade of Ugandan normalcy.

Nevertheless, the manifest and manifold injustices of South Africa's system make economic sanctions a temptation, because they can make us feel good. But should they?

Right-mindedness is not right behavior. If the aim of sanctions is described modestly enough, the success of sanctions is assured. That is, if the aim is to express disapproval, sanctions cannot fail. Richard Lugar (R-Ind.), chairman of the Foreign Relations Committee, says sanctions would say "how we feel" about apartheid. But American opinion already is clear, indeed almost unanimous, in disapproving apartheid.

President Carter's grain embargo and Olympics boycott in response to the Soviet invasion of Afghanistan were useful. They were useful not because they could do serious damage to the Soviet Union, still less because they would alter Soviet behavior, but because the measures helped awaken Americans from slumbers that Carter, among others, had induced with talk about "inordinate" fear of communism. Economic pressure against the Soviet empire should be continuous because it is our mortal enemy and its militarism should be burdened as much as possible.

But what of South Africa? Are sanctions supposed to destabilize it? One reason there is a Reagan administration is that the preceding administration helped bring down the shah and Somoza, two exercises in making matters worse. Are sanctions to remain in place until Pretoria changes policies? If so, which policies?

Simon Jenkins of *The Economist*, writing in *The Spectator*, notes that force, not the sanctions, settled disputes involving Rhodesia and Argentina. The Arab oil embargo did not erode U.S. support for Israel; it stimulated conservation and development of alternative energy sources, which have weakened Arab economies.

Thanks to an oil embargo against South Africa, it is nearly self-sufficient, with the world's best process for producing oil from coal. Thanks to an arms embargo, South Africa, which was 60 percent dependent on imported arms 20 years ago, today is 90 percent self-sufficient and a net arms exporter.

Sanctions would raise the costs of apartheid, but as Jenkins says, "Apartheid is not a white tribal hobby to be dropped from the household budget when things get tight." Sanctions, he says, please people who believe they are entitled to reorder the world and that the reordering can be done without violence: "The modern crusader sits at home ripping up IBM stock. . . . Defeat is someone else's fault and only the poor get hurt." In southern Africa, the 40 million poor would include many millions in states which are, and will remain, linked economically with South Africa.

Before the American Civil War, some abolitionists considered dissolution of the Union—secession by the North—preferable to continued association with slave states. This policy would have left the slaves to their fate, but their fate was not the most important thing to those abolitionists. The most important thing was the abolitionists' self-regarding fastidiousness about their own moral hygiene. Some advocates of sanctions and other measures to isolate South Africa seem most eager to isolate themselves from what is apt to be a long, tedious, morally ambiguous and largely unsatisfying process of constructive pressure through continued engagement.

August 26, 1985

Why Study Hitler?

In World War I (Corporal Hitler and Colonel Churchill were once just a few miles apart) Hitler was decorated for bravery, at the recommendation of a Jewish officer. But he never was promoted because, an officer said, "we could discover no leadership qualities in him." Until age 30 he neither gave a speech nor joined a party. In the "party" he then joined he got card number seven. Thirteen years later he led its conquest of the state.

The unquenchable thirst for information about this man is evidence that evil is more fascinating than virtue: There are more biographies of Napoleon than Lee. But the main reason for Hitler's hold on the world's imagination is that, as biographer Joachim Fest says, "He enormously widened the horizon of mankind's experience."

Hitler showed how fast the civilized can be barbarized. His regime rested in the heart as well as on the neck of a cultured nation. As Sebastian Haffner says, Hitler was no democrat but he was a populist, basing his power on the masses. From 1933 through 1945 the state was run, as all modern states are, by bureaucrats who would not have cheated at cards. Nazis were called "Neanderthals in airplanes," but their leader was skillful at using modern technologies of warfare and social control (radio, cinema, bureaucracy).

Hitler's 1,000-year Reich fell 988 years short, but his career, like Lenin's, shows the power of simplifying obsessions. Marx said: "The history of all society so far is a history of class struggle." Hitler said: "All events in Western history are merely the manifestation of the self-preservation drive of the races." Hitler's career refuted his (and Marx's) notions about the impotence of individuals in a world governed by iron laws and autonomous processes. But persons driven by obsessions cannot master their mainsprings. They cannot stop. Had Hitler stopped in October 1938, after Munich, or in June 1940, after the fall of France, he would have won. But he would have died of boredom administering Europe.

He was as radical as it is possible to be. When Einstein was telling the world that matter is energy, Hitler began practicing the politics of pure energy. His essence was restless dissatisfaction. A boyhood friend recalls young Adolf walking through Linz planning alterations of everything in sight. As shells fell on the bunker, the Führer, still an architect manqué, brooded over plans for rebuilding Linz. Today the Berlin wall, an architectural consequence of Hitler, runs almost directly over the bunker.

Napoleon was not French, Stalin was not Russian and Hitler did not become a German citizen until seven months before he became chancellor. He was no nationalist. He believed in race, not nation. The party superseded the state, the party symbol (the swastika) superseded national symbols. Small wonder conservative nationalists resisted his consolidation of power in 1934 and tried to kill him 10 years later.

If you are foolish enough to accept the modern definition of freedom as the absence of restraints, you must say Hitler was the freest of men. He was utterly unfettered by any scruples or affections. He instinctively rejected what John Lukacs calls "the most widespread idiocy of the 20th century, the belief in economic man," that is, the belief that mankind is moved by economic calculations and history is just a story of conflicting interest groups. None of the five leaders of the war years—Hitler, Stalin, FDR, Churchill, de Gaulle—knew or cared about economics. That may say something about why they were leaders.

In an age awash with theories purporting to explain how this or that dialectic or other impersonal force controls history, leaving little room for an individual to make a difference, Hitler demonstrated the power of an individual to wrench history into new patterns. Unfortunately, change for the better generally requires the patience of decent politics, the persuasion of a public mind that moves more like molasses than mercury. Therefore the rapid acceleration of history is the business of bad men.

Most politicians sail with the wind. A few tack into the wind. Hitler raised the wind and blew the masses like dust. True, other events had reduced a community to dust. As Haffner says, Hitler invariably toppled what was tottering (the Weimar Republic, Neville Chamberlain, the France of 1940), but he had a gift for seeing what was tottering. History is the history of mankind's inner life, and Hitler, the failed painter, was a political artist: He knew intuitively what could assuage the ache of emptiness in persons humiliated by defeat and disoriented by inflation.

Ortega y Gasset defined genius as the ability to invent one's own occupation. Hitler never had a steady job until he entered politics, and his first public office was chancellor. He invented the occupation of being Führer. That occupation, like serious Nazism, vanished with him. He had made politics an extension of inner turmoils and had seen history as his biography.

Early postwar writings about Hitler involved many butler's-eye views, memoirs of subordinates who stood near and saw much but understood nothing. One critic called this the "I was Hitler's toothbrush" genre. Since then there have been brilliant writings but there still is a widespread impulse to explain Hitler by explaining him away, making him disappear into some abstraction. For example, he is treated as some category of demon or mental illness, or some continuity in Germany's national character. But people know better. Fascination with Hitler is unabating because he is a dark mirror held up to mankind.

Macbeth is timeless not because Macbeth himself is some wholly alien creature but because he is too close to us all for comfort. Othello's jealousy is a "green-eyed monster," but Othello is no monster. He is a man, or there would be no serious drama and no audience for it across the centuries. Here you have Europe's best and worst: Shakespeare is one kind of guide to human possibilities, Hitler is another. The proper study of mankind is man, and Hitler was a man, however hard that fact may be on the reputation of the human race. An understanding of Hitler, as of disease, can conduce to health. The study of medicine begins, in a sense, with the study of death. The study of modern politics begins with Hitler.

May 9, 1982

Hitler's Inkwell

East German radio proudly announces that 60,000 people donated blood last year at a single center. The broadcast says: "Most of them were volunteers."

As the lyricist says, little things mean a lot. After a century of barbarities, it is hard to hold people's attention with stories of big outrages, like genocide in Afghanistan and conquest in Indochina. Perhaps one way to illustrate the nature of the communist regimes that threaten decency everywhere is with small episodes which, properly understood, no longer seem small.

If people had paid proper attention to Hitler's inkwell, a lot of trouble, including World War II, might have been avoided. Hitler, who fancied himself an architect, received from an architect an inkwell that Speer described as "a mass of ornamentation, scrolls and steps—and then, alone and forlorn amid all the magnificence of this 'inkwell for the chief of state,' there was a tiny pool of ink." It was inexpressibly vulgar. Hitler adored it. The extreme excess and giantism of the architecture Hitler loved provided a map of the man's mind, which was a swamp of seething, demented ambition. The map went largely unread because few people understood that taste tells character and character is destiny.

Consider some Soviet vignettes.

Recently Soviet television offered viewers a rerun. There on the screen was Khrushchev, who was thrown down the memory hole two decades ago. He was a nonperson until this February. When authorities decided to broadcast a Soviet–Indian movie about Nehru in January, they snipped out footage of Khrushchev's tour of India. But three weeks later, when it was rebroadcast—by popular demand?—lo! there he was.

It was only the fourth time since Khrushchev's fall in October 1964 that he had been mentioned on Soviet television. The other times were a denunciation of his memoirs, a report of his death and a mention of his role in the battle of Stalingrad, a city that had its name tossed (by Khrushchev) down the memory hole. Why the decision suddenly to admit that he existed? Who knows? It is impossible to fathom a mind as rotted with mendacity as the mind of that regime.

When Beria, head of the secret police, was liquidated in 1953, owners of the *Great Soviet Encyclopaedia* reportedly were mailed razor blades with instructions to cut out the two pages on Beria and replace them with two new pages on the Bering Sea. Scrubbing pictures has been a Soviet industry since it became necessary—Stalin could be *very* insistent—to erase Trotsky from photographs showing him friendly with the sainted Lenin. Three weeks ago, when the waxy, wheezing, doddering Chernenko was rolled out to vote in an "election," television showed a man supporting him. But in newspaper photographs the man was—pfffft!—gone. So, too, is the world chess championship match—pfffft!—after five months.

Gary Kasparov, 21, came recklessly close to defeating Anatoly Karpov, 33, the champion who is the darling of the Soviet regime. How darling? How about the Order of Lenin, $1 million in hard currency and a telephone in his German car. Yep, Karpov is a Soviet Yuppie. Kasparov is OK, a party member and all that. But—talk about reckless—he is half Jewish. He seemed about to beat Karpov until the head of the International Chess Federation, whose job depends on Soviet support, astonished a Moscow press conference by canceling the match. He said, "Until reaching this podium I did not know what I was going to do." Oops. The Soviet "news" agency Tass had announced his decision 12 minutes before he reached the podium.

Such swinishness is part of a seamless fabric of behavior that includes what Edward Girardet, writing in *The New Republic*, calls "migratory genocide" in Afghanistan. That policy involves devastation of the basis of life in the 80 percent of Afghanistan controlled by freedom fighters. Also in *The New Republic*, Jeri Laber of Helsinki Watch and Barnett Rubin of Yale report that immediately after the first communist coup, in 1978, Soviet advisers arrived at Kabul University and began changing the curriculum. A course in the history of Islamic art was abolished and a course of Islamic civilization, formerly the centerpiece of the curriculum, was relegated to minor status. New subjects included dialectical materialism, history of the workers' movement, history of Russia and the Spanish language, taught by Cubans.

The Soviet regime recently promulgated a law providing fines for motorists who alter their lights or grills or otherwise make their cars distinguishable. A regime that makes it a crime to personalize a car is apt to make it a crime to transmit a cultural heritage.

It has been 20 years since the first American combat troops arrived in Vietnam. Two Marine battalions arrived March 8, 1965, to help prevent a communist conquest that would result in a blood bath and fulfillment of the "domino theory." That theory was that if South Vietnam fell, so would Laos and Cambodia, and communist troops would be on the Thai border. *On* the border? The blood bath produced the boat people, who are more fortunate than those being "reeducated" in concentration camps or bartered to the Soviet Union as slave laborers, in payment for Soviet military aid. That aid was at work last week, as reported in this dispatch from Bangkok to the *Washington Post:* "Thai forces called in air strikes today in a fierce battle to repel Vietnamese units that crossed the Thai-Cambodian border in a drive to wipe out the last Cambodian guerrilla base along the embattled frontier . . . "

Recently six noncommunist nations of Southeast Asia condemned Vietnam for ignoring "the established rules of orderly and peaceful conduct of relations between states." Those nations should save their breath and should adopt the "Hitler's inkwell principle" of political analysis. The essence of communist regimes, their contemptible taste and detestable character, is apparent in their behavior toward everything—chess, universities, history. Taste tells character, character is destiny, and a dismal destiny is in store for people who cannot read the abundant signs, large and small, that communist regimes are not interested in "orderly and peaceful conduct."

March 18, 1985

Sophistries About Poland

Slogging through the sleet and mire of sophistry, Western leaders are using language unconnected with reality but fine for rationalizing passivity. The important thing regarding the suppression of Poland, they say, is that Russia must respect the principle of "nonintervention"—whatever that means in an Eastern Europe now in its 36th year of Russian "intervention."

Secretary of State Haig warned Russia to respect the principle of nonintervention. So did West German Chancellor Schmidt, speaking behind the Berlin Wall, where he was meeting with the leader of a regime planted and sustained by Russian bayonets. The West's reflex has been to define the crisis with language implying an alibi for complacency: Only Russian tanks count as intervention.

Solidarity's dilemma always has been that its only weapons—strikes—damaged an already desperate economy. The crisis was at hand last week when the regime began attacking Lech Walesa by name (and began calling him names, like "swindler"). The countdown to the current crisis began many months ago when Brezhnev defined Solidarity as "anti-Socialist" and "anti-Soviet," thereby emphasizing that if Solidarity prospered, no elite in Eastern Europe would be safe. And even before Brezhnev spoke, suppression was dictated by the logic of totalitarianism, which can not tolerate rival sources of social authority.

But the day after the suppression began, a *Washington Post* headline announced, "Soviets Reacting with Restraint." And in a national radio broadcast, a *Post* editor put much blame for the crisis on . . . you guessed it: the Reagan administration. He said that more U.S. aid probably could have averted the suppression.

Like frozen pizzas popped into a microwave oven, the familiar axioms of American liberalism were served piping hot in a matter of minutes: Russia was only "reacting" to events, not acting as an initiator. (Can't you just hear the laid-back fellows in the Kremlin reacting with restraint? "Hey, Leonid—have you heard? Those live wires in Warsaw are giving martial law a fling.") And the crisis reveals not the unchanging essence of the Soviet system but the folly of Americans who failed to seize the opportunity to save that system from another excess.

Within months after the 1968 suppression of Czechoslovakia, the allies were pressuring America to be "realistic" and get on with business as usual with Russia. Henry Kissinger notes that it is two years after the invasion of Afghanistan, four years after 20,000 Cubans commanded by a Russian general arrived in Ethiopia, six years after Cubans appeared in Angola. Thirty Soviet divisions are intimidating Poland (presumably in a way consistent with the principle of nonintervention). Yet there is a European "peace" movement operating on the premise that America is a threat to peace.

As Kissinger says, America is today in the role of supplicant, entreating Europe to allow us to deploy weapons that respond to European complaints that we have ignored Europe's vulnerabilities. These weapons would function to couple America to Europe in the event of Soviet aggression against Europe. (If we only need intermediate-range missiles for use against the Soviet Union in the event of a U.S.–Soviet conflict, we could put them at sea.) Now the suppression of Poland probably will demonstrate that NATO lacks political as well as strategic coherence.

Europe's political climate, and the role of corporate interests and free-market ideology in this Republican administration, make it unlikely that the unpleasantness in Poland will interfere with the Russia-to-Western Europe pipeline, or the sales of U.S. grain and technology that ease the strain that militarism places on Soviet society.

But surely the Reagan administration will reject additional measures that would ease Poland's shortages and debt burdens. The principal reason that had been heard for bailing out Poland was to prevent the regime from reverting to type and cracking down. Whatever merit that argument ever had (it was suspiciously useful as a rationalization for rescuing Western banks from the consequences of improvident loans) vanished last Sunday morning.

Furthermore, America should block Poland's application for membership in the International Monetary Fund. There is no humanitarian duty to ease communism's internal contradictions. On the contrary, the West's duty is to maximize the price Moscow pays for asserting sovereignty over Poland.

No happy ending was probable in Poland, but what is happening is the worst possible outcome for America. Russia is using a satellite regime to suppress Poland and chill all of Eastern Europe while Western statesmen beguile themselves with sophistry about

Russia's "nonintervention." This, because General Jaruzelski is as Polish as Pierre Laval was French.

December 17, 1981

Revel: The Essential Pessimist

Defense of democracy depends on pessimists who are not defeatists. It depends on spirited realists such as Jean-François Revel. For the first time since 1922, when Mussolini seized power, all of Western Europe is democratic. But Revel fears that democracy could prove to be a brief parenthesis in history, because democracy practices intellectual self-disarmament.

Part of the problem is the notion that nations that are merely imperfect have no standing to despise nations that are atrocious. Thus in Holland in 1981, a substantial portion of an opinion sample agreed that the Dutch could not criticize Soviet actions in Poland and Afghanistan "as long as housing conditions in Amsterdam fail to meet the highest standards of modern comfort, as long as women remain exploited and the legal rights of heterosexual married couples are denied to homosexual married couples."

Part of the problem is a reflex for self-delusion. It involves representing defeats as victories. For example, the State Department hailed the building of the Berlin Wall as a victory for the West because it revealed the "insecurity" of the East. Actually the wall, like another "victory," the Berlin Blockade, showed that the Soviet Union could abrogate U.S. rights without fear of serious reprisal.

Revel's new book, *How Democracies Perish*, is a catalog of folly, at once hilarious and hair-curling, especially regarding the lingering death of détente. Either economic links to the West are unimportant to the Soviet Union, in which case détente was even dumber in theory than in practice, or they are important, in which case they should be used for leverage. But what happened when the Soviet Union, showing toward the West's warnings the disdain the warnings deserved, imposed martial law in Poland?

France's prime minister declared that, were the West to retaliate by denying new loans to the Eastern bloc, that would be equivalent to "an economic blockade" and "an act of war." Amazing. There is no bankable economy in Eastern Europe. Poland, especially, is hopelessly in hock to the West and without the ability or intention to repay. Yet it is "an act of war" to refuse to stop the piling of bad loans onto the mountain of bad loans.

George Kennan is a tireless auditor of the errors, as he sees them, of people who regard the Soviet regime as radically unlike other regimes. Ten weeks after the invasion of Afghanistan, he said: "Their immediate objective was purely defensive."

Now, leave aside the question of what the Soviet Union had to fear from the communist regime in Kabul that the invading Soviet forces replaced. But what if what Kennan says is true? What does it say about the possibility of détente with a regime that says its vital interests are incompatible with an imperfectly attuned communist regime in Afghanistan, an independent trade union in Poland and an Anatoly Shcharansky outside prison walls?

When Cambodian communists buckled down to the drudgery (the work of idealists is never done) of murdering three million Cambodians, the communists almost certainly suffered horribly from blisters on their palms, a result of using clubs in what Revel calls "an orgy of exploding skulls." It was like the killing of baby seals, except the killing of the seals evokes more protests, and does not result in movies deflecting the blame from the seal-killers.

A new movie, *The Killing Fields*, earns the "Blame America First" Oscar by preaching (it is nothing if not preachy) that communists killed millions but the blame falls on—hey, you peeked—America. Why? Because American bombing of the communists drove them crazy. And you thought you had seen every wrinkle in the insanity defense? This version is: The guilty party is the one that deranges the killer by resisting him.

But as Revel notes, genocide can be discreet: "At a time when the entire world was anathematizing the war in Vietnam, an almost flawless program of genocide was being carried out in total secrecy a few thousand kilometers away on the same continent." The killers of millions of Tibetans were Chinese. One Tibetan had this experience: "Accused of having failed to stack the corpses correctly, he was forced to go down into the pit, where he sank into the heap of decomposing flesh. He was hauled out just in time to avoid asphyxiation."

America's conservative President refers to the regime responsible for killing the Tibetans as "so-called Communist China." Ponder that phrase. It is a symptom of the syndrome by which democracies perish.

January 17, 1985

Reagan's Dim Candle

The Reagan administration, measuring itself by a less than exacting standard, is proud of itself for being slightly firmer about Poland than Chancellor Schmidt and West Germany have been. But the administration has responded to the crisis in the center of Europe even less vigorously and coherently than did Carter to a crisis in southwest Asia (Afghanistan). Schmidt lagged behind even Italy's Communist Party in criticizing Russia. His erratic, hectoring behavior and the decay of his party have made Germany the most obstructionist member of an alliance that runs on consensus and can be held hostage by its most hesitant member. But what has the Reagan administration done in the dim light cast by its protest candle? It has refused to take potent measures. It refused to embargo grain, continuing (in the *Washington Post's* words) "to solve the Soviet Union's farm crisis for it." And it has refused to declare Poland in default on its debts.

That would immediately and severely burden Russia, which already is so hard pressed it is selling gold to supplement the $60 billion it has borrowed in the last decade from the West's banking system. Declaring default would sharply raise the cost and drastically decrease the amount of borrowing by the entire East bloc, thereby impeding Russian militarism. Reagan opposes the Russian gas pipeline that will be financed by Western capital, that will earn Russia hard currency to buy Western technology indispensable to its military machine and that will further the already far-reaching "Finlandization" of Germany. But as Russia goes to German banks for $137 million more in credits, Reagan refuses to inconvenience Russia's parasitism.

Last week the administration declared the Polish crisis over. It did so by deciding not to withdraw International Harvester's license to sell to Russia the technology and know-how for a $300 million factory (almost the value of all U.S. industrial goods sold to Russia last year). The factory will be able to produce 30,000 combines a year, approximately the total U.S. output. An administration advocate of the sale said it might boost Soviet grain yields 25 percent. U.S. experts on armored vehicles visited International Harvester and came away convinced that this plant could be used, as Russia's farm implement plants often are, to assemble armored personnel carriers, too. Even if it is not so used, it will enable Russia's dual-purpose plants to be shifted to a single military purpose.

While grousing about Europe's "selfish" nonresponse to Poland, America has exempted grain (75 percent of the value of U.S.-Russian trade), advanced one of the biggest industrial sales in the history of U.S.-Russian trade and propped up the East bloc's credit to keep the commerce flowing.

The unseriousness of America's response may wreck relations with China, which values America only as a counterweight to Russia. China sees that the administration that says it believes in "linkage" evidently will allow the Geneva negotiations and Secretary Haig's meeting with Gromyko to proceed as though nothing has happened. All diplomatic contacts continue, even though there are thousands of Poles in concentration camps. The Polish crisis is over.

But a crisis of American conservatism is at hand. This administration evidently loves commerce more than it loathes communism. And as Poland dies, the administration has, with ludicrous reluctance, decided it can coutenance draft registration, in part because to do otherwise would send a bad "signal"—this from folks sending the grain, debt and International Harvester signals and trumpeting their opposition to a draft. Conservatism that is so reverent about free trade and so unwilling to infringe private freedoms for public purposes is incompatible with the avowed aims of conservative foreign policy.

Haig's fear of what he calls "unilateralism" (acting not in concert with the allies) may reflect the fact that his strongest constituency is in Europe. Haig was appointed, in part, to assuage European, especially German, anxieties about an inexperienced President from the Republican right wing, which is critical of America's Europe-oriented foreign policy establishment. Haig's misadventures within the administration may have deepened a determination to keep his European constituency friendly. His policies neither invigorate the alliance nor emancipate America from the alliance's stupor. Rather than strong actions against Russia, we get tough talk about Cuba, without any likelihood of commensurate actions.

The suffocation of Poland is an era-ending event, marking the exhaustion of the West's alibis. If, after Vietnam, Angola, Ethiopia, Yemen, Libya and Afghanistan, not even Poland can rally the West, then "the West" is just a geographic, not a political, expression. A nation in the center of Europe is being crushed because it asserted its Europeanness. And the unspoken but unmistakable hope of many Western elites is that the crushing will be quick so that they can get on with business—not business as usual, business better than usual. The contradictions within the capitalist world are quite different from those Marx diagnosed, but just as dangerous.

Last April 24 (while Russia's Suslov was in Warsaw measuring Poland for its casket), Reagan lifted the grain embargo. Shortly thereafter he said: "The West won't contain communism, we will transcend communism." The second half of that is unintelligible, but the first half seems truer every day, with the State Department increasingly run by unreconstructed détentists. The German and American responses to Poland's agony demonstrate the bankruptcy of the détente theory that multiplying commercial links would bind Russia down. It is the West that is immobilized by the centrality and banality of its commercial values.

Republicans tend to believe that the business of America is business, so perhaps this administration is just doing what comes naturally. But Schmidt leads one of Europe's great democratic socialist parties. They once believed their mission was to raise politics above the morals of the marketplace. The Republicans and the socialists seem equally unequal to today's tasks. That is why Washington may soon see a rare event, a resignation from high office in defense of high principle.

January 18, 1982

Pepsi Marxism

Senator Bob Dole, speaking by satellite from Paris, was on his first visit to that city where distractions abound and dissipations tempt, so perhaps he should be forgiven for speaking sentences that gave listeners the sensation of sinking into fudge. Appearing on ABC's *This Week with David Brinkley*, Dole was fresh from a mission to moscow with U.S. businessmen eager for commerce with the Soviet Union.

When dealing with Moscow, Western businessmen have clothed their commercial instincts in a geopolitical theory. The theory is that trade will weave a "web of interdependence" leading to more civilized Soviet behavior. (This is a version of the old theory that fat communists will be torpid communists—like elderly gentlemen after lunching heavily at the Conservative Club.) Furthermore, the theory was that trade would quicken Moscow's interest in consumer goods, and in improving the Soviet standard of living rather than the military.

But the increase in trade in the 1970s coincided with increased Soviet aggressiveness and defense spending. Nevertheless, asked why the United States should be eager for Soviet trade, Dole answered:

"I understand the profit motive that some of the companies had; the U.S. Trade Council, the U.S.S.R. Trade and Economic Council met. They are very sophisticated businessmen. . . . They believe . . . that if we can improve our trading relationship with the Soviets, it might lead to other areas of improvement. . . . "

Might? Statesmanship is a balancing of probabilities, not a hunt for soothing possibilities. Again, Dole:

"[It] would seem to me that if we can increase our relationship in this area, it might lead to some easing of pressures in other places."

Again, "might"? Oysters "might" write sonnets tomorrow— "might" in the sense that it is not a logical impossibility, it is only an improbability.

Dole was followed on ABC by one of those very sophisticated businessmen, Don Kendall, head of Pepsico (Pepsi and other stuff), which does a lot of business with Moscow. Kendall offered an economic theory of history so sweeping it might make a Marxist blush. He said:

"I think that if we had continued on the course that we were on with the Soviets originally, back in the Seventies, and hadn't had the Jackson–Vanik [amendment, which linked trade to emigration of Soviet Jews], that we'd be living in an entirely different atmosphere today."

Well, yes, perhaps. After all, we can unilaterally change the atmosphere any time we decide not to care about Vietnam, Cambodia, Yemen, yellow rain, Angola, Ethiopia, Afghanistan, the Soviet arms buildup—all the things that characterized Soviet behavior in the Seventies.

People often think that whatever they do is the hinge of history. Many poets think poetry is, many journalists think journalism is, many businessmen think business is. But Kendall's doctrine about the potential history-shaping effect of trade implies a peculiar theory of Soviet motivation. What missile now deployed would not be deployed, what Cuban soldier now in Africa would be at home, what nation now being molested would have gone unmolested—Afghanistan? Poland?—if trade had flourished? Is the theory that disappointment about trade caused the Kremlin to pout and have a tantrum?

Asked what might make him abandon his theory about the efficacy of "communication" (read commerce) with Moscow, Kendall said he would "never" abandon it because "the alternatives are God-awful. I don't want to see the world blown up. I think that regardless of how long it takes, we have to try to find a way to communicate with the Soviets, and I happen to think trade is a very good way to do that."

That is an increasingly popular rhetorical tactic: "Freeze this, ratify that, expand trade, vote for him . . . or else be blown up." But such an apocalyptic posing of choices is not an argument about U.S.–Soviet relations; it is a means of drowning out argument.

We are communicating constantly with the Soviets: in Washington, Moscow, Geneva, Vienna, Madrid. Faith in the inevitable efficacy of "communication" suggests that the conflict between the United States and the Soviet Union is some sort of misunderstanding, rather than a clear understanding of differences that can not be split. Such faith in "communication" suggests that history contains no irreconcilables, no tragedy. It suggests that relations between nations—any nations—are analogous to relations between rational individuals, and hence can turn on "gestures" communicating "goodwill."

Soviet behavior has been killing frost in the garden of such dreams. At least it would have been a killing were those dreams open to evidence.

November 25, 1982

Demoralization by Agreement

A Western diplomat at the Madrid conference on "security and cooperation" noted a Russian delegate's suntan. The Russian said he had just returned from Spain's Atlantic shore. It was, he said excitedly, his first sight of an ocean. The tanned fellow was Igor Andropov, 41, son of the Soviet leader.

That episode, says Max Kampelman, chief U.S. delegate, expresses, metaphorically, the purpose of the process begun at Helsinki in 1975 and continued in Madrid. The purpose is to teach the insular Soviet elite the geography of the Western mind, "to bring the world to them."

But the effect on them is negligible. The effect on us is debilitating.

After 34 months of meetings, the 35 participating nations are about to accept a 35-page document. It sharpens some definitions of the obligations Moscow will continue to ignore. It also calls for future meetings to clarify commitments (such as peaceful settlement of disputes and reunification of families) that were clear enough at Helsinki.

The Helsinki accord was a dubious achievement. The West acknowledged what the Red army had settled 30 years earlier: Soviet domination of Eastern Europe. In exchange, Moscow made numerous empty human-rights commitments, and promptly smashed those of its citizens rash enough to act as though the Helsinki agreement was more than parchment.

Kampelman argues, convincingly, that the Helsinki process—an ongoing arraignment of Soviet tyranny—has constructively shaped public opinion in Western Europe and has facilitated public acceptance of new NATO missile deployments. The value of the Helsinki agreements is that they are not honored, and thus produce a court in constant session. But there is a cost to the West that may be more important.

Demoralization is generated by an international agreement

that is violated in virtually every particular by one side while the other side merely negotiates follow-on agreements that also will be largely disregarded. Furthermore, as the public becomes used to the sight of Western and communist diplomats deliberating about freedom of expression, travel, trade unions and other matters, the public concludes that the people talking so earnestly, for so long, share a political vocabulary and frame of reference.

Actually, there are few possibilities for real communication, let alone accommodation, between nations with diametrically opposed definitions of all important political concepts, from freedom through justice. So the Helsinki process spreads a fog of false but soothing assumptions. (We now speak routinely about Soviet "trade union leaders" and "journalists," although there are no such Soviet persons, within the Western meaning of the terms.)

Kampelman asks: The process begun at Helsinki will continue, so what is the U.S. alternative to participation—boycott it, leaving our allies to wage political warfare alone? Kampelman is convinced that Soviet officials are deeply distressed by the Western consensus against them on human-rights questions since Helsinki. The purpose of the Helsinki process, he says, is to keep Moscow on the defensive and force it to pay a political and moral price. He believes Soviet leaders do not possess the moral indifference of vigorous barbarians. Rather, theirs is an other-directed regime, desiring respectability as well as power.

Perhaps. Certainly for educating the educable there is no better teacher than Kampelman, a tough, intellectual Democrat. But teaching civility to Moscow is like teaching golf to wolves.

Some East European countries are complying reasonably well concerning matters such as family reunification. But the West knew from the start that it would be futile to hope the Soviets would agree at Madrid to stop jamming Western radio broadcasts which, if words mean anything, Moscow agreed to do at Helsinki. Fifty-one Russians who believed in the Helsinki agreement and organized to monitor their government's compliance are in jails, labor camps, "psychiatric hospitals" or internal exile. Since the Madrid meeting began, 500 Soviet citizens have been convicted for political or religious "crimes," Jewish emigration has virtually stopped and Poland has been suffocated.

Still, one salutary effect of the Helsinki process is on the morale of a few valiant persons—dissidents in the Soviet sphere, including many in prison. Recently, when a dissident released from the Soviet

Union was introduced to Kampelman, he kissed him, exclaiming that while in prison he and others had been heartened by Kampelman's relentless indictment of Soviet noncompliance with Helsinki undertakings.

Kampelman has quietly but effectively achieved relief for many persons suffering Soviet persecution. However, dissidents will be devastated if the Madrid conference ends with no tangible gains for those who risked—and lost—so much because they took Helsinki seriously. Specifically, no document should be signed with Anatoly Shcharansky in prison.

Were even a significant fraction of the Helsinki obligations fulfilled by Moscow, the Soviet system would be changed, and so would Soviet international behavior. That will not happen. And the release of a thousand Shcharanskys would not change the Soviet system. But it would release heroes and partially redeem the Helsinki charade.

August 24, 1983

Iron Curtain, Rubber Words

There are occasions, and this is one, when I am even more acutely aware than usual of my limitations as a writer. Only a Dostoyevsky could express the deep depression I feel after reading a two-part conversation with Max Kampelman, conducted by George Urban in *Encounter* magazine. Kampelman, chief U.S. arms negotiator, was chief U.S. representative at the Madrid conference on the Helsinki accords. You remember those: Signed in 1975, they expressed U.S. and Soviet "accord" about human rights. It seems that Kampelman, and presumably the Reagan administration, take the Helsinki "process" seriously in a way that is seriously at odds with reality. If a person as experienced, intelligent and representative of the Reagan administration as Kampelman can miss the mark so thoroughly regarding the Soviet Union, it is reasonable to despair of this nation's ability to face facts.

In the ongoing Helsinki process of negotiations, Kampelman says, we have engaged in a struggle for "hearts and minds" and have "tarnished" the Soviet image. Besides, we have to participate in the process because democratic publics demand governments "perceived to be always willing" to negotiate. But Soviet ideology has long since lost its luster, and Soviet society has lost its allure as a model, so Soviet power is not a function of the Soviet "image," which can hardly be tarnished through speeches in Madrid more than it has been by 68 years of domestic failure and foreign atrocities. Actually, any hearts and minds not revolted by Soviet behavior are apt to be anesthetized by the spectacle of the Helsinki process. That process is an elaborate pretense that we and the Soviets are in accord about the vocabulary and value of free expression, free trade unions, the right to travel and other matters. The effect of the process on minds is to muddle many in the West.

Kampelman is asked about negotiating a code of behavior with a power that espouses global revolution and extermination of all "class enemies" and "hostile social orders." He answers that we have forced the Soviets "to take some of our moral requirements into account." Wrong. What do our "requirements" require of the Soviets? The Helsinki process, like its arms-control counterparts, reassures the Soviets that they need not take anything into account. Kampelman says, "We are in the process of turning [the human-rights provisions] into a binding document." Binding? Where is Kampelman now? In Geneva, trying to negotiate more arms agreements with the regime that is violating all the major arms agreements it has entered into. Soviet arms negotiators can read the lesson of the Helsinki process: There is no penalty for treating agreements contemptuously; the Americans will come back for more, thereby blurring any indictment of Soviet wrongdoing.

"I am sustained," Kampelman says, "by the hope that at some point somebody in the Soviet system will say: 'How long can we go on being isolated in this manner?'" Isolated? Our negotiators and theirs troop together to Helsinki and Belgrade and Madrid and Geneva to multiply the agreements the Soviets break with impunity Kampelman refers to the Helsinki process as an "accountability process." But in what does accountability consist when the report negotiated during the Madrid session, which coincided with the suppression of Poland and Solidarity, mentioned neither?

During the Madrid proceedings, Kampelman says, he "systematically mentioned the names of dissidents," "raised issues" of rights, "talked about" the Czech dissident group Charter 77, "put pressure on" the Soviets on behalf of Western principles. Kampelman is a man of such decency it is a shame to have to respond: "So bloody what?" After all that jaw-jaw, Shcharansky is currently in an extremely cramped jail cell for the crime of trying to monitor Soviet compliance with the Helsinki accords.

When Kampelman says we participated in this process "in the hope of modifying their behavior," he is applying mild psychotherapy to a sociopathic regime. He says Soviet behavior derives not only from Leninism but also from a Russian component, a desperate desire for "respectability." Kampelman, representing the Reagan administration, evidently subscribes to the unslayable theory that Soviet leaders do not mean what they say. They say they do not care a fig about bourgeois respectability. They say that only innocents believe there is an ethic beyond revolutionary utility.

Kampelman answers critics with a question: "What are the alternatives to establishing standards and insisting on accountability?" The answers are: Stop disorienting Western publics by pretending that standards asserted unilaterally by the West and shredded by the other side are "established." Stop mangling the word "accountability" by applying it to a process devoid of penalties. Stop saying the Madrid accord "tightens the vise," or that it is "significant" that the agreement requires signatory nations to "take the necessary action" to comply. The "necessary action" would be that the Soviet regime dismantle itself.

Kampelman says: "We need to proclaim the fact that, in the Madrid document, the totalitarian Soviet leadership and the Polish military authorities had to accept the principle of free trade-unionism because of Western pressure." Please, spare us the proclamation. "Had to accept"? That rubber language about unions is precisely the empty invoking of Western values that the Soviets must be tickled to accept. Kampelman is asked: Is it not the case that this "requirement" of free trade unionism is made a mockery because there also is a nullifying provision that says the requirement "will be exercised in compliance with the law of the State?" Kampelman answers: No, because the Soviet state is bound by the International Labor Organization conventions which "guarantee" free trade unions. But then the question for Kampelman is: If the ILO matters, then why was the Madrid agreement on unions necessary?

Actually, abundant rights are "guaranteed" in the Soviet Constitution, including, by the way, the right of the member republics of the U.S.S.R. to secede. That Constitution is the moral equivalent of the Helsinki process, which the administration takes seriously.

April 1, 1985

Raoul Wallenberg: Lost in a Gauze of Lies

The gauze of lies that the Soviet regime wraps around reality has never been thick enough to muffle this question: Where is Raoul Wallenberg?

Now it is asked again, in the wake of the most recent in a long series of tormenting reports. A Russian immigrant in Israel says that when he was hospitalized in 1972 on the way to prison, he met a man who "looked Jewish, so I asked who he was. He answered in accented Russian that he was Swedish and was there because he helped the Jews. He said his name was Raoul Wallenberg." That occurred a quarter of a century after 1947, the year the Kremlin says Wallenberg died.

Last May, when tardily releasing documents about the Wallenberg case, a Swedish official said, "We are working on the supposition that he is still alive." (Sweden's lethargy concerning the case—lethargy born of cowardice—hardly constitutes "working.") If alive, he is 70. It is 38 years since he disappeared from Hungary into the Soviet Union.

On January 17, 1945, he was seized by Soviet forces that were "liberating" Hungary from their former allies, the Nazis. Three weeks later he was in the emblematic institution of the Soviet regime, Moscow's Lubyanka prison.

At 32, representing neutral Sweden, Wallenberg was in Budapest at America's request, working with breathtaking bravery and saving scores of thousands of Jews from Adolf Eichmann's final chapter of the "final solution," the destruction of Hungarian Jews. He bought buildings and draped them with Swedish flags as diplomatically protected territory. He dressed "Aryan-looking" Jewish men in S.S. uniforms to protect Jewish havens. He distributed fake passports and used sheer audacity to intimidate Nazi soldiers into opening the doors of cattle cars. Thanks to him, the 120,000 Jews in Budapest were the most substantial Jewish community surviving in Europe when the war ended.

One certainty is that Andrei Gromyko lied in the 1957 memorandum asserting that Wallenberg's "sojourn in the Soviet Union"—Gromyko's words—ended with a heart attack in prison in 1947. This memorandum came after 12 years of Kremlin denials that Wallenberg had ever been in Soviet hands. Gromyko cited the evidence of two Soviet functionaries, both conveniently dead, and said the body had been cremated—a transparent fabrication, given Soviet practices.

There has been a steady trickle of reports about Wallenberg, first from returning German prisoners of war, then from released political prisoners and Jewish emigrants. The reports give dates and places—prisons, cell numbers—that trace a tantalizing trail across the years and through the gulags.

For example, in 1961 a Soviet professor of medicine told a visiting Swedish physician that he had recently examined Wallenberg in a "mental hospital." In 1977 a Muscovite just released from the gulag called his daughter in Israel and mentioned meeting in a Moscow prison a Swede "who had served 30 years." Two years later the Muscovite was back in prison because, his wife said, he wrote a letter about Wallenberg. Sources in Eastern Europe report that in 1981 Wallenberg was moved to a prison hospital near Leningrad.

Why was he arrested in the first place? The Soviet machinery of brutality operates so automatically it leaves little room for, and certainly does not require, much mind. But Soviet repressors certainly did not want brave witnesses to the breaking of Eastern Europe. Why was he kept? Perhaps, in part, to show contempt for Western disapproval. Why did Soviet troops using horses and ropes drag away the statue erected to him in Budapest in 1948? Because the Kremlin disapproved of what he did.

It is prudent that we insistently ask what happened when Wallenberg ended his dance of death with the Third Reich and fell into the hands of its moral twin. When the Soviet Union gets away with such acts—acts that are as contemptuous as they are contemptible—it gets the idea that it can unleash "yellow rain" and can shoot the pope with little to fear from the West's fitful disapproval.

Besides, if this case is not America's business, what is? On October 5, 1981, Wallenberg became only the second person (Winston Churchill was the first) to be made an honorary American citizen.

Signing the bill conferring this honor, President Reagan said "we're going to do everything in our power" to locate Wallenberg. But we have not done that. So before Reagan agrees to meet with Yuri Andropov, he should receive an answer, beyond the routine mendacities, to this question: Where is Raoul Wallenberg?

January 6, 1983

Raoul Wallenburg and the Price of Neutrality

Like a northern pike rising at a lure, Sweden's ambassador has risen to defend his country against an accusation in a recent column. I welcome the opportunity to amplify the offending remark.

Writing about Raoul Wallenberg, the savior of thousands of Hungarian Jews, who disappeared into Soviet prisons in 1945, I quoted a Swedish official saying that, "We are working on the supposition that Wallenberg is still alive." I said: "Sweden's lethargy concerning the case—lethargy born of cowardice—hardly constitutes 'working.'"

In a letter to the *Washington Post*, the ambassador calls this "grossly unfair." He admits Sweden believed initial Soviet lies, but he says Sweden "has pursued this matter with a vigor and perseverance that probably exceeds what any government has done for one of its citizens."

Well.

Sweden's statement about its supposition was made when Sweden released documents pertaining to the case. Representative Tom Lantos (D-Cal.), who as a boy in Budapest was saved by Wallenberg, wrote to the *New York Times* (May 26, 1982):

"It is both ironic and deplorable that Sweden has waited 20 years to release some 42 volumes of reports and eyewitness accounts. . . . Had the information been made public earlier to those in a position to help Raoul Wallenberg, he may have been able to live his life with dignity—with his family—instead of in the infamy of the Soviet gulag. For years, the government of Sweden has engaged in ineffective silent diplomacy. . . . Now they tell those of us who have fought so hard for his release that we can finally see their documents. If . . . the Swedish government is now 'working on the supposition that he is still alive,' then it's about time."

Just after the war, Sweden's foreign minister was urged to press the case and disregard the fact that Soviet Foreign Minister Vyshinsky said that the Soviet Union did not have Wallenberg. The Swedish minister said: "What! Do you believe that Mr. Vyshinsky is lying?" Vyshinsky, the prosecutor in Stalin's show trials, lie? "Absolutely unheard of," said the minister.

The ambassador's claim that Sweden has done more for Wallenberg than any nation has done for a citizen is refuted by many cases, but especially that of Harald Feller, a Swiss diplomat who was in Budapest when Wallenberg was, doing similar rescue work. He, too, wound up in Soviet hands. But he was released in 1946 because his country arrested six Soviet spies and negotiated a swap.

Although Sweden found neutrality profitable between 1939 and 1945, after the war it discovered morality and ever since has been urging it on others, especially the United States, which frequently falls short of Sweden's exacting standards. Sweden has generally considered swaps beneath its dignity. "Sweden," said a Swedish foreign minister, "does not do such things." By the time (1979) Sweden proposed a swap, the Kremlin reacted with disdain.

Olaf Palme, who is again prime minister, and the world's moral tutor (he considers the United States an especially backward student), was prime minister in 1976. When Palme met with Kosygin, the Wallenberg case was not even on the agenda. Palme's administration dismissed the case in a word: "utagerad" (settled).

Even before the invasion of Afghanistan, Wallenberg's supporters urged Sweden to boycott the 1980 Olympics in Moscow. Even after the invasion, Sweden did not boycott.

In October 1981, a Soviet submarine ran aground while violating Swedish territorial waters. Wallenberg supporters urged using the submarine for leverage. When the Soviet Union asked for its boat back, Sweden could have said: Boat? What boat? We know nothing of any boat—just as you know nothing of Wallenberg.

But appearing on ABC's *Nightline* (October 30, 1981), the foreign minister was asked if Sweden "might want to propose a trade." He said that "would certainly not serve any useful purpose." Do Swedes wonder why Soviet submarines show such contempt for Sweden's sovereignty? Cringing neutrality has not noticeably immunized Sweden from the aggressive disdain of Soviet submariners.

In her new biography, *Wallenberg*, Kati Marton, a Hungarian-born journalist, concludes that Wallenberg fell victim to "Sweden's near-pathological fear of Russia":

"The scorn with which the Kremlin treated Stockholm's queries about Wallenberg was not altogether unjustified given the Swedes' lack of conviction following his imprisonment. The dim memory of an early 19th-century Russian invasion, Sweden's first and last, is not sufficient explanation for the country's spineless behavior on behalf of its captured diplomat."

Marton also says: "At Wallenberg's expense, Sweden has

learned a painful lesson: the price demanded to maintain one's neutrality can sometimes be too high." The lesson certainly has been taught to all of Europe; whether it has been learned is increasingly doubtful.

January 16, 1983

Death on Waterloo Bridge

The view from London's Waterloo Bridge—down the Thames toward Wren's dome on St. Paul's, up toward the House of Parliament—encompasses striking symbols of the West's attainments. But the bridge itself is now a symbol of the brazenness of the West's enemies.

Georgi Markov, 49, was walking across the bridge on September 7, 1978, heading home from his work at the studios of the BBC External Services. Suddenly he felt a sting on the back of his thigh and, turning, saw a man bending to retrieve an umbrella. The man, with a foreign accent, murmured "I'm sorry."

Markov did not mention the incident to his wife, but early the next morning he suffered a raging fever and said: "I have a horrible feeling that this may be connected with something which happened yesterday." Markov, Bulgaria's leading man of letters before he defected, had received many threats and warnings. One warning said he would be poisoned by a substance, tested in Moscow, that causes a high fever.

Scotland Yard announced that doctors found in his thigh a tiny pellet containing ricin, a rare poison extensively studied in Eastern Europe. There is no known antidote. The pellet was a highly sophisticated bit of murder technology. It was made of a platinum-iridium alloy which the human body does not reject. It was the size of a pinhead and had four openings to hold the poison. A similar pellet had been used in an unsuccessful assassination attempt against another Bulgarian defector in Paris. A few days after Markov died, a lieutenant general in Bulgaria's security force delivered a speech expressing "the deepest gratitude to our Soviet comrades-in-arms of the KGB for their constant help and comradely assistance."

You can read the book that got Markov killed. *The Truth that Killed* (published by Ticknor & Fields) is the autobiography he broadcast to Bulgaria, thereby enraging the regime. Markov's only child, who was just two when he died, asked her mother, "Why did daddy write those things if he loved us?" Her mother replied that daddy thought Bulgaria's rulers would not risk the scandal that might result from killing him. However, the real scandal is that there is so slight, and so fleeting, a sense of being scandalized by such crimes. The fact is illustrated by, and may have helped bring on, the so-called crime of the century—the Bulgarian plot to kill the pope.

The mills of Italian justice grind slowly, but they grind exceedingly small and are grinding to dust the pretense that the Turkish gunman acted alone. There is now not the slightest reason to doubt that his attack was organized by Bulgarians, who would not have undertaken such an audacious crime without the approval of the highest Soviet authorities.

None of this is news to anyone who has read Claire Sterling's book *The Time of the Assassins*. Her work on this case is the journalistic achievement of the age. Her most appalling evidence strongly suggests complicity by some democracies, including this one, in covering up the Soviet crime. The cover-up that Italian authorities are pulling apart, thread by thread, demands this action:

The U.S. Senate Intelligence Committee should call in U.S. intelligence leaders and march them through Sterling's book, page by page, asking why she singlehandedly learned so much more than the intelligence agencies, collectively, did. The Intelligence Committee should dwell on her accounts of attempts by U.S. agents to discourage her investigations. The real "crime of the century" is the complicity of democracies in suppressing evidence of the Soviet crime, lest relations between East and West become unpleasantly realistic.

What are relations to be with a nation like the Soviet Union, a nation now killing its dissidents by medical neglect? Describing the kidnapping, "in familiar urban-terrorist style," of the Sakharovs, *The Economist* (of London) says that the extraordinary fact is that this atrocity was not the work of a mere terrorist gang, but an action "approved by Soviet ruling circles," in violation of Soviet law and the equally worthless 1975 Helsinki human-rights undertakings.

It is serendipitous that the six-month anniversary of that kidnapping falls on the eve of the U.S. election. And it is splendid that the machinery of Italian justice has synchronized with the machinery of American electoral politics. This is the tenth consecutive election in which all issues should be secondary to this one: Who best understands the task of describing and containing the evil empire of which Bulgaria is a loathsome instrument? That issue is not the main reason why Reagan will win, but it is the main reason he should.

November 1, 1984

The Boot in Afghanistan's Face

The small, torn fragment of dull-green plastic does not arrest the eye or arouse the imagination—until it is explained. Then it is mesmerizing evidence of the Soviet regime's essence: unfettered brutality.

The plastic is from the casing of an antipersonnel mine used in Afghanistan. But the term "antipersonnel" suggests traditional usages of war: It suggests that the personnel against whom the mines are used are military. Actually, the intended victims are civilians, and often children. The mines are especially dreadful because they are not meant to kill, at least not instantaneously.

They are scattered by the hundreds of thousands—green in vegetation, brown in arid areas, white in snow—near villages. They are designed to blow off a foot or lower leg. Occasionally they do more: One man's foot was blown off and as he fell his hand hit another.

These weapons of indiscriminate yet limited violence express a military strategy of unlimited war by the world's largest army against an entire population. The mines are designed to maim—or to kill lingeringly. Soviet tacticians know that wounded persons are a drain on the community because of the constant care they require. Lethal infections often result, so the Soviet tactic demoralizes everyone exposed to the hideous suffering of victims, and especially children, dying from gangrene, staphylococcus or gram-negative septicemia.

Such savageries are the subject of an article in the current issue of *Foreign Affairs*. The author, Dr. Claude Malhuret, is executive director of Medecins sans Frontieres (Doctors Without Borders) and has been one of the 162 physicians and nurses rotated in and out of Afghanistan, managing hospitals. Because the MSF people are among the few foreign witnesses of the war that world journalism has largely forgotten, their hospitals have been bombed by Soviet planes. But MSF people have seen enough to substantiate Malhuret's thesis, which is:

The Soviet regime has analyzed various failures, including America's, in counterguerrilla warfare and has concluded that the key to success is a kind of ruthlessness that only a totalitarian regime will practice. Guerrillas succeed, as Mao said, with the aid of the local population, in which they live like fish in water. American, British and French strategies were aimed at winning the allegiance of the water—the population. Soviet strategy is to kill the fish by draining the water.

Reprisals, exterminations and other tortures are so unremitting that much of the population leaves, and that which remains is immobilized by physical and emotional traumas. Twenty-five percent of the Afghan population of 1979 is now in Pakistan and Iran. Hundreds of thousands are refugees within Afghanistan.

As Malhuret says, this ocean of suffering is not the unintended consequence of a war's unavoidable collateral effects. It is the bitter fruit cultivated by Soviet strategy. "This does not involve a warm bath/cold shower tactic, but the exclusive use of boiling water—again and again and again, until both the guerrilla fighters and the population ask for mercy."

Today the United States should be supplying Afghanistan's freedom fighters with as many hand-held rockets as they can use—the kind that can bring down helicopters. Soviet forces, having declared all Afghans of all ages to be enemies, live by helicopters that supply their isolated garrisons—and sow the landscape with mines.

The sowing is so thick that it is common to see goats and cows wearing bamboo splints tied with wires. Not content with causing random suffering among those who do not watch their step, Soviet forces booby-trap household artifacts, such as clocks, in villages they sweep through. They also scatter booby traps made to resemble pens or red toy trucks. "Their main targets," says Malhuret, "are children, whose hands and arms are blown off."

Malhuret denounces the "negligence" of the news media. He says that if organizations like MSF can maintain a constant presence in four provinces, in spite of violent Soviet opposition, the world's powerful news organizations could do as much.

The Red Army has now been engaged against the freedom

fighters longer than it was against the German Wehrmacht. But what is being done in Afghanistan in 1984 is more akin to the Ukrainian genocide of 1933. Then, as now, Soviet ruthlessness prevailed, and the West's denial reflex kept the unpleasant business out of most minds.

But one mind understood. George Orwell said that if you want to imagine the future, imagine a boot in your face—forever. The future came to Afghanistan four winters ago.

January 5, 1984

Brezhnev's Successes

Out in the Gulag Archipelago, where November wind scrapes the prisoners' faces like a dull razor blade, there are persons who remember that Brezhnev's first political job involved inflicting Stalin's unimaginably brutal collectivization of agriculture. Brezhnev's last state ceremony also reeked of death. He looked cadaverous as he stood atop the tomb displaying Lenin's corpse and watched the weapons roll by. The parade marked the 65th anniversary of the Bolshevik coup.

In November 1917, some Bolsheviks barged through the servants' entrance of the Winter Palace and arrested government ministers. Six persons were injured by Bolshevik shooting, five of them Bolsheviks. Thus began the Soviet state. Two months later Lenin wrote to Trotsky: "This is a moment of triumph. We have lasted a day longer than the Paris Commune." Since then the state has swollen but still is just camped on the country. It still is without legitimacy, without even the capacity to conduct a legitimate succession process—one that is not essentially conspiratorial.

Brezhnev was the most effective politician of the last two decades. His brutality bankrupted a cottage industry among Western academics—the business of discerning "liberalization" and predicting "convergence" between Soviet and Western societies. With the Helsinki pacts he won Western ratification of Soviet hegemony in Eastern Europe and reduced the language of human rights to applesauce. He launched the largest military buildup in history. Simultaneously he manipulated détente to paralyze U.S. procurements and divide the West. With SALT I he won formal recognition of political and military parity. SALT II, sealed with a Carter hug, confirmed Soviet strategic superiority.

Brezhnev took power exactly two years after the Cuban missile crisis began. A decade later he was dispatching Cuban forces to serve the Soviet Union's global reach. His commitment to a blue-water navy expressed his determination to project power. He engaged proxy troops in areas not contiguous to the Soviet empire (Ethiopia, Angola, South Yemen). He underwrote the destruction of the Paris accords and a U.S. ally, then underwrote Vietnam's invasion of Cambodia, where he made possible Vietnam's use of chemical warfare. He used force to snuff out a slightly milder form of communism in Czechoslovakia. Thirteen years later he did not need a single Soviet soldier to cause the suppression of an aroused Polish people. In Afghanistan he sent the Red Army into battle for the first time since the second world war (not counting its uses against satellites).

Neither "containment" nor détente nor the "web of interdependence" that trade was supposed to produce has altered the aims of the Soviet elite. Today Soviet forces are designed and trained to seize territory, not defend it. A leadership change matters less in the Soviet Union than most places because the winnowing process is certain to produce insular, ignorant and brutal elites from which the leader claws his way to the pinnacle. Also, the militarization of Soviet society is so comprehensive that the regime's controlling priorities do not change.

Nevertheless, beginning with Stalin's death, every transition has triggered wishful thinking about how economic troubles, ideological sterility and internal disputes will radically reduce Soviet strength. Now, ere many suns have set, we shall hear another theory, one that is both soothing and hectoring. The theory will be that Brezhnev's successor is a closet liberal threatened by hawks lurking in Kremlin closets (the Kremlin is all closets), so the United States should make some concession to strengthen the liberal. The theorist will not be inhibited by the fact that the successor, Andropov, is a product of the KGB.

Optimists note that the Kremlin is surrounded by a sea of trouble—social stagnation, Poland, Afghanistan. But although Brezhnev's nation cannot grow grain, it can land a warhead a few hundred feet from a missile silo in South Dakota. Poland? Brezhnev died the day Jaruzelski's thugs deterred Poles from heeding Solidarity's call for a strike. The next day Warsaw moved to release Lech Walesa. The West's fatuity machine cranked out the opinion that this was a "hopeful" sign. Rubbish. It was a sign of Brezhnev's last victory, the crushing of Eastern Europe's most resilient people. Afghanistan? A tiny fraction of Soviet forces are engaged there, and the outcome is not in doubt.

Reagan's administration has lifted the grain embargo, subsidized Poland's martial law regime and stumbled away from the pipeline sanctions it stumbled into. Having accelerated the erosion of the federal government's revenue base, the administration is forcing Congress to choose between cutting domestic programs and cutting defense. The consensus for rearmament, nurtured so painstakingly, is about to crumble. Andropov can take comfort from the fact that all this is the work of America's hawks.

The Economist has suggested that unless Brezhnev's successor risks reform, "Brezhnev will have been his country's Metternich: the man who made the eventual detonation worse by merely delaying it." But if Poland, an incandescent and cohesive people, has been suppressed so easily, what detonation must Brezhnev's successor fear? Henry Kissinger argues that the difficulties confronting the democracies are all amenable to solution by the democracies, whereas the problems confronting the Soviet Union require changes in the Soviet system. But perhaps the inability of the democracies to summon the will to solve their problems is itself a systemic failure—a result of the political culture of affluent consumer societies. If so, the Soviet system, for all its stupidity and cruelty, may be superior in the political-military competition that will decide our fate.

In the 1930s, when rumors circulated in Moscow that the figure in Lenin's tomb was wax, a chemist took some correspondents to the tomb. Saying the body would last a century, he opened the glass case and tweaked the nose on the mummified remains of the man who had felt triumphant when the Soviet regime lasted two months. It is fitting that this regime of slave labor and yellow rain has made a relic of a corpse.

November 22, 1982

Ivan X, Jogger, Maybe

Konstantin Chernenko's strength is reportedly ebbing, and not surprisingly: Building the New Soviet Man and a worker's paradise worthy of him involves long hours and heavy lifting. So, just to be ready, here is a generic news story to be run whenever a Soviet "leader" (an odd term for the head of a nation where people have no choice but to follow) dies:

WASHINGTON—The death of the Soviet leader is viewed here as a promising "opening" in U.S.–Soviet relations. His successor, Ivan X, is considered a "moderate."

State Department officials warn that it would be "superficial" to draw "premature" conclusions based on the "mere facts" of his life, which "on the surface" follows the traditional career path of the Soviet elite. "True," a U.S. official says, "Mr. X has spent 27 years arresting people, but he probably has got all that out of his system."

As evidence of Mr. X's moderation, State Department analysts note that although no one has actually seen him jog, the consensus in the diplomatic community is that he jogs in New Balance shoes, which are made in Massachusetts. Also, he is said to use a Walkman, on which he listens to Bruce Springsteen tapes.

"He is a high-tech, 'new ideas,' Gary Hart-type appealing to Soviet yuppies," said a Yale Kremlinologist. A Harvard professor of Détente Studies, noting that Springsteen's current hit is "Born in the U.S.A." infers that Mr. X may wish to "normalize" relations with Afghanistan.

It is common knowledge that Mr. X snacks on Twinkies delivered by diplomatic pouch. "Clearly," says a State Department Soviet expert, "he is cosmopolitan, breaking the mold of insularity."

The State Department acknowledges some gaps in its knowledge of Mr. X. For example, equal numbers of experts are certain that he does and that he does not speak English.

Although Mr. X has published many articles, the State Department says little is known about what he "really" thinks. "Did *Mein Kampf* tell us Hitler's mind?" cautions an official. Mr. X's writings include attacks on freedom of expression, a defense of the "export of socialist fraternity to Afghanistan," and "Against Bourgeois Sentimentalism: A War-Winning Strategy for Nuclear Weapons."

A State Department official explains, "True, a literal reading of his writings might suggest he is occasionally somewhat muted in his enthusiasm for the spirits of détente, Geneva, Helsinki and San Clemente. But sophisticated Western observers understand that obeisance to traditional rhetorical modes is required for advancement in a society as 'conservative' as the Soviet Union, which is utterly unlike our society.

"Furthermore, Americans must understand that in the Soviet system, just as in ours, the role of personality is paramount." Asked how U.S. optimism could rest on the assumption that Soviet society is radically unlike and essentially similar to ours, the official said: "Nevertheless."

The official notes that "seasoned observers" believe Mr. X opposed the Soviet suppression of East Germany, Hungary, Czechoslovakia and Poland, favors "liberalization" of concentration camps, and is a middle-of-the-roader regarding the psychiatric "hospitals." The State Department considers it "encouraging" that Mr. X has risen to power while privately opposing every significant Soviet policy in his lifetime.

At a recent Moscow reception for the American peace group, Clergy and Faculty Mightily Concerned, a Soviet official confided that Mr. X, 69, is a "Young Turk" who wants arms control so that Soviet living standards can rise. The Soviet official said Mr. X is "a pragmatist—sort of a Soviet Howard Baker," but is threatened by "hawks" in the Politburo.

State Department officials concur that Mr. X and other "doves in the Kremlin closets" need a sign from the United States that it "means no harm." U.S. diplomats are formulating "new approaches" that will show U.S. "flexibility" in arms control negotiations. "The Soviets made a concession by returning to the talks they had broken off," a U.S. official observes, "so a U.S. concession would be symmetrical." The Commerce Department is organizing a trade delegation committed to "prophylactic unilateralism," meaning credits to underwrite Soviet purchases of U.S. goods.

A White House official, paraphrasing Churchill, explains that all U.S. policy rests on the principle, "Jaw-jaw is better than even prime rib."

At the State Department, a reporter recalled that optimism

about the "moderate" Khrushchev died with the Hungarian invasion, the Berlin Wall and the Cuban missile crisis, and optimism about the "moderate" Brezhnev died in Prague, Afghanistan, Yemen, Angola, Ethiopia and Poland. A State Department official replied: "Yes, but."

January 20, 1985

George Bush's Surmise

Vice Presidents are virtuosos at the art of funeral-attending, and at Brezhnev's funeral George Bush, the former CIA director, had a 40-minute chat with the successor, Andropov, former head of the KGB. They talked, Bush said, "as spook to spook." That was an interesting thought: The CIA director and the head of the Soviet secret-police/psychiatric-hospital/slave-labor empire are in essentially the same craft.

Anyway, Bush brought back a hopeful surmise. Andropov, he said, had spent 15 years reading all Soviet intelligence reports and "anyone who has had access to all the data must objectively know that if a country goes in peace, it has absolutely nothing whatsoever to fear from the U.S.A."

Swimming beneath the surface of that surmise, like a school of sluggish pike in brackish water, are some interesting implications. The Cold War is to a significant extent a misunderstanding to be cured by better "data." Soviet policy is defensive and reactive, driven by neurotic fear of U.S. motives. Therefore, U.S. foreign policy must be psychotherapy to get the Soviet Union thinking "objectively." As Bush's boss says, we must convince the Soviets that we mean them no "harm."

George Orwell said it requires not just intellect but imagination to comprehend Soviet behavior. American leaders are most imaginative when concocting reasons for misapprehending Soviet motives. Comprehension is the enemy of cheerfulness, and cheerfulness is mandatory for leaders of democracy, especially when it is irrational.

American leaders will believe uncountable things to avoid believing the depressing truth, which is: The Soviet regime is intellectually deranged, morally bankrupt, politically corrupt and economically lunatic, and therefore is utterly dependent for whatever legitimacy it can claim, and whatever élan it can muster, on its role as liberator of everyone from everything but communism.

When Stalin died, Western leaders said, cheerfully: Fundamental change will soon be afoot because Stalin was the last old Bolshevik and, besides, his successor has given a speech praising "peaceful coexistence." Georgy Malenkov did that, in a speech saying war is bad. But he was not really the successor. He succumbed to a Stalinist attack from Khrushchev, who then became an anti-Stalinist regarding everything except government and culture.

Khrushchev, said Westerners cheerfully, is an earthy peasant, in touch with Soviet Everyman. Surely, therefore, he is more interested in raising living standards than in missiles. Two years after the Cuban missile crisis he was replaced by what Westerners thought was to be a troika—Podgorny, Brezhnev and Kosygin. Kosygin was cheerfully regarded as dominant, and as a worldy moderate, partly because he had an intellectual son-in-law.

The moderation of the new regime did not pan out, as Czechs, Poles, Ethiopians, Afghans, Yemenis, Vietnamese, Cambodians, Laotians, Nicaraguans, Angolans and others can attest. But when Brezhnev fell, well there was Andropov who—be of good cheer—had been reading the data and therefore knew that the United States meant no harm.

Today think tanks are hard at the task of pondering What It All Means— the fact that Gorbachev is the first leader too young to have fought in the war with and then against the Nazis; the fact that he is a lawyer; the fact that he has failed upwards through agriculture. All—all!—that is known for sure is that he rocketed to the top of the Soviet elite during the slightly more than a decade (from the invasion of Czechslovkia to the invasion of Afghanistan) when Soviet behavior was even more brutal than before.

After Stalin, the last Bolshevik, came Khrushchev, the last leader to have profited mightily from Stalin's purges. Then came Brezhnev and Andropov and Chernenko, the last leaders who were—what?—brutalized or sensitized or something by the war. Now comes Gorbachev, and from Western leaders comes the "new generation" theory: Be of good cheer, because the new generation is, well, younger, and, therefore. . . . Besides, his wife has a well-turned ankle—a matched set, in fact.

I am not being sexist. I respect her for her mind, but ankles are geopolitical facts. They occasioned favorable comment during a tour of Britain. The tour was like a Broadway show previewing in New Haven to rave reviews. He and she cut graceful figures, she by having one, he by talking of contracts for British industry. He smiled a lot, at least until a Member of Parliament, perhaps remembering Lady Astor's question to Stalin (When are you going to stop killing people?) asked about persecutions.

Gorbachev's charm slipped. He said: So's your old man. Actually, he said: What about Ireland and unemployment? This guy is apt to be around for a long time, and it is apt to seem like a long time.

March 14, 1985

Miss Manners's Diplomatic Message

From Harvard, of all unlikely places, but of course from someone just a visitor there, comes something useful. It is a tract for these troubled times. Its title is *Common Courtesy: In Which Miss Manners Solves the Problem that Baffled Mr. Jefferson.*

Miss Manners (a.k.a. Judith Martin) writes a splendidly authoritarian (and, in the bargain, authoritative) column for readers who like the smack of firm government. Although she reigns in Washington, she does not write about government as this is narrowly understood here. But Harvard's Kennedy School of Government, having sensibly despaired of perfecting the Republic with laws, invited Miss Manners to lecture on the role of manners. Her lecture supplies what the Founding Fathers forgot, "a philosophically acceptable and aesthetically pleasing standard of American etiquette."

The problem (my opinion, not Miss Manners's) began in early July 1776, when Jefferson was asked to go upstairs and draft a declaration of insubordination. He had a journalist's weakness for a snappy lead, so he began with that stuff about everyone being equal. Predictably, American etiquette suffered vertigo, and 200 years later a philosopher (Peter De Vries, who also writes novels) says that the trouble with treating people as equals is that they are apt to start doing the same thing to you.

The problem Jefferson left was: How do you express such American values as equality, individual liberty, social mobility and the dignity of labor in etiquette? As Miss Manners says, "The abolition of ancien-régime etiquette by French revolutionaries was all very well, but who wants to watch a bunch of revolutionaries eat dinner?" America's revolution was almost a black-tie affair, having been launched, in large measure, by landed gentry. But it has been laxly translated into an etiquette whereby you are assaulted in restaurants by: "Hi! I'm Donald and I'm your waiter!"

Donald is a practitioner of a common vice, instant intimacy through the universal use of first names: "All men are created . . . familiar." Donald may be of impeccable personal virtue and so perhaps should not be horsewhipped. But if he is not checked, the result will be, as Miss Manners says, "social chaos and the end of civilization, or about what we have now."

Miss Manners's target is the Jean-Jacques Rousseau School of Etiquette, which involves the belief that natural behavior is necessarily beautiful and that rules only impede the spontaneous flowing of such beauty. She notes that the idea that Nature is benign is especially popular in earthquake- and flood-ridden California.

She also notes that we live in an age in which it is easy to insult people inadvertently. Ask any gentleman who has opened a door for a woman who is so bellicosely emancipated that door-opening is an affront.

And it is hard to insult people intentionally. Ours is an age of nonculpability; pop psychology has washed away personal responsibility with a blanket amnesty. If you say to someone, "You are disgusting and your necktie is vulgar," the person is apt to reply, with dreadful tolerance, that you are just feeling hostile because you are depressed and you will feel better tomorrow.

Miss Manners knows that a harmonious society depends on not treating all impulses as equally worthy of expression. It depends on reticence and decorousness, just as a durable marriage depends on the ability to say, with a straight face, "Why, I don't know what you're worrying about. I thought you were very funny last night, and I'm sure everybody else did too."

Miss Manners's theme—that armageddon, not affection, is produced by substituting "honest self-expression" for the artifice of manners—has an application to diplomacy. The American weakness for the Rousseau Etiquette translates into the belief that "frank" and "honest" dialogue between nations is bound to increase understanding, and understanding is synonymous with comity. Hence the American enthusiasm, not to say giddiness, about summits.

Hence, also, the unslayable faith in the Middle East "peace process." (The word "process" is popular with people who have an ideological or vocational interest in something sterile. Hence: "the arms-control process.")

Miss Manners recalls being president of a school board and differing with another member on every question. That member suggested taking the board on a retreat so they all could get to know one another better. Miss Manners said to him:

"You don't understand. The only reason I haven't murdered you is that I really don't know you all that well, so I feel I have to give you the benefit of the doubt. Do you want to remove that doubt?"

Messrs. Reagan and Gorbachev are going to Geneva to get to know one another. Thanks to Miss Manners, they, and you, have been warned.

October 20, 1985

"Fresh Starts" and Other Fictions

It is paradoxical. It also is true. The conservatives' task is to pull this conservative President, and U.S. diplomacy generally, out of the 19th century and into the 20th. This conclusion is compelled by President Reagan's peculiar and opaque rhetoric about a "fresh start" in U.S.–Soviet relations.

This conclusion is paradoxical because conservatives have a retrospective cast of mind. Their cardinal virtue, prudence, involves mining the past for instructive precedents and proven institutions and procedures. Furthermore, the greatest figures of 19th-century diplomacy—Metternich, Wellington, Bismarck, Disraeli—are in the conservatives' pantheon.

Nevertheless, the conservatives' problem today is that President Reagan, although a definer of contemporary conservatism, subscribes to a model of diplomacy that reflects the 18th-century liberal mind. This is so even though the model was adopted, not unreasonably, by those 19th-century conservatives.

The problem is the radical newness of a kind of 20th-century regime, and the depressing oldness of rhetoric about a "fresh start." What did Reagan mean by that? Indeed, what could he mean?

He is painfully fond of the least-conservative sentiment conceivable, a statement taken from an anticonservative, Thomas Paine: "We have it in our power to begin the world over again." Any time, any place, that is nonsense. But that may have been how things looked in 18th-century America, on the thinly populated fringe of an unexplored continent, or in revolutionary France, in the first flush of upheaval.

Many people then believed in "fresh starts" because society was not planted thick with institutions; or old institutions suddenly seemed fragile. They believed that people everywhere were similar, essentially good and easily educable. "The present age," said Paine, "will hereafter merit to be called the Age of Reason, and the present generation will appear to the future as the Adam of a new world." Some people also believed, with Paine, that the "science of government" is "of all things the least mysterious and the most easy to be understood," because "men have but to think and they will neither act wrong nor be misled."

Reagan has repeatedly used Paine's words about beginning the world "over again" concerning domestic policy. One result of his sincere belief in "fresh starts" is the deficit. The theory was that we would cut taxes and then compensate for the lost revenues by cutting spending. We would start "over again," making a "fresh start" in defining federal social roles, as though the New Deal and Great Society never happened. But it is, it seems, impossible to start over again at even, say, 1965 levels of social spending. It is not even possible to make a "fresh start" without Amtrak.

Applied to domestic policy, the idea of a "fresh start" has produced fiscal problems. Applied to foreign policy, it can produce disaster.

Americans believe in "fresh starts," meaning limitless possibility, because they think all people, and all regimes, think "economically," rationally calculating how to enhance their essentially similar interests. That assumption would be true, or true enough, were the world as Paine thought it was. He said there were just two types of government: those "by election and representation" and those "by hereditary succession." He predicted that all governments soon would be representative and then "nations will become acquainted, and prejudices fomented by the intrigues and artifices of courts will cease."

The 19th century was not that serene, but it was relatively tranquil. Irving Kristol, writing in *The National Interest,* a new foreign policy quarterly of conservative bent, says that 19th-century diplomats represented regimes that regarded one another as permanent presences. They defined national interests in limited and familiar ways that allowed conflicts to be resolved by splitting differences. Sometimes the splitting was done after wars—but they were limited wars. Governments maneuvered to alter, but not obliterate, the "equilibrium" among powers. The rules of that game of nations allowed for time-outs and fresh starts.

The rules changed radically with the eruption in this century of totalitarian regimes whose foreign policies reflect domestic arrangements resting on lies and terror. Regimes that derive their claims to legitimacy from ideologies that legitimize limitless violence are not interested in the 19th-century ideal of "equilibrium."

Today's synonym for "equilibrium" is "stability." We seek a "stable" relationship in strategic arms and "stability" in regional conflicts. The Soviet Union derides stability in theory and assails it in practice.

America is a nation of poker players. Poker is a game of fresh starts—play a hand, shuffle the deck, deal again. The Soviet Union plays chess and pursues endgame.

October 31, 1985

Trotsky Assassinated, Yet Again

GENEVA—For a regime that fancies itself the vanguard of revolution, the vessel of history, fountain of progress, destroyer of reaction and consigner of outmoded things to the ash can of history, the Soviet regime is remarkably tradition-bound in one regard. It clings to its animosities.

Some societies define themselves in their admirations, some in their animosities. America defines itself in admiration of Washington, Jefferson, Lincoln. The Soviet regime (Soviet society has no voice) bristles with defining animosities, the most durable of which is for poor old Leon Trotsky.

Not content with having driven him into exile, even into rural Mexico, and having sent thither an assassin to drive an ice axe into his skull, the regime took the trouble to erase him from history books and even from photographs (some of which showed him distressingly close to the sainted Lenin). But now Trotsky is back, for another bashing. A *Los Angeles Times* headline says: "Trotsky Revived as Villain in Soviet Play." The subhead is: "Discredited Old Bolshevik Portrayed as Double Agent."

Decades ago Trotsky was slung down the memory hole. It was as though he had never existed. That was rude treatment for the creator of the Red Army that saved the Russian Revolution. But Trotsky had run into trouble with Stalin. Trouble with Stalin was fatal for millions. For Trotsky it was singularly obliterating. Yet now he has been resurrected so that he may be condemned to death yet again, this time by a play that portrays him as Stalin did—as an anti-Bolshevik.

The Trotsky–Stalin feud was dressed up in ideological nuances. Trotsky, who had a powerful if warped and narrow mind, said Soviet Russia could not survive isolation, so there must be world revolution, pronto. Stalin, who would have lowered the intellectual tone of the St. Valentine's Day Massacre, argued for "socialism in one country." But the real issue was that the Soviet Union, which spans 10 time zones, was too small for the two of them.

What does the reemergence of Trotsky, if only for another drubbing, mean? It probably is additional evidence of the de-Stalinization of the Soviet Union, the rehabilitation of Stalin, the most prolific killer of the most killing century. (An enchanting rumor is that Volgograd, which was Tsaritsyn until 1925 and then was Stalingrad until 1961, may soon be Stalingrad again.)

The anti-Trotsky play certainly is evidence of the amazing continuity of the basic impulses that animate the Soviet regime. Denial of such continuity is an essential component of the mental makeup of Western enthusiasts for the arms control process. They always see the Soviet Union on the verge of "fundamental" change.

In totalitarian societies little things, such as the reappearance of Trotsky, mean a lot. So they are not really little. Churchill knew this.

In April 1933, less than two months after Hitler seized power, Churchill warned Parliament of such German "martial and pugnacious manifestations" as "appeals to every form of the fighting spirit, from the reintroduction of dueling in the colleges to the Minister of Education advising the plentiful use of the cane in the elementary schools." Churchill noted these things because he knew what many of today's arms-control enthusiasts ignore: There is a link between the internal dynamic and external behavior of a totalitarian society. A system sustained by the Gulag Archipelago is not tamable by "dialogue" or by parchment covered by arms control phrases. That is why it was right for Avital Shcharansky, the wife of the most famous Jewish prisoner of conscience in the Soviet Union, to be here in Geneva haunting the proceedings.

Now, return to the *Los Angeles Times* story about the redenouncing of Trotsky in accordance with Stalin's old mythology. The story contains this hilarious sentence: "Western observers of cultural trends say that publication of the play may reflect increased official willingness to be more realistic about Soviet history."

Of course. The reappearance of an utterly traditional, utterly tendentious fable of Stalinist history is evidence of—what else?— new "realism," and therefore is grounds for optimism about U.S.-Soviet relations. So say the usual suspects, those "Western observers of cultural trends."

The moral of this little story about Trotsky is timely and should be spelled out in neon across Geneva, the host to the world's recurring illusions. The moral of the story is this:

There is a mobile army of "Western observers" whose observations condition the atmosphere that produces things like the arms control process. These observers can be counted on to announce that anything—absolutely anything—that happens in the Soviet Union is heartening, the harbinger of "realism" and a reason for hastening to Geneva and expecting "fundamental change."

January 13, 1985

No-Fault Murder

As U.S. Army Maj. Arthur D. Nicholson Jr.'s life bled slowly away into East German soil last month, two Soviet generals, a brigadier and a three-star, arrived at the scene separately. These generals—not simple soldiers, but commanders who rose to high rank by knowing what behavior satisfies Kremlin expectations—were there during the withholding of medical care from Nicholson. During Nicholson's long dying—the slow-motion murder—the three-star general asked Nicholson's sergeant, who was being kept away at gunpoint, why he had shot his major.

The Reagan administration's response to this crime has been

to treat it like a traffic accident covered by no-fault insurance, but the Soviets are having too much fun to do what the administration wants to do—change the subject. The Soviets now say, with exuberant malice, that the administration wrongly reported that they have agreed not to murder more Americans.

Six days after the murder, the irrepressible State Department exclaimed that it was pleased that there were going to be talks about preventing such "episodes." The talks occurred and the State Department was, of course, pleased: "We obtained agreement from the Soviets that they will not permit use of force or weapons against members of our military liaison mission in the future."

But now the Soviets, who clearly are enjoying this, say:

No, we meant what we said at the time. The United States was to blame for Nicholson's death, Soviet soldiers acted properly, we retain the right to act similarly in the future and, by the way, the State Department statement also "does not correspond to the facts" when it says we are considering compensation for Nicholson's death.

Not even the State Department could say it was pleased about that, so it said something even worse. It called the Soviet statement "unacceptable." In State Department usage, "unacceptable" is an adjective that invariably modifies a noun that denotes Soviet behavior that the United States will respond to only by attaching to it the adjective "unacceptable."

The *Washington Post* story about this shambles contained the generic paragraph found in all such stories: "State Department sources said they were puzzled and taken aback by the unexpected Soviet blast, and speculated that it arose from differences between military and civilian authorities in Moscow."

What is never unexpected is State Department speculation that Soviet misbehavior is merely a tactical concession by Soviet civilian leaders to military leaders. But in this instance, the Soviet military seems to have been almost reasonable in the talks in Germany, and seems to have been overruled by the civilians—moderate Mikhail Gorbachev and company—in Moscow.

Of course the State Department professes itself "puzzled" by yet another "unexpected" instance of the Soviets saying that they meant what they said in the first place. Were the State Department ever to concede that the Soviets mean what they say (e.g., Nicholson's death was America's fault), we would not need an army of State Department experts to explain what the Soviets "really" mean and why U.S. policy can be more accommodating than Soviet policy "seems" to be.

There is one great presidential power—the power to persuade. That is why any serious diminution of a President's stature subverts him comprehensively. Does Ronald Reagan understand that his nonresponse to Nicholson's murder has something to do with the fact that, six months after carrying 49 states, he and aides are engaging in eight-hour bargaining sessions with legislators, parceling out presidential authority, negotiating the micro-management of foreign policy, niggling about who might administer "nonlethal" purchases from the micro-sum ($14 million) at issue in the Nicaragua controversy?

There is a civil war on there, the most bitter sort of war, the sort least susceptible to negotiated solution. In England, Russia, Spain, China, Greece and the United States, civil wars were won, not dissolved through negotiations. Yet in a dizzying series of retreats, the freshly inaugurated President has been negotiating about "nonlethal" (shaving cream? cheese spread?) aid to the democratic side in the civil war while a freshman senator leaves the negotiations to appear on the White House lawn to tell a network news audience that this President is moving his, the senator's, way.

Words, the carriers of ideas, have consequences. When you call the contras the moral equivalents of the Founding Fathers, and call Nicaragua a Soviet "beachhead," and then ask for a trivial sum trivialized by restrictions, and describe the principal alternative plan as "worse than nothing" and a "shameful surrender," and then negotiate in the hope of splitting the difference with this shameful-worse-than-nothing, you are asking for trouble of the most ruinous sort: laughter, in the form of snickering.

Congress, too, is in the burlesque. Before the House voted to destroy Nicaragua's anticommunist resistance, it voted 394–2 to proclaim that the "murder" of Nicholson was "inconsistent" with a 1947 U.S.–Soviet agreement. Have a care, Kremlin: Congress considers such, er, inconsistencies to be, well, unacceptable.

April 28, 1985

The Cold War as a Misunderstanding

Several years ago, I heard President Reagan say approximately this:
"I would like to take the Soviet leaders up in a helicopter over Los Angeles." (Here I thought: Good, he is going to push them out. But no.) "I would point to all the small houses with swimming pools and I would say, 'Those are the workers' houses!'"

Surely Ronald Reagan does not think the hard men of the Kremlin are misguided Lane Kirklands, labor leaders mistaken about how best to raise living standards. But Reagan may illustrate the great, and perhaps fatal, paradox of American politics:

He is thumpingly successful because he is thoroughly American—moderate, amiable, reasonable and convinced that others are, too. That is, he has the constricted political imagination natural in a sheltered, liberal nation to which history has been kind. Hence he is, as the most successful American leaders are most likely to be, especially apt to underestimate the terrible dynamic of the Soviet system. One manifestation of this misunderstanding is the sweet thought that the regime's leaders would be susceptible to the taming example of American freedom and affluence.

I mention this now because the *Washington Post* reports that recently the President was flying over New Hampshire and said to the governor how much he would like to take Gorbachev to "any house down there" to meet "the working people." What does the President think such a visit would accomplish? Perhaps: The Gorbachev palm slapped to the Gorbachev forehead, and a thunderstruck exclamation, "Marx goofed! I have seen the future, and lots of kitchen appliances, and it and they work. So dismantle the gulag!"

Is this another "It's-all-a-horrid-misunderstanding" theory of the Cold War? Usually the "misunderstanding" is a mutual misassessment of the other's peaceful intentions. In this case, the supposed misunderstanding concerns how best to satisfy the common man.

This theory founders on the fact that the thin slice of Soviet society that has power also has material comforts. The regime is driven by the need to justify the exemption of the privileged few from the dismal life led by the many. The regime derives its legitimacy, such as it is, from the pretense that it is custodian of History's progressive impulse. That is why the Soviet regime is not—cannot be—in the live-and-let-live business.

If the leader of this regime were not following in the shuffling footsteps of three cadaverous leaders, he would be seen to have the charisma of suet pudding. Yes, he is "resplendent" in his "gleaming white shirt" (words from the introduction to his self-interview in *Time*). But he is also a truculent liar: He is truculent when dismissing as "insubstantial" all complaints about Soviet violations of its Helsinki undertakings. He is a liar explaining how tickled Jews are about the privilege of remaining in the Soviet Union.

The "bold, new" arms control proposal is bold in offering something so old. It is traditional Soviet algebra: $X = X + Y + Z$. The Soviets offer X (50 percent reduction of "strategic" forces), the United States will give X, and will count its intermediate-range forces as strategic, and will kill its attempt to catch up with the Soviet strategic defense initiative. The Soviet side wins not by getting us to accept their equation, but by getting us to talk, exclusively, the arcane, antiseptic algebra of arms control.

It is axiomatic: Control the agenda and you control the meeting. Regarding summit meetings, the axiom is: Control the pre-summit conversation and you control the event. And look what is happening. Throughout the 1970s conservatives sensibly criticized the policy of treating arms control as the centerpiece of U.S.–Soviet relations. Today we see a Gresham's law of political discourse. The dry arcana of arms control has driven out talk of all other things, including: Afghanistan, Poland, Angola, Nicaragua, yellow rain, terrorism, arms control violations, Helsinki violations, etc.

In another way, too, America is paying the price of its arms control obsession. So eager were the Nixon and Carter administrations for agreements, they prenegotiated (in Washington) proposals compatible with the Soviet buildup. Then they settled for agreements that were, essentially, mere snapshots of the rising force levels. But Soviet levels rose faster. Today they are so large and varied that a mutual cut of 50 percent could be tailored that would leave the Soviets with an enhanced strategic advantage.

The lament of correct thinkers within the administration is: The Soviets would never attend a "Sakharov Summit" or an "Afghanistan Summit," but here we go to a "Star Wars Summit." And the (definite article, "the") question already is: What will Reagan give up to make it a "success"? This, too, is a reason why when I hear people praising summits I want to take them up in a helicopter and . . .

October 10, 1985

Lenin's Children

In a century of steel and war, Switzerland has made industries of chocolate and the pursuit of peace. Above-the-fray Switzerland thinks of itself as unoffending. But it has much to answer for. It was Lenin's haven until Germany sent him in a sealed train to Russia to ignite the revolution that would take Russia out of the war. Germany used Lenin (in Churchill's phrase) "like a typhoid bacillus." It found the disease in squeaky-clean Switzerland.

While in London Mrs. Gorbachev vetoed a visit to Marx's grave in Hightower Cemetery, preferring to visit the crown jewels in the Tower. But she will go as a pilgrim to Lenin's Geneva haunts. She will be celebrating the man who vowed to purge Russia of "harmful insects" and ordered "shooting on the spot one out of every ten found idling." He pioneered modern genocide by ignoring individual guilt, enforcing collective guilt against "class enemies," a.k.a. "harmful insects."

The Gorbachev family's division of labor is between theory and practice. She is a university lecturer in "Marxist–Leninist philosophy," which is an oxymoron. He is concerned with practice. While she is genuflecting at Geneva's 10 Rue du Foyer, where Lenin lived with Krupskaya, Mr. Gorbachev will, we are asked to believe, be seeking world tranquility, to enable him to build communism in one country.

The theory, advanced by many Western intellectuals, is that the Soviet elite does not mean what it says when it says, as it constantly does, that it embraces Lenin. He did not believe there could be communism in just one country. He said: "As long as capitalism and socialism exist, we cannot live in peace. In the end, one or the other will triumph." However, there never is a shortage of Westerners eager to assure the West that Soviet leaders do not mean the menacing things they say, that what they really mean is. . . .

Today's theory is that Gorbachev wants a respite from the arms race, and especially from one involving technologically exotic defense systems, so he can "solve his economic problems." But it is absurd to say that military spending is causing the regime's economic problems. Military spending is the regime's raison d'être. The regime has never given priority to the comforts of the masses. It has never made a serious effort to provide a Cuisinart in every apartment, or even a separate apartment for every family.

Yet the West's wishful thinkers insist: Gorbachev wants to build communism. Which means . . . what?

In *Travesties*, Tom Stoppard's antic play that turns on the fact that Lenin, James Joyce and the Dada artist Tristan Tzara were in Zurich during 1917–18, a character is told that a "social revolution" has erupted in Russia. He asks: "A social revolution? Unaccompanied women smoking at the opera, that sort of thing?" He is told: "Not precisely, sir."

Even communists have had trouble saying precisely, or even vaguely, what communism is supposed to be. Lenin said, with nice concision: "Communism is Soviet power plus electrification of the whole country." If Lenin was right, communism has come to Russia. Is Leninism right? Ask Mrs. Gorbachev, who teaches the stuff.

Lenin liked electrification but loved terror, and said: First things first. Trotsky said: "We shall not enter into the kingdom of socialism in white gloves on a polished floor." Lenin said you do not make an omelet without breaking eggs. He established an egg-breaker: Cheka, the secret police. By 1919, Cheka was killing 1,000 persons a month for political offenses. In the preceding 80 years, the number of executions in the Russian empire had averaged 17 a year.

When the First Lady of the Soviet state makes pilgrimages to places made sacred by association with Lenin, she reaffirms the iconographic role of the man who unified the theory and practice of mass murder. She is not a peasant; she is what passes for a philosopher in a society where the humanities are illegal. She knows what Lenin said and did, and what she is doing. Let us do her and her husband the honor of taking them seriously when they say they take Lenin seriously, even reverently.

In 1907 Lenin wrote to his mother from Geneva, saying he was weary but was getting a "wonderful rest" in restful Switzerland: "No people and nothing to do is the best thing for me." Indeed. But by March 1908, he had his pep back. He told a Geneva meeting that during the Paris Commune, the proletariat was guilty of "excessive magnanimity. . . . It should have exterminated its enemies."

His placid Swiss listeners probably murmured, "Well, of course, by 'exterminated' he really just means. . . . "

We know what he meant. And we know what Soviet leaders mean when they say they are Lenin's children.

November 17, 1985

America's Therapeutic Impulses

When tranquil, as he usually is, George Shultz resembles an Easter Island statue. When aroused he is more oyster-like, unquestionably alive but undemonstrative. However, he reportedly was quite exercised in Moscow when Mikhail Gorbachev treated him to a rude and ignorant lecture about the pathologies of American society. That episode probably strengthened the President's tendency—a tendency as quintessentially American as Ronald Reagan himself—to regard his Soviet adversary as either a patient or a pupil, someone to be treated or taught.

When statesmen's heads touch Swiss pillows, the heads often acquire the pillow's attribute: soft. But the President's peculiar hopes were acquired in Washington and reflect an alarming continuity grounded in national character.

At the first meeting between a President and a Soviet leader—Tehran, 1943—Roosevelt decided he could apply to Stalin the American therapeutic and didactic impulses. The theory was that his charm, and the wartime alliance with democracies, would wean Stalin from his paranoia and misunderstandings.

Because a prophet's most important qualification is an adequate memory, it was easy to predict that Reagan, whose politically formative years were Roosevelt years, would see the summit as a chance to dispense "reassurance" and information to Gorbachev. Reagan, who in five years has failed to modify Tip O'Neill's views of America, came here convinced, according to a senior aide, that "personal dialogue" would alter Gorbachev's views of America. But those views are products of the ideological prism through which reality is refracted for Leninists. Presidential dialogue will change those views when the sky rains artichokes.

A wit once asked: If a little knowledge is a dangerous thing, who has enough to be out of danger? Fair enough. But how much is needed to refute Reagan's notion that the summit could "eliminate some of the paranoia, if we could reduce the hostility, the suspicion that keeps our two countries at odds"?

Paranoia is a condition susceptible to therapy and cure, and hence is a comforting diagnosis of Soviet behavior. Also comforting is the Reagan thought (reported by an aide) that Soviet "mistrust" is rigid in a historically "understandable fear of aggression from outside." However, the Soviet army has been fighting in Afghanistan two years longer than it fought Hitler. It is fighting not because of a paranoid fear of invasion, but because the Soviet system is organized for aggression.

Rumors flitting like barn swallows in and out of Washington windows recently included this one, which I believe: One briefing paper suggested that Reagan begin the summit by telling Gorbachev that our countries have had similar experiences. Our country had to settle the West, his had to conquer Siberia; and indeed, California and Siberia are sort of similar accomplishments. The foreign policy bureaucracy has lots of ideas, and consistently proves the old point that a man is not necessarily intelligent because he has many ideas, any more than a man is a good general just because he has many soldiers.

Like most Presidents, and especially like the one who set out to seduce Stalin 42 years ago, Reagan does not have an inclination toward theory. Rather, he has an experiencing nature. He responds to individuals and individual situations, and assumes other leaders are like him. Furthermore, politicians in democracies prosper through persuasion, and those who prosper most spectacularly acquire Rooseveltian vanity or Reaganite serenity regarding the amount of ice that will be melted by the sunshine of their personalities.

The desire to deal with an adversary in "human terms," with the adversary somehow shorn of his culturally acquired attributes (such as Leninism), is understandable. But it leads to confusing psychology with politics. To believe an adversary is adversarial only because of "unreasonableness" rooted in historical experiences is to recast diplomacy as therapeutic anthropology.

There may be a guileful side to this talk about soothing and instructing the Soviets. A summit that is described in advance as therapeutic in intention can be called a success simply because it occurs. By this semantic fiat, frothy ideas such as cultural exchanges—Beach Boys for ballerinas—are not beside the point, they are the central point: more therapy-through-"communication."

Whether the President's rhetorical run-up to the summit has been naïvely optimistic about modifying Soviet behavior, or cunningly calculated to lower expectations for concrete results here, or a bit of both, clearly the Soviet side is investing a lot in "communication." It has deployed an unprecedented number of briefers and interviewees.

The Soviet Union is (in Orwell's words) a place where yesterday's weather can be changed by decree, and Soviet respect for the power of words is proportional to Soviet disrespect for the integrity of them. The Soviet regime relies on overkill in all things, and for this summit has borrowed the capitalist form of it: When the product is shoddy, double the advertising budget.

November 21, 1985

The 20th Century Has Not Happened

A dictator's lot is not a happy one because his work is never done. He must have many opinions, on the assumption that his subjects have none. Mikhail Gorbachev is finishing the fine-detail work—the finials and newels, as it were—on utopia. So he is polishing the Communist Party's new programme. Of course the draft may be changed in February in the heated debate and rough-and-tumble that makes a Soviet party congress so entertaining. But the draft gives a reader, in addition to a migraine, a sense of the dismal continuity of the Kremlin's creed.

The programme is just the fourth in the party's history. The first was in 1903. Forty-two years passed between the second (1919) and third (1961). The West's strongest tendency is wishful thinking, and Western voices have hailed the fourth programme as proof of Gorbachev's anti-ideological moderation. That judgment rests on a slender reed: The programme avoids the sort of rash prophecies of Khrushchev's 1961 document that said the Soviet economy would surpass America's in 1970, when workers would be working six-hour weeks. No wonder the new programme promises punishment of "windbaggery," not to mention "toadyism" and "fawning."

The Soviet Union is in the 68th year of building communism, a phase that used to be called (until the title became embarrassing) The Glorious Transitional Period. The transition is supposed to be from mere socialism to nifty communism. The new programme, written in a literary style that can best be described as proletarian prolixity, has a prefatory exclamation: "Workers of the world, unite!" That seems odd, considering Soviet fury when Polish workers did just that. The text begins at full gallop: "Because of the Great October Soviet Revolution the land of the Soviets has traversed a long and glorious road . . . " It ends lyrically: "Under the leadership of the party, under the banner of Marxism-Leninism" socialism has been built and—hold your horses—communism is coming soon.

What will communism be? "A new qualitative state in society." You say that is vague? Hush. The programme says the party does not deal in "detail" about "full" communism. Why should it, when the master was virtually silent? Marx left only a sketchy map. He said communism would be like a symphony orchestra—a peculiar thought, given that he considered the division of labor "alienating." But a symphony needs an authoritarian conductor, and the Soviet Communist Party has volunteered for that role. The party's mind is revealed in the new programme's old rhetoric:

" . . . The principle of democratic centralism . . . enhanced efficiency of centralized guidance . . . " " . . . the inviolable alliance of the working class, the collective-farm peasantry and intelligentsia . . . " "Atheistic education, pressing for the strict enforcement of the constitutional guarantees of the freedom of conscience . . . " " . . . the party's ideological education work to conduct military-patriotic upbringing . . . " " . . . practice confirming the Marxist-Leninist concept of . . . " " . . . the dialectics of developments are such that . . . " "to rectify errors of a subjectivist, voluntaristic nature . . . " " . . . displaying Bolshevist fidelity to principle and a self-critical approach . . . "

Stalinism is the practice of Leninist theory. With this programme Gorbachev announces himself yet another Stalinist. "The entire course of world development confirms the Marxist-Leninist analysis of the character and main contents of the present age." "[Nothing can] take the historically doomed capitalist system out of its state of all-permeating crisis . . . " To read this programme is to fall through a crack in time. The 20th century has not happened. The Soviet elite subscribes to a "science" utterly insulated from evidence. The Soviet regime, armed to its iron teeth and ignorant as a stump, is lurching around on the world stage preening itself on its "science" while subscribing to the superstitions of a 19th-century German who sat scribbling in the British Museum, imagining the future.

Decades ago the Soviet elite accommodated its creed to the need to seek world hegemony without a final spasm of total war. But the distilled essence, the *sine qua non* of Leninism remains. It is the belief in irreconcilable conflict between the capitalist and communist camps, and the inevitable triumph of the latter. In Leonard Schapiro's metaphor, the Soviet regime's ideology is less a blueprint than a compass. But it points to worldwide communism. Hence all compromises and accommodations are temporary.

Marxism-Leninism sits like a squat rock unmarked by the waves of evidence that it is nonsense. Nowhere in the new programme's profuse expenditure of words is there a paragraph an educated person can read without blushing for its author. To read this coagulated cant is to see how appallingly provincial the Soviet elite is, how utterly disconnected from international culture, how completely intolerant of all other social systems on earth. As Robert Conquest says, the point is not that a Gorbachev reads from *Das Kapital* as from a breviary, any more than Richard Coeur de Lion was constantly studying theology. The point is that any Soviet leader has been thoroughly marinated in the ideology that legitimizes him.

What is important is not precisely how the ideology is believed but whether the regime acts in accordance with it. The Soviet elite is devoted to its own continuity and will not jeopardize itself by domestic reforms or a nonaggressive foreign policy that would call into question the Leninism that legitimizes its monopoly of power. The new programme (let's assume Gorbachev can wheedle support for it from the turbulent party congress) is a reaffirmation that clangs like the door of a mental prison, a restatement of the "scientific" basis of the "privilegentsia." The programme is proof that the most powerful arsenal of the 20th century is in the service of the most durable fallacy of the 19th.

December 9, 1985

PART 4

Midday

Well, Actually, You Can't Have It All

This is the saddest story ever told. A whole generation believed the Michelob beer commerical and, consequently, got its heart broken. Many baby boomers expected a pot of gold but have settled for a DoveBar.

Baby boomers were born between 1946 and 1964. There are 78 million of them, and many are depressed because they were told something that is not true. But it just *had* to be true: It was on television. And in the believable part of television, the commercials. It did not just say, "Where you're going it's Michelob." (The yous are those young go-getters wearing suspenders but careful to call them braces and hard-charging young women heading for "the top" in business suits and running shoes.) Michelob's commercial also said, "Who says you can't have it all?" Sadly, the answer is: reality, that's who.

I am talking about just some of this generation. Come over here and I will whisper the word: YUPPIES. Now, Yuppie-bashing has gone too far, but Yuppie discontents are fascinating. Some baby boomers are suffering a form of the mental disease known as "'60s envy." The phrase is Joseph Epstein's. He used it of today's students who are seeking a cause (antiapartheid will do) as a way of getting the sort of cachet students enjoyed way back when. Many baby boomers are suffering "'60s nostalgia," remembering applause and tingles of importance. How else explain the otherwise inexplicable—the fact that Bob Dylan can still draw a crowd?

But the baby boomers' discontent goes deeper—or perhaps still shallower—than that. A *Wall Street Journal* report on "strapped Yuppies" quotes one such: "We can't afford houses and cars, but we'll spend $2 on a DoveBar so we can try to tell ourselves we aren't doing as badly as our pocketbooks say we are." A DoveBar is ice cream. It is a flimsy prop for self-esteem. Many baby boomers are big spenders, but often their foreign travel, pricey audio systems and gourmet mustards are compensatory consumption. It may be a substitute for such things as adequate housing, but whose fault is that? Their nagging sense of scarcity—they are even nagged while in their high-tech kitchens making broccoli purée—has something to do with the 1970s inflation, especially in housing. But it has more to do with the drop in consumer savings and soaring consumer debt.

Many baby boomers are not "into"—as they gratingly say—deferral of gratification.

Professionals among baby boomers are suffering "generational crowding." It is ironic. The fact that there are so many of them gave their generation a sense of specialness and even moral superiority. Pat Caddell, political consultant and card-carrying baby boomer, says of his generation, "All through its existence it has experienced itself as the center of events." Many came to political consciousness during Vietnam and basked in the flattery of media swooning about "the most moral generation in history." But today they have glutted the market for professionals, depressing salaries. "As a generation," says a member of it, "we were brought up to think we could have tremendous jobs; wonderful houses, exotic travel, great marriages, beautiful children." All these came to be considered entitlements, things that come automatically.

Not quite. The *New York Times* reports that some of the city's dingy single-room-occupancy hotels, which often are homes for the poor, increasingly have tenants who "come carting their books, stereos and tape decks, their button-down shirts and Adidas running shoes." A Brown University graduate with a master's degree says, typically, that he simply cannot afford Manhattan apartments. One young woman says her bathroom is so filthy she showers with shoes on. She works for a "better government" group called "Fund for New Priorities." You, gentle reader, may think she needs a few. You may be thinking the unthinkable: "Why don't these folks just face the fact that they cannot afford Manhattan? Lots of people live elsewhere—New Jersey, Indianapolis—and still find life worth living." You, gentle reader, must be kidding. Understand: Leaving Manhattan is the Death of the Dream, a.k.a. growing up. It is impossible for balanced minds, like yours and mine, to understand how much of the Yuppies' sense of moral superiority is bound up with despising the suburbs. Of course it was in those suburbs that the many baby boomers' parents gave the babies that sense of material entitlements that today causes them to complain that the universe is unfair. One no-longer-really-young professional says, "It used to be you moved to the suburbs for the children. But on some level we still think of ourselves as children." Peter Pan, call your office.

Still, baby boomers have not repealed biology, and many have decided that they would rather push strollers (they *must* be Apricas) than Nautilus equipment. So, last July there was an epochal event, the publication of Tony Schwartz's article "Second Thoughts on Having It All." It appeared in *New York* magazine, the *Our Weekly Reader* of Manhattan's you-know-whos. Schwartz told the harrowing story of a couple with two incomes and one child. Weary of the helter-skelter life required to scrape by in a cramped Manhattan apartment on $90,000 a year, husband and wife picked themselves off the floor in the living room where they slept and made the shattering sacrifice. They—are you ready for this?—decamped to *New Jersey.* I mean, the ultimate ick. (It was appropriate that in 1984 Gary Hart, a consumer perishable much favored by Yuppies, injured himself by telling a New Jersey joke.)

A frazzled Phyllis told Schwartz, "I fantasize about retiring, buying a farm, moving to fresh air and space." Her husband intervened: "We don't like farms." Phyllis: "I guess I'm addicted to New York. You walk down Broadway and it's a scene . . . " She got that right. Now, get her some psychological methadone for her addiction. And Phyllis: where you're going—perhaps even New Jersey—there's Michelob.

February 3, 1986

H. Rap Brown, Radical at Last

ATLANTA—From the sun-dappled park comes the background rhythm of urban life, the slap-slap-slap of basketballs on blacktop. Across the street, in a small convenience store, and in profound peace of mind, sits the proprietor, selling eggs and reading the Koran.

He is Jamil Abdullah Al-Amin. He is 41. He used to be H. Rap Brown. But that was long ago and, in a sense, in another country. It has been a winding and ascending path from his boyhood in Baton Rouge to Atlanta's west end. The hyperkinetic human torch of urban unrest, circa 1967, is, in 1985, enveloped in a strange serenity in a city known for its hum of energy. The man who was the hammer of Amerika, or at least of Cambridge, Maryland, has become a merchant, but with this distinction: He is, at last, really radical.

That 1967 radicalism was a short candle. It was rhetorical rad-

icalism, elicited from young people by older flatterers and ampli-
fied by the media 18 years ago. Today, and for the long haul, Jamil
is in inner emigration, out of his country and into Islam.

He burst upon the nation in the 1960s, when the social air was
composed of (in the words of a Rex Stout character) "oxygen, ni-
trogen and odium." He succeeded Stokely Carmichael as head of
the Student Nonviolent Coordinating Committee, which soon
changed the second word to "National." He said the sorts of things
that then passed for trenchancy: "If you give me a gun I just might
shoot Lady Bird." The only lasting legacy of his brief blast of prominence is an aphorism: "Violence is as American as cherry pie."

The 1960s were God's gift to conservatism, a decade domi-
nated, not numerically but culturally, by overreachers. Those years
were noisy with the voices of fundamentally frivolous people feign-
ing seriousness, people convinced that sentiment is the measure of
virtue, that rhetoric is the measure of sentiment and that morality
is a state of mind: I feel, therefore I am. This radicalism helped to
produce two significant effects: the "backlash" candidacy of George
Wallace and the presidency of Richard Nixon.

"Many people," Jamil says, "reckon time from the '60s. Time
stopped for them then. I don't miss the '60s." Now that Brown is
someone else, and quite quiet, he is, at last, impressive. He is 6 feet,
5 inches tall and gestures slowly as he speaks, pointing with fingers
that should belong to a pianist.

There are many Muslims in his neighborhood. The store next
door sells incense and Arab-style garments. Many of his customers,
including a three-year-old seeking six eggs, wear the kind of cro-
cheted cap he wears beneath a gray cloth. His shelves are sparsely
stocked, but his customers are buying only Cheerios and milk, a
few dollars' worth at a time, and anyway, commerce is not the
point. The Koran is the point—every point.

After inciting riots in Maryland and elsewhere and getting into
a shootout with police in New York, he served five years in jail. But
by 1971 he had converted and had concluded that the change that
matters is the one the changer can control: the soul. Democracy is
less a creed than a climate of opinion. His interest is in a creed. He
prays five times a day and fasts during the month of Ramadan.

The transmission of religion to the rising generation is never
easy, and inoculating Muslim children in the middle of a metropolis
against the temptations of American youth culture will be espe-

cially difficult. To that end he and neighbors (he has been chosen Imam of his community) are founding a religious school.

Kierkegaard said that Christianity is not glad tidings to the unserious because it seeks first to make them serious. Religion has done that for Jamil, who shows a flicker of levity only when asked if he goes to see the undistinguished Atlanta Hawks play basketball: "No, I go to see the other teams play."

Driving a Toyota van on one of the freeways that has made this city a symbol of Dixie transformed, Jamil reaches behind him for a plastic carrying case, removes from it a cassette, slips it into the dashboard tape deck and the van is filled with the almost musical sound of passages from the Koran recited first in Arabic and then in English. This might seem like another example of America's amazing capacity for absorption. But to give Jamil his hard-won due, he has not been absorbed.

Members of Atlanta's large black middle class are driving all around him on the freeway. But H. Rap Brown, a boy from America's South, has become a man of a distant East.

September 22, 1985

Conservatism and Character

When God decided to get things rolling, he separated light from darknoo. Whon intellectuals get a similar itch, they start magazines. Twenty years ago some intellectuals launched a quarterly that shaped conservatism. In the 20th-anniversary issue of *The Public Interest*, Daniel Bell, Irving Kristol, James Q. Wilson, Nathan Glazer, Mark Lilla and others trace the changes since the epochal year 1965.

That was the year of Vietnam escalation, the eruption of Great Society legislation, the apogee of confidence in management of the economy. The reign of professionals in initiating policies was supposed to complete the "end of ideology," replacing political passions with economic analysis. However, one result was a surfeit of "reforms" generated not by political demands, but by the vocational interests of the theory class. Another result was the rise of conservatism. It rose from three layers of rubble, the fragments of collapsed consensus about the U.S. world role, the efficacy of federal compassion and the utility of macroeconomic theories. But in 1985, conservatism is waist-deep in rubble of its own making. That is the debacle of public finance: the deficits. This is not merely, or even primarily, an economic matter. It reflects moral failing, a defect in the formation of the public's character and conservatism.

There is nothing new about the possibility of groups (including whole generations) maximizing their interests by voting themselves benefits to be paid for by borrowing—by transferring wealth from future generations to present ones. That temptation has always been inherent in democracy. Why, then, have large peacetime deficits become normal only recently? Why has the temptation been surrendered to, utterly, under the most self-consciously conservative administration? One reason, says Wilson, is the declining moral force of the idea of self-restraint. An unwillingness to defer consumption to facilitate future benefits has become a willingness, even eagerness of voters to "beggar their children."

From 1789 until the 1960s, debates about new government activities were usually about whether it was proper for government to do this or that, such as run social security or Medicare systems. Since 1960, debate has been solely about how to pay for such things—or how to fob off the costs on future citizens. The rise of conservatism has not reversed, it has not slowed, it has accelerated the supplanting of the ethic of self-control by the ethic of self-absorption.

Bell notes that 100 years ago there was severe laissez faire regarding economic life and strict regulation of morals. By the 1970s that pattern was reversed. In the 1980s there has been a modest and mostly rhetorical readjustment. Contemporary conservatism has a contradiction between its cultural moralism and its ascription of moral dignity, not mere utility, to market mechanisms. Markets are splendid allocators of resources. But conservatism's increasingly "populist" tone flows from a form of idolatry known as market worship. Markets measure mass appetites at a given moment. Populist conservatism is uninterested in deferral of gratifications.

Antipopulist conservatism says many public problems can only be understood as arising from citizens with inadequate habits of virtue, with virtue understood as self-control, respect for others' rights and concern for distant consequences. Antipopulist conservatives must say that the Reagan administration—judged, as it increasingly must be, by its deficits—has delusions of adequacy. Wilson says Keynes was not just an important economist, he was a moral revolutionary, because he said deficit spending should be judged by its practical effects in paticular contexts, not any inherent moral qualities. Reagan has completed that revolution by demoralizing borrowing, and hence public finance. He has shown that even a conservative, even in a period of high economic growth, feels only negligible restraints on saddling future generations with the costs of today's consumption.

One cost of bad character, and of years of condescension about "Victorian morality," is apparent in the growth of a black underclass of single-parent families in ghettos where upwards of two-thirds of all children are born out of wedlock. In the mid-1960s Pat Moynihan's report on the disintegration of black families was denounced as a racial insult. Today single-parent black families are twice as common as they were in 1965. Some scholars, who are braver than many black "leaders," argue (as Glenn Loury has in *The Public Interest*) that the principal challenge is improvement of "the values, attitudes and behaviors of individual blacks."

Many black leaders derive their status and other psychic income from mediating the allocation of federal relief. But "society" does not cause and Congress cannot cure the calamity of sexual irresponsibility among lower-class blacks. As Kristol says, "What is wanted is a black John Wesley to do for the 'underclass' in the ghettos what Wesley did for the gin-ridden, loose-living working class in 18th-century Britain. Reformation has to be on the agenda, not just relief."

Conservatism is a doctrine of disapointment and consolation. Its hopes for social regeneration through improved character—for statecraft as soulcraft—are almost always unrealized. The consolation is that conservatism is thereby confirmed: A nation is a mysterious organism, not a Tinkertoy to be pulled apart and reassembled willfully.

However, conservatism does not conclude that the "underclass" is paradigmatic of problems beyond the reach of ameliorative policy. Since 1965 we have learned that the ability of schools to instill competence and serve social mobility cannot be gauged by the objective, "quantifiable" variables such as pupil–teacher ratios or per-pupil expenditures. More important is a distictive school ethos. Social competence is grounded in good character, and good schools have a "structured" approach to encouraging that. Such a rediscovery of common sense may seem like reinventing the wheel.

But conservatism aims not to be electrifying, just useful. Antipopulist conservatism is sufficiently unsentimental about mankind to say this: Even the most obvious must be repeatedly rediscovered.

November 11, 1985

Billy Graham, an Embarrassing Export

When Vladimir Bukovsky, a Russian dissident, was being sent into exile, a KGB agent noted that the handcuffs on Bukovsky's wrists were made in America. But handcuffs are not America's most embarrassing export.

Billy Graham's sojourn as a guest of the masters of the Gulag coincided with the anniversary of the Nazi surrender, so he said (according to the *New York Times*): "I want to remind you that the United States and the Soviet Union were allies at the time against a common enemy. Now we have another common enemy—the possibility of a nuclear war."

Graham did not remind anyone that the Soviet Union and the Nazis began the war as allies, and their falling out was not a Soviet initiative. But Graham's delicacy is less interesting than his "common enemy" formulation.

Is it his notion that the threat of nuclear war is a mysterious "third force"? Or the result of some odd misunderstanding, some mutual mistake? Whatever, his language suggests a moral symmetry between his country and the Soviet Union. Evidently they are equally innocent victims—but of what? Physics?

The Kremlin is sponsoring the—take a deep breath—World Conference of Religious Workers for Saving the Sacred Gift of Life from Nuclear Catastrophe. The Kremlin's audacious cynicism is wondrous. A "gift"—from whom? Marx? And when did the Kremlin begin speaking of "the sacred"?

This travesty, this exploitation of clergymen's vanities and naïveté, is designed to strengthen the "peace movement"—but only in the West. In East Germany, a new law makes it a crime to wear a button saying "Swords into Plowshares." In Moscow, "Ground Zero Week" lasted the minutes it took the police to pounce on the handful of people who unfurled a banner.

The *Washington Post* reports that when Graham spoke in two

churches, both "were heavily guarded with police sealing off all roads leading to them. Hundreds of KGB security agents . . . were in the congregation." Graham told one congregation that God "gives you the power to be a better worker, a more loyal citizen because in Romans 13 we are told to obey the authorities." How is that for a message from America?

According to the *Post*, Graham is "a star attraction" at the conference and "is being driven around Moscow in a Chaika limousine while others are shepherded around in a fleet of buses." He has conferred with Georgy Arbatov, the Kremlin's foremost stroker of Americans. Graham calls Arbatov "wonderful."

Graham is America's most famous Christian. Solzhenitsyn is Russia's. The contrast is instructive.

When advocates of a "nuclear freeze" recently showed their movie (the one that says war would be terrible) to some Senate wives, Jane Denton, the wife of the Alabama senator, noted that there would be no showing for the wives of Politburo members. Not to worry, Jane. The *Baltimore Sun* recently reported on two local "peace" activists:

"When the Reverend Hope Harle-Mould and his wife, the Reverend Linda Harle-Mould, returned nearly a year ago from a trip to the Soviet Union, they were struck by the strength of a 'grass roots' movement there against the nuclear arms race."

The Washington Cathedral (Episcopal) has Gothic architecture but trendy politics. One service last Sunday was a prayerful rally for ERA. And here is Bishop John Walker preaching at the Cathedral last November. "We must know that all we did between 1900 and the independence of Cuba was designed to make Cuba turn away from us. Perhaps if we had the strength and security of who we are, we might say we were wrong. We might reach out a hand of brotherhood and forgiveness to the Cuban people even as we seek their forgiveness of us."

Forgive Walker's mussy language. (Surely he does not mean "designed.") Forgive the hyperbole ("all" that we did?) in the service of facile guilt-mongering. But don't forgive the intellectual vacuum at the core of his thought—the idea that dealings would be with "the people" of Cuba, rather than with the regime that is their jailer.

People pray for different things. There was a London church where, between performances, an actress prayed to be delivered from the attentions of Edward VII. I pray that some of today's clergy, on the left and the right, will stop acting as though pious intentions are substitutes for intelligence, and excuses for irresponsibility. A crusty 19th-century Briton, A. W. Kinglake, wanted skeptical words inscribed on all churches: "Important If True." Skepticism becomes more necessary as churches become more political.

May 13, 1982

The Moral Limits to Peace

From Britain have come some words in season.

Not much about Europe's temper can be inferred from evidence about Oxford's temper, but the Oxford Union (a debating society) vote against pacifism is, if not portentous, at least instructive. The emphatic (416 to 187) rejection of the motion that "this House would not fight for Queen and country" came exactly 50 years after a similar "king and country" resolution passed.

The 1933 vote was a referendum on the Great War, in which the futility of the tactics—fighting machine guns with young men's chests—matched the absurdity of the motionless slaughter: When Germany surrendered in 1918 there were no foreign soldiers on German soil. Oxford undergraduates had been junior officers, a very brief vocation. Understandably, postwar Oxford was receptive to pacifism.

Today, as the most recent Union debate showed, pacifism has no such dignifying explanation. It is inseparable from anti-Americanism, and the postulation of a moral symmetry between American and Soviet motives. Furthermore, it rests on the belief that physical survival is a value superior to any other.

The day after the recent Union debate, the governing body of the Church of England rejected (338 to 110) a resolution endorsing unilateral nuclear disarmament for Britain. The Archbishop of Canterbury cited the "moral inconsistency" of Britain's opting out of the risk involved in a deterrent system from which Britain would continue to benefit. Well, yes. But that argument is terribly limp compared with the editorial words of the *Salisbury Review*, a new British journal of conservative thought:

"Just as the Church has traditionally taught that war has moral limits, so it should now be teaching that there are moral limits to peace. Otherwise, presumably, any humiliation may be tolerated. A desire for world peace should not be allowed to dissolve all other moral commitments in our society . . . The Greek word for peace in the New Testament is more correctly translated as an equilibrium based on justice. Any Western society, therefore, that were to accept the 'better red than dead' argument would necessarily be abnegating its legitimacy."

If only the churches could speak as clearly. America's Catholic bishops, in a draft pastoral letter, have offered this pretzel-like twist of logic: Possession of nuclear weapons is tolerable only if rendered pointless by disavowing any declared intent to use them. The Pope, who thinks otherwise, should urge the bishops to think more spaciously, avoiding the constricted focus on two sets of weapons. Such a focus gives rise to an unthought assumption of moral symmetry between the two regimes.

There seems to be reluctance to inject the great themes of political argument—such as justice and legitimacy—into the argument about defense policy, because that would require unblinking scrutiny of the Soviet regime we are deterring. And that would make such groups as Germany's Green Party seem less winsome.

The Greens' pacifism is in part distinctively contemporary and in part recalls cultural fermentations of 50 years ago. Jane Kramer of the *New Yorker* explains the "expiatory" and "redemptive"—the religious terms are apt—fervor of Germany's pacifists: "They have no history to attach to with any pride, and it is intoxicating for them now to think of themselves as victims of a madness other than their own."

In *The Long Weekend*, their social history of Britain between the wars, Robert Graves and Alan Hodge titled a chapter "Pacifism, Nudism, Hiking." All three were forms of this century's characteristic groping for secular faiths. Today, socialism having lost its luster, the groping finds expression in disarmament. Again.

In November 1932, the once and future prime minister Stanley Baldwin told the House of Commons that the new superweapon—the airplane—had invalidated traditional moral reasoning about war ("The bomber will always get through.") and urged on young Britons the pacifism that found expression in the famous Union resolution three months later. He said that the world's youth would be to blame if they allowed old men to make war:

"When the next war comes . . . do not let them [youth] lay

blame on the old men. Let them remember that they, they principally or they alone, are responsible for all the terrors that have fallen upon the earth."

Wrong. The truth was more banal, and more germane to today's controversies. When war came the blame came, rightly, to those in authority who had not maintained the balance of power. They had rationalized their dereliction of duty by sentimentalizing youth, and by judging intellectual movements by the most benign motives behind them rather than their probable consequences.

February 20, 1983

Whittaker Chambers's Winding Staircase

In awarding the Medal of Freedom to Whittaker Chambers, President Reagan has shown loyalty and pugnacity that become him well. His loyalty in this instance is to one of the profoundest passions of American conservatism. His pugnacity is toward the cultural forces that disdained Chambers and rallied round his adversary, Alger Hiss.

Subsequent scholarship has vindicated the jury that convicted Hiss of perjury. (Hiss should have been tried for committing espionage when he was a diplomat and Chambers was a Soviet agent, but the statute of limitations had run out.) Nevertheless, Hiss—how he must taste ashes today—has led a life of enigmatic fanaticism: He has stuck to his shredded story.

And the life of the Hiss cause is a study in intellectual corruption. Never has so much ingenuity been invested in a cause as futile and often cynical as the campaign to assert Hiss's innocence. The investment has been made by people who rushed to judgment on his behalf, embracing him as an emblem of the innocence of any "idealism" on the left and regarding his "persecution" as vindication of their anti-anticommunism.

Chambers's life illustrated the axiom that all rising is by a winding staircase. His tortured journey was from left to right, from the most sectarian politics, communism, to a nondenominational Christianity; from the shadows of conspiracy to the spotlight of public controversy. He was a man of urbanity whose final years were spent with his wife in rural solitude.

It is a terrible thing to be treated as an abstraction. Both Hiss and Chambers were so treated when they came to be considered— by a narcissistic minority of a generation—as symbols of an entire generation's divisions.

Hiss was Harvard Law, aide to Justice Holmes, member of a Boston law firm with the name of Choate in its title, successful diplomat. At the time of his fall, when he swore he had never known Chambers, he was head of the Carnegie Endowment for World Peace. Tall, thin, well-tailored and elegant in manner, he was, to those who imprudently sprang to his defense, a symbol of cosmopolitanism under siege from Yahoos.

Portly and rumpled, with a disreputable past and too much intensity for a drawing room, Chambers's inelegance was complete. But he had two advantages: the truth, and Hiss's ruinous arrogance in a bluff that Chambers called. Chambers's victory was, however, costly. It has been said that an intellectual hatred is the most vicious. Torrents of it were directed against Chambers because discrediting him was considered useful to a political agenda—establishing America's paranoia and Russia's innocence.

As a young man, Chambers worshipped a God that failed, the myth of collective salvation through political action. His lasting legacy, indeed his triumph, was that most solitary of things, an act of sustained introspection. His extraordinary memoir *Witness* is, although the product of a quite different temperament, comparable in depth and power to the memoir of another American alienated from his times, *The Education of Henry Adams*.

Chambers's magnificent prose is at times too charged with passion for contemporary sensibilities. Adams is less unsettling. Adams's pain was a product of an incurable sense of emotional disconnection from his times. Chambers's prose of pain, almost rising to poetry, derived from the 20th-century disease of misplaced engagement.

Witness was published in 1952, when another American was beginning a political journey less dramatic but, in its outcome, momentous. Ronald Reagan read *Witness* and, 30 years later, could quote the passage describing an epiphany: Chambers contemplating the delicate convolutions of his daughter's ear and saying: No, this thing is not the result of a chance aggregation of atoms; it requires design, and that means God.

Chambers writes about another person's awakening from dogmatic slumbers. A German diplomat in Moscow had been well-disposed toward the communists, until one night. In what Chambers called five annihilating words, the diplomat's daughter said: "One night he heard screams." The great political literature of our time, from Orwell and Koestler and Chambers through Solzenitsyn and beyond, makes us hear the screams.

Chambers's book is an unrivaled account of the costs of the totalitarian temptation. When he died, Arthur Koestler said, "The witness is gone, the testimony will stand."

Today the West is unevenly divided between those of us who are and most persons who are not preoccupied, even obsessed, by the fact that the stakes of politics were forever transformed by the eruption in our century of the radical evil of totalitarianism, and by the necessity to make antitotalitarianism the touchstone of all politics. To us, Chambers, an ungraceful man touched in the end by the blinding grace of painful truthfulness, led a life worth honoring.

February 26, 1984

The Take-for-Granted Quotient

Remember the reaction to the writing on the wall at Belshazzar's feast? Old-fashioned Old Testament fear took the fun out of the feast. In Ohio and in Maryland there have been episodes like that, involving savings and loan institutions.

There has been a spurt of panic, some of it reasonably related to the condition of some mismanaged and inadequately insured institutions. But there is another and remarkably simple explanation for the kind of panic that can produce runs on thrift institutions. The simple explanation is complexity. But, of course, nothing is simple in a world in which a "run" on a bank involves lines of people sitting in line in lawn chairs.

Do you know how your bank works? Sure, you know you rent your money to it. The bank does stuff with it, and makes money, and gives some of it to you in interest and services, such as checks decorated with scenes of Cape Cod. However, that is a pretty sketchy knowledge of something as crucial—if you think about it—

as the whereabouts and activities of your money. But, then, you rarely have to think about it, which is something to think about.

Thrift institutions are examples of this facet of modern life: We are surrounded by things we cannot do without and do not understand. Banks are not incomprehensible. Bankers understand them—at least some do, somewhat, some of the time. But the rest of us have to take it on faith that the banking system works swimmingly.

We must take much on trust. If we took time to understand everything, we would never get the lawnmower sharpened or the screen door repaired. When that trust begins to crack, it can crumble quickly, producing panic.

A century ago transportation—say, a horse and buggy—was comprehensible, in the sense that all the moving parts were visible and uncomplicated. Well, OK, the horse was complicated, but you know what I mean. Today we go to an airport, step into a thin tube of aluminum, are hurled 35,000 feet up and 3,000 miles along, and few of us have even the foggiest notion of how a jet engine works, why a plane flies or how the air traffic control system keeps the planes from bumping one another.

In the 19th century, when doctors were loved, they could not do much for patients, other than make them somewhat comfortable while waiting for nature to heal or kill them. Today doctors are vastly more potent. They also are proportionately less intelligible— and, not coincidentally, less revered.

In the 19th century, when, of an evening, a family wanted entertainment, it could try conversation (ask grandmother; she can tell you what that was) or books. There was nothing mysteriously technical. Today families stare at devices that bring sights and sounds into their living rooms. Although we are sure there is a reasonable explanation (for the physics of television, not, Lord knows, for the sights and sounds emitted by it), not one American in 10,000 can do justice to a child who asks, "How does that work?"

A flourishing economy, indeed a functioning society, depends on the mass of men and women not thinking about a large and growing number of things they depend on in daily life. One measurement of the modernity of the modern world is the TFGQ—the Take-for-Granted Quotient. A crucial task—crucial, although often mundane—of modern government is to enlarge the TFGQ.

It does this by inspecting restaurants, so customers need not calculate the risk before deciding to trust an unfamiliar kitchen. It certifies the safety of elevators so we never need to make a prudential calculation before inserting ourselves in a box hauled aloft by (I am guessing) pulleys and cables and things.

Of course government, as is its wont, often gets carried away and tries to reduce to zero life's risks. Nevertheless, to keep modern society flowing, government must act in many small ways to take large amounts of hesitancy out of life. It does this, for example, when it provides insurance for deposits in thrift institutions. Such insurance removes the drag of anxiety from a crucial social activity—saving.

"We may fling ourselves into a hammock," wrote Chesterton, "in a fit of divine carelessness. But we are glad that the net-maker did not make the hammock in a fit of divine carelessness." Modern society requires government that looks over the shoulder of, and occasionally nags, the makers of the many networks of institutions on which we depend.

May 23, 1985

The Madison Legacy

Jefferson called James Madison "the greatest man in the world," which was a smidgen strong, considering that Edmund Burke was then in the world. All that many Americans know of Madison is that his wife was a pistol. But he, more than any other founder, clearly understood and unsparingly articulated the nation's premises, which contribute to today's problems.

If we really believed the pen is mightier, or even more dignified, than the sword, the nation's Capital would be named not for the soldier who wielded the revolutionary sword, but for the thinker who was ablest with a pen. It would be Madison, D.C. Until recently there was not even a government building named for him. And what has now been named for him? A *library*, for Pete's sake. What a put-down in a city with the world's highest ratio of action to reflection. In a city where the regard for books can be gauged by the number of adequate bookstores (one), there now is the Madison Building of the Library of Congress.

Madison wrote many of the Federalist Papers, the newspaper

columns that argued the case for ratifying the Constitution. The founders are famous for their institutional ingenuity in devising the system of checks and balances, but Madison, more than the others, also had sociological sophistication. His two concerns were "the extent and proper structure of the union"—not only government ("structure"), but geography ("extent"). Previously, philosophers had said that if democracy were feasible at all, it could only be in a small society. A small society can be homogeneous and free from "factions," which were assumed to be ruinous. Fiddlesticks, said Madison, whose revolution in democratic theory involved saying of factions: The more the merrier.

America's Madisonian philosophy involves a negative catechism. It asks not how the best in government and citizens can be attained, but how the worst can be avoided. What is the worst political possibility? Tyranny. To what form of tyranny is democracy prey? Tyranny of the majority. How can that be prevented? By clever institutional arrangements (separation of powers, federalism), but also by having so many minority interests that there is no stable majority, only shifting coalitions of factions.

The most fertile source of factions is, he said, "the various and unequal distribution of property." So "the first object of government" is "protection of different and unequal faculties of acquiring property." From "different degrees and kinds of property" there ensues a salutary "division of the society into different interests and parties." An "extensive republic" would provide scope for the multiplication of economic diversities, and hence of factions. Jefferson did not act from Madisonian motives, but he served Madisonian purposes when he seized the opportunity for the Louisiana Purchase.

Ronald Reagan, who comes from California, where Manifest Destiny (a Madisonian impulse, in part) ran out of room, said nice things about Madison at the library dedication, but he must regret the multiplication of factions. The increasing Balkanization of the public, combined with the increasing sophistication of pressure tactics, accounts for much of the growth of government and for the paralysis of government when it attempts anything (such as Reagan's program of budget cutting) that requires broad consensus.

Reagan recently wielded, for the first time, the presidency's only formidable formal power, the veto. It is a Madisonian instrument; it is a negative, blocking power. A faction—one-third plus one in either house of Congress—can sustain it. With the fiscal year two months old and most appropriations bills still to come, the veto power may become, as never before, the central fact of government. But as Reagan thanks Madison for this sort of power, he must have dark thoughts about Madison's complacent, even proud, comment that in our affairs, public and private, we have a "policy" of supplying by opposite and rival interests the defect of better motives.

The suggestion that America's system can work without anyone having good motives—without public-spiritedness—gives people an easy conscience about pursuing private interests through public policies. And as Reagan tries to incline the public toward deferring gratifications—asking less of government, saving more and consuming less—he must regret the restlessness and impatience built into America's public life by Madisonian cheerfulness about the uninhibited self-interestedness of the multiplying factions. Alas, conservatives, being stout Madisonians, are ill-equipped to criticize this. They see no social costs in the culture of capitalist acquisitiveness. And they define politics negatively as the business of drawing a protective circle—as wide a circle as possible—around the individual's sphere of private action. So conservatives say public concerns are, by definition, secondary to private concerns.

Madison Avenue in Manhattan is, symbolically, the Main Street of the Madisonian republic. Advertising tries to be a pyromaniac, igniting conflagrations of desires for instant gratification. It is fuel for our Madisonian society. It spurs economic growth, and hence specialization, diversity and the multiplicity of factions that Madison favored.

Aside from the aptly named Madison Avenue, there is a striking disproportion between Madison's importance in shaping the nation and the nation's estimate of his importance, as reflected in memorials to him. But he has received justice of the poetic sort in Washington, from (appropriately) the private sector. Washington's poshest hotel is the Madison. There, in the lap of luxury, leaders of the private sector (read: factions) restore their tissues after hard days' laboring to bend public power to their private advantage. They can labor serenely, to the extent that serenity comes from knowing that they are acting as Madison anticipated. But the churning of the government by factions is more violent than anything he envisioned.

The lobby of the Madison is a gently undulating dark sea of fine worsted, an array of "different and unequal faculties of acquiring property." Madison might be pleased; then again, he might be chagrined at what his philosophy has promoted.

December 7, 1981

The Splendid Legacy of FDR

Anyone who contemplates this century without shivering probably does not understand what is going on. But Franklin Roosevelt was, an aide said, like the fairy-tale prince who did not know how to shiver. Something was missing in FDR. The average politician has so many pieces missing that you could assemble another politician from the missing pieces. But what FDR lacked made him great. He lacked the capacity even to imagine that things might end up badly. He had a Christian's faith that the universe is well constituted and an American's faith that history is a rising road.

FDR's life supports the idea that all history is biography. To tell his story is to tell the story of the nation while he lived. And his life shows why biography is the form of nonfiction that can come closest to high literature. The great themes of literature are love and disappointment. Those are keys to the mystery of character formation. FDR was formed late, not in childhood but in manhood, by an unfulfilling marriage, an unfulfilled love and a devastating disease. Many persons in high public stations become as hardened to the sufferings of the common man as a physician can be to the pains of patients. Perhaps the fierce pain of polio gave FDR his gift of empathy.

The crucible of his middle years made him into one of the three presidents who were larger than the government. They were Washington, who established the central government's authority; Lincoln, who preserved it; FDR, who settled old arguments about its supremacy and the sufficiency of its powers. Jefferson is a saint of the Democratic Party, but FDR, the maker of the modern Party, secured the triumph of the principles of Jefferson's rival, Hamilton, who favored a nation with a strong central government driven by executive energy.

A revolutionary (a Lenin, a Hitler) sees large forces and tries to make them larger. A conserving politician like FDR tries to bring them within the scope of constitutional government. By a "New

Deal" he meant, he said, a new "concept" of government's duty. Hitherto government had acknowledged only a duty to produce "conditions" in which people could pursue happiness. Henceforth "government has the final responsibility for the well-being of its citizenship." Government would be an agency for delivering a measure of happiness, defined as material well-being.

Social security exemplifies how FDR did what only great leaders do; he changed the citizen's sense of what citizenship entails. Social security expresses the bonding of the generations and the nation's commitment to an ethic of common provision. Today, as constantly since FDR, the argument concerns only the scope of that commitment, not the commitment itself.

FDR's measures to regulate the national economy brought to a head constitutional controversies that had raged intermittently since the eighteenth century. His constitutional philosophy, if it can be called that, began and very nearly ended with this axiom: The constitutional powers allocated to the Federal government in the text of the Constitution are inherently sufficient for the national purposes enumerated in the preamble of the Constitution. Today that thought seems banal, but a mark of greatness is the ability to settle great controversies so decisively that a few generations later the controversies are barely intelligible.

The Depression and a high-technology war melded the government and the economy. Between 1787 (the drafting of the Constitution) and 1942, America escaped full-scale involvement in a protracted foreign war. But when FDR died in 1945 America was more supreme than Great Britain after Waterloo, than the France of Louis XIV—than any power since the Roman Empire. And it had a central government commensurate with that role.

Twentieth-century history is in large measure a story of the economic consequences of war and the political consequences of mass communication. Radio made FDR America's first "intimate" public figure, one always popping up in everyone's living room. FDR had none of Churchill's eloquence, but he had a flair as a phrasemaker: "rendezvous with destiny," "day that will live in infamy," "economic royalists." No wonder he once said that if he had not gone into politics he might have gone into advertising.

FDR, like another master of radio, Churchill, met the challenge of the dictators by mobilizing the language without debasing it, and mobilizing free people without rupturing the institutions of freedom. Hitler came to power 32 days before FDR and died eighteen days after FDR. Had it not been for FDR, Hitler might have won his war—but Stalin might have won less from the war. FDR had a progressive's provincialism, the belief that the basic threat to freedom comes from the right, and that history's natural tendency is toward democratization. Poland's crisis casts a cold light on the centenary of the man who did not understand what he was dealing with at Yalta.

But on balance FDR still casts a splendid shadow forward across the years. Radiating in infectious zest, he did the most important thing a President can do: He gave the nation a hopeful, and hence creative, stance toward the future. To a crippling extent American conservatism still is, strictly speaking, reactionary: It defined itself in reaction to the New Deal. It remains ambivalent about something the nation is emphatic about—FDR's irrevocable redefinition of the relationship of the citizen to the central government. Hence, the Republican Party remains in danger of being regarded as political castor oil, to be taken occasionally for medicinal purposes, and put aside as soon as possible so that Democrats can restore the sense of fun.

The grandeur of a great capital—the imposing buildings and monuments—gives government the appearance of solidity. But American government is like a soft leather glove, taking the shape of the Presidential hand. And once stretched by a large hand, it never fully contracts. Lyndon Johnson was the last President who knew FDR personally; Ronald Reagan may be the last with vivid memories of FDR at the peak of his powers. But all presidents now occupy an office FDR transformed, an office that is the head and heart of a government whose duties he defined.

February 1, 1982

The Unsentimental Man from Missouri

Stylistically, Harry Truman was utterly unsuited to follow FDR, whose eloquence and elegance set the standards for the modern presidency. But Truman, born 100 years ago May 8, has come to represent a distinctive style—or perhaps an antistyle. Today many Democrats who claim to revere him reduce him to a mere mannerism—an unfocused feistiness—as they reject his substance.

Sentimentality about this unsentimental man developed partly in reaction against the perceived deviousness and insecurities of Presidents Johnson and Nixon, and in reaction against the slickness of politics in the media age. Enthusiasm about Truman expresses a preference for plain speaking and a nostalgia for plain living.

Truman was the last President to live approximately as his countrymen do: He strolled across Pennsylvania Avenue to do his banking. He probably was the last President without a college education—although he was better read than most Presidents who came before him and all who have come after. He was the last candidate before television. In 1948 he appeared on television once, for three minutes, urging people to vote.

Soon after death put the haberdasher in the patrician's place, British voters did something similar. They replaced Churchill with Clement Atlee. Plain speaking was in fashion. (Here is the full text of a letter from Atlee to a left-wing colleague: "My dear Zilly: Thank you for sending me your memorandum which seems to me to be based on an astonishing lack of understanding of the facts. Yours ever, Clem.")

As in the late 1930s, when a President resisted the pull of an isolationist public, in the late 1940s elite opinion was at odds with popular opinion, and was correct. Public opinion forced an almost immediate reduction of the armed forces from 11 million to one million. But even more swiftly—between Yalta and Potsdam—the question preoccupying clear-sighted people changed from, "Will the Soviet Union abide by agreements?" to "Is Soviet appetite for expansion insatiable?"

Aided by extraordinary talent—Marshall, Acheson, Kennan, among others—Truman made 1947 the most creative year of U.S. diplomacy. On March 12, 1947—arguably the most important date in postwar history—Truman went before Congress to seek $400 million in military and economic aid for Greece and Turkey: "I believe it must be the policy of the United States to support free poeple who are resisting attempted subjugation by armed minorities or by outside pressures." That "Truman Doctrine" expresses the essence of the Kennedy–Johnson policy in Indochina and the Reagan policy in Central America. It is a formulation uncongenial to Messrs. Hart and Mondale.

On June 5, 1947, George Marshall spoke at Harvard, proposing what became the Marshall Plan. Also in 1947, George Kennan formulated the doctrine of "containment," and the first steps were taken toward a North Atlantic alliance to implement containment. That year was the apogee of Truman's career. Soon Alger Hiss was on trial, Mao was in Shanghai, there was an atomic explosion in the Soviet Union, and Americans were being asked to "die for a tie" in Korea. A week after Truman ignited a firestorm by firing—tardily—Douglas MacArthur, the death of Senator Vandenberg, the Michigan Republican, deprived the nation of the leading exponent of bipartisanship in foreign policy. Washington knew bitterness that had not been seen since the debate on the League of Nations and was not seen again until the Vietnam War.

Three of the eight postwar Presidents have been "accidental," and the first of them was an especially fortunate accident. In the nick of time—the 83d day of FDR's fourth term—the nation acquired a President with the realism and stamina to contain communism. Had FDR died a year earlier—and from what is now known of his condition, it is a wonder he did not—Henry Wallace would have become President as the Red Army poured into Europe.

FDR met with Truman only eight times in his last eight months and only twice after the Inauguration. But there was an astonishing difference between Truman's quick comprehension of the communist challenge and the unrealism of FDR and many of his aides. (Patrick Hurley, FDR's personal representative in China in 1944, saw Mao as an agrarian populist: "The only difference between Chinese communists and Oklahoma Republicans is that Oklahoma Republicans aren't armed.") No less astonishing is the difference between Truman's views regarding U.S. capacities and responsibilities and the views of those in his transformed party who today praise him.

Acheson thought it revealing that Americans refer to problems as "headaches." That is a revealing synonym because Americans believe they can banish headaches with pills, quickly and easily. The President who built the structure of postwar security knew that nothing but disaster comes quickly and easily.

May 3, 1984

The Least Artistic Great Artist

Exposure to the large spirit of Charles Dickens should be on a grand scale. It is, for those who spend eight and a half hours in early Victorian England at the Royal Shakespeare Company's splendid production of a play wrought from Dickens' sprawling novel *Nicholas Nickleby*.

This is an age choking on products that are frivolous in conception and shoddy in execution. But 42 actors playing 137 roles on a set that is a masterpiece of stagecraft have produced, with passion, a gem. They have recreated the world that Dickens, godlike, created and filled with a riotous variety of the sort of people we shall forever describe as Dickensian.

Much has been made of the $100 ticket price. That is 20 cents a minute (three cents a minute less than a lot of Broadway fluff). When the 14-week run ends January 3, just 55,000 people will have seen it (about half the attendance at a University of Michigan football orgy). And the producers will have about broken even. By bringing *Nicholas Nickleby* to Broadway, they have done the sort of thing Nicholas and other Dickensian heroes do—a glittering deed in a naughty world.

Dickens has been called the least artistic great artist, and he certainly is the most popular fine novelist in the language. Most of his writings appeared first in serial form in popular publications, cheek-by-jowl with journalism, as entertainment, sort of like today's comic pages. Sort of.

It is sometimes said, dismissively, that Dickens wrote "cartoons," meaning that he simplified and exaggerated virtues and vices. But today's cartoons are . . . cartoons. We have declined from Dickens to Doonesbury. Doonesbury and *M*A*S*H* and other entertainments dabble at wisecracks and call the dabbling "social commentary." But Dickens changed society, improving and saving lives. Debtor prisons, courts, the "Yorkshire schools"—those prisons for unwanted boys that are one subject of *Nicholas Nickleby*—are among the many wrongs that he helped to right.

He may have been too sentimental for today's "realists," but he left a legacy of improvement, which they are not apt to do. He was an especially effective advocate for children. In his day, children were still tried in courts with adults, and "education" still aimed at "breaking the child's spirit." Few novelists write much about childhood, perhaps because its complexities are as many, and more mysterious, than those of adulthood. Most adults have pruned their dreams and narrowed their focus and become relatively (relative to children) simple. Dickens, in *Nicholas Nickleby* and elsewhere, took the terrors of childhood with the seriousness of a man who could really remember being a boy.

A critic, arguing that evil is more interesting than good, says: "Take someone to the zoo and he wants to see the snakes." At the end of the play *Nicholas Nickleby*, audiences rise and applaud, rapturously, the kindly creatures in the human zoo. Is Nicholas, standing there at the end with an orphan in his arms reminding us that there is always another child to be comforted, "too good to be true"? He is, if we think so. Thinking of him as impossibly noble can make us unnecessarily discouraged about our capacities.

G. K. Chesterton, a Dickensian figure in his physical abundance and his more than ample confidence in the common people, wrote that whereas a poet in the Middle Ages inscribed "Abandon Hope All Ye Who Enter Here" over the gates of Hell, modern writers inscribe that over the gates of this world. But over the gates of Dickens's tumultuous world is inscribed the injunction to abandon hopelessness and all the pleasures of pessimism.

Dickens defies the persistent attempts to force him into the ranks of the political left. As George Orwell said, in every attack on society Dickens is "pointing to a change of spirit rather than a change of structure." Dickens is the keeper of the flame that lights the world's dark corners, the faith in social regeneration through personal regeneration.

Orwell, with his disdain for "smelly little orthodoxies," distilled Dickens's doctrine into 10 words: "If men would behave decently, the world would be decent." That lacks metaphysical flourish, but it has the not inconsiderable virtue of being true.

Unlike John Osborne and the other "angry young men" of the postwar theater, Dickens was, in Orwell's phrase, "generously angry." In Osborne's *Look Back in Anger*, the protagonist, Jimmy Porter, says: "There aren't any good brave causes left." Dickens's message, which has found an avid audience on Broadway, is that the worthiest cause is kindness, and it is timeless.

October 22, 1981

Miss Manners: Between Anarchism and Stalinism

In Washington, you can dine with senators or ambassadors, if you are not careful. But you can also at least dream, as I do, of dining with Judith Martin. Anyone who does dine with her should be careful, but may feel free to eat cold asparagus with his fingers.

Regardless of anything you may have heard to the contrary, Ms. Martin is the National Bureau of Standards. Under the name Miss Manners she writes columns, a selection of which has been published as *Miss Manners' Guide to Excruciatingly Correct Behavior*. It is rich with maxims (such as: Always use the fork farthest to the left), mastery of which will make you as swanky as Anthony Eden or Audrey Hepburn. However, if your children are, like some I know, inclined to eat even mushroom soup with their fingers, the news about asparagus should be kept from them.

Her book should not be praised for anything so vulgar as utility. Read it for the snap, crackle and pop of Miss Manners's prose, which, like any distinctive style, expresses a personality. Hers is compounded of verve, wit, irony, archness, and an adamancy never achieved by Pope Pius IX, whose Syllabus of Errors was, compared to Miss Manners's syllabus, half-hearted.

She insists, wrongly, that she deals with manners rather than morals. Perhaps she wants to distinguish what she does from what Ann Landers and Phil Donahue do—dispense advice about staying chaste in junior high, or winning civil rights for avocados. Actually, her book is the most formidable political book produced by an American since *The Federalist Papers*, and it took three Americans to produce that. Her subjects are conventions, restraints, social elbow room—in fine, correct conduct. Between anarchism and Stalinism lies civilization and Miss Mannersism.

As Plato understood, there is really only one serious political topic. It is more serious than war, or even the New Federalism. It is the upbringing of children; all else turns on that. Concerning children, Miss Manners advocates strong central government. For public occasions, "a parent must develop a way of smiling at a child, perhaps with narrowed eyes, or a way of holding the child's wrist, which conveys to the child that he is storing up serious trouble." A parent also must know how to stare at a child in a way that will cause him to utter whatever phrase is called for, such as, "I'm sorry I broke your lamp."

Miss Manners knows she is leaning into the wind—a sirocco, really—of an age in which disagreeable table manners are considered evidence of democratic sympathies, and coarse speech a sign of perfect honesty. In an age absurdly sold on sincerity, Miss Manners is rehabilitating hypocrisy. Without it, people will say what they think and do as they feel—a prescription for civil war.

I am sure a becoming blush mantles the cheeks of Miss Manners when she deals with the subject uppermost in the public's mind. Letters, which it is her humanitarian calling to answer, indicate that the topic is sex:

"Q. Dear Miss Manners: What should a lady keep on hand for the comfort and convenience of a gentleman guest who may be spending the night unexpectedly? An extra toothbrush? Shaving equipment? Perhaps a comfortable bathrobe? Slippers? Should I keep them in different sizes (small, medium, and large)? I'm only interested in being a gracious hostess.

"A. Yes, Miss Manners can see that. But what are you running there? Or rather, as Miss Manners deals in manners, not morals, what do you want to appear to be running? Suppose you were overcome with passion while visiting and were then offered a wide choice of sizes and styles in nightgowns?"

Modern life does make one think, and it is nice to delegate some thinking to Miss Manners. This is an age of "liberation" from the gentling delicacies that make liberty endurable. It is an age with new vices (such as "self-gossip"—nattering on in public about one's private life) and a jarringness, exemplified by the telephone, which Miss Manners likens to a postman who compels you to read the mail the instant he delivers it.

Miss Manners's task is the daunting one of defending conventions in a nation in which the word "conventions" calls to mind only quadrennial occasions for bad political manners. Her guide for the perplexed contains 700 pages, every one pleasurable, but she—ever considerate—distills them to two guidelines, one of which will serve in any situation:

1. Don't.
2. Be sure not to forget to.

July 29, 1982

The Black Sun

Americans have a habit—often considered a virtue, which it often is—of looking on the bright side of life. But occasionally it is salutary to look at the dark side. In a few years, Americans will be able to do this in Washington, adjacent to the Mall, in two old buildings the government has allocated for a Holocaust museum.

This decision to locate a grim, disturbing display amidst the Mall's patriotic and celebratory symbols may cause controversy. But the decision is wise.

The Mall, one of the world's magnificent urban spaces, is a shrine to which Americans come as pilgrims. Its openness is an analogue of our society; its vistas open receptive minds to the symmetry and temperateness of our political arrangements.

But the Mall has no single motif. It is surrounded by museums and monuments, art galleries and government offices. The latest addition to the Mall, the Vietnam Veterans Memorial, is designed to remind visitors of some sobering experiences and stern values. It occupies prime public land because the government decided that it is in the public interest for the public to contemplate these experiences and values.

Government performs many such pedagogic functions, from providing public schools to organizing patriotic observances designed to arouse civic sentiments. The government created the Holocaust Memorial Council, which will raise private funds for the museum. The council already has done much to add the annual Days of Remembrance (in mid-April), the anniversary of the liberation of the camps, to our liturgy of civic religion.

But some persons will ask: What has the Holocaust to do with this nation? That is a fair question. The answer is that no other nation has broader, graver responsibilities in the world, so no other nation more needs citizens trained to look life in the face.

Leave aside the scandal of this nation and its allies—the fact that they did not act on the knowledge that the Holocaust was occurring. They refused, for example, to bomb the rail lines and crematoria at Auschwitz when 10,000 were dying there daily. Never mind. The museum should be an institution of understanding, not accusation.

The theme of the Holocaust memorial in Jerusalem is: Remember. But remembrance without understanding is betrayal. It occurs when people try to democratize the Holocaust, making it something general, symbolic, abstract and other than a Jewish catastrophe.

Yes, before the killing of Jews became systematic, the killing of the mentally retarded was systematic in Germany. Yes, the Nazis killed gypsies and others. Yes, Mao and Stalin were much more prolific killers than Hitler. Yes, between 1975 and 1980 the Khmer Rouge did to Cambodia what the Black Death did to Europe in the 14th century.

But we falsify and trivialize the Holocaust when we bend it to our convenience, making it a symbol—of general beastliness, or whatever. It was not a symbol; it was a fact. The flight into such generalities is a flinching from this fact: The Holocaust was directed murderously against particular victims: Jews. Their tragedy cannot be appropriated by others as a useful metaphor.

However, a general good for the nation can flow from an unblinking understanding of it.

The two shattering events of modern politics were the First World War and the Holocaust. The war shattered governments and empires, and patterns of civility, clearing the ground for primitivism. The Holocaust—the eruption of primitivism in the heart of our civilization—overturned the idea that there are limits on evil.

What is life like when lived beyond a sense of limits? You could tell from the smoke the sort of persons consumed in the crematoria. Newcomers to Auschwitz, who still had some fat on their bones, made black smoke. Persons who had been there for a while made white smoke. There: That is an emblematic fact of 20th-century politics.

The Holocaust was the bureaucratization, almost the domestication, of the most volatile passion, hatred. The memory of the Holocaust is the black sun into which we cannot bear to stare. But we should stare, because this mentally soft Republic is threatened by the inability of its citizens to comprehend how radically the untamed world—from the brutalized elite in the Kremlin to the pandemic savagery of El Salvador—differs from their mild experiences and assumptions.

The Holocaust museum, located at the epicenter of our collective life, can be a mind-opening reminder of the furies beyond our shores. The museum is needed because nothing in nature is more remarkable, or dangerous, than the recuperative power of innocence in a liberal society.

March 10, 1983

Keeping Faith with Mengele's Victims

Irena Kirkland is, among many other excellent things, a life-affirming person and one of Washington's dozen or so CTs—Correct Thinkers. One reason she is both of these things is that she passed through a furnace few of us can even imagine and emerged an alloy of steel and laughter. Somewhere in Latin America, perhaps in Paraguay, there lurks an evil man who today has fresh reasons to fear the kind of steel and spirit he helped to produce in people like her.

Irena Neumann (as she was before she married Lane Kirkland) and her sister Alena, arrived at Auschwitz in October 1944. They tumbled from cattle cars with 2,500 other Jews. She and Alena had been sent from Czechoslovakia to a concentration camp for a year before they arrived at the Auschwitz depot under the eye of Josef Mengele.

All but 200 of the 2,500 were immediately dispatched to the gas chambers. Those spared were thought suitable for labor. Any sign of infirmity—even wearing glasses—could get a person selected for death. Irene and Alena (who today lives in Geneva) may have been spared because, although they were nearsighted, their youthful vanity caused them not to wear glasses.

A "kapo"—a prisoner functioning as a guard—asked their birthdates. Having long since lost all documents, they could have said anything, but they told the truth. When the kapo heard the identical birthdates (with their heads shaved they did not stand out as identical twins), she told them to give different birthdates. Otherwise they would be sent to Mengele, the sadistic pseudo-doctor and science quack who conducted lunatic experiments, especially on twins, who mesmerized his small, warped mind.

Recently in Jerusalem, at a meeting of twins and others who survived Auschwitz, a mother recalled that Mengele was enraged when she gave birth. He had not noticed she was pregnant. Novel forms of abortion interested him, so a chance had been missed. He forced her to cover her breasts with tape so that he could see how long the child would take to starve to death. He was enraged when she killed her own child with a morphine injection, an act of mercy.

The Lord said, Vengeance is mine. But in Los Angeles, the Simon Wiesenthal Center is giving the Lord a hand concerning Mengele. The Center has discovered documents that suggest U.S. authorities may have had Mengele in custody in 1947, and that in 1962 he may have sought admission to Canada. The Center wants to know what the government knew and when it knew it, and what is now being done about tracking him to Paraguay, or wherever. Good questions, all.

A federal magistrate has just held that Andrija Artukovic, 85 and infirm, is mentally competent to cooperate with his lawyers in fighting extradition to Yugoslavia. He faces prosecution for complicity in the murder of 770,000 persons while he was minister of the interior in the Nazi puppet government of Croatia. After four decades, Nazi crimes still resonate in this season of sickening commemorations, such as the commemoration of what is ludicrously called the "liberation" of Warsaw by Soviet oppressors.

Why, it is frequently asked, continue trying to prosecute old men like Mengele and Artukovic? Certainly the reason is not deterrence, not the prevention of Holocausts. No punishment can affect the calculations of the genocidal, who are not careful calculators of cost-benefit ratios.

Yes, prosecutions foster awareness of the Holocaust and, yes, pursuit of the genocidal is an obligatory response to life in an age of genocides, in Uganda, Cambodia and, today, Afghanistan. But regarding the real bedrock reason for pursuing the criminals, Irena Kirkland has a more correct idea.

She knows there can be no proportionality, no punishment that "fits" the crimes. But she also knows the truth of this Italian proverb: Revenge is a dish best eaten cold. Her reason for feeling deeply pleased about the continuing pursuit of Mengele is this: Somewhere, Mengele is feeling fear.

That reason may seem to lack metaphysical flourish, and it is not "forward-looking" in the sense of having a utilitarian, reforming purpose. But who cares? Irena Kirkland's reason satisfies an intuition so deeply felt that it surely expresses some constituent of our moral nature. It is the conviction that someone who has caused so much pain should never know ease. Let us just say that Irena

Kirkland's thinking is correct thinking, and get on with the prosecutions, by which we keep faith with the persecuted.

February 14, 1985

Mesmerized by the Moment

In 1940, a British officer on Dunkirk beach flashed to London
a three-word message: "But if not." It was instantly recognized as
a quotation from the Book of Daniel, where Nebuchadnezzar commands Shadrach, Meshach and Abed-nego to worship the golden
image or be thrust into the fiery furnace. They say, defiantly:
" . . . our God who we serve is able to deliver us from the
burning fiery furnace, and he will deliver us out of thine hand, O
king. But if not, be it known unto thee, O king, that we will not
serve thy gods, nor worship the golden image. . . . "

The message from Dunkirk is stirring evidence of a community
deriving cohesion from a common culture. Today many universities
do little to equip rising generations with a sense of being legatees
of a shared and valuable civilization.

The process of neglect accelerated in the 1960s, with the celebration of "relevance" (meaning teaching relevant to the recon-
struction of society along radical lines) and the belief that a university's purpose is not to put something into students but to let
something out—"liberation" and "self-expression" and all that. But
before the 1960s, intellectuals had become (in Harold Rosenberg's
deathless phrase) "a herd of independent minds."

The herd embraced the notion that intellectuals should constitute an "adversary culture." This notion is part of the self-dram-
atization of persons who strive for importance by imagining that
they are oppressed. If you believe (as the novelist Stanley Elkins
does) that Disneyland is "just like Auschwitz or Dachau," you can
believe that scholarship is a "struggle" against a disease called Western Civilization.

To slay the dragons of "genderism" and "ethnocentrism," universities have encouraged factional disciplines, a kind of "special
interest scholarship." First came "black studies." But when, in disregard of logic and scholarly standards, any social group is made

the basis of an academic discipline, the sluice gates of silliness are open.

Today there hovers over "women's studies" an aroma of politics ("consciousness raising") and paranoia. "Women's studies," says a professional enthusiast, "empowers us to learn what we have never been taught and what, I suspect, they don't want us to know." (The capacious pronoun "they" encompasses the other sex.)

A leader in "feminist scholarship" says: "St. Augustine, Aristotle, Erasmus—these men return us to the monstrous misogyny of the past, which we must of course understand, but which, as the mainstay of the curriculum, is hardly sufficient." She speaks the minds of many others when she says "teaching is a political act." She does not just mean that ideas have consequences. She means that the proper ideas to teach are those congruent with a particular political agenda of social "transformation."

And now, with an inevitability both depressing and comic, there are "men's studies." These, according to a professor, concern (he is serious) "the disadvantages of being the privileged group."

William Bennett, chairman of the National Endowment for the Humanities, says that a humanities curriculum often is "an obscure interpretation of literature here, a skinny piece of somebody's history there, a dose of a few philosophical dilemmas and conundrums, a dash of anthropological relativism and then an exhortation to think of all this in connection with current events."

The 1983 Mt. Holyoke catalog says all students must take one quarter that "offers exposure to a Third World perspective." The menu includes "Field Studies in the Black Community," "Spirituals and the Blues," "Images of the Feminine in Indian Literature and Culture," "Black Women in America."

In 1982–83, every Amherst freshman had to pick one course from a list that included "Food" (the course concerned "issues" about hunger, especially in the Third World) and "In Search of a Land Ethic" (wherein students "construct one or more ecological ethics").

Bennett says such courses are a symptom of academics "mesmerized by the moment. Students who haven't been introduced to the magnificence of the Renaissance or the drama of the U.S. Constitutional Convention are invited to explore the legacy of the Sixties. Students who haven't studied Aristotle, Aquinas or Kant are urged to examine ethical dilemmas on their own."

As this century staggers to a close, note that at the turn of the century at Fisk University, the black school in Nashville, the freshman curriculum included Tacitus and Horace (in Latin) and Sophocles and the Bible (in Greek). By the end of another century of progress, millions of freshmen will have "constructed" millions of "ecological ethics," but the idea of a core curriculum will have vanished, and with it the civilization that such a curriculum should transmit.

May 6, 1984

The Real Utility of Education

The title of the commission that was created in 1981 and has just issued its findings is itself heartening: The National Commission on Excellence in Education. Its subject was excellence, not equality or some other facet of social justice peripheral to the purposes of education. One measure of recent confusions is that it seems almost bold to extol the pursuit of excellence, and to do so without worrying about "elitism" or the imposition of "repressive" standards that will inhibit the free flow of self-expression from students.

Noting that "history is not kind to idlers," the commission says the nation has "lost sight of the basic purposes of schooling" and has committed "an act of unthinking, unilateral educational disarmament." This act was perhaps unthinking in the sense that it was unreflective. But it was the result of ideas.

One idea is that education is less a matter of transmitting a cultural legacy than of instilling skills useful in tomorrow's markets. Another idea is that education is less a matter of putting something into students than of letting something—"self-realization" or whatever—out.

The commission rightly notes the link between a nation's educational excellence and commercial vigor. But the commission stresses that its concern "also includes the intellectual, moral, and spiritual strengths of our people which knit together the very fabric of our society. . . . A high level of shared education is essential to the fostering of a common culture, especially in a country that prides itself on pluralism and individual freedom." A continental nation steeped in capitalist individualism must make provision for nurturing some collective consciousness.

The four words on the seal of one of the first land-grant colleges (Michigan State) expresses the practicality of much of America's educational effort: "Agriculture and Applied Science." Such education accords with a premise of modern politics: A good society is one in which citizens' passions are absorbed in commerce. But the fact that American education has always aimed to serve commercial vigor has imposed on education a special duty. It is the duty to strengthen the social bonds that are weakened by the dynamism of a restless society of atomized individuals preoccupied with getting and gaining.

In their wonderful book *Shakespeare's Politics*, Allan Bloom and Harry Jaffa say that today no books play the role that the Bible, Shakespeare and Bunyan once played in the education of English-speaking peoples. No generally read works supply civilizing and unifying models of virtue. *M*A*S*H* and *Star Wars* will not suffice. The thinness of the stream of shaping culture is, in part, a result of the contemporary assumption that school curricula should be academic cafeterias catering to students' whims.

The central symbol of American life is the little red schoolhouse, representing faith in education. There were public schools in Boston in 1635. In 1880 England had a population of 23 million and four degree-granting institutions; Ohio had a population of three million and 37 such institutions.

John Adams, the most dour of the Founders, expressed typical American optimism about one thing: "The virtues and powers to which men may be trained by early education and constant discipline, are truly sublime and astounding." But Adams also said something that reveals why education and equality are American values in tension: "Education makes a greater difference between man and man, than nature has between man and brute." If so, the more the resources that are invested in education, the more stratified society may become.

If education is going to create and widen disparities between citizens, it must take care to inculcate some commonality. Otherwise, links of shared values and understandings become dangerously attenuated.

American education has rarely been accused of being insufficiently utilitarian. Indeed, it sometimes has seemed to reflect the belief that in order to produce good citizens, education must merely produce persons competent to participate in the economy.

Certainly we want lots of American engineers who can run rings around the competition in whatever high-tech tomorrow is coming at us. But even more than we need persons conversant with new technologies, we need a citizenry acquainted with the ancient patrimony of our civilization. That patrimony is a renewable resource, but it will not regenerate spontaneously. It needs urgent attention when a California college student asks a professor of English if Julius Caesar resented Shakespeare's portrayal of him.

It has been said that the trouble with the younger generation is that it has not read the minutes of the last meeting. One of the commission's implied recommendations is that schools should make that reading mandatory.

May 1, 1983

Journalism and Passions

Journalists, like surgeons and second basemen, generally do what they do better than they talk about what they do. But journalists talk a lot about their craft, sometimes disquietingly, as in the case of Van Gordon Sauter, president of CBS News, as reported by Ron Rosenbaum in November's *Esquire*.

Sauter was converted from print to television journalism by a moment in Mississippi. In 1964 three civil-rights workers were missing, and Sauter saw an old black man in a boat dragging for bodies, "and you just knew from looking at the expression on his face that he knew those kids had been murdered.

"So I started writing right there and I devoted my first six paragraphs to depicting that situation, the color of the water, the total ambiance. I was feeling absolutely elated until suddenly I turned around and there, at the other end of the bridge, was a TV crew with a mobile truck getting film of that same guy in the boat and I suddenly realized that no matter how good a writer I was, that TV crew *possessed* that moment in a way I never could."

Well, Faulkner had a way of possessing such scenes but, yes, television has its own way, and there are more cameras than Faulkners. But there is an unsolved, perhaps insoluble, problem of television journalism: A camera is a deficient news-gathering instrument. It is used most naturally and potently not to transmit information but to convey scenes, some of great emotional impact. Scenes can be informative; information can have emotional impact. But it is one thing for emotional impact to be a consequence of reporting. It is something else for an emotional response to be the aim of journalism.

Rosenbaum discerns at CBS a "theory of moments." He quotes Dan Rather saying, "Van keeps saying we need stories that reach out and touch people. Moments." Sauter says:

"The kind of thing we're looking for is something that evokes an emotional response. When I go back to the [control room], I tell them, goddam it, we've got to *touch* people. They've got to feel a *relationship* with us. A lot of stories have an inherent drama, but others have to be done in a way that will bring out an emotional response."

Rosenbaum describes this as "the exaltation of the emotional communion of the 'moment,'" and he wonders: "Feelings. Emotions. Relationships. Reach out and touch. . . . Is this the evening news or some kind of encounter session?"

Intentionally eliciting emotional responses is a legitimate function of literature. But of reporting? Changing minds—and hearts—is an explicit aim of much of what appears on editorial and op-ed pages of newspapers. Furthermore, good reporting about all sorts of situations can stir all sorts of feelings. But if journalism becomes a quest for "moments" the point of which is to provoke emotions, then journalism becomes avowedly manipulative. Pursuit of such "moments" involves editorial judgments that are problematic and, at bottom, political. They are judgments about the emotions viewers should have, and how to cause viewers to have them.

I am associated with ABC News. I rarely see evening news programs, because at 7 P.M. I am too busy subduing children to watch reports about other violent conflicts. I do not know whether ABC or NBC attempts to trigger emotions with "moments." But the technology of television may drive television journalism in that direction.

Compared to the English language, a camera is a crude, superficial instrument of communication. It generally deals with surfaces. Pictures—of police dogs attacking civil-rights workers, of Vietnamese clinging to helicopter skids, of a bankrupt farmer watching his land being auctioned—can have extraordinary impact. They tell us things and can pack a larger punch of truth than all but the rarest writers can pack into prose. But when there is an attempt to elicit emotional responses to reality, it is time to ask: Is this journalism, or literature carried on by camera, or political agitation?

Given the camera's capacities and television's time constraints (there are 22 minutes of news in a 30-minute broadcast), there may be a temptation to make the most—the most emotional wallop—of every moment. But in a world of conflict, suffering and scarcity, there is no shortage of emotions. It remains unclear how television, a slave to the camera, can best serve a society in which the public generally has a high ratio of passion to information.

October 31, 1982

Conservatism and Cheerfulness: Bill Buckley at Sixty

This is a truth: It is better to light a candle than curse the darkness. This is a fact: When (the third day in his cradle, I'll wager) Bill Buckley decided that darkness was descending on Yale and the rest of the West, he resolved to light a giant festive bonfire.

He did. It is called contemporary conservatism. He has just turned 60, and his magazine, *National Review*, has just turned 30, so it is time for me, whose writing career began at *NR*, to write an appreciation.

There is a misapprehension that to disagree with Bill is to risk disintegrating, scorched and crinkled, beneath the fire of his ire. Actually, he knows that anger is a useful servant but a bad master. When he decided that Yale (like much else, including me) was unsatisfactory, he did not reduce his loyalty, he redoubled his allocation of energy toward improving it. It will be impossible to write a history of America in the last half of the 20th century without acknowledging the weight of Buckley's works. Of how many journalists can that be said?

Bill once wrote that sailing and skiing are the purest sports because they involve sublime collaboration between the participant and natural forces—wind and gravity. That thought is quintessential Buckley, a flash of insight couched as cheerful dogmatism. His degree of dogmatism often is inversely proportional to the gravity of the issue.

Thirty years ago, when *NR* nailed its colors—no pastels, please—to its mast and set sail, bobbing out upon the blue water of American controversy, the list of best-selling books included Sloan Wilson's *The Man in the Gray Flannel Suit* and Norman Vincent Peale's *The Power of Positive Thinking*. Launching *NR* required positive thinking, because there was then so much conformity in the nation's intellectual life, which was swathed and smothered in the gray mental flannel of a bland liberalism.

As a sailor, Bill knows the truth of this maxim: Voyaging is victory. There can be ample exhilaration in the mode of venturing. His voyage to the victory of the conservative movement began as a lonely journey in a small sloop. The early years were spent tacking into strong winds. But Prince William the Navigator undertook something no mere Magellan ever tried. He worked to change the wind. He did change it, using words.

And such words. As someone once said of a poet: "He kept, as it were, a harem of words, to which he was constantly and absolutely faithful. Some he favored more than others, but he neglected none. He used them more often out of compliment than of necessity."

Throughout his exuberant public career, Bill has been stigmatized (yes, stigmatized) as "clever," meaning "merely" clever. People who have lost arguments to him have said they lost only—only!—because he is articulate, whereas they just cannot quite give voice to their razorlike thoughts. But Bill's career as a controversialist has underscored, at the expense of adversaries, the fact that you cannot think what you cannot say. There is a book to be written on why this country ever came to consider verbal facility the way English Puritans considered church ornamentation: as Satan's work.

Politically committed people live in constant danger of becoming politically obsessed and winding up like Gatsby, whose warped personality was the price of living too long with a single dream. The occupational hazard of political movements is terminal earnestness. Political journals often become lumps of dullness leavened only by outbursts of hysteria. What was said of Gladstone is true of them: They do not exactly lack a sense of humor, but they are not often in the mood to be amused.

Furthermore, because conservatism is realism about mankind's limitations, it does not lend itself to the flattering of the species.

Conservatives are healthily disposed to detect signs that the clock of time is running down and things are going to wrack and ruin. This disposition frequently gives them a certain grimness. Bill's singular achievement has been a compatible marriage between conservatism and cheerfulness.

The range of Bill's pleasures—sailing, harpsichords, peanut butter, Bach—are so numerous that none of them can really be a source. As has been said, happiness is not a what, it is a how. It is a talent and, hence, happy people have no particular reason for being so; they just are. Bill is fortunate, but not more so than we who have profited from his example.

December 5, 1985

Murray Kempton, Craftsman

Time out.

The usual business of this column—issuing edicts to a world too naughty to obey—is today suspended so that I can celebrate the Pulitzer Prize awarded, at long last, to columnist Murray Kempton, the class of our class.

In 1957 Kempton, a craftsman, watched another, Edward Bennett Williams, the lawyer, defend Jimmy Hoffa, and Kempton wrote: "To watch Williams and then to watch a Department of Justice lawyer contending with him is to understand the essential superiority of free enterprise to government ownership." The superiority of Kempton to the rest of us is a pleasure to proclaim. The man who wrote, "It is hard for a man who has enjoyed both the taste of our beer and the flavor of our politics to say which of these national glories has gone flatter in his lifetime," has given contemporary journalism some of its tang.

Thomas Jefferson said all men are created equal, but Jefferson never read Kempton, an unequaled producer of pearls like this (December 4, 1962): "One reason why the garment unions have so sedulously promoted the slogan that man cannot live by bread alone may be that they would prefer not to limit judgment of their worth to their success at providing bread alone."

When in 1958 I came out of the Illinois wilderness to reconnoiter the East, I, wary of exotic metropolitan things, gingerly opened a *New York Post* and discovered Kempton. In the 1950s he was writing sentences like this one about an Eisenhower campaign trip (October 30, 1956):

"In Miami, he had walked carefully by the harsher realities, speaking some twenty feet from an airport drinking fountain labeled 'Colored' and saying that the condition it represented was more amenable to solution by the hearts of men than by laws, and complimenting Florida as 'typical today of what is best in America,' a verdict which might seem to some contingent on finding out what happened to the Negro snatched from the Wildwood jail Sunday."

A 75-word sentence, sinewy and ironic and demanding, is something newspaper readers rarely see. And they rarely see Kempton. He has been hard to syndicate because he has written so much about New York City affairs, which are an acquired taste. Also, he cannot get the hang of having enthusiasms. After Willie Mays and Adlai Stevenson, the list of persons enjoying Kempton's unalloyed approval ends, and the list of approved causes is even shorter. It has been said that to his dog, every man is Napoleon, hence the popularity of dogs. To Kempton, no cause is as pure as every cause considers itself, hence, perhaps, the difficulty of making Kempton as popular as he deserves to be.

And then there is Kempton's prose style. It is part of the problem, and a national treasure.

Many people now flinch from a prose more elaborate than that spoken on television. But the eye is superior to the ear as a recipient of language, in part because a reader can pause, think, reread. Some Kempton sentences, climbing a winding path up a pillar of thought, must be read twice to be properly enjoyed. But why complain about a second sip of vintage claret?

Kempton is a direct descendant of George Mason, author of the Virginia Bill of Rights, a nicer piece of work than that of Kempton's great-great-grandfather, who wrote the Fugitive Slave Act of 1850 and later was Confederate ambassador to Britain. Kempton was born in H. L. Mencken's Baltimore in 1917, the year this republic tumbled into modern history, and he has cast a cold eye on the molten history being made around him.

There may be a better book on the 1930s than Kempton's *Part of Our Time*, but I doubt it. In it he wrote of ideological writers on the left: "It seems to me to have been one of the tragedies of the thirties that so many people substituted an exterior for an interior passion, and nowhere is this process more damaging than to literature." One reason Kempton's columns rise to the rank of literature is that although he knows that news is necessarily about the surface of things, he also wants to tell the stories of persons who are not all surface, and wants to save the Republic from those who are.

One reason I became a columnist is that, long before I did, I had in my mind's eye a "role model." That is a phrase sometimes used by people too embarrassed to use the word "hero." I am not embarrassed. I know how good a journeyman pitcher in the mid-1960s must have felt just knowing that Sandy Koufax was a pitcher and a contemporary. It is deeply satisfying to be able to say I am in a craft adorned by Murray Kempton.

May 2, 1985

Raymond Aron, Anti-Ideologue

Raymond Aron was one of those men on whom age settles almost playfully. His wittiness made him seem increasingly elfin. Two weeks ago in Paris, when I last saw him briefly, he strode out of the offices of *L'Express* into the sunlit Avenue Hoche and toward what promised to be an autumn of international acclaim.

It is hard to identify an American who has enjoyed comparable preeminence in our nation's intellectual life. Emerson? William James? Lippmann? Aron, who died last week at 78, was a bit of all three. Last month this scholar and journalist published his memoirs, and they went immediately to the top of the best-seller list. The book has 780 pages, not one of which tells how to combat cellulite. Strange country, France.

Aron, a Jew, was born in 1905. Dreyfus was on Devil's Island. In a nation where anti-Semitism was strong, and still is not negligible, and in an era when radicalism of the left was standard among intellectuals, Aron adhered to moderate conservatism. His schoolmate, Jean-Paul Sartre, found fame as a philosophical irrationalist and political Stalinist. Aron became more exotic, because rarer: a philosophical anti-ideologue, combining the life of the mind with political moderation.

His death stilled the pen of the world's most formidable journalist. He wrote more than 30 books, many of them theoretical, and taught at many of the world's finest universities, but he was always a public man. His career was an echo of a healthier age, before the handling of ideas was thought to be the business of an academic clerisy, and before academic specialization sharpened minds by narrowing them.

In the past decade, there has been a transformation of French intellectual life, a thorough "de-Marxification." Events, especially in Afghanistan and Poland (with which France has complex historical ties) have helped, but so, to a large extent, have ideas, words, books. Foremost have been the words of Solzhenitsyn, and of such French writers as Jean-François Revel and Alain Besançon.

Besançon says no French intellectual of note now calls himself a Marxist. Many consumers of ideas—many teachers, parish curates, civil servants—call themselves Marxists, but producers of ideas do not. The Communist Party is no longer a party of mass conviction.

The ground for the transformation of French intellectual fashion was prepared by Aron, and especially by his book, *The Opium of the Intellectuals* (1955). Solzhenitsyn is the most consequential contemporary exposer of the practice of Marxism. Aron was the most effective critic of the theory.

He did not just refute the doctrines espoused by enemies of open societies. He also served such societies by dealing unsentimentally with their sentimentalities. The political problem, he said, is to reconcile "the equality of men as men with the inequality of their functions in the community" and to "obtain from the subordinate recognition of his superiors without causing him to suffer constraint or lose his dignity." In a democracy, the expression of such thoughts is as necessary as it is impolitic.

In a book with a deliberately paradoxical title—*In Defense of Decadent Europe* (1978)—he argued that Europe can be praised for its freedoms, but he wondered about a connection between those freedoms and Europe's diminished capacity for collective action. "In spite of its wealth, in spite (or because) of its culture and its freedoms," Europe will not defend itself without U.S. assistance. Aron died on the eve of a campaign against even that assistance. His voice would have been invaluable during the "hot autumn" of protests against the new NATO missiles.

"Anyone who reflects on wars and strategies today," he wrote, "raises a barrier between his intelligence and his humanity." But the man who in 1933 saw Nazis burning books in Berlin was, to the end, a passionate intellect, accepting the role of military power:

"Other people live from other emotions. How could I, as a Frenchman of Jewish origin, ever forget that France owes its liberation to the power of its allies, and that Israel owes its existence to its weapons and any chance of survival to its own determination, and that of the Americans, to fight if it proves necessary . . . ?"

It is almost past now, Europe's great generation of "Atlanticist" intellectuals who in the crucial postwar period defended Western values, and Western defense measures, against many detractors. The detractors multiply like rodents. Defenders like Aron are as rare as eagles.

October 23, 1983

Philosophy and Fierceness

Five years ago, while the Tall Ships, as buoyant as the Republic, converged on New York harbor, an Israeli force swept into Entebbe airport. July 4, 1976, was a great day to be an American, and a great day to be Jewish, and was, I am assured, an absolutely sensational day to be American and Jewish.

As Shimon Peres, then Israel's defense minister, wrote about the rescue of the hostages held in Uganda, Entebbe "proved that Israel is capable of maintaining not only defensible frontiers but also a defensibly erect stature. . . . At a distance of over 4,000 kilometers from home, in one short hour, the posture of the entire Jewish people—in fact, the posture of free and responsible men all over the world—was straightened."

Only one Israeli soldier—the leader of the storming team—died in the rescue mission now known as "Operation Jonathan." So let us now praise Jonathan Netanyahu.

You can get to know him in *Self-Portrait of a Hero*, a collection of his letters written between 1963, when he was 17 and studying in America, and 1976. The impact of these letters is related to the fact that, as novelist Herman Wouk says in his introduction to the book, "Like Anne Frank's Diary, it is a fortuitous, not a deliberately created, work of art." These letters also have a tragic fascination for the reader, who knows from the start that the destination is death at an early age.

Jonathan's temperament, like that of the Zionist movement that founded Israel, was an extraordinary mixture of philosophy and fierceness—especially fierceness turned inward as he drove himself through a life of ever more demanding dedications. It does not derogate the virtues he exemplified or the nobility of his death to say that Israel will be a happy nation—made happy in security by men like Jonathan—when it no longer so desperately needs so much exhausting intensity from its best citizens.

In an age when a subsidy forgone is called a "sacrifice," Jonathan's life, as told in his letters, is an antidote to the exhaustion of the vocabulary of civic virtue. And some letters illustrate today's headlines. As the noose closed around Israel before the Six Day War in 1967, Jonathan wrote:

"We sit and wait. What are we waiting for? Well, its like this: An Englishman, an American and an Israeli were caught by a tribe of cannibals in Africa. When they were already in the pot, each of them was allowed a last wish. The Englishman asked for a whiskey and a pipe, and got them. The American asked for a steak and got it. The Israeli asked the chief of the tribe to give him a good kick in the backside. At first the chief refused, but after a lot of argument he finally did it. At once the Israeli pulled out a gun and shot all the cannibals. The American and the Englishman asked him: 'If you had a gun all the time, why didn't you kill them sooner?' 'Are you crazy,' answered the Israeli, 'and have the U.N. call me an aggressor?'"

Israelis live life *in extremis*, and Jonathan's life was a distillation and intensification of Israel's experience. His last letter, written six days before his death, just before the Entebbe operation was planned, expresses his relentless self-reproach. But the last words of the last letter are, "It'll be okay." We shall see.

When just 17 he wrote, "There's no reason why the tower I build around myself, around my person, whatever it may be, should not stand forever." Nothing stands forever, but legend comes close. Jonathan was not only Achilles, he now is, through his letters, his own Homer. The tower he built is the imperishable example of the compatibility of the civilized virtue of reflection and the martial virtues that stand between civilization and its multiplying enemies.

Ours is an age of antiheroism, eager to define away heroism, or to dissolve it through analysis, psychological or sociological. Heroism expands mankind's sense of possibility, and therefore destroys alibis and creates duties. But for Israel especially, and for all challenged nations, much depends on the power of heroic example to elicit more such examples.

The motto of Israel's officer corps is "After me." The point of the Fourth of July, here as there, is to remember that we come after heroes. Because of Entebbe, Israel and the United States, linked in so many ways, now share a sacred day.

July 2, 1981

Jack Swigert's Example

Newspapers exist primarily to inform. But the first and finest columnist (Samuel Johnson) rightly insisted that men more frequently require to be reminded than informed. So let us now be reminded of Jack Swigert's gifts to his country. He gave examples of bravery when he did not die, and when he did.

Some public persons take too much to heart Longfellow's announcement that life is real, life is earnest. They are oppressively somber, their backs bent, figuratively speaking, beneath the weight of Responsibility. Swigert was not like that. He had life in perspective, perhaps because he had felt the breath of death.

The first time was with the world watching. To be precise, the world was listening to the laconic space-speak between Houston and Apollo 13. It was April 13, 1970—a great day for the superstitious.

Suddenly, crackling across 206,000 miles came words more memorable to those who heard them than "the Eagle has landed." The words, spoken in a tone of tenseness not hitherto heard from space, were: "We've got a problem." Suddenly, the space program stopped being automatic and antiseptic and became a matter of desperate improvisation to save three men outbound at 2,200 mph.

An oxygen tank had exploded, damaging the command capsule's electricity, computer, water and fuel cells. Instead of heading for a moon landing, astronauts Swigert, James Lovell and Fred Haise were in danger of dying as no one ever had, hurtling into deep space. But with superb help from Houston, they launched themselves into a maneuver that whirled them around the moon and homeward.

Last summer, when Swigert was running for Congress, a small malignancy was removed from his nasal passage. When a physical examination in August left him with mysterious back pains, he underwent extensive tests, which revealed cancer in his bone marrow. By then it was too late for Colorado Republicans to field another candidate so, like a spacecraft locked in orbit, he continued, adding chemotherapy, with its debilitating effects, to the wear-and-tear of campaigning. He lost some hair and frequently looked ravaged, but he gave an imperishable example to a national constituency—the three million Americans who have cancer and are summoning the physical and emotional stamina to carry on.

There was reason to hope, if not to expect, that the therapy would arrest the disease. In 1982, as in 1970, Swigert acted on the principle that however long the odds, you are not beaten until you concede. But shortly before Christmas, pain drove him into a Washington hospital.

There, to the end, he was what he had been all his life: in control. Surrounded by and attached to the paraphernalia of high-technology medicine, he monitored his condition. He had a mind disciplined by close encounters with danger (he survived a plane crash while an Air Force fighter pilot in Korea), and eyes trained to extrapolate reality from electronic impulses on gauges and screens.

At one point he told a doctor that he thought one lung was filling and that he should have an X ray. The doctor disagreed, so Swigert bet him a steak dinner. Before 24 hours had passed, Swigert had died at age 51, a week before he was to have been sworn in as a congressman.

Heroism is not as promiscuously distributed as President Reagan said in his Inaugural address, when he baptized us all heroes. But there are humble, hidden forms of heroism. A gifted professional basketball player (Spencer Haywood), asked how it felt to be a hero, responded that if you want to see heroism, watch a welfare mother raising a large family.

But public acts of heroism, although not morally grander than private bravery, have special power as models of virtue. The communication of patterns of excellence once was a function of literature. However, the tutelary task once performed by, say, the Bible, Bunyan and Shakespeare is no longer performed by any corpus of great books that shape the community's moral imagination.

Walker Percy writes novels of moral seriousness, but his characters do not make virtue vivid. John Updike is a gifted writer, but his Harry "Rabbit" Angstrom and other residents of Brewer, Pennsylvania, are not intended to do for us what Homer's and Dante's creations did for Greece and Italy—supply unifying patterns of excellence. Contemporary literature is doing some serious things, but not that serious thing.

Nations always, but especially in an era of nonheroic or antiheroic literature, need conspicuous real heroes. This nation just lost one.

January 2, 1983

The Finest Public Servant I Have Known

A silly person once said that only silly persons have heroes. But only exceptionally small people will not acknowledge the exceptionally large persons among us. Heroes make vivid the values by which we try to live. I say, with many others: Henry Jackson was my hero.

He was an insoluble problem for the image-tinkers and a splendid puzzle for the label-makers who infest contemporary politics. Because he was uninterested in the cosmetics of politics, dull persons considered him dull. Discerning persons considered his kind of character as exciting as it is rare. Persons who, under the pressure of fashion, are as flexible as fly rods found Jackson incomprehensible. They came to the absurd conclusion that he had departed from the liberal tradition.

He was a pioneer of environmentalism. He was the preeminent champion of civil rights. He fought for the full domestic agenda and authored legislation that put teeth into U.S. pronouncements on behalf of Jews and others persecuted by the Soviet regime. And if Jackson's proposals for substantial force reductions had been adopted, we might have had arms limitation agreements that actually limit arms.

Jackson was one of those persons—Felix Frankfurter was another—whose constancy was mistaken for change. He never wavered from his party's traditional belief that there is no incompatibility between government with a caring face at home and government with a stern face toward adversaries.

From Wilson confronting Lenin and FDR confronting Hitler, through Truman confronting Stalin, Kennedy confronting Castro and Johnson confronting Ho Chi Minh, the Democratic Party has been the foremost opponent of this century's foremost evil—totalitarianism. Jackson was an anchor against weariness, wishful thinking and apostasy in the world's oldest party.

He nurtured in this Republic something without which no republic can long endure: a sense that problems are tractable. To be in his presence was to experience the wholesome infection of a reviving spirit. This was especially remarkable because he, more than any contemporary, looked unblinkingly at, and spoke uncomfortingly about, the terrors of our time. He taught less clear-sighted, less brave persons how to combine realism and serenity.

He missed the ultimate prize of our politics, perhaps because he lacked the crackling temperament that marks persons who burn on the surface with a hard, gemlike flame. If his political metabolism seemed uncommonly calm, that is because he had the patience of a mature politician—a gift for planning, thirst for detail, and a sense of ripeness in issues. He had a flame, but he had depth in which he kept it.

In committees and on the Senate floor, he was a cannon loaded to the muzzle with knowledge born of diligence. His unrivaled effectiveness was a rebuke to the less industrious and a refutation of the theory that fancy footwork is necessary and sufficient.

A legislature is a face-to-face society, where character and moral force tell. What Jackson did in committees and on the floor was awesome. But it was only a small fraction of the work he did during four decades of 18-hour days, working with one member after another, one member at a time, building coalitions of common sense.

His legendary energy flowed as much from his spirit as from his physiology. His biography is an essay on the sources of American vitality. He was the son of immigrants, and of the American West. His parents crossed not only an ocean but a continent, seeking an open future in our most open region.

For longer than I have been alive, Congress has been embellished by his presence. And for longer than I live, public life shall be enriched by the radiating force of his character.

If you wonder who real leaders are, find out who has real followers—persons who follow a leader onto a path of life, who adopt careers where they navigate by stars he taught them to see. The social geology of this city is layer upon layer of persons pulled into public life by the example of lives worth emulating. In numerous public offices, and in law and journalism, there is a thick layer of Henry Jackson's men and women.

There are those, and they are legion, who call themselves "Jackson Democrats." I can say with absolute authority that there is such a thing as a "Jackson Republican."

Henry Jackson mastered the delicate balance of democracy, the art of being a servant to a vast public without being servile to any part of it. He was the finest public servant I have known.

September 8, 1983

In Praise of Mortality

Fred is dead and philosophic thoughts fill all minds at the Will home. One mind is especially somber. On the eve of her fifth birthday, Victoria, special friend and confidante of Fred the goldfish, has seen death and has decided, after mature deliberation, that life is still good. The time will come when she will see that there is much to be said for mortality.

Fred was named by Victoria for Fred Lynn, the Baltimore Orioles centerfielder. (Victoria certainly has got her father's number.) Fred lived into the sear and yellow leaf and died of the most natural cause, old age. Neither cholesterol nor automobiles nor handguns played a part. Irrational eating and drinking, negligence about exercise, and similar foolish behaviors kill only creatures who can think and who therefore stand at the pinnacle of creation.

Victoria noticed Fred's decline the night before he died. Her attention wandered to the tank beside her bed, even though her father was giving an especially stirring reading of *Bread and Jam for Frances*, a cautionary tale about a young badger who has an incontinent appetite for bread and jam. Victoria noticed that Fred, usually a trencherman, was peckish. At 10:23 the next morning, he died.

Victoria, having glimpsed, for the first time, the skull beneath the skin (in this case, the scales) of life, needed a few words from Leon Kass, a University of Chicago philosopher and biologist and medical doctor. Kass has just published a collection of essays to which I shall refer again in December when I award it the citation as the year's best book. It is *Toward a More Natural Science: Biology and Human Affairs* (Free Press). The essay Victoria needed in her sorrow is "Mortality and Morality: The Virtues of Finitude."

Kass says that retarding senescence and preserving youthfulness is part of the scientific project of controlling biological aging. These objectives are continuous with the aspirations of medicine—longer life, better health. But suppose sensational success; imagine an indefinite extension of life. Consider, Kass says, what would be lost.

Could life without the limit of mortality be serious? Homer's immortals are beautiful and vigorous—and shallow and frivolous. Their passions are only transiently engaged. They are spectators of the moral dramas of life. Those dramas are the monopoly of mortals. As Kass says, "Mortality makes life matter—not only in the chemist's sense." This is in part because finitude—the sense of not having world enough and time—is a spur to achievement.

Kass argues that not only seriousness but some beauty, too, is related to impermanence. He refers not just to the beauty of a flower or sunset, but especially to the distinctively human beauty of good character, of virtue. Immortals, says Kass, cannot be noble. They cannot meet the challenge of transcending concern with mere survival; they cannot put their lives at risk. (This indicates why pacifism, far from being a form of idealism, is a renunciation of all ideals in favor of a mere material thing, biological existence.) "Immortality," says Kass, "is a kind of oblivion—like death itself."

The case Kass makes for mortality does not make a virtue of necessity. Rather it says that the necessity of death is the mother of virtue. The human longing that is assuaged by love and addressed by religion—a longing deriving from the sense of incompleteness—cannot be cured by longevity, however protracted. It cannot be cured by "more of the same."

Far from bringing happiness, the obsessive pursuit of longevity distracts us from the soul's natural quest. It is a distraction from the duty to master the fine art of living well, which requires rising above concern for mere bodily continuance.

Biology teaches what moral philosophy concludes: We are social, communal creatures, with strong impulses, physical and spiritual, for reproduction. We are constituted for concern for the species; our lives point beyond themselves, toward perpetuation. Children are our participation in the enduring.

A craving for physical immortality is childish in the sense of being narcissistic and incompatible with a mature devotion to posterity. It also is hostile to children. Children are the bearers of our hopes, and if they are to flower, Kass notes, "we must wither and give ground."

Those who come after, who take our place, are "life's answer to mortality, and their presence in one's house is a constant reminder that one no longer belongs to the frontier generation." That is why to have children is to come as close as is possible to reconciliation with the human condition.

That is what Fred's death, and Victoria's tears, caused me, with Kass's incomparable help, to think. But all I told Victoria is that Fred is in fish heaven. She can read Kass when she has mastered *Frances*.

Fred now rests beneath Maryland soil. His tank is home to a member of the next generation, Eddie. Eddie is named for Eddie Murray, the Orioles first baseman. Victoria, obviously, is fine.

September 8, 1985

Baseball, Before Night Descends

Like the fellow in the Bible who tried to reason with the deaf adder and did not get to first base, Mrs. Will has been telling me that at 42 I should grow up. I see no merit in her suggestion, but have agreed to think about something other than baseball during the wasteland that stretches like the Sahara between the World Series and spring training.

Before that long night descends, let me note that the Baltimore Orioles, with the best record in baseball during nearly the last 27 years, are one of two American institutions of consistent excellence. The other is the telephone company. The government is fiddling with that, so the Orioles may soon have cornered the market on quality.

Considering the way some less-than-excellent players are paid today, Joe DiMaggio has a point when he says that if he were negotiating a contract with Yankees owner George Steinbrenner, he would be able to say, "George, you and I are about to become partners." Oh, for the days of innocence when the Pirates' Honus Wagner, the greatest shortstop ever, rejected a salary offer of $2,000 by declaring: "I won't play for a penny less than fifteen hundred dollars." (An NFL running back got those numbers confused this year when he said his goal was to gain 1,500 yards or 2,000 yards, "whichever comes first.")

Amazingly, the beauty of baseball is not apparent to everyone. When baseball gave lifetime passes to the 52 hostages released from Iran, a football fan asked, "Haven't they suffered enough?" Some critics say baseball is just another opiate of the masses, another of the distractions that American society produces so prolifically, diverting attention from the class struggle or the Iowa caucuses. But not all distractions are created equal. Some numb the mind (alcohol, the Iowa caucuses); others engage the mind (baseball).

Besides, reasonable people want to be distracted from the world's horrors, which sometimes include a baseball team. When Miro's avant-garde sculpture *Chicago* was unveiled in that city, a lady with a lived-in face was asked if she liked it. "Yeah," she said, "it keeps me from thinking about the Cubs."

It is said that baseball is "only a game." Yes, and the Grand Canyon is only a hole in Arizona.

Proof of the genius of ancient Greece is that it understood baseball's future importance. Greek philosophers considered sport a religious and civic—in a word, a moral—undertaking. Sport, they said, is morally serious because mankind's noblest aim is the loving contemplation of worthy things, such as beauty and courage. By witnessing physical grace, the soul comes to understand and love beauty. Seeing persons compete courageously and fairly helps emancipate the individual by educating his passions.

Professional sports can be a melancholy business, because an athlete's career compresses so much of life's trajectory into a short span. But as the Pirates' Willie Stargell said, "The umpires always say 'Play ball.' They don't say 'Work ball'." That is why once when Stargell was boarding another 3 A.M. plane after a night game, he said: "I'm not crying; I asked to be a ball player."

Baseball players are less subject than most athletes to the cruelty of the calendar. Look at the Phillies. They are balm to the spirits of middle-aged men. The leadoff batter is 40, the next batter is 42, the star pitcher is 38. They have between them 61 years in major league baseball. (I leave to philosophers the question of whether the pinball game the Phillies play on that plastic carpet is really baseball.)

My spiritual adviser (Tom Boswell, baseball writer, *Washington Post*) notes that such longevity, although not normal, is not unheard of. Henry Aaron and Warren Spahn got better after they turned 35. Aaron hit 245 home runs; Spahn won 20 or more games seven times, 180 in all. As Boswell says, no other team sport is so fascinated with the process of aging as baseball, perhaps because none of our other sports are based on skill and timing rather than brute force. No other sport has so many 10- and 15- and even 20-year careers.

Great sporting events are unifying events for the communities directly involved. For the nation they are exceptions to what sometimes seems to be a rule—that our shared experiences are either sad, such as the assassination of President Kennedy, or divisive, such as the firing of General MacArthur. The World Series occurs four times as frequently as the Iowa caucuses. What a wonderful country America is.

October 13, 1983

Huck at a Hundred

Land o' goshen, time flies. It seems like only yesterday that he was just a sprout of a boy, and now look at him. Huck Finn is 100 years old. His story was published in America on February 18, 1885.

Another boy from the banks of the Mississippi—downstream, at St. Louis—was T. S. Eliot, and no one was ever less like Huck, but he said Huck's tale was a masterpiece, in part because it was the first novel written entirely in natural speech. Natural? Darn tootin'. I, too, am a son of the middle border, hailing from about 150 miles due east of Hannibal, and I say Huck speaks pure American. People who speak otherwise are speaking dialects and should seek help.

We who write, and therefore think, in column-length chunks, are connoisseurs of concision, and my hat is off to Huck. Consider his one-sentence summation of all that needs be said about the art of cooking. He is complaining about the Widow Douglas's practice of cooking different parts of the meal in separate pots: "In a barrel of odds and ends it is different; things get mixed up, and the juice kind of swaps around, and things go better." Huck is pithy even when engaged in literary criticism, a craft that makes most folks garrulous. In an Arkansas house he sees some books: "One was 'Pilgrim's Progress,' about a man that left his family it didn't say why . . . The statements was interesting, but tough." That is a perfect précis, but it also is the kind of breezy talk that has gotten a lot of mud slung at our boy.

There always have been ninnies who say that Twain's novel is disrespectful of blacks. But only someone suffering terminal solemnity can take offense from passages like:

"We blowed out a cylinder-head."

"Good gracious! Anybody hurt?"

"No'm. Killed a nigger."

"Well, it's lucky; because sometimes people do get hurt."

Such talk still gets some people lathered up more than somewhat. But tarnation, you knew which side Twain was on when Huck shouted to Jim, "They're after us!"—*us.* Accusing Huck of racism is cuckoo considering what caused some 19th-century moralists to say Huck should be kept from the tender eyes of children. It was the passage where Huck's conscience is nagging him because he violated church teaching and Missouri law and mores by helping Miss Watson's slave escape. He writes a letter to her, telling her where Jim is. But he thinks about what a boon companion Jim has been, "and then says to myself: 'All right, then, I'll go to hell—and tore it up." Some folks thought that passage would throw the nation spang off its moral rails. (T. S. Eliot's parents would not let him read the novel. He snuck off to London and read it.)

Huck choosing hell was Huck listening to his sound heart rather than his deformed conscience. Twain thought a conscience is a social product, as bad as society. Being a believer in a boy's pure heart, Twain was a sentimentalist and like most such was fated to be an angry man. He was angry about the violence of the river towns where there were bloody feuds and cruel murders and people were tarred and feathered and it was considered fun to douse a dog with turpentine and set it aflame. He was angry about the coming of industrialism, which he thought was debasing the nation's physical and moral beauty. At the risk of torturing too much meaning out of the text, is the steamboat that wrecks Huck's raft—his pristine island of self-government—a symbol of the machine despoiling America's garden?

Huck's story resonates in America's heart because it is about freedom understood in a distinctively American way, as the absence of social restraints, and obedience to the promptings of a pure heart. Twain, like Tocqueville, feared the invisible shackles of social conformity almost as much as he feared oppressive institutions. And Huck? Heck, he did not even cotton to new clothes, which made him "feel all cramped up." And he took to the river when he found out "how dismal regular and decent the widow was" who was bent on "sivilizing" him. Twain's novel about this shrewd boy is for grown-ups as much as children, but it has a childish notion at its core. It is that (in today's jargon) "authenticity" and "self-realization" are achieved outside of or against society, not through it. Huck is—dare I say it?—an "alienated" 14-year-old.

The American idea of freedom is Huck going down the Mississippi or Thoreau going up the Merrimac. To be free is to be foot-loose in a pathless wilderness, unbounded by geography or history, utterly unconstrained by social bonds. But why must we speak of "bonds," in a way that suggests ropes biting into wrists? Human beings are social animals whose capacities, including the capacity for virtue, can be realized only in a social setting, not isolated on a raft borne ceaselessly past communities where individuals acquire only corrupt consciences.

Four decades after Huck's raft began its endless voyage through America's consciousness, there appeared, in 1925, another equally emblematic creation of America's imagination. Jay Gatsby was citified but not really more "sivilized" than Huck. His story, like Huck's, is about integrity of personality. Huck, in flight from society, has it, or, more precisely, achieves it. Gatsby, the synthetic man, is a warning about one unpleasant possibility for a social animal.

As Gatsby's story ends, the narrator, Nick, looks out across Long Island Sound and thinks how "for a transitory enchanted moment man must have held his breath in the presence of this continent." Gatsby had had a faint doubt about the quality of his happiness, and now Nick imagines the houses of West Egg, Long Island, melting away and the island once again being "a fresh, green breast of the new world." Pessimism about the ability of Americans to measure up to America's promise is, in its way, Twain's theme.

"I thought of Gatsby's wonder when he first picked out the green light at the end of Daisy's dock . . . Gatsby believed in the green light, the orgiastic future that year by year recedes before us . . . So we beat on, boats against the current, borne back ceaselessly into the past." I imagine Huck sitting on Daisy's dock, loafing and smoking and fishing, and thinking: I got to light out, the blue lawns of Long Island are too cramping. An American boy belongs on the river, that rolling road where the current carries you effortlessly away from confinement.

February 18, 1985

Acknowledgments

Debts of gratitude are a pleasure to pay and I owe large debts to William Dickinson and Anna Karavangelos, and their associates at the Washington Post Writers Group, and to Rick Smith and his associates at Newsweek, especially Olga Barbi. They make writing a column even more fun than it naturally is. I have now published three collections of columns with three publishing houses, but with only one editor: Erwin Glikes. He is so talented I follow him around. Much that I do is made possible by, and all that I do is made better by, the work of my infallible associate Dusa Gyllensvard, to whom: Thanks.

Index